Dolores LaChapelle

EARTH WISDOM

A New Natural Philosophy Series Book ■ Photographs by Steven J. Meyers ■ Drawings by David LaChapelle

Joint publication of Way of the Mountain Learning Center and International College

FINN HILL ARTS
P.O. Box 542
Silverton, Colorado 81433

Library of Congress Catalog number: 77-93140
ISBN 0-917270-01-0

Printed in the United States of America

Second printing 1984

The *Tewa Prayer* on pages 7 and 129 is reprinted with permission from *The Tewa World: Space, Time, Being and
Becoming in a Pueblo Society* by Alfonso Ortiz, © 1969 by the University of Chicago Press.

Contents

Introduction .

When *Earth Wisdom* came off the press in November of 1978 it immediately gained recognition as a source book for individuals, as well as college classes and environmental groups, involved in the on-going efforts to define a new social paradigm more conducive to harmony between human beings and nature. Even when International College dropped its Press in 1980 and the book was out of print, its influence continued. Now, with the emergence of Deep Ecology as a step toward this new social paradigm the growing demand for copies of *Earth Wisdom* has resulted in both a second printing here in the United States and a translation of the book to be published in West Germany next year.

This new introduction for the second printing gives me the opportunity to trace the early history of specific aspects of the Deep Ecology movement.

New Natural Philosophy   In the spring of 1977, while working on the manuscript for *Earth Wisdom* I took time out to travel to Claremont, California for a meeting with Paul Shepard and Joe Meeker for discussions which eventually led to the development of New Natural Philosophy. The original impetus toward this movement came in 1971 when Joe Meeker received a grant from NEH for a year's research into the relationships connecting literature, philosophy and ecology, during which he worked not only in this country but with Konrad Lorenz at the Max Planck Institute near Munich and with Arne Naess of the Eco-philosophy program at the University of Oslo in Norway. During the next few years Meeker taught environmental philosophy at U.C. Santa Cruz, worked on his book, *The Comedy of Survival: In Search of an Environmental Ethic,* and was Senior Tutor in Humanities at Athabasca University, a new Canadian institution built around a core of environmental studies. Paul Shepard is professor of Human Ecology at Pitzer College in Claremont and the author of numerous books on the human/nature interaction. His most recent book is *Nature and Madness,* published by the Sierra Club.

The name, New Natural Philosophy developed out of a leisurely Sunday morning discussion between Meeker and Shepard in January of 1977. Natural Philosophy, a search for divine order as revealed through natural creation, in ancient Greece, persisted until the rise of empirical science some three centuries ago. New Natural Philosophy, as Meeker and Shepard conceived of it, is a search for ways in which human thought and understanding can once again proceed more compatibly with nature. As Meeker further explains in his introduction to the New Natural Philosophy Program, "Humans can no longer assume a godlike role as lawgivers and manipulators of nature, but must create for themselves a new role as informed participants in natural processes within and around themselves." When Meeker presented the idea to Paul Proehl and Linden Leavitt of International College, a meeting was set for April in Claremont. I drove down from Colorado and Arne Naess flew in from Norway for the meeting. In addition to those mentioned above, the New Natural Philosophy Program included Vine Deloria Jr., David Klein, Sigmund Kvaløy, Paul Lee, Peter Marin, Loree Rackstraw, Paolo Soleri and Gary Snyder.

Earth Wisdom was the first volume to be published in the New Natural Philosophy Series. No further volumes were published for the series because in 1980 International College found it financially expedient to drop the Press and concentrate instead on their tutorial program. Publication of *Earth Wisdom* thus reverted to The Way of the Mountain Learning Center.

Eco-philosophy   This movement at the University of Oslo, involving Sigmund Kvaløy and Arne Naess, a specialist on the philosophy of Spinoza, has been defined by Naess as "a philosophy of ecological harmony or equilibrium." In an interview in 1982 Naess stated that we need "a tremendous expansion of ecological thinking in what I call ecosophy. *Sophy* comes from the Greek term *sophia,* 'wisdom,' which relates to ethics, norms, rules, and practice. Ecosophy, then, involves a shift from science to wisdom." Eco is derived from the Greek word, *oikos,* meaning household with the ultimate meaning of earth household or the biosphere. The change in nomenclature from eco-philosophy to ecosophy is a useful step in that the word, *philosophy,* literally "love of wisdom," has the connotation of wisdom solely from the intellectual efforts of human beings while the word, *ecosophy* implies a wisdom derived from the whole of the biosphere.

Deep Ecology   Arne Naess' first mention of Deep Ecology occurred in his Introductory lecture at the Third World Future Research Conference held at Bucharest in September 1972, when he pointed out the difference between "a shallow, but presently rather powerful movement" and "a deep, but presently less influential movement." He defined the shallow movement as a "fight against pollution and resource depletion. Central objective: the health of people in the developed countries." The Deep Ecology movement was defined as "Rejection of the man-in-environment image in favor of *the relational, total-field image.*" Among the more important objectives of Deep Ecology are: "Every form of life has the equal right to live and blossom; diversity and symbiosis; and local autonomy and decentralization."

Shortly after Arne Naess' lecture at Bucharest was published in the journal, *Inquiry* in 1973, George Sessions, philosophy professor at Sierra State College in

California, began his *Ecophilosophy Newsletter*. This publication continues to be the single most important influence on the growing Deep Ecology movement in the U.S. Bill Devall, professor of Sociology at Humboldt State College, who first became acquainted with Sessions when they both taught at Humboldt, wrote an in-depth study, "The Deep Ecology Movement," which was published in the *Natural Resources Journal* in the spring of 1980.

In 1980 the University of Denver sponsored the Earthday X Colloquium in which the progress of the ecology movement since the first Earthday in 1970 was examined by 23 scholars from universities throughout the country. Two papers: George Sessions' "Deep and Shallow Ecology: A Review of the Philosophical Literature" and my paper, "Systemic Thinking and Deep Ecology: An Historical Overview" brought the term, Deep Ecology, to the attention of a wider academic audience.

In the decade following Arne Naess' lecture at Bucharest, Deep Ecology has grown throughout the world by means of local, decentralist action. The resulting newsletters have been started by individuals, not by institutions. The latest newsletter is *The Deep Ecologist* coming from John Martin in Australia. Three books on Deep Ecology are scheduled to be published within the next two years.

Mind Underlying every aspect of the emerging new social paradigm is a reassessment of Mind as such. Gregory Bateson, perhaps the seminal thinker of this century, pointed out that "the most interesting — though still incomplete — scientific discovery of the twentieth century is the discovery of the nature of mind." New research, coming from a number of different areas, is beginning to provide information about the interaction of mind-within the human being and mind-at-large in the environment. Understanding of this interdependence of mind will, of necessity, lead to a change in our ideas about the land itself. And, as Aldo Leopold wrote long ago, "To change ideas about what land is for, is to change ideas about what anything is for."

In Nature there are innumerable processes going on all the time — manifestations of simultaneous energy patterns — which are so complex that the human mind cannot begin to comprehend the whole, much less have the intelligence to direct all the action; yet we are conditioned to believe that human culture enables us to do so! Aldo Leopold spent almost forty years of his life studying the land and decided, "This land is too complex for its inhabitants to understand." More recently, John Todd said that his New Alchemy Institute began "with the realization that none of us and no one we knew had the knowledge or even the wisdom to make a tiny piece of the world work."

Each of these men came to the realization that only the earth itself has the wisdom to teach us what we need to know. Although the earth's billions of years of experimental wisdom is still available to us we have lost the knowledge of how to communicate with it. For millenia, traditional cultures communicated with the earth and all its beings through rituals and ceremonies. *Earth Wisdom* is a beginning step toward restoring this lost communication.

> "The challenge is to fit ourselves to this place . . . so that our cultures are once again a ceremony of interaction between species and ecosystem . . . A community of beings joined by rim and basin, air and watershed, food chains — ceremonies. We will be informed by earthworms and plankton. We will study that authority which resides in place and act out our lives accordingly. There is no separate existence."
>
> from "Future Primitive"
> by Linn House and Jerry Gorsline

The structure of this book

Part I begins with a particular experience in my life, which both crystallized my feelings toward the earth and led to an intuitive understanding of the relationship of mountains and mind in the beginnings of the major religions. After historically documenting this relationship, I explore the particular break in this relationship which is part of our European heritage.

Part II investigates the nature and the boundaries of mind in relation to Nature.

Part III delineates the practical results of healing the split between human consciousness and Nature as a whole.

Part IV provides immediate help for those of us who would live as Nature intended us to live, not as our limited left hemisphere knowledge tries to program us to live. We must become aware of the complex interrelationships of a place before we can proceed to live responsibly in a particular ecosystem; therefore, we must take time to learn from the land itself.

The total responsibility of primitive peoples for their lives and their land has been gradually eroded from the time of the earliest civilizations until today most people have lost all ability to act responsibly. True responsibility—the ability to respond—depends on total awareness of the environment, on our learning to communicate with the ecological wisdom of the earth itself. Once this occurs, the realization comes that no one—not the bureaucrat in his Washington office or the expert in the university research laboratory knows more than what your own place can teach you about how to live in that place.

Finally, this book should in no way be considered a definitive study but rather a preliminary report on how we can once again begin to learn from the earth.

Acknowledgments

Permission to quote extensively from the following works is gratefully acknowledged by the author:

The Sacred Pipe: Black Elk's Account of the Seven Rites of the Oglala Sioux, recorded and edited by Joseph Epes Brown. Copyright 1953 by the University of Oklahoma Press.

"The Most-Sacred Mountain," poem by Eunice Tietjens in *New Voices*, edited by Marguerite Wilkinson. MacMillan Publishing Co. By permission of Janet Hart and Marshall Head.

"Hewn and Cleft from this Rock," by Holmes Rolston III. In *Main Currents in Modern Thought*, January-February, 1971. By permission of the author and *Main Currents in Modern Thought*.

Specified excerpts from *Poetry, Language, Thought*, by Martin Heidegger (translated by Albert Hofstadter). Copyright © 1971 by Martin Heidegger. Reprinted by permission of Harper & Row, Publishers, Inc.

"Open Letter to the People," by Ian (Sandy) Thompson. In *Deep Creek Review*, Summer, 1975. By permission of the author.

"Future Primitive," by Jerry Gorsline and Linn House. In the North Pacific Rim Alive Bundle of PLANET DRUM. By permission of the authors.

"Divine Madness," tape by Alan Watts. Big Sur Recordings. By permission of Mark Watts and the Electronic University, Box 361, Mill Valley, California, 94941.

"Part of a Winter," by George Sibley. *Mountain Gazette*, No. 40, By permission of *Mountain Gazette* and the author.

The Tewa World: Space, Time, Being and Becoming in a Pueblo Society, by Alfonso Ortiz. Copyright © 1969 University of Chicago Press. By permission of the publisher.

"Have you ever wanted to keep on walking until something happened?" by Alan Furst. *the Weekly* (Seattle, Washington), June 8-14, 1977. By permission of *the Weekly* and the author.

A Quest for Vision, by Tom Pinkson. By permission of the author.

"The Memorial," by the Unsoeld family. By permission of Willi Unsoeld.

The Tao of Painting, A Study of the Ritual Disposition of Chinese Painting, by Mai-Mai Sze. Bollingen Series XLIX, copyright © 1956, 1963 by Princeton University Press. Reprinted by permission of Princeton University Press.

Search for Gods, by Vincent Vycinas. Copyright © Martinus Nijhoff Boekhandel en Uitgeversmaatschappij B.V., The Hague. By permission.

Between Heaven and Earth, by Gaston Rébuffat. Published by Kaye and Ward Ltd., London, England. Reprinted by permission of the author.

Magical Child, by Joseph Chilton Pearce. Copyright © 1977 by Joseph Chilton Pearce. Reprinted by permission of E. P. Dutton, Inc.

The Meaning of Shinto, by J. W. T. Mason. Copyright © 1935 by E. P. Dutton, Inc. Reprinted by permission of E. P. Dutton, Inc.

The Earth, the Temple, and the Gods: Greek Sacred Architecture, by Vincent Scully. Copyright © 1962 by Yale University. By permission.

"By Frazier Creek Falls," by Gary Snyder. *Turtle Island*. Copyright © 1974 by Gary Snyder. Reprinted by permission of New Directions.

The Ecology of Imagination in Childhood, by Edith Cobb. Columbia University Press. By permission.

No Foreign Land, by Wilfred Pelletier and Ted Poole. Copyright © 1973 by Pantheon Books, a Division of Random House. By permission.

The Death of Classical Paganism, by John Holland Smith. Copyright © 1976 Charles Scribner's Sons. By permission.

The Tender Carnivore and the Sacred Game, by Paul Shepard © 1973 Charles Scribner's Sons. By permission.

Riprap and Cold Mountain: Poems, by Gary Snyder. Four Seasons Foundation. By permission of the author.

Eleusis: Archtypal Image of Mother and Daughter, by C. Kerenyi (translated by Ralph Manheim). Bollingen Series LXV, 4. Copyright © 1967 by Princeton University Press.

The Long-Legged House, by Wendell Berry. Harcourt Brace Jovanovich, Inc. By permission of the author.

Masked Gods, by Frank Waters. Copyright © 1950 by Frank Waters. Reprinted by permission of Joan Daves.

The Way and the Mountain, by Marco Pallis. Published by Peter Owen, London. By permission.

Report to Greco, by Nikos Kazantzakis. Copyright © 1965 by Simon & Schuster, Inc. Reprinted by permission of Simon & Schuster, a Division of Gulf & Western Corporation.

The Way of the White Clouds, A Buddhist Pilgrim in Tibet, by Lama Anagarika Govinda. Reprinted by permission of Rider & Company, London, England.

I wish to acknowledge with gratitude the following libraries and staff for their help: King County Library of Washington and Margaret Baunsgard; University of Washington Libraries, Tom Kaasa of the East Asia Library, and Helen Eilertson in cataloging; Ft. Lewis College Library, Dr. Harrold S. Shipp Jr., and Mrs. Schilling; Silverton Public Library and Stanna Meyers.

I also want to thank Beverly Bradley, Deborah and Tom Hart, Nancy and Jerry Hoffer, Ed LaChapelle and Dottie Smith for their special assistance.

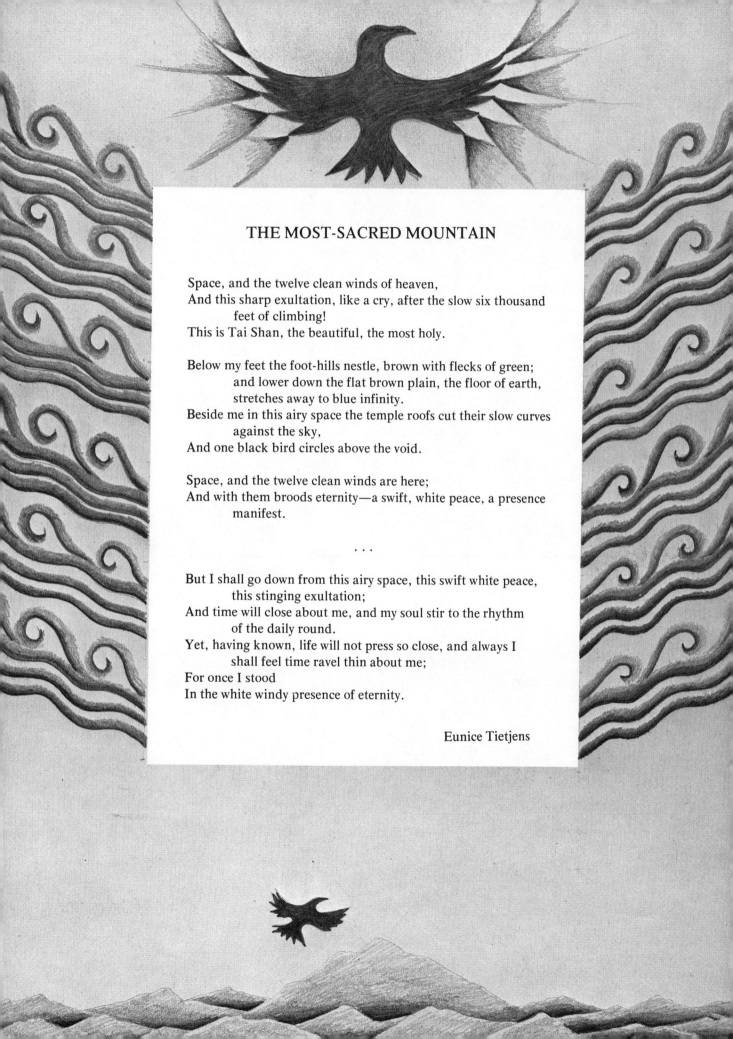

THE MOST-SACRED MOUNTAIN

Space, and the twelve clean winds of heaven,
And this sharp exultation, like a cry, after the slow six thousand
　　　feet of climbing!
This is Tai Shan, the beautiful, the most holy.

Below my feet the foot-hills nestle, brown with flecks of green;
　　　and lower down the flat brown plain, the floor of earth,
　　　stretches away to blue infinity.
Beside me in this airy space the temple roofs cut their slow curves
　　　against the sky,
And one black bird circles above the void.

Space, and the twelve clean winds are here;
And with them broods eternity—a swift, white peace, a presence
　　　manifest.

　　　　　　　. . .

But I shall go down from this airy space, this swift white peace,
　　　this stinging exultation;
And time will close about me, and my soul stir to the rhythm
　　　of the daily round.
Yet, having known, life will not press so close, and always I
　　　shall feel time ravel thin about me;
For once I stood
In the white windy presence of eternity.

　　　　　　　　　　　　Eunice Tietjens

VIEW FROM PANIC PEAK, looking south toward the summit of Mt. Olympus and the Snowdome. The glory was seen to the west of Panic Peak. Olympic National Park, Washington.   (Photograph by Ed LaChapelle)

Within and around the earth, within and around
the hills, within and around the mountain,
your authority returns to you.

A Tewa Prayer

The unitary fourfold of sky and earth, mortals
and divinities . . . we call—the world.

Martin Heidegger

This is the predilection of two warriors . . . This
earth, this world. For a warrior there can be no
greater love . . . This lovely being, which is alive
to its last recesses and understands every feeling,
soothed me, it cured me of my pains, and finally
when I had fully understood my love for it,
it taught me freedom.

Don Juan

Note to the reader

It is difficult to convey an understanding of wholistic natural systems by means of reading and writing in the prose form, which are predominantly left-brain activities. In an effort to overcome this limitation, I make use of poetic quotations which deal with the same material but in a totally different manner. The juxtaposition of the two will, I hope, bring greater understanding. Therefore, if a particular section seems unduly difficult, turn to the nearest meditation section (indicated by the drawings) in order to integrate the two hemispheres of the brain. Then, when you return to the previous section, you may find the difficulties resolved because some of the limitations of fragmented thinking have been by-passed.

In general, I have used the slightly awkward expression, *human being*, instead of man or mankind, not merely to avoid the sexist connotations of the latter terms; but, more specifically, to reinforce the fact that we human beings are only *one* kind of being on this earth and not necessarily wiser or more important for the whole organism, the earth itself, than any other being. Secondly, I have used the lower case *g* to begin the word *god* whenever I am not referring directly to the God of organized religious systems, in an effort to by-pass the stereotyped thinking associated with the word *God*.

Because this book is designed for the general reader, I have used a somewhat unusual reference system in order not to interrupt the narrative flow unnecessarily, yet still provide instant information on the sources used. The numbers in brackets refer to the numbered list of references in the back of the book. If there is a second number within the bracket, it is the page number in that reference.

Dolores LaChapelle
Way of the Mountain Center
Silverton, Colorado

Part I

1. The Glory

Each summer for sixteen years I lived on a small rock outcrop surrounded by the ice and snow of the Blue Glacier, 7,900 feet high, on the side of Mount Olympus in the middle of the Wilderness Area of the Olympic Peninsula in Washington. We were there to study the glacier as part of a long-range research project connected with the University of Washington. Throughout these years, every evening we would all climb up to the top of Panic Peak and watch the sun set. During the day, whenever I had free time from my other duties, I would climb up there to check the wild flowers, do Tai Chi, or just gaze at the mountains.

One misty morning in 1971 I climbed up toward my usual spot. But as I came onto the summit, there, filling the sky, was a giant shadowy figure surrounded by all the glory of three circular rainbows. It was such a powerful sight that I staggered and almost fell. Realizing the danger, so near the 2,500-foot drop of the cliff, I sat down. I sat there stunned for some time before I suddenly realized what it must be. To test it, I stood up and raised my right hand. The gigantic, three-mile high figure raised its arm. My gesture dominated a mile of glacier and towered over the valley as far as the next glacier, giving me a feeling of incredible power over all below me. Suddenly, there came into my mind all the stories from religious legends of the "devil" tempting the saint with "power over the world" from the heights of mountains. Then it occurred to me that, although I knew the scientific explanation of the glory, I was still impressed and awed by the "vision." For a person who had never even heard of a glory, such a manifestation would be even more awesome, in fact, miraculous. At that point, I realized that this meteorological phenomenon was possibly the origin of certain religious visions; furthermore, that probably it was also the underlying reason for the tradition of the haloes around the heads of saints.

The glory was gradually fading when I ran down to tell the others. Rushing into the cabin I said, "I just saw a triple glory!" Their first comment was, "Did you get a picture of it?" When I admitted that taking a picture was the furthest thought from my mind at the time, I was told that I could have made a fortune because no one has ever taken a photograph of a triple glory. I had to laugh. It was the time-honored reaction to a vision from on high: a mundane practical statement—"You could have made a fortune." Concretely, of course, I knew I had not seen a "vision"; instead, I had been privileged to witness a very rare natural meteorological phenomenon.

The only other person I know who has seen a glory is Ron Lindsay, who was working at the same Blue Glacier research station two years later when he saw a glory. When I asked him about it he said that it was a triple rainbow and he could see the shadowy figure within it. He went down to get his camera and brought two other persons back with him. The glory lasted a long time, almost half an hour. Then the clouds obscured the sun. He told me of his great excitement when he first saw the glory. And then he remembered thinking how fortunate he was to have seen this rare phenomenon, and that he had some idea of what caused it. Then, after he had waved his arms to test it, he told me that he thought, "Aha, now I really know where the custom of putting haloes around people's heads came from."

The best description in literature occurs in Henry Miller's *Big Sur and the Oranges of Hieronymus Bosch*, where he writes: "If it be shortly after sunup of a morning when the fog has obliterated the highway below, I am then rewarded with a spectacle rare to witness. Looking up the coast toward Nepenthe . . . the sun rising behind me throws an enlarged shadow of me into the iridescent fog below. I lift my arms as in prayer, achieving a wingspan no god ever possessed, and there in the

drifting fog a nimbus floats about my head, a radiant nimbus such as the Buddha himself might proudly wear. In the Himalayas, where the same phenomenon occurs, it is said that a devout follower of the Buddha will throw himself from a peak—'into the arms of Buddha.'"
[220, 95]

It was not until years later, when I read a book on Mount Omei, one of the four Buddhist sacred mountains in China, that I found a written account of a vision by the Abbot of Chieh Yin Tien:

Suddenly, I became aware that the Boddhisatva Samantabhadra had bequeathed his manifestation to this human world, displaying many varieties of visible phenomenon. Perhaps it is a matter of fore-ordained causation. The singular wonder is that every time, when winds and clouds change suddenly and fantastically, there appears unexpectedly a huge round bright circle, floating across the mountain, full of strange colors, gathering into splendour. At the moment, peaks, ridges, grass, and trees are all fresh, gleaming and magnificent. Even when the clouds and mist have already dispersed, this bright sphere still remains illuminated all by itself. Certainly this is the universally shining "Buddha's Glory", amidst which appears a world of encircling clouds. A further wonder is that before this colorful circle appears, clouds and mist must first come into sight . . . Again, this is another verification that the Boddhisatva Samantabhadra makes suggestive revelation to all living beings.   [130]

The English editor of the modern edition of the book has inserted a footnote which states: "Fu Kuang [the Chinese for "Buddha's Glory"], a corona of rainbow colors, lying on the cloud floor below the cliff [whence the "Buddha's Glory" is usually viewed] in which the spectator's shadow is cast." [130]

Thus, I finally found proof that a religious vision seen by this Buddhist abbot was, in reality, a glory. The history of Mt. Omei is closely intertwined with this vision, which was first recorded in the reign of Ming Ti (58–75 A.D.) when an official climbed up the lower slopes of Mt. Omei looking for herbs. Through the mist he saw the footprints of a deer but they were not like an ordinary deer. He followed the tracks up the mountain. They led him up to the summit and at the edge of a fierce precipice they disappeared. When he looked over the edge he beheld a wondrous sight: "a sphere of circling light; around its edges were five colours in seven layers." [130] Awed by this miraculous sight he rushed down the mountain to an old hermit and told him the strange story. The old hermit told him: "What you have seen is no other than a special manifestation to you of the glory of the great Boddhisatva P'u Hsien; fitting it is, therefore, that this mountain should be the centre from which his teachings may be spread abroad. The Boddhisatva has certainly favored you above all men." On the spot where he had seen the glory, the official built the first of the Buddhist temples, the Hall of Universal Glory. Since then, the hope of seeing the Buddha's glory has drawn many pilgrims to the mountain, but the monks say that, "One cannot behold it unless he possess foreordained good luck." [130]

Adam's Peak, a mountain in Ceylon, which is sacred to four religions, has a phenomenon called "Shadow of the Peak." Sir James Emerson Tennent, in a book published in 1859, states that phenomena of this kind may have "suggested to the early painters the idea of the glory surrounding the heads of beatified saints." He adds this description: "To the spectator his own figure, but more particularly the head, appears surrounded by a halo as vivid as if radiated from diamonds. The Buddhists may possibly have taken from this beautiful object their idea of the *agni* or emblem of the sun, with which the head of Buddha is surmounted. But, unable to express a *halo* in sculpture, they concentrated it into a flame." [317, 72]

In Coleridge's poem, "Constancy to an Ideal Object," written in 1826, he refers to a somewhat similar phenomenon called a *Heiligenschein* caused by the sun on a snowmist. The poem concerns a woodman walking up a glen:

> The viewless snow-mist weaves a glistening haze,
> Sees full before him, gliding without tread,
>
> An image with a glory round its head;
> The enamoured rustic worships its fair hues,
> Nor knows he makes the shadow, he pursues!

Coleridge had himself experienced such a phenomenon and refers to a book titled *Aids to Reflection*, published in 1825, which states: "The beholder either recognizes it is a projected form of his own Being, that moves before him with a Glory round its head, or recoils from it as a Spectre." [60]

In Alpine climbing, it is usually referred to as the "Spectre of the Brocken." The first Englishman to see this phenomenon was climbing with a guide on a peak named *Brocken*. In Goethe's *Faust* there is a line: "Near to the Brocken the witches fly." The diverse meanings of the words *spectre* and *glory* indicate the different states of mind of those viewing the same phenomenon. Apparently religious-minded persons such as the Chinese abbot, or those who have a love of nature, call it a glory. Those who fear the mountains, such as the peasant guide, or who are out to conquer nature, such as the English climber, call it a spectre, which has a demonic connotation. In the early climbing days in the Alps, it was not generally realized that the figure seen in the circular rainbow is that of the viewer.

After completing the first ascent of the Matterhorn in 1865, Whymper and six others were on the way down when one of the members of the party slipped. He fell against one of the guides, knocking him off, and pulled two more along before the rope broke, leaving Whymper and the two remaining guides safe. Very slowly and very fearfully the three remaining men climbed down the mountain. At 6:00 p.m. they had reached the snow upon the ridge descending towards Zermatt "and all peril was over . . ." They looked down the snow, still hunting for any sign of their friends. Whymper writes, "Convinced at last that they were neither within sight nor hearing, we ceased from our useless efforts; and, too cast down for speech, silently gathered up our things, and the little effects of those who were lost, preparatory to continuing the descent. When, lo! a mighty arch appeared, rising above the Lyskamm, high into the sky. Pale, colourless, and noiseless, but perfectly sharp and defined, except where it was lost in the clouds, this unearthly apparition seemed like a vision from another world; and, almost appalled, we watched with amazement the gradual development of two vast crosses on either side . . . The Taugwalders thought it had some connection with the accident, and I, after a while, that it might bear some relation to ourselves . . . The spectral form remained motionless. It was a fearful and wonderful sight; unique in my experience, and impressive beyond description, coming at such a moment." [357, 399]

On the opening page of Whymper's book, *Scrambles Amongst the Alps*, is a drawing which he made of this sight. It shows an almost complete circle with one partial cross or line in the center and two complete crosses on either side of it. Since three men were involved, their shadows would make the three figures. The shadows would be very indistinct because Whymper refers to the bow as pale and colorless.

One of the most incredible accounts of a glory which I have ever read is that of one which occurred in the spring of 1953 at the Grand Canyon. In an article entitled "The Brocken Spectre of the Desert View Watch Tower, Grand Canyon," Donald Black wrote in *Science* magazine that it was first noticed at about 9:00 a.m. but lasted all day. The glory stayed with the shadow of the tower as it was shortened by the sun high in the sky and it moved from the west toward the east as the sun moved across the sky. "As late as 4:00 p.m., the spectre was still visible in a small side canyon lying about ENE of the tower; the shadow was then about 400 feet in length." The author describes the spectre as consisting "of a series of colors which are or bow around the shadow of the tower." [30] He points out that it is rarely seen. Charles Farmer, tower supervisor, stated that during his twenty years of duty at Grand Canyon he had never seen the spectre before 1953.

As the book on Mt. Omei states: "Not a ray of the felicitous Glory can any brush portray . . ." The illustrator of the book settled for putting the Chinese characters for "Buddha's Glory" in the circular bow. It is equally impossible to capture anything of the power of the spectacle with a camera.*

The best color photo is in Rébuffat's book. It is labeled "Brocken Spectre" and was taken on the Matterhorn by Pierre Tairraz. Although this photograph is the best of a glory taken throughout the 120 years that the Chamonix family of Tairraz have photographed the mountains, it can give no real idea of the impact of the glory when actually viewed from a mountain. First, the glory is an unsaturated color phenomenon, so the camera cannot register the colors as brightly as the eye can. Second, the figure is shadowy and indistinct and the seeming height of the figure is barely discernible because the valley floor is only vague through the mist. The enormous figure, filling the sky, which I saw and which I will refer to again in the following chapter when I go into detail on the visions of religious figures, cannot be discerned in photographs. The immense height of the figure is due to the fact that one sees the valley or lower cliffs behind the fog. The figure I saw seemed to be three miles high because it covered all the land between the cliff I was on and the terminus of the White Glacier some three miles away. Of course, I realized later that it wasn't that high but the intuitive, immediate feeling is that it *is* three miles high because it covers three miles. This is the reason that both Ron Lindsay and I, when we saw it, tested it by waving our arms. It is almost impossible to believe that the huge figure is one's own shadow.

In the New World it is very likely that the small circular arc of a rainbow, shown over the head of the figure in American Indian visionary drawings, actually stands for a glory. These visions were usually experienced on mountains. The only drawing which shows plainly that it is a glory is one done by Geronimo which shows a figure in the air surrounded by a circle.

Until recently, the glory was a rare spectacle because it requires an unusual relationship between the sun, the observer, and a cloud composed of droplets of uniform size. Now that air travel is common, the glory is seen more often because the sun can project the plane's shadow onto the clouds below it, providing a configuration conducive to the glory appearing.

The first scientific record of the glory dates back to a French expedition to Peru in 1735. A free translation of what Pierre Bouguer wrote follows: "The small distance made it possible that one could distinguish all parts of the shadow; one saw the arms, the legs, and the head. That which astonished us the most was the appearance of a Glory or Aureole which encircled the head and which consisted of three or four small concentric rings

*Photographs in color of a glory:
1. Gaston Rébuffat and Pierre Tairraz. *Between Heaven and Earth*. London, Kaye and Ward (unpaged).
2. Richard Scorer. *Clouds of the World, a Complete Color Encyclopedia*. Harrisburg, Pa.: Stackpole Books, 1972 (page 139). This is taken from an airplane and shows the plane's shadow surrounded by a glory.
3. Howard C. Bryant and Nelson Jarmie. "The Glory." *Scientific American*, July 1974.
Black and white drawings and photographs:
1. Edward Whymper. *Scrambles Amongst the Alps in the Years 1860–1869*. London: John Murray, 1871 (frontispiece).
2. M. Minnaert. *The Nature of Light and Colour in the Open Air*. New York: Dover, 1954 (frontispiece).

consisting of intense colors, each ring having the same color distribution as the main rainbow with red on the outside." [327]

Early scientific efforts to understand the glory date back to 1895 when C.T.R. Wilson built the first cloud chamber to try to reproduce a glory in the laboratory. He had seen one in 1894 from the top of Ben Nevis in Scotland.

Simply stated, the glory is produced by the scattering of light from water droplets back toward the sun, thus enhancing the light. This enhanced light is what can cause the valley below the glory to be seen in psychedelically bright colors, such as described by the abbott on Mt. Omei when he wrote: "Peaks, ridges, grass and trees are all fresh, gleaming and magnificent." Often it is possible to see backscattering when a car's headlights strike a cat's eyes at night. The light from the headlights is brought to a focus on the cat's retina and then some of it is scattered back toward the lens of the cat's eye and refracted back toward the car, so that the cat's eyes seem to glow from within.

In a glory, the light is scattered backward from the spherical edges of hundreds of water droplets instead of from a cat's two eyes. According to Bryant and Jarmie, the authors of "The Glory" in *Scientific American*, in explaining how this occurs, "we approach some current frontiers of optics and particle physics." In 1908 the physicist Gustav Mie showed that the intensity of the light scattered backward can be "represented as a sum of a series of algebraic terms." But the complexity of this method is enormous. It would take some 6,300 algebraic terms evaluated and added together to determine the wavelength of only one color for only one droplet.

Modern techniques in physics allow us to bypass the difficulties in evaluating this series. It turns out that there are two types of contributions to the glory: one stems from internal reflections within the droplet (higher-order rainbows), and one is contributed by surface waves.

The internal reflections involve complex angular momentum calculations. To trace the actual pattern of the scattering of the light rays, Bryant and Jarmie mention research done at the University of New Mexico: "Their results can be interpreted to obtain the probability of finding a particle of light (a photon) at a given point in space . . . The peaks and troughs in the probability curve can be interpreted in terms of waves reflecting around the inside of the droplet and interfering with one another constructively (the peaks) and destructively (the troughs). These waves correspond to light rays bouncing around inside the droplet at close to the critical angle." [43]

The paths of the light in the water droplets which form a glory differ from those which form rainbows. For a glory, "The paths consist of light that is reflected repeatedly at an angle of 82.8 degrees within the droplet, together with small segments of surface waves in which the light clings to the surface of the droplet and is conveyed the rest of the way around the droplet to the backward direction. When a number of different paths give rise to light waves that are in phase, there is a resonance, or enhancement, in the backscattered light. The glory is believed to be due principally to the paths in which the light travels halfway around the droplet and those in which it travels three and a half times around the droplet before being sent straight back." [43] The colors of the glory are thus due to the different wavelengths of the sunlight going through cycles of maximum and minimum brightness at different angles.

The contributions to the glory from surface waves are described by the concept of Regge poles. As Nussenzveig, in his article, "The Theory of the Rainbow," points out, "Instead of a great many terms, one can work with just a few points called poles and saddle points. In recent years the poles have attracted great theoretical interest in the physics of elementary particles. In that context they are usually called Regge poles . . . Multiple internal reflections that happen to produce star-shaped polygons play an important role, leading to resonances, or enhancements in intensity." [235]

Bryant and Jarmie, in summing up their article, write: "Thus we find that an important component of the explanation of the glory is quite similar to one concept in the theory of elementary particles." [43] In quantum mechanics, elementary particles are described as having wave characteristics, which are related to the probabilities of finding a particle at particular points in space and time. I will go into this further for those with little knowledge of physics. Both light and matter at the subatomic level behave like separate particles and also like waves. Capra, in *Tao of Physics*, explains this further: "Light . . . is emitted and absorbed in the form of 'quanta,' or photons, but when these particles of light travel through space they appear as vibrating electric and magnetic fields which show all the characteristics of waves." [48, 152] Heinsenberg's "uncertainty principle" states that we can never accurately determine both the position of a particle and its momentum simultaneously. The more accurately we know its position the less accurately we know its momentum and *vice versa*. Heisenberg further explained the implications of this relationship: "Natural science does not simply describe and explain nature; it is part of the interplay between nature and ourselves." [122, 81]

Bryant and Jarmie close their article by characterizing the glory as a "striking demonstration of the wave nature of light and a colorful reminder of the underlying unity of the physical world." [43] Although the reference to "underlying unity" by these scientist-authors is to the fact that the wave-particle duality exhibited by light is shared by all the elementary particles which make up matter, an even deeper level of this underlying unity is demonstrated by the *relationship* between the human being, the mountain, and the sky (sun and cloud) which allows the glory to *be* a visible phenomenon. If the human being, the mountain, the sun, and clouds are not in a particular relationship at the time, there simply is *no* glory. The following chapter explores some particular relationships between human beings, mountains, and sky which have been important in human history.

2. The Glory, The Mountain, and the God

The human eye, the sun, and the cloud droplets must be in a particular relationship for the glory to occur. The glory appears in the opposite direction from the sun and, since the sun is usually above the observer, it follows that the glory is seen below. Thus, the mountain is crucial for the manifestation of the glory with its accompanying feelings of unity, power, and awe-feelings usually labelled "religious". If we look further into this, we find a definite relationship between mountains and the beginnings of religions.

According to our European tradition, the highest achievements of religious thought have occurred in the "prophetic" religions. Going back to the beginnings of the oldest of the prophetic religions, we find the mysterious semi-legendary figure of Spitama Zarathustra, commonly known as Zoroaster.

Zoroaster

According to the sacred writings of the Zoroastrian religion, the *Zend Avesta*, Zoroaster wandered, searching for the truth, for ten to fifteen years. Then, on the "mountain of the Holy Communing Ones" [133, 33], Zoroaster encountered the "soul of the Earth." From this high mountain, Zoroaster looked out over the devastated, over-grazed country and intoned the first Gāthā:

> With hands in prayer uplifted
> To Mazda the quickening spirit,
> I fain would give due honour
> To all who, by good works, win favour
> From him the Good, the Holy (Ahura Mazda)
> And from the soul of earth, our mother.
>
> [133, 212]

He heard the "soul of the Earth" lamenting to heaven:

> For whom did ye form me? Who made me?
> On me all ills are working,
> Drought and murder, and force and rapine . . ."
>
> [133, 224]

The "soul of the earth" is complaining of the conditions brought about by the nomadic branch of the Aryan tribe. According to Haug:

The Aryan tribes, after they had left their original home, which was in all likelihood a cold country, led mainly a pastoral life, and cultivated only occasionally some patches of land for their own support . . . [They] were given to this nomadic life as long as they occupied the upper part of the Punjab, whence they afterwards emigrated into Hindustan proper. Some of these tribes, whom we may style the Iranians proper, became soon weary of these constant wanderings, and after having reached such places between the Oxus and Yaxartes rivers and the highland of Bactria as were deemed fit for permanent settlement they forsook the pastoral life of their ancestors and their brother tribes and became agricultural. In consequence of this change the Iranians estranged themselves from the other Aryan tribes, which still clung to the ancestral occupations and allured by the hope of obtaining booty, regarded those settlements as the most suitable objects for their incursions and skirmishes. [111, 292–293]

Zoroaster, belonging to the Iranian branch of the Aryan tribes, equated the "good" with the settled life, with cultivating the earth and caring for it.

During the seven or eight years following the first vision, Zoroaster had six more visions on at least four different mountains. The account of these visions is contained in the early Gāthās (songs) where it is frequently pointed out that the true rites are fire-worship and agriculture. [111, 165] The earth is praised: "I praise the earth, the wide-stretched, the passable, the large, the unbounded, the mother . . ." [111, 184]

Only the Gāthās are thought to be the work of Zoroaster himself but even after his time in the *Zamyâd Yasht*, the earth is directly invoked. The word, *Zamyâd*, refers to the earth. This *Yasht* "is chiefly devoted to the praise of the glory (quarenô)." This glory is closely related to mountains with names such as "creator of light" and "district of light," which may indicate an actual meteorological glory, but at this late date there is no way to determine the facts about this. The Zamyâd describes the origin of all mountains out of the heart of the central and primeval mountain, Alborz. [111, 216]

The basic duality of Zoroaster is reflected in the word *Ahuras*, the "living ones" (Zoroaster's people) who were opposed to the Devas. The Supreme Being, Ahura Mazda, means the Ahura who is called Mazda. In modern Persian this word becomes Hormazd or Ormazd. "Ahuramazda [creates] all that is good, bright, shining." [111, 216]

There is a close similarity between the religious rites of the Brahmanical Indians and the people of Zoroaster. The fundamental difference concerns the word *deva*. In the Vedas, the sacred writing of India, the gods are called *devas*; however, in the writings of Zoroastianism, this same word *deva*, Persian *div*, is the evil spirit—a demon or devil. [111, 267] The word *devil* came into the Jewish religion from the time when the Hebrews were captives in Babylon and thence into Christianity.* According to Zoroaster, devas or devils "are the originators of all that is bad . . . and are constantly thinking of causing the destruction of fields and trees." This connotation has its origin in the fact that their former fellow tribesmen, the Indians, were running their cattle, sheep and goats over their fields, destroying them. [111, 267] At the head of the list of evil devas, according to Zoroaster, was Daevanam Daevo, or archdemon. Following him was Indra (who was the king of the Vedic gods of India), and third was Saurva (the Shiva of the Hindus).

Zoroaster's followers fenced their fields off from this destruction which created further fighting with the "deva worshippers." The Persian word *pairi-daêza*, meaning a "beautiful garden fenced in," was taken over into the Old Testament as the word *paradise*, and thence spread over the whole civilized world. [111, 5] The origin of the words which, even to this day, convey our ideas of good and evil come from the treatment of the earth long ago, in the time of Zoroaster in the seventh or sixth century before Christ.

This basic dualism of the good creation and the bad creation fighting for control of the earth persists in later sacred writings. Its roots can be traced back to Zoroaster's experience of the sheep-ravaged, dry, barren, rocky hillsides where the nomads wandered and the well-watered, cared-for, enclosed gardens (paradise) of the Iranians. Agriculture became a religious duty to the Zoroastrians. In the *Vendidad* this chant occurs:

> When barley occurs, then the demons hiss;
> When thrashing occurs, then the demons whine;
> When grinding occurs, then the demons roar;
> When flour occurs, then the demons flee.
>
> [111, 232]

The *Vendidad*, which originally meant "against the Devas", [111, 173] lists the most evil of all actions: "performing burning (of the dead), and idol-worship, and causing oppression, and cutting down trees" [111, 217]. Earth and fire were equally sacred, so the dead could neither be burned nor buried, which led to the practice of exposing the dead bodies on scaffolds so that birds could devour them. Some of the Amerindian tribes also exposed their dead on scaffolds—perhaps for the same reason, that Mother Earth is sacred.

How strange that the very lands which the ancient Zoroastrians so carefully protected are now among the most seriously eroded lands on earth! However, we see the beginnings of the problem in the later *Vendidad*, where the Zoroastrian fear and hatred of the devas, no longer related to an existing nomadic people, becomes an abstract concept of devils and demons, with a resultant complexity of rites, rituals, and exorcisms. When religion lost its contact with the earth of Zoroaster's original teaching, the people lost their awareness of the earth's need. Combined with an increasing population, it led to the destruction of the soil.

The Importance of Mountains and Sacred Standing Rocks in the Beginnings of Judaism

Biblical revelation began with Abraham (about 2000–1500 B.C.), the father of the Jewish religion. [212, 6] His father and all of his clan left Ur of the Chaldeans to go to the land of Canaan. They settled in Haran, where Abraham's father died, for some years, and then travelled on toward Canaan, passing through the land as far as Shechem, which means "shoulder of the mountain" [212, 797]. The Book of Genesis tells how, at the famous oak tree of Moreh, the Lord appeared to Abraham and told him he would give his descendants the land. "So he built there an altar to the Lord . . . Thence he removed to the mountain on the east of Bethel . . . and there he built an altar to the Lord and called on the name of the Lord." Modern excavations at Shechem unearthed a large temple, with walls sixteen feet thick, which was probably a temple of Baal-berith. This was a Canaanite sect, the religion of the people who inhabited this land before the arrival of Abraham: "Standing stones were found before the temple; these are the cult symbol (massebah) mentioned so frequently in the Old Testament." [212, 798] For more about these stones see below.

In the final test of a long series of tests, God called Abraham to take his son and go to the land of Moriah and offer him as a burnt offering "upon one of the mountains which I shall tell you." Abraham travelled three days and on the third day "lifted up his eyes and

---

*Ernesto Buonaiuti, former professor of the history of early Christianity at the University of Rome, summed up the importance of Zoroaster when he wrote: "Today no one can deny the influence of the Iranian cult of Zoroaster upon the postexilic Hebrew religion, and, more generally speaking, upon the whole development of spiritual life in the Mediterranean basin, from the end of the sixth century on." [44, 221]

saw the place afar off." Then, taking his son Isaac and the wood and the knife he set out for the mountain. His son said, "Behold, the fire and the wood; but where is the lamb for a burnt offering?" Abraham said, "God will provide himself the lamb for a burnt offering, my son." On top of the mountain, just as Abraham put forth his hand to slay his son, the angel of the Lord called him and told him not to slay his son. "I know now that you fear God, seeing you have not withheld your son, your only son, from me." He saw a ram caught in a thicket by the horns and Abraham offered it instead of his son. "So Abraham called the name of the place The Lord will provide; as it is said to this day, 'On the mount of the Lord it shall be provided.'" Then the angel of the Lord told Abraham, "I will indeed bless you, and I will multiply your descendants as the stars of heaven and as the sand which is on the seashore." (Gen. 22:17)

The great rock on the top of the Temple Mount, "Abraham's Hallowed High Place," the spot where he offered up Isaac, became the altar and the center around which Solomon built the great temple a thousand years before Christ. Later, a church was built there by the Crusaders. Finally, 1200 years ago, "Caliph Ab El Melek built a mosque upon the spot and left the naked top of the bold mountain bare, as devout Mussulmen believe that Muhammed ascended to heaven from it. This rock, 56 feet long by 42 feet wide, is surrounded by a richly wrought railing, and is directly under a noble dome . . . [This] is the most historic rock in the world . . . virgin rock that has remained the same for thirty centuries carefully guarded by all schools of religious faith." [340, 234]

Returning now to the "standing stones," the *massebah,* upright stone pillars of raw unhewn stone, according to McKenzie these were the symbols for Baal. "The Baal was worshipped on the high places." The Old Testament often speaks of Baals in the plural because in different localities the God Baal took different forms. "Baal worship appeared early in Israel; the Israelites worshipped the Baal—Peor of Moab . . . Several of the kings of Israel and Judah permitted or patronized the cult of the Baal. Yahweh was sometimes given the attributes of the Baal and worshipped with the rites of the Baal." [212, 72] The beginnings of the Old Testament religion used the language of Baal worship, as well as the sites and the very altars. The worship of Baal continued to be a danger to Israelite belief, and the Old Testament contains traces of the lingering fear of the old religion of the sacred places on the mountains. In Psalm 121: "I will lift up my eyes to the hills: From whence does my help come? My help comes from the Lord, who made heaven and earth." The question mark in this psalm is ignored in modern times; however, the real meaning is clear when we look at Jeremiah 3:23, "Truly the hills are a delusion, the orgies on the mountains. Truly in the Lord our God is the salvation of Israel."

Abraham knew God under the name, El Shaddai, the name by which the God of the Israelites was known until the time of Moses. Many authorities translate it as "The One of the Mountain." In Canaanite mythology, north was the seat of divinity, "the mountain of the north," and the god lived on this mountain. [212, 316 and 260]

In later writings of the Bible, and indeed down to the present day, the God of the Jewish religion is often referred to as the God of Abraham, of Isaac, and of Jacob. A brief look into the Old Testament shows that each time God revealed himself to each of these patriarchs, it was in a particular place. The revelation came out of a particular relationship between the man and the *place.* Abraham was told to travel three days until God designated the mountain where the sacrifice of Isaac was to take place. Later, for Isaac, the *place* was called Gerar. There was a famine and the Lord appeared to Isaac and said, "Do not go down to Egypt; dwell in the land of which I shall tell you. Sojourn in this land, and I will be with you, and will bless you; for to you and to your descendants I will give all these lands . . . So Isaac dwelt in Gerar." Jacob, the son of Isaac and younger brother of Esau, journeyed to Paddan-Aram, partly out of fear of his brother's vengeance and partly because his father wanted him to marry one of his kinswomen and not a Canaanite woman. Jacob started on his journey, and when the sun set, he stopped for the night. He took a stone as his pillow and dreamed of the ladder leading from earth to heaven, with angels on it. The Lord stood above it and said, "I am the Lord, the God of Abraham your father and the God of Isaac; the land on which you lie I will give to you and to your descendants . . . Behold I am with you and will keep you . . . and will bring you back to this land." Then Jacob woke up and said, "How awesome is this place! This is none other than the house of God, and this is the gate of heaven." Early the next morning Jacob took the stone on which he had slept, set it up as a pillar, and poured oil on it. He called it Bethel, or *bet el*, "house of El (god)." [212, 91]

When Cyrus the Great liberated the Jews and permitted them to return to their homeland, they took back with them influences of Zoroastrianism. The prophet Ezekiel, exiled to Babylon by Nebuchadnessar in 597 B.C., was a link between pre-exile Israel and the Judaism of the restoration. Ezekiel's vision occurred in the month of the ancient god Tammuz, the season of the summer solstice when the descent of the sun-god from the sky occurred. The crucial parts of the vision are found in the first chapter of Ezekial: "As I looked, behold, a stormy wind came out of the north, and a great cloud, with brightness round about it . . . their wings touched one another; they went . . . without turning as they went . . . In the midst . . . there was something that looked like burning coals of fire, like torches moving to and fro among the living creatures; and the fire was bright, and out of the fire went forth lightning . . . I saw a wheel upon the earth . . . as it were a wheel within a wheel." The form on the throne "was a likeness as it were of a human form . . . and there was brightness around about him. Like the appearance of the bow that is in the cloud on the day of rain, so was the appearance of the brightness round about. Such was the appearance of the likeness of the glory of the Lord. And when I saw it, I fell upon my face . . ."

Ezekiel's vision was of an enthroned man surrounded by a rainbow-like form. It might have been the meterological phenomenon of the glory but the context of the biblical passage does not seem to indicate that Ezekiel was on a mountain. It is more likely that he was seeing a halo complex.*

After the people of Israel were led by Moses out of Egypt into the wilderness, the glory of the Lord appeared often, as when the Israelites complained of hunger and for having left Egypt. Exodus records that "As Aaron spoke to the whole congregation of the people of Israel, they looked toward the wilderness, and behold, the glory of the Lord appeared in the cloud." The most famous occasion was when Moses went up to Mt. Sinai, and the cloud covered the mountain. "The glory of the Lord settled on Mt. Sinai . . . Now the appearance of the glory of the Lord was like a devouring fire on the top of the mountain in the sight of the people of Israel." "The glory of the Lord appeared to all the congregation" is reported several times in Leviticus and Numbers.

Elsewhere in the Bible, as McKenzie points out, "the glory of Yahweh appears rather as a brilliant light, and it is visible to men only when it is veiled by a cloud which is rendered luminous by that which it contains . . . In later books the concept of glory loses some of its primitive concrete reality, and to see the glory of Yahweh means to witness His saving acts." [212, 313] This may mean, however, that with the growing loss of contact with nature, the glory no longer appeared to the people as reality. They could imagine it only as a spiritual activity of God. What these manifestations really were—glory or sun halo—we cannot determine, but the fact that the Israelites were travelling through the wilderness in close contact with the mountains and the sky makes it more likely that they would see this type of optical phenomena than at later times in their history, when they led a more settled existence.

Before we leave the Old Testament, mention must be made of the prophet Elijah and the celebrated contest on Mt. Carmel. Elijah lived during the reign of King Ahab of Israel, whose wife, Jezebel, favored the worship of Baal. Rain had been scarce for some time. Elijah told Ahab that he had forsaken the commandments of the Lord and followed the false gods, the Baals. Elijah affirmed the "supremacy of Yahweh over nature" [212, 232] and told Ahab to gather the 450 prophets of Baal on Mt. Carmel, one of the sacred mountains of Palestine associated with the ancient worship of Baal. Carmel is only 2,000 feet high, but it rises steeply from the Mediterranean Sea. It presents a vertical appearance and access is difficult.

Elijah proposed that the prophets of Baal be given one bull and he another; that each bull be cut into pieces and laid on the wood, but that no fire be put under it. The priests of Baal, the Book of Kings tells us, "called on the name of Ba'al from morning until noon . . . And *as midday passed* they raved on . . . but no one answered, no one heeded." Elijah then prepared his offering and called on the Lord. "Then the fire of the Lord fell, and consumed the burnt offering." Elijah seems to have been wiser than the priests of Baal because clouds are more likely to gather around a mountain in the afternoon.

The name, Mt. Carmel, has since passed into mystical writings as a synonym for the Ascent to God, as exemplified by the Spanish Carmelite, St. John of the Cross, in his famous poem, "A Poem for the Ascent of Mount Carmel." The original order of Carmelites was founded at Mt. Carmel by the Crusader Berthold in the twelfth century. The Spanish mystic, Saint Teresa of Avila, was a Carmelite nun.

Jesus and Mountains in the New Testament

Six mountains are closely associated with significant events in Jesus' adult life. The first is the Mountain of the Temptation, where, at the beginning of his public career, he fasted for forty days and forty nights and wrestled with the devil. Traditionally it is thought to be Jebel-Quarantal, [42, 80] a barren rocky peak which rises a thousand feet from the plain of Jordan west of Jericho. Today, part way up this mountain, there is a Greek monastery hewn out of the living rock where Jesus supposedly sat. From this rock Jesus looked out over the depths below as far as the Arabian desert. The final temptation took place on the summit of the mountain. From the summit can be seen the oasis of Jericho with its fruit groves and springs of water. Between the reeds, the Jordan can be seen winding toward the Dead Sea, with mountains of Moab on the eastern shore. "All these things will I give thee, if thou fall down and worship me," the devil said. Jesus, for the third time, repulsed him: "Get thee hence, Satan, for it is written: Thou shalt worship the Lord thy God, and him only shalt thou serve." The similarity to Zoroaster's view over fertile fields and barren, overgrazed slopes is striking.

On the western shore of the Sea of Galilee lies the mount called "The Horns of Hattin." "The horn-like crests [of black basalt] rise against the sky with the sweeping curve of their high valley between." [340] In the grassy valley between the horns, looking out over the

---

*Alistair B. Fraser, of the Meterology Department of Pennsylvania State, speculates that this may have been the case. [92, A92]

Sea of Galilee only three miles away, Jesus told the waiting multitudes of the Beatitudes which outline the basis of the Christian life.

The word *horns* in the name of the mountain and its shape indicate that it was probably an ancient Mother Goddess shrine, thus a sacred mountain for the surrounding locality from ancient times. Jesus, who lived in a close relationship with the earth, would naturally choose such a "place of power" to deliver an important teaching such as the Beatitudes. Here he spoke, teaching "as one having authority . . . Six times the words rang out across the hillside: 'Ye have heard that it hath been said by them of old time . . . But I say unto you . . .' So the great Lawgiver, the Moses of the New Covenant, made an end of Israel's Sinai and exalted the Mount of the Beatitudes into the Sinai of all mankind." [42, 118]

The hills were covered with wildflowers and of them Jesus said, "Consider the lilies of the field, how they grow; they toil not, neither do they spin: and yet I say unto you, that even Solomon in all his glory was not arrayed like one of these." Jesus had faith in the goodness of Nature: "Take no thought for your life, what ye shall eat, or what ye shall drink; nor yet for your body, what ye shall put on . . . Behold the fowls of the air: for they sow not, neither do they reap, nor gather into barns; yet your heavenly Father feedeth them . . ."

There are two possible sites of the Mountain of the Transfiguration, Mt. Tabor or Mt. Hermon, but as McKenzie states of Mt. Tabor, "the probable presence of a village on the summit in New Testament times makes this identification improbable." [212, 865]

Mt. Hermon, 9,232 feet high, is crowned with perpetual snow on its summit. It is the source of the life-giving Jordan river and a landmark for nearly all of Palestine, as it can be seen from as far as the Red Sea. [340, 208] It was a sacred mountain for a number of peoples even before the time of the Israelites. The Amorite people called it Senir; the Phoenicians, Sirion; and the Hittites dwelt at the foot of it and called it Mt. Sariyana. Sariyana is included in the list of deities who witnessed the treaty of the Hittite King Mursilis and Duppe-Teshub of Amurru. [269]

Soon after the first prediction of his passion in the New Testament, Jesus went into the mountains to meditate, taking Peter, James, and John with him.

At the top of the mountain, the Transfiguration occurred. St. Matthew wrote, "His face shone with the brightness of the sun and his garments took on the whiteness of light itself. They became shining." Jesus was joined by two figures who likewise appeared transfigured. The disciples said it was Moses, the giver of the Old Law on Mt. Sinai, and Elijah, the great prophet and forerunner of the Messiah. But then a cloud overshadowed them and hid them. The voice of the Lord was heard, and the disciples fell on their faces in terror. It was only when Jesus touched them they dared to look, but they saw no one there but Jesus as they knew him.

St. Peter, especially, was struck by the Transfiguration. Wherever he went, he proclaimed the Transfiguration of the Lord. In his second letter, he writes, "We were eye-witnesses of His majesty. For when He received honor and glory from God the Father and the voice came borne to him by the Majestic Glory, 'This is my beloved Son,' we heard the voice borne from heaven, for we were with Him on the holy mountain."

McKenzie says: "The revelation made to Peter, James, and John in this passage has no parallel, in the Old Testament or New Testament." [212, 897] There are some interesting similarities to the meteorological phenomenon of the glory. The shining splendor of Jesus' garments recalls the brilliant colors of the landscape as seen through the glory on Mt. Omei. The vision ended suddenly with the coming of the cloud "overshadowing them", which often happens when the glory is destroyed by the clouds moving in closer. Finally, there were three men at the spot below where Jesus was praying; if there was a glory, there would be three figures in the glory.

The Mount of Olives is the main hill east of Jerusalem. It is mentioned in the Old Testament in Samuel: "When David came to the summit, where God was worshipped . . ." The triumphal entry of Jesus into Jerusalem began on this mountain, and Gethsemane lay on its lower western slopes. It was the scene of the agony in the garden and Jesus' arrest, as well as the scene of his Ascension. The Mount of Olives is conspicuous from every part of Jerusalem.

Golgotha, also called Calvary, means "the place of the skull." It lies just outside the city of Jerusalem. Traditionally this site of Jesus' crucifixion was on a hill, but no definite proof of the actual location is possible. [340, 319]

Not only during the last three years of his life, when he was actively engaged in teaching the multitudes, but throughout his early life, Jesus was influenced by mountains. Nazareth, where he lived for some thirty years and began his mission, "lies cradled in a valley, surrounded and protected by hills." [42, 49]

Muhammad

Muhammad, "the praised one," is considered the founder of the last of the prophetic religions. He was born at Mecca about 570. For many years he spent the month of Ramadan in a cave on Mt. Hirā, fasting and praying.

Mt. Hirā is a huge, cone-shaped mountain about two miles from the city of Mecca. In the year 610, during the night, the angel Gabriel brought Muhammad the command of God. Gabriel showed him the brocade covered with writing and told him: "Read!" Muhammad did not understand but was pressed by the angel to read, so he did, and the words were as though written on his heart:

Read in the name of thy Lord who created,
... Read!
Who created man of blood coagulated.
Read! Thy Lord is the most beneficent,
Who taught by the pen,
Taught that which they knew not unto men.

Muhammad awoke from his sleep much disturbed as he despised ecstatics and thought he must be possessed. So he went out to throw himself from the top of the mountain and be rid of this possession, but ... "When I was midway on the mountain, I heard a voice from heaven saying, 'O Muhammad! thou art the apostle of God and I am Gabriel.' I raised my head towards heaven to see [who was speaking], and lo, Gabriel in the form of a man with feet astride the horizon, saying, 'O Muhammad! thou art the apostle of God and I am Gabriel.'" [183, 106] The figure was so huge it filled the sky. Muhammad stood gazing at this apparition until his wife sent messengers to look for him and bring him back. She reassured him that he was not possessed but was truly a prophet. She went to her cousin who had become a Christian and had read the Torah and the Gospel, and he told her that Gabriel, who had come to Moses before, had come also to Muhammad and that he "is the prophet of his people."

From the first prophetic religious figure, Zoroaster, to the last, the encounter occurred on a mountain. And, of special interest in Muhammad's case, the figure filled the sky, reminiscent of the figure in a glory; but Muhammad mentions no other manifestations of the glory. It may have been because he was so sure that he was possessed and that the vision was evil, he would not notice its beauty, just as many of the early climbers in the Alps called the manifestation a spectre and failed entirely to mention its beauty.

Mt. Safa is the mountain referred to in the famous legend of Muhammad. Three years after his mission began, he was asked for miraculous proof. He then ordered Mt. Safa to come to him, and as it did not move, he said, "God is merciful, had it obeyed my words, it would have fallen on us to our destruction. I will therefore go to the mountain, and thank God that He has had mercy on a stiffnecked generation." [25, 675]

Before ending this account of religious figures and mountains, it is worth noting that the Buddha came from the Sakya clan, which lived in the foothills of the Himalayas, and was in sight of mountains as he grew up. Concerning the exact location of Buddha's area, Thomas states in his book, *The Life of Buddha:* "Modern investigation has placed it in the northeastern portion of the United Provinces, and along the borders of Nepal between Bahraich and Gorakhpur." [318, 16] The Buddha did not found a religion; he taught a method of practicing awareness which his followers transformed into a religion.

The brief accounts of these historical figures reveal that the original insight of each came from an intense relationship to a mountain in a particular place. Later, followers developed their teachings into the structured religions we have come to know as Zoroastrianism, Judaism, Christianity, and Muhammadism.

3. Sacred Mountains of China and Japan

To understand the full depth of the relationship between the human being, the mountain, and religion, it is necessary to turn to China's sacred mountains. Because of the influence of Taoism in China, the primitive relationships between human beings and mountains came directly down through the ages to modern times. Furthermore, due to the very early use of writing in China, at about 1600 B.C. [228, 86], written records concerning these matters were made long before any influence from the West could disrupt the continuity.

The basic structure of the universe was symbolized in Chinese astronomy by a central polar region and four peripheral regions. On earth these pillars of Heaven were symbolized by the Five Sacred Mountains which marked the cradle of Chinese civilization and stood for the harmony of everything in nature under the one vast sky of heaven. Hêng Shan in the north, Tai Shan in the east, Hua Shan in the west, and Hêng Shan in the south marked off the four corners of the square of the Earth, centered on Sung Shan in the center, which was the *T'ai Chi* (Great Ridgepole), the axis and the still center. [313, 87] The symbolism of the One and the Four is the manifestation of the One of Heaven on the square of the Earth. The importance of these five points led to the number five being a sacred number to Chinese: five elements, five planets and five virtues. [313, 25]

The Chinese character for five, *wu*   X , indicates the cardinal points of the four directions and the center. The lines going out to the four directions and meeting in the center indicate completeness and perfection. In fact, the upper and lower halves of this character can be seen to consist of two triangles, one pointing up, standing for the sacred mountain of Earth and the other pointing down, standing for the sacred mountain of Heaven. The triangle form is the primary symbol for mountain. Three triangles made up the old form of the Chinese character, *shan* (mountain).

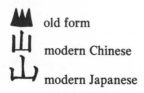

old form

modern Chinese

modern Japanese

The Five Sacred Mountains of Taoism

The most famous of the five Taoist mountains is Tai Shan, sacred mountain of the East, in the western part of the mountainous peninsula of Shantung, a coastal province. The fame of the mountain was so great that the province was named Shantung (East Mountain). [97, 46] Veneration of this 4,500 foot-high mountain goes back to at least 2000 B.C. [75, 228]

The name Tai Shan has been translated as "the Honorable" because it sits in the seat of honor, the East, from which all life springs. In fact, its ancient name Tai Tsung, according to Dyson's source, means "First Womb" or "Beginning", which would translate into First Beginning, or Mount Genesis. [75, 46] According to early historical records of China it was visited by the founders of the three most ancient dynasties: Yü in 2205 B.C., Ch'eng-t'ang of Shang in 1741 B.C., and King Wu of Chou in 1117 B.C. [75, 229] It is associated with the Chinese element wood and with the color green.

In ancient times, the Emperors made tours of inspection to the four quarters of the empire every five years and performed the Imperial Fêng and Shan Ceremony at each of the five sacred mountains. At Tai Shan, the Fêng and Shan Ceremony—which was the veneration of Heaven and Earth—was celebrated near heaven, on a mound heaped up on the summit, and near earth, on a low hill at the foot of the mountain. [97, 62]

Confucius and Mencius wrote of the importance and beauty of the mountain, and Confucius made the pilgrimage up the mountain. Geil writes, "It is difficult to exaggerate either the number of the pilgrims who have come here or the influence which has spread out from this place. I suppose that a sum total of billions of human beings, throughout the millenniums of its history, have assembled at the foot of this Sacred Mountain." [97, 47] Lane reports that "in the early part of this century as many as 10,000 people daily climbed up the mountain." The path up the mountain is called the "way to heaven" and on this path there are 6,700 steps carved from the living rock. [168, 262]

On most of the Sacred Five mountains there is a "Throw-Body Precipice," where the pilgrims, overcome by their ecstasy, would throw themselves into the depths to achieve paradise. Tai Shan had such a "Throw-Body Precipice." [97, 107]

Geil quotes from the official and scholar, Wan Kung, concerning the highest pinnacle of all, which bears the name of Great Peace: "In the year Jen-shen, 9th Monkey of Lung-ch'in, when my work on the Yellow River was completed, the Son of Heaven was pleased, and issued to me a command in the following terms: 'You shall offer a pure sacrifice in the East.' Accordingly, in the 8th moon, I sacrificed on Tai Shan . . . I passed the ups and downs, jumped over dangers, touched the Chin tablet, ascended the Sun-gazing Peak, and finally climbed to the very summit of the Mountain, where I visited the Temple of Heaven." A black, robed figure beckoned to him and said: "This is the topmost stone of Tai Shan." "Astonished, I looked at the rock and saw that it was solidly cemented at the top, and firmly embedded in the earth at the bottom . . . I sighed deeply and said to myself: 'Alas! Tai Shan claims the place of honour among the Five Peaks, and this topmost stone claims the place of honour on Tai Shan. Yet it has been built over, levelled down, and trodden under foot. If I do not cause this venerable relic to be exalted, and its spirituality to be manifested, I shall be greatly to blame.'" So he had the temple removed and the earth removed from the rock, and the topmost living rock once again stood forth. It had been hidden, Wan Kung went on, "But now it emerged and returns at last to its true position on Tai Shan, keeping its dignity intact. We trust that those of future generations who come to gaze upon it will refrain from chipping, damaging, or chiselling that which was perfected by Heaven." [97, 112] To the left of the entrance portal on the summit stands a four-sided stone monument at least 2,000 years old, inscribed with the single word, *Ti* (God). [168, 262]

The sacred mountain of the North and the sacred mountain of the South have names which sound exactly alike, Hêng Shan, although the written characters are different. To avoid confusion, the southern one is generally called Nan Yo or South Peak. It is some 2,000 feet high and rises just west of the Hsiang River, south of

Tungthing Lake in the province of Hunan. According to Dyson, the Emperor Huang Ti, who ascended the throne in 2697 B.C., deified Hêng Shan (which means Cross-Wise Mountain) as guardian god of the South. [75, 22] It is associated with the Chinese element fire and the color of red. [97, xvi]

The sacred mountain of the West is Hua Shan and is south of Tungkuan at the great bend of the Yellow River in the province of Shensi. The name Hua Shan means "Flower Mountain" because the various peaks of the mountain open out like flower petals. [54, 476] Hua Shan is the most precipitous of the five sacred mountains. It not only has the usual footsteps carved out of rock, but also chains strung along the cliffs to hold onto. It has hundreds of caves for hermits. Some were actually carved out by the Shan-jen themselves. Shan-jen is a term which means "Mountain-men" but, in old writings, is a title bestowed on thinkers whether or not they lived in seclusion on mountains [97, 253] Fire is the element of the sacred mountain of the West and the color is white. [97, xvi]

Hêng Shan, 2,200 meters, is the sacred mountain of the North. It is at the extreme north end of the Thaihang Shan range not far from Peking, in Hopei province. Its element is water and the color, black. [97, xvi]

Sung Shan, the last of the Sacred Five, is the Central Peak, 2,240 feet high and located in Honan province. It is an outlier of the Funiu Shan just south of Loyang. *Sung* means High Mountain, or Great Mountain. [97, 172] It is associated with the element earth and its color is yellow.* [97, xvi]

Since earliest times the Imperial Fêng and Shan Ceremony was performed on the site of each of the Sacred Five mountains. The purpose of these rituals was to order the life of the community in harmony with the forces of nature by worship, propitiation, and celebration. The ancient *Book of Rites* declares that while the rules of ceremonies "have their origin in heaven, the movement of them reaches to earth. The distribution of them extends to all the business of life . . . They supply the channels by which we can apprehend the ways of Heaven and act as the feelings of men require." [173] This idea of harmony with the forces of nature is central to Taoist thought.

Taoism

Taoism had two origins: The older root of Taoism was the ancient shamanistic influence involving earth, religion, and magic, which "entered Chinese culture at a very early stage from its northern and southern elements respectively." [229, 3] The newer aspect came from the philosophers of the Warring States who followed a Tao of Nature rather than a Tao of Human Society. They went off into forests and mountains seeking to understand Nature with the purpose that only through a deep knowledge of Nature could human beings hope to live in order. They avoided the courts of the feudal princes—not so much because they renounced the world as Christian ascetics did—but because they so loved the earth they wished to live in harmony with all of Nature. For the Taoists, the Tao, or way, was not merely concerned with the right way of life within human society. This was much too narrowly anthropocentric for them. They were concerned with something much larger—the way in which the universe worked. By not imposing their preconceptions on Nature, but by yielding to Nature insofar as they could understand it, they hoped to learn how to fit their lives into the greater life of Nature.

The Great Harmony is known as the *Tao*, a basic concept of Chinese philosophy. "The Tao . . . however being inexpressible—in fact, beyond intellectual comprehension—could not be defined, although it was constantly referred to." [313, 15] The Tao Te Ching, "Canon of the Power of the Tao," goes deeply into the Tao but never limits it by trying to put an ultimate definition on the concept. "The Tao never does; yet through it all things are done." (Tao Te Ching XXXVII) Mai Mai Sze, in the *Tao of Painting*, devotes some time to analyzing the basic Chinese characters which make up the word, *tao:*

In Chinese, a single character or a combination of two or more characters to form a word depicts an object, act, or thought with a vividness possible only in pictographic writing. Associated ideas contribute overtones of meaning and greatly enlarge the import of the words. The choice of *tao* (road, path or way) and not another character denoting a path or way must therefore have been based on ideas intrinsic in the pictograph . . .

The character for *tao*,

is made up of two pictographs: *ch'o* representing a foot taking a step, and *shou*, a head. The use of *tao* in the simplest sense of 'path' can easily be deduced from *ch'o* (foot).

1. 道
tao: road, path, way; method, principle, standard, doctrine; the Way

ch'o: a foot taking a step, step by step

shou: head

ch'ih: to step with the left foot

chih: to halt; foot, footprint

ch'uan: hair

shou: head

There is evidence that the combination of *shou* (head) and *ch'o* (foot) symbolized the idea of wholeness . . . as to soul, mind, and emotions. Dissection of the *ch'o* (foot) pictograph supports this meaning of *tao*, for it is composed of *ch'ih* (to step with the left foot) and *chih* (to halt). Step-by-step progress requires care and deliberation and, by extension, careful and deliberate conduct or behavior from an inner motivation.

[313, 8-9]

---

*Unless noted differently, general information on the Sacred Five mountains comes from Couling [64] and the specific locations from Needham. [228, 55]

This is as far as Mai Mai Sze goes in analyzing the character for foot. What is of great interest here is that the only activity where this particular type of walking, to step with the foot and then halt, is regularly used is in mountain climbing where it is called the *rest step*. Notice, above, in the old form of *ch'o*, one foot is down and the other is actually held in the air. Without the *rest step*, climbing requires great effort even on small peaks. On high peaks it is a necessity. Furthermore, the *rest step* must be coordinated with the breathing. On high peaks, where the air thins out, inhalations and exhalations must become more pronounced.

Old Swiss guides are known for their ability to travel all day at the same, unvarying speed, no matter what the altitude, with never a stop. Younger men *seem* to travel much faster but require stops, so they cannot cover as much ground as the old guides in the same time. I've known many strong men who do not have the experience necessary to use the *rest step* and either get altitude-sick or fail to make the summit of 14,000-foot peaks. From my experience with old climbers in their late 'seventies and 'eighties who know and use the *rest step*, their performance on mountains is almost magical. I'm sure that the ordinary man in ancient China would have had a similar feeling of magic about the old sages who could travel so effortlessly on mountains. It is the mountain that teaches this *rest step*.

When the *rest step* is skillfully done, the human being flows with the mountain, with nature itself; without the *rest step*, the human being puts forth a great deal of effort; there is much *doing*, but little is accomplished. In fact, on a 14,000-foot peak, if the *rest step* has been done automatically from the base of the mountain, the *flow* of the climb gets better and better, and less effort is expended the higher one gets. Without the *rest step* above 12,000 feet, the going gets more and more difficult, producing labored breathing, laboring heart, and eventually altitude sickness—much *doing* with little result. The contrary is at the heart of the Taoist concept *wu wei*, "non-doing."

Although *wu wei* is usually translated as "non-action" or "inactivity," Needham believes that "the majority of sinologists have been wrong here" and that the real meaning, as far as the early Taoist philosophers were concerned, was "refraining from activity contrary to Nature," [229, 68] which the *rest step* exemplifies. Needham goes on to quote from the Tao Te Ching: "Let there be no action (contrary to Nature), and there is nothing that will not be well regulated." About 300 A.D. Kuo Hsiang, in his commentary on *Chuang Tzu*, wrote: "Non-action does not mean doing nothing and keeping silent. Let everything be allowed to do what it naturally does, so that its nature will be satisfied."

Ordinarily, the character *tao* is simply described as a drawing of a head (symbolizing a person), somewhere on a road, hence 'way', hence, 'the right way.' This is from Needham (Vol. 2) and his reference is Karlgren.

[148] This is the usual analysis, but the problem with this is that the character for foot is not further analyzed, thus leaving out a crucial clue as to the origin of the character, *tao*. Mai Mai Sze, in the further analysis of the character for foot uses as references Giles [97] and Wieger. [358]

In addition to the importance of mountains in the analysis of the Chinese charcter for *tao*, mountains are central to the beginnings of another important concept, *yin* and *yang*. In the old form of these Chinese characters *yang* is represented by the sun with its rays, together with the character *fu*, meaning hill or mountain. The character for *yin* was a coiled cloud along with the character *fu*. According to the definition in the Êrh Ya, a dictionary of the Chou period, *yang* describes "the sunny side of the mountain" and *yin*, "the side in the shadow." This relates directly to the changing relationship of the sun and the mountain. In the morning, when the sun is behind the mountain, the trees are dark—almost black; in the afternoon, when the setting sun shines directly on these same trees, they are bright and glowing with light.

The usual symbol for *yin* and *yang* is the Tai Chi disk. According to Mai Mai Sze, "The Tai Chi disk might be described as a view from directly above 'the mountain' referred to in the definitions of the characters *yin* and *yang*, so that the result is a stylized figure of its sunny and shady sides . . . The mountain also represents the central sacred point or peak of the Center [the Center peak of the Sacred Five Peaks] . . . among which the point in the middle indicates the Tai Chi, the core and fixed point of reference that is the Tao." [313, 38–39]

By further extension, *yin* and *yang* have come to mean that the essence of Heaven is *yang* and of Earth, *yin*; male is *yang*, female, *yin*; light, the sun, is *yang*; darkness, the night is *yin*. These qualities are fluid, always moving, just as the sunny and shady side of a mountain are not fixed and firm, but dependent on the movement of the sun in relationship to the mountain and the human being.

Chinese painting began as a "making sacred" of the ritual objects to be used in religious ceremonies. Even in its later developments, when Chinese landscape painting was referred to as *shan shui*, mountain-water, it continued to be an act of reverence in praise of the harmony of Heaven and Earth. Confucius wrote: "The wise man delights in water, the good man delights in mountains. For the wise move, the good stay still. The wise are happy; but the good, secure." [345, 120]

Chinese paintings of mountains are remarkable examples of "the capacity for accurate observation and representations of geological forms." [230, 592] From as early as 1100 A.D. and the Sung painter Li Kung-Lin, Chinese illustrations of mountains were of such accuracy that modern geologists can discern the type of rock as well as the geologic forces at work. They depicted the real world as they saw it from close observation.

The emphasis on close observation of Nature is evident in the fact that Taoist temples have been known as *kuan* which means "to look." [229, 56] As Needham points out, "in their beginnings magic, divination, and science were inseparable," so we find the roots of Chinese scientific thought among the Taoists. [229, 57] Needham began his monumental, multi-volume work on *Science and Civilization in China* when he read a passage in a Chinese document from 1088 concerning the magnetic compass. This was over a century before we can find any mention made in Europe of the compass. Needham, in a footnote, writes: "I shall never forget the excitement which I experienced when I first read these words. If any one text stimulated the writing of this book more than any other, this was it." [231, 250] He went on to devote years to the work and in the process discovered over and over again that in many fields, from mathematics through many of the sciences, the Chinese made discoveries which antedated similar European discoveries by three to six centuries. For instance, in the late Thang period (8th or 9th century A.D.), the Chinese knew of the declination as well as the polarity of the magnet, antedating European knowledge by some six centuries. [231, 333] These Chinese discoveries eventually reached Europe in the earlier centuries through Arab intermediaries and, more recently, by means of Jesuit missionaries' letters in the late Sixteenth Century.

Needham shows that the "mystical naturalism" of the Taoists was essential for their discoveries in science, and he emphasizes the difference between mystical naturalism and other forms of mysticism. Mystical naturalism asserts "that there is much in the universe which transcends human reason here and now . . . but . . . the sum total of incomprehensibility will diminish if men humbly explore the . . . relations of things . . . Religious mysticism . . . dotes upon the arbitrary residuum and seeks to minimize or deny the value of investigations of natural phenomena." [229, 97] Needham also argues that it is sometimes "authority-denying mysticism" rather than rationalism which aids the growth of experimental science.

The Taoists were in favor of a primitive undifferentiated form of society and against the feudal form. The roots of this went back to the matrilineal cultures based on the ancient Chinese creation-goddess myths. They felt that in the political area *wei* was forcing things in the interests of private gain and *wu wei* was "letting things work out their destinies in accordance with their intrinsic principles." [229, 71]

The Four Sacred Mountains of Buddhism

The four sacred mountains are referred to as the four corner-stones of Buddhism, thus bringing them into mythical association with the four elements of the Buddhist cosmos: earth, air, fire, and water. [231, 243]

Mount Omei, site of the Buddha's Glory, is the sacred mountain of the West and is associated with fire. Located in Szechuan Province, its Permian basalt cliffs rise precipitously from the plain forming a precipice about 6,000 feet high. [229, 596] From the summit of 10,163 feet, the eastern ramparts of the Himalayas, one hundred miles away, can be seen.

The oldest of the mountain's temples still standing, Wannien (Myriad Years), was built in the 4th century. On top of the mountain is the monastery of the Golden Summit, connected to the Hall of the Patriarchs. Behind is the Terrace of the Buddha's Vision, where one can look down the 6,000-foot precipice and see the Buddha's Glory when conditions are right:

Something not cloud nor mist is rising through layers of space,
Unearthly iridescence and mysterious lights curve in strange
  patterns.
Will you not try standing on the high level of the Stone Terrace,
  and look out?
For everyone is within the Glory of the Buddha.   [130]

Chao Hsün-Pai writes in the foreword to the *Omei Illustrated Guide,* "Since the time that Buddhism first entered China nearly three thousand years ago, Mount Omei has been filled with its glorious fame. Almost a hundred temples, large and small, strewn all the way from the foot of the mountain to its highest peak and adding beauty to the mountain, attest this fact. Its reputation has been fortunately preserved by countless monks and 'worshippers of the mountain.'" [130]

Each section of the long route to the top has a special name, such as Bridge of Murmuring Waters, Somber Dragon Abyss, Pool of the Gleaming Moon, Monastery of the Thundering Cavern. Each has its own legend. One of the most vertical sections of the path is Heaven-Piercing Hill. Its several thousand steps are cut out of the solid limestone. The Imperial Inspector Shou P'u described it: "When descending, travelers go crab-fashion, with one man's feet on another man's shoulders. when ascending, they go like ants, stuck onto each other, with one holding another's foot in his mouth. The high winds growl angrily, mad as a furious tiger. The huge rocks lean out, fierce as fierce devils" [130]

Legends reveal that Mount Omei was a sacred mountain long before Buddhism came to China. A particular spot is known as "the site where Hsuan Yuan, the Yellow Emperor inquired of the Way." Hsuan Yuan was a legendary sovereign, B.C. 2697, who, tradition has it, once was supposed to have visited Omei. Commentaries on the Taoist books claim that Omei is Ti Ch'i Tung T'ien, the Seventh Cavern of Heaven. [130]

The Lolos, a primitive people from the mountains to the South who are not Buddhists, worshipped a triad of deities of their own on Mount Omei. In the early 1900s they could be seen as pilgrims on Mount Omei, according to Johnstone. [135, 55] These people left independent Lolo country about 1850 due to a tribal feud. They were allotted lands in China for which they paid rent. When they migrated they were in the habit of taking their gods with them and giving them a new site, so they chose Mount Omei.

Johnstone refers to the glory: "It has been likened to the famous Brocken Spectre, and to the Shadow of the Peak in Ceylon, but the brilliant and varied colours of 'Buddha's Glory'—five colours, say the Chinese—give it a rainbow-like beauty which those appearances do not possess." [135, 101] Johnstone climbed to the top in hopes of seeing the glory, but the day was clear and he was unable to see it.

The Buddhist sacred mountain of the North is Wu-t'ai Shan, which means five terraces, so-called because of the five high peaks on it. It is about 10,000 feet high and is associated with the *bodhisattva*, Wênshu, representative of Wisdom. Its element is air. The sacred mountain of the South is Chiu-hua Shan, in Anhui province. Its name means Nine Splendid Blossoms. Li Po, viewing it from afar, described it as nine hibiscus flowers. [54] The *bodhisattva* connected with it is Ti-tsang, and its element is earth. The last of the Buddhist sacred mountains, the Eastern one, is P'u-t'o Shan on Chusan Island, so it is naturally associated with water and with Kuan Yin, the goddess of mercy. The fourth Buddhist element, fire, is associated with Mount Omei.

Japanese Sacred Mountains

The most famous sacred mountain in Japan is Fuji-no-yama. Fuji comes from *Huchi* or *Fuche*, the Ainu word for the Goddess of Fire. [328] O Yama means "honorable mountain." According to Mariani, more than 100,000 people climb Fuji each summer. [199, 113]

In every part of Japan there is a local mountain deity; furthermore, there is a special religious sect, Shugendō, founded in the seventh century which combines Shinto, Taoist, and Buddhist elements. The followers of this sect are called *yamabushi*, "those who sleep on the mountains." Long ago the *yamabushi* were shaman-type mountain hermits, who practiced great austerities among wild mountains. Even today in modern times *yamabushi* climb mountains as part of their religion. [198, 84]

In Japan, due to the influence of Shinto, sacred mountains are even more important than in China; however, to begin to understand the meaning of these mountain deities it is necessary to know more about Shinto. This is discussed in Chapter 10.

Mountains have been an important subject in Japanese literature from the very beginning of recorded history. The first Japanese anthology of poetry, the Manyoshu (8th century), is filled with lyrical references to mountains. For example:

> From to-morrow ever
> Shall I regard as brother
> The twin-peaked mountain of Futagami . . .
>
> Princess Oku   [197, xvii]

4. Power-filled Rocks and Sacred Mountains

In the oldest religion, everything was alive, not supernaturally but naturally alive. There were only deeper and deeper streams of life, vibrations of life more and more vast. So rocks were alive, but a mountain had a deeper, vaster life than a rock, and it was much harder for a man to bring his spirit, or his energy into contact with the life of the mountain, as from a great standing well of life, than it was to come into contact with the rock. And he had to put forth a greater religious effort.

D. H. Lawrence   [170]

In China and Japan an unbroken tradition of mountain veneration dating back to the earliest times simplifies the tracing of the history of sacred mountains. Details of such a tradition in the rest of the world are not as easy to document; still, a brief survey of sacred rocks and mountains throughout the world gives some idea of both how basic and how widespread such beliefs are in human culture.

Human beings have felt that certain rocks were sacred since the very beginnings of human culture in the Paleolithic age. The Australian aborigines sometimes conceive of rocks as the sources of the souls of newborn babies, and sometimes as their ancestors, "who passed that way in the dreamtime." But, as Coon points out in his *Hunting Peoples*, the aborigines may not explain their sacred rocks at all but merely say, "You see that rock? It has power." [63, 194]

The idea that stone possessed a certain power was extended to setting up of stones to make a sacred place, where the spirit could be reached by rites. The stone itself was also an altar where the worshippers communicated with the spirit of the stone by pouring oil or blood over it. Blood indicates a sharing of life while oil has to do with fertility and abundance of life. [274, 124] Sacred standing stones were not merely a "token that the place is frequented by a God, but a permanent pledge that in this place he consents to enter into stated relations with men." [155, 207] Mircea Eliade provides further insight into the standing stone by pointing out that it is a "boundary" where two realms meet. The human being has access to another realm through the stone. In cultures which conceive of three cosmic regions, heaven, earth, and the underworld, the pillar provides access to all three worlds. [274, 40]

Later, groups of stone pillars were set up: sometimes double pillars, as in the Phoenicians' culture and sometimes groups of pillars imitating groves of trees. In the next stage, three pillars were arranged with two pillars as supports and the third lying across the top. In some cultures, this was a table of offering, and in others it was considered a gateway to the world of the dead. In Megalithic times it became the doorway to the temples and tombs, as well as marking the solstices and equinoxes.

Exactly where the Megalithic culture began is unknown, but it is thought to have been somewhere in Asia Minor. From there it spread across the Mediterranean to Africa and also along the southern shore of Asia, up the northeastern seacoast and over to Alaska and Japan and the islands of the Southwest Pacific. [180, 151 and 155, 149]

The classical civilizations of Greece and Rome rested on a foundation of Megalithic people. The Greeks had many references to men once having been "stones." In Italy there were a number of earth goddesses whose names contain the root, *la,* meaning stone. Laverna, goddess of a cleft in the rock on the Aventine, was one. From this same root come the words lapidary, worker in precious stones; labrys, a stone axe; and labyrinth, which means a "place of stones." [155, 149]

The living rock itself sometimes has a decisive influence on how it is used. Stonehenge, the foremost Megalithic religious construction, could not have been built had it not been for the inspiration which the great sarsen stones provided. Jacquetta Hawkes, in *The Land,* [114, 132–133] described the geologic formation of these famous stones. Salisbury Plain and the Wessex downlands in England are basically chalk, consisting of the remains of small forms of life which were deposited on the floor of an ancient sea. When this sea bed was tilted up by geologic forces, it was easily worn down by water creating the "downs" of England, which are gently rounded, low hills. In some localities, however, there was a layer of much harder rock over the chalk layer.

When this layer was eroded, it formed straight-edged, angular blocks of stone, entirely different from the underlying chalk. With their inadequate tools of stone and antler the Megalithic people could not have cut these stones from solid bedrock, but water, frost and wind had already done this for them. They could further shape them and lift them to build their monuments, such as Stonehenge. Unused blocks of these enormous, squared-off rocks discovered in later ages were called "grey weathers" by the local peasants because they looked like flocks of sheep from a distance. Later, in the alchemical tradition in Europe, the monoliths became the "philosopher's stone," according to Knight. [155, 168]

Rocks have been important in most religions. For instance, the great rock on top of the Temple Mount in Jerusalem where Abraham offered Isaac is sacred to Jews, Christians, and Moslems. The "black stone" in the Kaaba shrine at Mecca, the central place of worship for Moslems, is a meteorite. To this day devout Moslems perform the ritual circumambulation of this stone. Walking around or dancing around a sacred stone is a rite commonly used in many parts of the world. There is slight, but persisting evidence from myths and legends, and the experience of modern "sensitives" that human beings can get in touch with some actual physical energy from the rocks. Other evidence along these same lines comes from the study of ley lines in Britain and the energy currents in China labelled "Green Dragon" (*yang*) and "White Tiger" (*yin*) by the feng-shui. [229, 360]

Francis Hitching, member of the Royal Institute of Archaeology, spent considerable time investigating the megalithic stone monuments in Britain. He believes that the power of stones has "something to do with electromagnetism . . . It may have something to do with the unique qualities of quartz, which . . . seems to be a constituent of every active stone. The molecular structure of quartz is spiral . . . It is also piezo-electric: That is, it expands slightly if given a slight charge of electricity. If placed under pressure—as it would be if charged while inside another stone—alternate edges of its prism give off positive and negative voltages on what can reach a dramatic scale: a force of 1,000 pounds applied on each face of a half-inch crystal of quartz creates 25,000 volts." [124, 285]

In pursuing the effect of electricity on humans, James Beal, in a paper on "Electrostatic Fields and Brain/ Body/Environment Interrelationships" suggests that shamans, for instance, may have felt "the power of a place" because of a number of factors, some to do with changes in the earth's local magnetic field causing changes in electrostatic field strength and some to do with negative ion concentrations. He goes on to say that the shaman "did not know these things—he could not know them, but he sensed them, in the excited electrochemical processes in his own nervous system, and that these, in turn, triggered the neurons and synapses in the circuits of his brain." [22] These "places of power" were not only felt by primitive shamans and medicine men of long ago, but they have continued to be felt by various peoples down through the ages to modern times.

Experienced rock climbers sometimes feel certain very definite, but unexplainable, effects. Once, in Canada, trying a rarely climbed route, I had been leading up a fairly difficult pitch when I came to a level spot with a very easy chimney going on up. But I could not bring myself to step up onto the first foothold (which was as easy as taking a step up a stairway). I tried a couple of times, but simply could not do it. Thinking I must be tired, I told the second rope to take over the lead. No sooner had the the first man moved into the chimney when the whole thing avalanched out. He was not seriously hurt but was severely shaken. I have no way of explaining what I felt, but now, years later, I think it may possibly have had something to do with the pressure generated inside the rocks pushing against one another, generating sufficient voltage for my body to sense it. What I do know is that one must be in tune with the rock and at ease with it from a great deal of climbing to feel it at all. The others were not as experienced rock climbers as I, and they felt nothing unusual until the rock slid out.

Rituals involving rocks occur in places as far apart as ancient Greece and modern Tibet. Hermes was the god of travellers and messengers. His columns were erected near the roads and were used as landmarks. Travellers passing by threw rocks at the feet of these columns. [343, 67] In Tibet, it is the custom for each traveller crossing the high mountain passes to leave a rock on the cairn at the top.

The Rock of Ishi in Japan provides perhaps the purest example in any religion of the religious presence of a rock. At the Ishi Shrine, there is no inner shrine building whatsoever, only a fence enclosing a large rock. People bow before it in respect. It is so ancient that its early history is no longer known. It is said to be the "seat of the Kami divine spirit." Mason explains: "The Rock of Ishi, representing creative divinity as the soil, properly received man's spiritual homage for the part it plays in Shinto symbiosis by helping man . . . both cooperate in advancing the creative development of divine spirit in the spatial universe . . . On the Rock of Ishi, Shinto declares man is not an outlaw in the universe but is one with universal divinity." [208, 211-212]

Down to this day, rocks are the central focus of meditation in Zen gardens such as the famous Ryonji Temple in Kyoto, where a few carefully placed rocks rise out of a sea of raked sand, giving the illusion of immense space. Later, it became fashionable for the nobility to have similar gardens, and nobles and samurai were known to pay enormous sums of money for one powerfully shaped rock as the focal point of a garden. [175, 94]

Rocks in Amerindian Culture

"*Inyan*—the rocks—are holy," Lame Deer said. "Every man needs a stone to help him." [167, 113] Lame Deer, a Sioux Medicine Man, went on to explain: "Also you are always picking up odd-shaped stones, pebbles and fossils, saying that you do this because it pleases you, but I know better. Deep inside you there must be an awareness of the rock power, of the spirits in them, otherwise you would not pick them up and fondle them as you do." [167, 275] For the Oglala Sioux, one of the four powers which together are called *Wakan tanka* (the Great Spirit) is "the Rock," which *was* even before earth's creation and is the oldest of material things. The Rock is the power of the abiding mountains and the Winged Ones, the Thunders are associated with it. [4, 43 and 166] Natural monoliths in the Sioux country are the emblems of Inyan, the Rock. Standing Rock in South Dakota and *Inyan Kara,* which the white man named Devil's Tower, in Wyoming, are two outstanding examples.

The chants of the Pebble Society of the Omaha tribe, which were recorded by Alice Fletcher with the help of La Flesche, an Omaha, provide a clear example of the importance of "the Rock" for the tribe. The Pebble Society performed curing rituals. Examples of two such chants are:

Verily, one alone of all these was the greatest,
Inspiring to all mind,
The great white rock,
Standing and reaching as high as the heavens, enwrapped in mist,
Verily as high as the heavens. [90, 570]

He! Aged One, *ecka*
Thou Rock, *ecka*
Aged One, *ecka*
He! Unmoved from time without end, verily
Thou sittest,
In the midst of the various paths of the coming winds
In the midst of the winds thou sittest
Aged one . . .
He! This is the desire of thy little ones
That of thy strength they shall partake
Therefore thy little ones desire to walk closely by thy side
Venerable one. [90, 572]

The word, *ecka,* means "I desire" or "I implore." The "little ones" are the members of the society. The rock standing in the midst of the winds relates to the idea of the winds as "messengers of life-giving forces." The stones used in the sweat lodge represent the "Aged One," the Rock.

The Importance of Rock in C.G. Jung's Life

Jung had such a powerful encounter with a rock when he was a small child that it remained with him the rest of his life. Some detail on this experience is important for two reasons: first, it clearly shows that even in our culture the power of a rock in a small child's life may be just as great as it is in other cultures more attuned to Nature; and secondly, since Jung spent his entire life exploring the unconscious, he provides direct, first-person evidence of the depth of a child's relationship to Nature.

In his book, *Memories, Dreams, Reflections,* Jung tells of the period of his life, from seven to nine years old, when he played in the small caves formed by the spaces between the large blocks of stone in an old rock wall of the family garden. He tried to keep a perpetual fire alight in one of these tiny caves. In front of this wall was a slope with a rock sticking out on which he would often sit alone. At these times he played an "imaginary game that went something like this: 'I am sitting on top of this stone and it is underneath.' But the stone also could say 'I' and think: 'I am lying here on this slope and he is sitting on top of me.' The question then arose: 'Am I the one who is sitting on the stone, or am I the stone on which *he* is sitting?' This question always perplexed me, and I would stand up, wondering who was what now." [140, 20] There was never a final answer, but there was always a strong feeling of a secret relationship to the rock. He goes on to say that thirty years later, when he was a married man with children and his career was going well, he stood once again on that same slope. All at once he was again that child who had lit the secret fire and sat on the rock wondering if it was he or he was it. His adult life in Zurich seemed remote and completely unconnected to him. He states that it was frightening "for the world of my childhood in which I had just become absorbed was *eternal,* and I had been wrenched away from it and had fallen into a time that continued to roll onward, moving farther and farther away." It was only with a violent effort that he could pull himself away from the spot.

When Jung was older, he once again took up this close relationship to rocks. In 1923 he began work on the stone tower at Bollingen on the upper lake of Zurich. As he wrote, "Words and paper . . . did not seem real enough to me . . . I had to make a confession of faith in stone." [140, 223] He added to the tower through the years. After his wife's death in 1955 he added an upper story to the central section, which he discovered represented himself. From time to time he worked on particular stones. On one perfectly formed cube, he engraved alchemists' verses and ancient Greek on its four sides. The final words he carved on it were: "In remembrance of his seventy-fifth birthday, C.G. Jung made and placed this here as a thanks offering, in the year 1950." He calls the stone an explanation of the Tower "but one which remains incomprehensible to others. [140, 228]

And so Jung himself, possibly the modern man most in touch with his unconscious, in his old age felt the necessity of tactile contact with the living bones of the Earth Mother, rocks.

Outstanding Sacred Mountains Elsewhere in the World

India

"Long ago a Hindu sage, his mind aglow with memories of the icy Himalayas exclaimed, 'In a hundred ages of the gods I could not tell thee of the glories of Himachal where Siva lived and where the Ganges falls from the foot of Vishnu like the slender thread of the lotus flower.'" [168, vii] Mount Kailas is considered the throne of the god, Siva, and has been called the spiritual heart of the world. In the ancient Indian scripture, the *Mahabharata*, there are references to the "peaks of famed Kailasa." India, K.M. Panikkar claims, owes its "continuity of civilization" to the cult of the Himalaya. [197, xvi]

Lama Govinda, born in Germany of European descent, became a Buddhist monk long ago and spent a large part of his life in Tibet, leaving at the time of the Chinese invasion. He said "Above all the sacred mountains of the world, the fame of Kailas has spread and inspired human beings since times immemorial." [103, 198] Kailas "forms the hub" of the two most important civilizations of the world, China and India, and the center of the universe for Hindus and Buddhists. Its Sanskrit name is Mt. Meru, and it is considered not only the physical but the metaphysical center of the world. "Kailas forms the spire of the 'Roof of the World,' as the Tibetan plateau is called, and radiating from it, like the spokes from the hub of a wheel, a number of mighty rivers take their course towards the east, the west, the north-west and the south. These rivers are the Brahmaputra, the Indus, the Sutlej, and the Karnali." [103, 199] The mountain stands in such splendid isolation in the center of its plateau that it is possible to walk around it in two or three days. Each face of the vast pyramid rises thousands of feet directly from the floor of the valley. The pyramid is so regular that Lama Govinda says it is like "the dome of a gigantic temple,' [103, 200] As we shall see in Chapter 5, it is a Mother Goddess-shaped mountain.

The noted traveler, Sven Hedin, says that Kailas is "incomparably the most famous mountain in the world." [168, vii] Lama Govinda calls it the "most sacred spot on earth." [103, 204] and says that those who endure the dangers and hardships of the pilgrimage find that their lives "are rewarded by an indescribable feeling of bliss, of supreme happiness . . . Their mental faculties seem to be heightened, their awareness and spiritual sensitivity infinitely increased, their consciousness reaching out into a new dimension . . . It is as if their individual consciousness, which obscured or distorted their views of the world, were receding and giving place to an all-embracing cosmic consciousness." [103, 204]

Lama Govinda goes on to explain more about the power of sacred mountains:

The power of such a mountain is so great and yet so subtle that, without compulsion, people are drawn to it . . . as if by

27

the force of some invisible magnet; and they will undergo untold hardships and privations in their inexplicable urge to approach and to worship the centre of this sacred power . . . Instead of conquering it, the religious-minded man prefers to be conquered by the mountain . . .

To see the greatness of a mountain, one must keep one's distance; to understand its form, one must move around it; to experience its moods, one must see it at sunrise and sunset, at noon and at midnight, in sun and in rain, in snow and in storm, in summer and in winter and in all the other seasons. He who can see the mountain like this comes near to the life of the mountain . . . Mountains grow and decay, they breathe and pulsate with life. They attract and collect invisible energies from their surroundings: the forces of the air, of the water, of electricity and magnetism; they create winds, clouds, thunderstorms, rains, waterfalls, and rivers. They fill their surroundings with active life and give shelter and food to innumerable beings. Such is the greatness of mighty mountains.

[103, 197-197]

Marco Pallis was on a British mountain climbing expedition long ago when he discovered the Tibetan Buddhist tradition and spent some time in a monastery in Tibet. In his book, *The Way and the Mountain,* he writes of the effects of the high altitude air and light of Tibet:

. . .during one's stay there one did become very frequently conscious as of a mysterious presence, using that epithet, however, without any sensational connotation, but rather according to its primitive meaning of something not to be uttered, something that can only remain an object of the unbroken silence of the soul.

All one can do is to repeat that one became conscious more than once of a peculiar quality of transparency affecting the whole atmosphere of the place; it was as if the obstacles to the passage of certain influences had here been thinned down to something quite light and opaque . . . once out on the plateau . . . one finds oneself in a landscape of such ineffable contemplative serenity that all separate impressions coalesce into a single feeling of—how can one best describe it?—yes, of impartiality . . .

If some readers are inclined to dismiss this impression of Tibet as rather fanciful and in any case explainable as an effect, upon an imaginative nature, of a high mountain climate —the valleys are all over 12,000 feet and the air is indescribably exhilarating to both body and mind—this writer can only make answer that though much can reasonably be attributed to such a cause, this is nevertheless insufficient to account in full for the conviction . . . that Tibet is a focus of spiritual influence in a particular and objective sense and apart from any power of one's own to respond or otherwise, as the case may be. Essentially, this is a question that pertains to what may properly be called the Science of Sacred Geography, and Tibet is by no means the only example of the kind, though it is one of the most remarkable and extensive." [244, 112-113]

From the experience gained in many years of climbing in different parts of the world, I can agree with Marco Pallis. I have found conditions such as he describes in particular places in the mountains of Canada, the United States, and Japan.

Western Hemisphere

In the New World, the mountain which geographically fulfills a similar position is called Snowdome, in the Canadian Rockies. About 12,000 feet high, it is the hydrographic apex of the Continent. From this one mountain come the headwaters of the Columbia River, which flows into the Pacific; the Saskatchewan, which flows into Hudson Bay and thence to the Atlantic; and the Athabaska River, which joins the Mackenzie River, which flows on into the Arctic Ocean. Standing on the top of Snowdome, looking out over the tremendous expanse of the Columbia Icefield, one feels that one is at the very top of the world, with all that one sees below sloping off towards the edges of the world. Snowdome is certainly a sacred place and would be recognized as such in other parts of the world; yet in our culture it goes unnoticed.

Orizaba, 18,200 feet high, was venerated by the Aztecs, who called it Citlaltepetl, "The Mountain of the Star," most probably referring to Venus, the Morning Star. Orizaba is the most striking of the many sacred mountains of Mexico.

Mount McKinley, in Alaska, was called Denali and was considered sacred. Mount Rainier was called Tach —ho ma (Tachoma), "The Mountain that was God." The area now called Paradise Valley on the south side of Mt. Rainier was called a "Land of Peace" by the Indians. Any fugitive in trouble who managed to reach that area was secure from punishment or pursuit. Paradise Valley is an open area covered with wild flowers.

The random sampling of mountains given above shows that the idea of sacred mountains is widespread; however, to understand what is involved in the human relationship to sacred mountains, it is necessary to turn to the southwestern United States, where almost every Indian tribe has a group of sacred mountains which define its area.

The Tewa Pueblo world is bounded by four sacred mountains: North, Hazy or Shimmering Mountain (Tse Shu Pin); West, Obsidian Covered Mountain (Tsikomo); South, Turtle Mountain (Oku Pin); East, Stone Man Mountain (Ku Sehn Pin). On present day maps, the mountain of the North is Conjilon Peak; West is the same name, Tsikomo; South Mountain is the Sandia Crest, northeast of present Albuquerque, and the East Mountain is Truchas Peak. [241, 19] On each of these mountain tops is a keyhole arrangement of stones called the "earth navel" with the open end directing the energy toward the village. In the center of the village is "Earth mother earth navel middle place." This is the sacred center of the village just as Sung Shan in China was the Center Pillar of Heaven. The mountain earth navels of the Tewa gather in blessings from all around and point them toward the village, while the center mother earth navel concentrates and centers all this energy. The Tewa have a prayer which refers to the interaction between the people of the village and the mountains around them:

> Within and around the earth, within and around
> the hills, within and around the mountains,
> your authority returns to you.   [241, 13]

The sacred mountains of the Navaho are the Mountain of the East, which has been variously identified as Mount Blanca in Colorado; Wheeler Peak above Taos, in the Sangre De Christo Range; or Pelado Peak near the pueblo of Jemez. The Mountain of the South is Mount Taylor of the San Mateo range. The Mountain of the West consists of the San Francisco Peaks in Arizona, and a peak in the La Plata range or the San Juan range is the Mountain of the North. Although the Indians have a specific name for each of their sacred mountains, it is not always possible to get agreement as to which mountain on a modern map is the ancient Navajo sacred mountain. [350, 164]

The San Francisco Peaks are also sacred to the Hopi. What these sacred mountains mean to the Navaho and Hopi people is shown by testimony given before the Coconino County Planning and Zoning Commission in 1974 relative to a proposed housing and recreation development in the San Francisco Peaks area.

A 75-year-old Hopi of the Kachina clan, Forest Kaye, testified: "It has been told by my elders that the deity of Kachinas resides in the San Francisco Peaks area. Since time immemorial, shrines have been erected among and around these peaks; these shrines are used for offerings of prayer.

"Since the beginning of time, Hopis have made pilgrimages to these peaks for evergreens and religious offerings—evergreens which are essential for all ceremonies, offering of prayer feathers in the hopes of creating harmony for all mankind . . . Now I and the Hopi people are asking you to respect our humble wishes by refraining from desecrating the San Francisco Peaks area. Your continued infringement on the peaks for monetary gains will not only destroy the sacredness of the peaks, but also the reason why the Hopis exist." Alton Honahni, Sr., another member of the Kachina society added: "To the Hopi, it is our mother; we nurse from these Peaks for religious survival. If you are set on destroying the existence of Hopis, then don't listen to us."

Robert Fulton, Navaho medicine man, explained, "If we allow the white man to dig away at our sacred mountain . . . he is, in essence, destroying our very soul. We must not allow the white man to desecrate our religion and thereby our soul . . . we will no longer be able to see the clouds as they drift forth from Doko'o-sliid, bringing us rain, nor will we be able to seek comfort by the sight of our sacred mountain, for we will have violated her and we will not be worthy of her powers."

Fred Kaye, Navaho medicine man, said, "These sacred mountains are endowed with plants, food, and medicine.

They bring harmony and balance to the people. People live according to the mountains.

"The mountain is also a teacher. It teaches people the way of life. If the white man desecrates, ruins, or develops the mountains, its teaching will be lost to the people. The gods have ordained that these mountains are the bodies and lives of the people . . . Many times when all else fails, medicine from these mountains has healed the sick and wounded, and restored balance and harmony among the people. The mountains have protected us from destructive forces.

"Who are these white men who are making plans regarding the mountains? Do these men have pollen? Do these men have an offering to give to the mountains? Do these men know the prayers, legends, and songs from the feet of the mountain to its head?" [276, 174–178] This last sentence is reminiscent of the Chinese sacred mountains, Mount Omei and Tai Shan, where every foot of the path up the mountain has legends, poetic names for rocks, and shrines for venerating the mountain.

Thus, it can be seen that each tribe had its own sacred mountain or mountains, and the tribe maintained its existence through its abiding relationship to the mountain.

The tribes of the Great Plains also had their sacred mountains, and those seeking a vision went up to the top of the mountain. Perhaps the most important Amerindian vision on a mountain in modern times was Black Elk's vision when he was nine years old. When the famous Sioux medicine man was very old he took John Neihardt, his biographer, up to the top of Harney Peak in the Black Hills, the site of his long-ago vision. In that vision he had been taken to see the Six Grandfathers and these Powers of the world had shown him the "sacred hoop of the world." At the very end of his vision the Six Grandfathers and the throngs of faces in the cloud all cried out "He has triumphed"; but Black Elk, at the end of his life, thought he had failed, so he wanted to go up to give a last message to the Six Powers of the world. He and John Neihardt climbed up the mountain in the midst of a prolonged drought. Black Elk performed his ceremony and said his last prayer: "In sorrow I am sending a feeble voice, O Six Powers of the World. Hear me in my sorrow, for I may never call again. O make my people live!" [234, 39] Rain fell and thunder spoke while Black Elk stood weeping on the mountain. When Neihardt wrote his book, *Black Elk Speaks,* in 1932, it made no impression. But by 1961, when it was reprinted, times had changed and the words of Black Elk have since changed the hearts of thousands of white people. They are now learning the Indian's reverence for the earth, and because of that, the sacred hoop of all the people is coming together, as the Six Powers told Black Elk it would.

A Meditation: Hewn and Cleft from this Rock, by Holmes Rolston, III

The walk in has carried me backward, ten thousand years at every step, and here I must rest, for I am lost in the plethora of time. Pardee Point shall be an Ebenezer, a *stone of help*. Before me is the inclined contact located in the rock cut; now can I fix my bearings from the precambrian contact? . . . I am the sentient offspring of this rock; in this evanescent encounter Dust shall return and meet in retrospect the dust from whence he came. 'In the mother's body man knows the universe, in birth he forgets it.' If I can recollect my pre-natal past, my gestation in the geological womb, my genealogy, then I shall know who I am and where I am . . .

As the blood in my veins is but an inland sea, so the rock in my bones is but borrowed from the subterranean matrix in which I am re-immersed. Behind the hostility of plutonic depths, and interred with these sediments, and dissolved in the sea, are the nutrient powders of life. The waters of the oceans must, if I judge aright, have escaped juvenile from the earth. Proto-rock sired the seas. Volatile magmas belched fertile vapors and gases. Rains fell from methane-ammonia laden skies, and fell again to enrich the sea with salts of erosion for a billion years. Out of the lithosphere: atmosphere, and hydrosphere, and biosphere. Earth's carbonate and apatite have graced me with the carbon, calcium, and phosphate that support my frame. The iron of hornblende and augite is the iron of the blood in which courses my life. Those stains of limonite and hematite now coloring this weathered cut will tomorrow be the hemaglobin that flushes my face with red. So now would I, this rock parasite, return to praise my natural parents. Ephemeral, anomalous, if so I am, erudite, conscious, proud, I can no longer suppress, but yield to, rejoice in, and humbly confess yet another primitive intuition, only enriched by my intellectual sophistication. Here is my cradle. My soul is hidden in the cleft of this rock . . .

I shall linger and wait in wonder. I shall celebrate my geogenesis, my being in freedom, by conversing with this consanguine rock from whence I was hewn . . . to worship here at this sacred line. I come as *Homo admirans*. Knowledge begins in wonder, observed the sage of Athens. But it begets it as well, and, reveling in awe, I am who I am. So find I now my peace, my place as noble and aesthetic scion of stone.

5. Caves and Mountains in the Religious Heritage of Europe

In many cultures throughout the world the continuity of the relationship between human beings, mountains, and religion has continued right down to modern times; however, in Europe this continuity was ruptured. The next two chapters relate some of the events leading to this break in our European heritage which has contributed to the "nature-hating" which lurks beneath the surface of our modern culture.

Paleolithic Religion

In the Paleolithic Age, religion in Europe was deeply involved with the actual physical structure of the earth as in Asia. This is shown in the remarkable cave art created by Upper Paleolithic peoples, who flourished for at least 20,000 years from about 30,000–10,000 B.C., the time of the last of the four great glacial advances of Pleistocene times. Most of northern Europe was covered by great ice sheets and the glaciers spread far down from the Alps and Pyrenees; yet, under these forbidding conditions, the highly successful hunters began the "art of the caves" found in the caves on the slopes of the French Pyrenees and in the Cantabrian Mountains of northern Spain. "Their best work can be favorably compared with anything achieved since. They invented drawing, engraving, stenciling, painting, modeling in relief and in the round, and sculpture in relief and in the round— almost every process known to us today . . . they showed astonishing inventiveness. The bodies of the animals were beautifully modulated, with every bone and swelling muscle, every fold and hollow given its full value." [113] They developed great skill in using many colors, made from natural minerals, to secure a fully rounded, three-dimensional effect.

This sacred art is found deep in the innermost reaches of the caves, and to reach it often involves crossing dangerous chasms, waterfalls, and passing through narrow fissures in the rock. The reason the cave artists went to such lengths to hide their sacred drawings is related to the totem animal. According to Levy, the totem animal is a focus of life-energy embodied in the immortal ancestor. It is most often thought of as human, but able to assume an animal form in order to maintain the earthly life of the descendants who are incarnations of its spirit. The drawing, then, of the totem animal, although an abstraction, is felt to be nearer to reality than one's own life. That is why the drawing must be hidden and protected, so it is made deep in the unchanging stability of the cave. [180,39] Also, according to Scully, by painting these animals "in the splendid movements of full life . . . the earth was thus impregnated with them." [286,10] These drawings, according to Levy, showed "the spiritual and truly religious conception of a connection originally based upon the need for food, and sufficiently effective to hold the group in social and economic cohesion." [180,35] Some of the drawings were magical in that they showed the animal falling with the weapon in it, but most were truly religious. Levy defines the two terms: "Magic may be defined as the imposition of non-physical power to attain a specified end. Religion is the maintenance of abiding relationship." [180,35]

Levy gives the modern example of the Australian aborigines, who follow a winding path in their processional dance to a cave where they have hidden sacred objects. This winding path duplicates the wanderings of their divine ancestor in trying to reach the earth. Both this example from a living race and the drawings of spiral mazes just outside Palaeolithic caves indicate the idea of a pathway between the two worlds which is intricate and difficult. Emphasis on spirals and mazes in religious dances and rituals continues down to modern times.

Dancing figures with animal masks depicted in cave art "were a deliberate means of approach to the animal nature, and therefore to the divine. 'They are to us what prayers are to you,' explained an old Bushman." [180, 42] Levy sums it up: ". . . reciprocity was their aim, a participation in the splendour of the beasts which was of the nature of religion itself." [180,20]

Neolithic

Later, in the megalithic age, there developed the custom of burying the dead in massive communal tombs. Hawkes states that these tombs "were not intended simply for a backward-looking cult of the dead or the appeasement of ancestors, they were to suggest a return to the Earth Mother for rebirth, the association of death with fecundity, which inspires all the myths of the goddess and the dying god. In this sense they represented the timeless unity of the tribe, of its members, dead, living and unborn all enclosed within their common matrix, the rock and the earth." [114, 159]

The polished stone axe, "emblem of the gentle life of cleared forest and reaped harvest, as also of the sacrifice of the peaceful beasts," was an important symbol in the Neolithic times. It was connected both to that aspect of religion concerned with seasonal fertility and with the developing symbolism of stone—stone pillars and stone altars. [180,86]

The Mother Goddess connected both these aspects of Neolithic religion. The Goddess wore the cow's horns in Asia and Africa, indicating that the human being's reciprocal relationship with animals, which began in the Stone Age, continued with his domesticated animals. She retained her fundamental status as the earth out of which all birth comes and into which all life goes at death; but, added to this concept, was the newer one of the growing of grain, which springs up from the Earth Mother, is cut down, and used by human beings, but ever again grows up anew from fruitful Mother Earth.

As human beings became aware of the causes of seasonal change in sky phenomena, such as the sun and storms, there developed the concept of deities of the sun and wind. Another concept is the dying male god, the vegetation god, who is reborn and dies with the yearly growth and decay of the earth's vegetation. Thus, the Stone Age religion of reciprocity, which began with the ceremonies concerning the birth and death of the hunted animals, developed further into the ritual attunement to the rhythms of the seasonal change of the earth's vegetation. Ceremonies were developed in which human beings ritually give their energy to the process of assisting the New Year to be born, the harvest to be cut down, and the sun to rise or to return from his winter house and bring back the warmth.

Early Civilizations

Levy describes how, in the beginnings of the early civilizations of Sumer and Egypt, peoples from the hilly upland country migrated down into the fertile marshy lowland because of drought. At Ur, the center of the Sumerian civilization, there was a temple of the Goddess Ninkhursag, "Lady of the Mountain." Under this title, the Mother Goddess was worshipped in all the cities of Sumer, "another mark of the nostalgia of the immigrants into the marshy plains, who yet in imagination lifted their eyes to the hills." [180, 95] The later descendants of these people built the Ziggurats, artificial mountains for rituals. [134, 73] According to James, the Akkadian word ziqquratu means "pinnacle" or the "summit of a mountain." At the ancient site of Nippur, the temple was called the "House of the Mountain" to represent the lost ancestral mountain. [180,168] In Egypt, a similar movement of peoples from the upland occurred, down onto the terraces above the marshy valleys of the Nile. Hathor emerges from the Stone Age as the horned Mother Goddess. Her name means Dwelling of the God. She was both the protecting enclosure of the young God, Horus, and the body from which he emerges. Hathor is connected with mountains—again showing the nostalgia of the former upland dwellers. In Egyptian drawings she is seen between cleft mountains, "the horned Gate that divides the death-sleep and waking of the sun and is herself that mountain enclosing its cave tomb." [180,119] Levy does not mention the possibility, but it seems likely that just as the Sumerians built their Ziggurats in nostalgia for their lost mountains, the Egyptians may have begun their pyramids for similar reasons.

Mother Goddess Landscape Forms

Particular mountain shapes, generally called Mother Goddess mountains, played an important part in the religions of other cultures as well, and they continue to exert considerable influence on the unconscious level to this day. Two aspects of Paleolithic cave art contribute to an understanding of the symbolism of these mountain forms. The first is that of small female figures with very prominent hips and breasts and small heads, carved from rock, which have been found in many caves and are generally regarded as images of the Earth Mother. The second aspect is the emphasis which the cave drawings placed on the horns of an animal.

Levy mentions one of the most notable of these horn drawings is "the fine relief of a woman of a short type lifting a bison's horn; the horn through whose point, in later religious cults, the creative force of the beast was thought to be expelled." [180, 59] In various cultures, horns have been symbols of power, virility, strength, and fierceness. Concerning antlers and horns, Róheim writes: "They appear to be simply the penis displaced upwards; and it seems that this displacement upwards, this erection displaced to the head, is a necessary fore-pleasure phase, an introduction to the coitus in the case of some animals." [362, 352] Most animal horns are bent or curved, or usually come in pairs. According to Zeckel, "Human imagination had to create a horn which, without much fantasy, was the penis displaced upwards; single, but straight, unbent and very strong and long . . . the unicorn horn." [362, 352] The unicorn was called licorno in Italy. Corno means phallus. [362, 355] For all these reasons, the horn is used in initiation ceremonies and seasonal rituals as a symbol of fertility and abundance. Crests on helmets and ceremonial headresses, such as the British ceremonial guards, are further developments of the basic horn symbolism.

The broad spreading base of some mountains suggests the fertile female shape as shown in the broad, full hips and breasts of the stone carvings, while the horned peak of the summit suggests the power of the animal horn found in cave drawings. Archaeological evidence derived from the location of Cretan palaces clearly points to the importance of these mountain forms in the Bronze Age. In his book, *The Earth, The Temple and the Gods*, Scully explained the relationship between the palace and the Mother Goddess mountain.

The palace was set in an enclosed valley and oriented so that a gently mounded or conical hill was to the north or south with a double-peaked or cleft mountain some distance beyond the conical hill but on the same axis. A gently mounded or conical hill (see photo) symbolizes the caring, nurturing aspects of the Mother Goddess. The double-peaked or cleft mountain symbolized her power, as well as her nurturing aspect. The double-peaked mountain resembles a pair of horns but it also suggests raised arms or wings, the female cleft through which the baby moves in birth, or sometimes breasts. The eye naturally comes to rest in the valley or hollow between the two horns. Scully says this suggests the goddess' lap, similar to the lap of horned Isis upon which the pharaohs sat. [286, 14]

The combination of a conical hill and the double-horned mountain is the most impressive of all the Mother Goddess forms when the conical hill is seen standing directly behind the cleft or break in the ridge. Paul Shepard calls these cleft ridges "cross valleys." He explains that these cross valleys are "streams or rivers that cross ridges or mountains. They result from at least four situations: from the overflow of a basin, from being gently lowered across a buried ridge as the stream removes materials by erosion, from the stream's capacity to maintain its position as the ridge rises by uplift at right angles to it, and from erosion into the hillside until the crest of the hill is notched." [290]

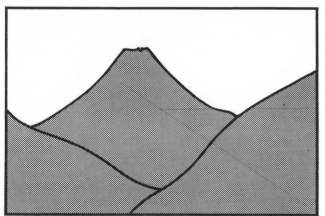

Cross valley Mother Goddess landscape form

For an understanding of the symbolism involved in the combination of the cone and the double-horned mountain it is necessary to consider, once again, the stone female figurines. Scully points out that these are "carved as the child knows the mother, all breasts, hips, and *mons veneris*, full and round." [286, 10] Notice the word *mons*, Latin for mountain in this anatomical word for the female genital region. The combination of the gently rounded *mons veneris* and the two breasts is the same combination as the conical hill between the cleft mountain or ridge, the "cross valley." Possibly, the power of this combination of landscape forms has something to do with the actual birth of the baby. Recent discoveries by Leboyer and others have proved that the new-born baby (if undrugged and coming out of an undrugged mother) can see her face and recognize it later. This may indicate that the first combination of shapes the baby sees after birth is the gently rounded *mons veneris* between the two breasts.

Scully points out that V cleft was connected with the female parts of the Mother Goddess in Paleolithic and Neolithic times, and the same V was a "a stylized form" for horns. "One may therefore legitimately surmise that the cleft or horned mountain may sometimes have been seen as embodying the *mons veneris* of the earth." [286, 15] In other words, the horned mountain is symbolically connected with giving birth; furthermore, the geologic origin of such mountains actually does connect them with fertility and birth. Horned mountains are caused by the intersection of three or more glacial cirques. These cirques are created by the scouring action of the glacier on the underlying rock. As the glacier scours deeper into the rock and carries away more finely ground-up rock particles, the cirques grow larger and deeper, eventually leaving only a narrow ridge between them and, at an even later stage, grinding away the ridge itself until the two cirques join. The higher rock, remaining after the three cirques intersect creates the horned mountain; thus such a mountain truly fulfills the function of a nurturing mother because her finely ground rock powder, carried down by the glacier and its meltwater streams, eventually provides the soil necessary for life.

Volcanoes, nearly perfect Mother Goddess conical forms, continually introduce new material into the rock cycle for the first time. Leveson explains this process: "In the operation of the real earth, the source of most volcanic material lies far beneath the more superficial levels where erosion, weathering, sedimentation, burial, and metamorphism take place. These latter processes occur within the outermost thirty miles or so of the earth's four-thousand-mile radius. But most rock melts originate not in the crust but in the underlying mantle, and from there make their way upwards toward the surface." [179, 44] Again, a Mother Goddess mountain form, the breast-shaped volcanic cone, nurtures all life on earth by contributing precious elements from deep

MOTHER GODDESS mountain (nurturing aspect).　　　　　　(Photograph by Steve Meyer

within the earth to replenish the soil, the ultimate source of life for all plants and animals.

Both types of Mother Goddess forms have figured in art in modern times even though Christian culture did not recognize the underlying meaning. El Greco's masterpiece, "View of Toledo," depicts a perfect combination of Mother Goddess forms. The conical hill in the background is seen through the cleft formed by the Tagus River flowing between two rounded hills. El Greco came from Crete to Spain in his thirties. "Toledo" is his only true landscape, and the power of the painting undoubtedly reflects the impression made on him by spending his early years among the Mother Goddess forms of the mountains in Crete. In Alpine regions of Europe, there is frequently a little mountain chapel on top of the conical hills.

In Japan there is always a Shinto shrine on a conical hill. Mother Goddess landscape forms were also an important consideration for the *feng shui* in China. These experts, who planned palaces and tombs to line up with energy lines in the earth, were responsible for the flowing lines and the beauty of the Chinese landscape as seen today. An interesting historical example of the influence of Mother Goddess forms in China concerns the King of Yüeh who defeated the King of Wu in 471 B.C. and built the first wall of his new capital in a specially chosen spot beside a lake (now in Nanking). The state of Yüeh got its name from the early Yüeh culture which introduced the veneration of sacred mountains and a matriarchal form of society into China as was mentioned in Chapter 3. The view from Nanking today shows two outstanding Mother Goddess forms visible—one horned and one cone. [54]

Mother Goddess Forms and Religion in Crete

The Minoan civilization of Bronze Age Crete did not build temples; although its art and culture reached a high level of development. Instead, Mother Goddess rituals were performed on mountain peaks, in caves, and in rustic shrines, in order to keep close contact with the earth by means of the cave, the rock pillar, and the tree. For example, a cave near the River Karteros, which is probably Homer's Cave of Eileithyia, the Goddess of Birth (one aspect of the Mother Goddess) shows evidence of continuous use for rituals down to the Roman occupation. Winding galleries lead to an area containing a circular stalagmite surrounded by a square made up of small stones. [180, 214] A stalagmite, although of entirely different geologic origin, has the same symbolism as a rock pillar. On Mount Dikte, there is another cave associated with a stalagmite, which is probably the legendary birthplace of Zeus, the god of the Greeks. [180, 215]

The relationship of the palaces and the Mother Goddess landscape forms is such, Scully explains, that "the natural and the man-made create one ritual whole, in which man's part is defined and directed by the sculptural masses of the land and is subordinate to their rhythms." [286, 11]

This can be understood from a more detailed description of a particular site such as the palace of Knossos. To reach Knossos, it is necessary to climb up through low hills from the old harbor. At the precise spot where the valley widens, the palace can be seen, set into the valley with Mount Jouctas directly behind it. The approach to the palace is by a narrow, raised stone path. Moving along this path, suddenly the eye can see down the long axis of the court to the mounded conical hill which closes the valley and the double horned peak of Jouctas in the distance. The palace seems to lie sheltered upon the very body of the recumbent Earth Mother. [286, 12]

Knossos was particularly susceptible to earthquakes, and this very fact may have been partly responsible for its sacredness. Because the Minoans lived in harmony with Nature, they trusted her so they could take full advantage of "the chthonian character of the place which, as an earthquake center, seemed to manifest the power of the goddess or of her creature, the horned bull —perhaps the King as Poseidon—as 'Earth-shaker.'" [286, 219]

Bull-dancing was a unique rite in Crete. It is shown on many art objects of ancient Crete. The dancer, often a woman, seizes the horns of the bull in each hand and leaps over the back of the bull. As has been mentioned, the horns of the animal were considered to be filled with the creative force of the animal. According to Scully, this ritual "celebrated both men and women together as accepting nature's law, adoring it, adding to their own power precisely insofar as they seized it close and adjusted their rhythms to its force." [286, 13] A form of this dance is still performed in the Corridas of Southern France. The dancers wait until the bull lowers his head to charge "whereupon they place their foot on the bull's forehead, nimbly allowing themselves to be tossed in the air and land on their feet at a safe distance." [215, 55]

The bull dance is associated with the labyrinth or maze. The use of the maze for ritual dancing, dating back to the caves of Palaeolithic times, continues in present-day Europe in maze-like dancing grounds used in folk dancing.

The bull dance is connected with the Greek legend of Theseus successfully penetrating to the center of the labyrinth and finding Ariadne (whose name means the "very holy," a name in Cyprus for the Goddess Aphrodite). [180, 248] He lost Ariadne again because she was a goddess, but he set up her image in Delos in Greece and taught the youths and maidens to dance before its horned altar through the windings of a labyrinthine dance. This labyrinthine-type dance was used to make a second wall of magic defense for Troy. [155, 202-249]

Greece

The first of the Indo-European tribes to invade Greece (about 1900 B.C.) were the Achaeans. These patriarchal herdsmen brought their male gods with them with the result that worship of the Sky-Father, thunder-wielding god, usurped some of the prerogatives of the local Mother Goddess worship. However, even Zeus, the King of the Gods, still retained remnants of the Old Religion: He was said to have been born of the Great Mother in a Cretan cave and suckled by a horned beast. At any rate, the old buried Minoan religion returned much later in the Mystery Religions of later Greece.

The relationship between the actual site of the temple, the Mother Goddess land forms visible from that site, and the particular deity connected with the site determined the total concept of the particular deity. The Greeks oriented their temples in relation not only to the Mother Goddess forms of the earth, but often to the particular point where the sun rose on the feast day of the specific god in the year of the temple's dedication. [286, 44] To illustrate this complex relationship, consider the goddess Artemis, who was the mother of wild beasts and guardian of the untamed wilderness areas. On the sites which had formerly been devoted to the Mother Goddess, the Greeks often built a temple dedicated to Artemis, the "maiden of the mountains." She represented the Goddess as mother of wild beasts, which was close to the oldest aspect of the Goddess, when the Paleolithic peoples painted the animals deep within Mother Earth. In order to bring Artemis within the Olympian pantheon she became a huntress herself, goddess of the moon and of hunting. She was the daughter of Zeus and Leto (a Mother Goddess type) and twin sister of Apollo. She is the Mother who avoids marriage and remains free of domination by males and their law. "Thus she protects the wild from rape by man, and her sites in Greece are haunted by that watchful, dangerous presence."[286, 80] She was sometimes called "the Mountain Mother." The lower ridges extending out from the main mass of some mountains do seem to resemble the outspread arms of a "mountain mother," protecting all beings sheltered below the ridges. This particular symbolism is expressed in the famous Boeotian vase which shows Artemis sheltering birds, snakes, bears, wolves, and fish beneath her wide-spreading arms. The Temple of Artemis near Mount Artemision presents a perfect view of the Mother Goddess form called a "cross-valley." The cone of Mukhli stands centered in the middle, between the two horns formed by the sides of the gorge. [286, 84]

Artemis was also goddess of the moon; her brother Apollo was god of the sun. Delphi, the seat of his greatest oracle, was previously a Mother Goddess site. Here, the temple site dramatizes the opening of earth through the V of the hills. At Delphi, the cleft rocks mark the site of Gaia, the Earth Goddess. It was from this cleft that the Pytheness originally prophesied.

The site of the Temple at Bassae clearly shows the reconciliation which Apollo affected between ancient wild nature and the rationalism of the Greeks. From a great distance, the horned cleft can be clearly seen; but the temple itself, located between the horns, is invisible. All that can be seen is the great shapes of mountains beyond. Shortly after reaching a spring of water, the temple suddenly appears "against the sky, so set that its columns, as clear cylinders of geometrical order, rise slowly, step by step in fact, above the broken rock of the hill." [286, 123] Nearer still, the long axis of the temple moves across the distant horns and, "as it does, so it locks the whole landscape into place. Temple and landscape are now one architecture, which clearly expresses a double reverence in its form: both for the mighty earth, with all its power, and for men, with the god." [286, 124] The pillars of the temple are Corinthian columns which are tree-like in form, reminiscent of Apollo's symbol, the palm tree, which in Crete had been a symbol for the Mother Goddess. During Apollo's birth, Leto, his mother, had grasped the palm tree for support. In the temple at Bassae, the tree-like pillars stand for both the god and the earth powers which Apollo had brought under his sway.

Zeus, the thunder-wielding sky god, became the supreme god of the Greeks and the successor of the old Goddess, whose power he usurped through marriage to Hera. Temples to Zeus were placed on the tops of mountains, the places which had been most sacred to the old Mother Goddess.

In general, the Greek temple attempted to reconcile sky-god orientation with earth-mother landscape. At Samos, for instance, a walled enclosure in the interior, a cave-like space for the goddess, is surrounded by a columned exterior which directs the eye out to specific Mother Goddess mountains. Samos was called "The Labyrinth" because the many columns created the type of space through which a labyrinthine dance naturally moved. In the great Ionic temples, the columns give one the feeling of standing in a grove of trees. In ancient times, of course, rituals took place in a grove of trees. As these were gradually cut down or destroyed by grazing, wooden columns were erected. These were later replaced by stone columns. The capitals of the Ionic columns evoke horns, but at the same time, because of the curling tendrils, they are also reminiscent of plant life. [286, 51, 52 and 54]

The most spectacular setting of all the temples is that of Poseidon, the god of the sea at Sounion. For the Greek sailor returning across the Aegean Sea, it was the first sight of home. The horned cleft rises just above the promontory of the temple site. Upon entering the temple from the land side and walking forward, the earth suddenly drops away and leaves one looking straight down into the sea. Upon turning around, there, framed between the columns, are the Mother Goddess cone and horns of the earth, thus balancing the earth and the sea, the ancient power of the Goddess and the sea-bright sky-god, Poseidon. Ultimately, the balance, represented in the temple of Sounion, tipped toward more complete supremacy of the sky-god principle, accompanied by growing distrust of the earth-Mother Goddess principle, which became a dark force threatening the brightness of human reason. As the idea that man is the "measure of all things" gained ascendency, Nature came to be considered as either irrelevant or antagonistic. The various stages of worship connected with the goddess Demeter of Eleusis illustrate these changing concepts of the Greek gods.

Eleusinian Mysteries

Although it is not generally recognized, the most famous of all religious rites, the Eleusinian Mysteries, are not only intimately connected with the earth, but additionally provide an outstanding example of the power generated by the on-going relationship of human beings to a particular place, thus reinforcing Levy's definition of religion as abiding relationship. Because these Mysteries were considered by the writers of classical Greece and Rome as the quintessential religious experience open to humanity, their influence has continued to this day through two different mediums: in literature and through the Church's adaptation of some of the Eleusinian rites to Christian ritual. (See Chapter 17 for more information on Christian rituals.)

Although the classical writers thought of the Mysteries as being absolutely unique to mankind, it will be seen below that they are actually a form of a very important basic human ritual relationship to Nature, as demonstrated specifically by Indonesian and Amerindian rituals.

"Within Greek religion, the Eleusinian Mysteries were unique of their kind, and this uniqueness was their characteristic trait, which was indeed stressed," according to Kerényi, the outstanding authority on Eleusis. He explains, "Whereas in the history of religion, doctrines and cults have laid claim to the one and only truth, Eleusis was held to be the one and only *place* where what happened before the eyes of the initiates . . . was permitted and true." [151, 115] The central feature of this "sacred place" was the Plutonian, the cave, which indicated the entrance to the underworld. In this cave was an *omphalos,* meaning "navel", a bond between the underworld, on the one hand, and heaven and earth, on the other." [151, 80]

The rites of the Eleusinian Mysteries center around the figure of the goddess, Demeter, and her daughter. Though she bears an Indo-European name, Demeter was really an ancient Minoan goddess of fertility of the earth and, after a period of time as part of the Olympian pantheon of gods, she was again worshipped in her essential Mother Goddess aspect when she became Mother of the Mysteries. The rite at Eleusis became the most famous of the ancient Mysteries because of the praise given it by such renowned Greeks and Romans as Homer, Plutarch, Cicero, Aristides, Sophocles, and Euripides. Its fame was so great that when a Ptolemaic king of Egypt in the Third Century B.C. wanted to found a Greek-Egyptian cult (of the god, Serapis) in Alexandria, he sent for a son of one of the high priests of Eleusis to head it. [284, 97] The early fathers of the Christian Church, such as Clement of Alexandria, greatly feared the power of the Mysteries.

The oldest written document pertaining to the Mysteries is the Homeric Hymn to Demeter. From this we learn that the Mysteries were established by the goddess herself, and those who took part in them could look forward to a blissful state after death. These people are called "Blessed" in the hymn, and Sophocles called them "thrice blessed." According to Isocrates, at the beginning of the 4th century B.C. Demeter gave two things when she came to Eleusis: "first, the fruit of the field, to which we owe our transition from an animal to a human life; and second, the rites, participation in which makes us look with joyful hope upon the end of life and upon existence as a whole." [243, 14-15] In 59 B.C. in Rome, Cicero, while introducing a deputation from Athens, pointed out that it was Athens "in which 'humanity', religion, and agriculture had originated." [243, 15]

Grain had an important part in the Mysteries. Not only is the first grain said to have been sown and harvested on the plain near Eleusis, but according to legend the goddesses themselves first gave grain to the Eleusinian hero Triptolemus, telling him to spread it throughout the world. James shows that Demeter's Mysteries at Eleusis were originally held at the time of the sowing of grain in the autumn, when the beginning of the winter rains allowed the parched fields to be worked. Originally Demeter's feast was connected to fertility rituals in the Mediterranean region, where women made bowers with couches of vegetation and sat on the ground to fertilize the crop which had just been sown. [134, 136] However, modern scholars hold that the agricultural aspect lost its importance in the later development of the mysteries.

It is certain that several different myths have been combined in the legend of Demeter. The basic Greek story, as given in Homer, is that Persephone or Kore, "the Maiden," was picking flowers in a meadow when Pluto, the king of the underworld, abducted her and took her into the underworld. (Originally, this was Plouton, the god of the wealth of the fertile earth, who later became confused with Pluto.) [134, 137] Persephone's mother, Demeter, searched all over for her, eventually reaching Eleusis, where she disguised herself as an old woman and sat on a rock to weep for her lost daughter. She was taken in by the family of the ruler, Keleos, and became nurse to the infant child of the family. She was secretly attempting to make him into an immortal when she was discovered. Before leaving she commanded the people of Eleusis to build her a sanctuary. After Persephone was found, as a compromise she spent part of her time below the earth with the King of the Underworld and part of the time above the earth. As long as Persephone remained above the ground with her, Demeter allowed the rain to fall and grain to grow again; when she was below the ground, the land was parched and barren.

Robert Graves points out that when a Greek legend concerns rape or abduction of a goddess it usually has to do with the patriarchal Greek attempt to impose a male god where formerly a form of the Mother Goddess ruled. In this case there is both a rape and an abduction. A possible explanation is that the Mother Goddess fertility role was at one time partly taken over by the imposition of the male god, Plouton. [243, 19]

It was formerly thought that it was the disappearance of Persephone that caused the earth to lose its fertility. Later it was found that it was after Demeter mourned for her daughter in Eleusis that fertility ceased. In Euripides' *Helena*, Demeter, angry at what has been done to her, withdraws into the mountains and withers the vegetation, allowing nothing to grow on earth. In the chorus of this play, Demeter is called "the mountain mother," thus equating her with the "Great Mother." [243, 18] We are dealing here with a primeval myth of the earth mother who is angry, perhaps at the invasion by patriarchal gods. Actually, Demeter did not make the actual gift of grain to the world until after Persephone's descent into the underworld. This agrees with the primitive belief as mentioned above: the return to the Earth Mother for rebirth and the association of death with fecundity in the Megalithic Age. Along with the gift of agriculture, Demeter gave humanity a ritual and a vision concerning bliss after death.

Aristides was an initiate into the Eleusinian Mysteries. He says that the Mysteries were the "most terrible and most luminous" of all the divine things and spoke of the "ineffable visions" that many generations of people had seen there. As the initiates were forbidden to disclose what actually happened in the initiation, the only information available has to do with the rituals up until this last step.

First, as most authorities agree, there was a day-long procession with singing and dancing from Athens to Eleusis, led by the sacred cult figure of Iacchos (a type of the young dying vegetation god). [38] Hartley Burr Alexander states that Athenian participation in the mysteries was a part of the covenant of agreement between the two cities which in very ancient times ended hostilities. [4, 127] According to Herodotus, a few days before the festival the call went out through all the streets of Athens: "To the sea, O mystai!" [284, 101] The processional journey began by a climb up to the pass of Daphni. Scully points out that all along the way the procession encountered key sites connected with Mother Goddess landscape forms. First, the procession came to a conical hill, the goddess nurturing form,

which guards the pass on the Athenian side. At the top of the pass, they saw the horns of Mount Kerata, which means horns. As the route wound down from the Pass, "the horns of Kerata slide once more out of sight: the mystic object found and lost." [286, 75] The way down was rocky and dry. Herodotus mentions that the dust of the great crowd could be seen from afar. Part way down, the hills to the left suddenly opened up and a mass of rock thrust up between them, another Mother Goddess form. At this spot, a sanctuary to Aphrodite exists. At this very point, also, the way turns and the horns of Kerata are replaced by the horns of Salamis. When they reached the shore of the gulf of Eleusis the initiates ritually bathed in the sea before continuing round the shore, arriving at Eleusis at night. Scully explains that: "Eleusis is clearly that passage between worlds, that 'Gate of Horn,' celebrated in the Odyssey and by Vergil . . ." [286, 74] Kerata, the horned mountain, rises directly above the sanctuary of Eleusis.

According to most authorities, the name Eleusis in antiquity meant "passage" or "the gate." Kerényi, however, states that grammatically, the actual name of the site of the Mysteries, Eleusis, differed by accent and inflection from the Greek word, *eleusis*, "arrival", although the words were related. The place name, Eleusis, "refers to the underworld in the favorable sense and may be translated as 'the place of happy arrival.'" [151, 23] Graves explains that the word came to mean *advent*, referring to the coming of the Divine Child, the god Iacchos, and that this word, *advent*, was adopted by the Christians for the weeks before the birth of Jesus, the Divine Child at Christmas. [104, 159] A further interesting point is that the season of Advent in the Christian church has combined these many levels of meaning— partly joy at the expected arrival of the Christ Child with salvation for mankind, and a combined solemnity and joy at the thought of one's own death. The solemnity derives from the awareness of preparing for a "happy death" by a good life; the joy is in expectation of death as the beginning of the future heavenly life. It is easy to see the continuity of these themes from the ancient Greek religion to Christianity.

The initiates entered "the Gate" and by torchlight crowded in among a forest of columns, which created a mysterious, shadowy labyrinthine grove. [151, 89] The final rite took place deep within the cave-like interior, where the initiates drank the sacred potion* used by Demeter herself, as recorded in the Homeric hymn. This central sanctuary was built directly over the site of a Mycenaean megaron, thus linking Demeter directly with the Cretan Mother Goddess. [134, 151]

The culmination of the rite is not known. It is concerned with an object shown to the initiates. "Happy is he who has seen it," says the Homeric Hymn. In Plutarch's "On the Soul," he compares the terror of death, which is suddenly transformed into the bliss of soul, with the transfiguration of the participant in the Mysteries once he has seen the vision. The Roman Christian Bishop, Hippolytus, says that the climax of the Mysteries is the display of an ear of wheat, cut and harvested and displayed "in silence." He further writes, "The immense life-giving power of the earth mother was impressed immediately upon the soul of the mystae." Otto explains that it was probably the same type of plant miracle as used in Nature festivals of primitive people: "The ear of wheat suddenly grown, silently harvested and displayed to the mystae is then really a revelation and pledge of the goddess, who first gave this fruit to mankind through the Eleusinians . . . More than that: it is an epiphany of Persephone herself, her mythical *first* recurrence in the shape of the grain, after her descent to the realm of the dead." [243, 25]

Demeter and Persephone can be considered as two aspects of the Mother Goddess. "For a Great Goddess could do just that: in a single figure which was *at once* Mother and Daughter, she could represent the motifs that recur in *all* mothers and daughters, and she could combine the feminine attributes of the earth with the inconstancy of the wandering moon. As mistress of all living creatures on land and sea she could reach up from the underworld to heaven." [151, 32] In fact, she governed all three parts of the world, heaven, earth, and underworld; thus she was a type of Robert Graves' "triple goddess."

On the last day of the celebration of the Mysteries occurred the "pourings of plenty," when liquid was poured out by overturning special unstable ritual vessels. According to Kerényi, this probably took place in the cave, the Ploutonion, and the liquid ran into a cleft in the earth, the *chthonian chasma*. [151, 141]

The myth was bound up with cult. The old story handed down ages past was not just remembered, but relived during the cult rite. "The cult of the Earth Mother Demeter bears all the traits of a firmly rooted family cult attached to a particular soil." [152] James further explains that the "seasonal cult-drama was enacted at Eleusis from very ancient times" and was essentially an ancient family cult of the Eumolpidae, so was a carefully guarded, secret rite for a specific place and occasion. [134, 151]

The Neoplatonic writer, Proclus, in the 5th century A.D. recorded that the initiates uttered a sacred formula while gazing up at the sky, "Rain (O Sky) conceive (O Earth), be fruitful." This undoubtedly refers to "the genuine ore of an old religious stratum sparkling all the more for being found in a waste deposit of Neoplatonic metaphysic." [134, 151]

The Eleusinian Mystery is tied to an actual physical *place*, actual earth forms (mountains and the sea), and an actual gift of the earth, the wheat. All the writers throughout the ages who wonder at the mystery and look for occult explanations overlook these very real ties with the earth, but from these very ties with the earth comes the power of the rite. To understand this, however, it is necessary to turn to Amerindian rituals because these have retained their meaning uncluttered by "Neoplatonic metaphysic."

Amerindian Rituals of the Hako and "Many Children"

Tahirussawichi, the Pawnee priest, says of the journey part of the rite, "Many Children": "Mother Corn, who led our spirits over the path we are now to travel, lead us again as we walk, in our bodies, over the land . . . She led our fathers and she leads us now, because she was born of Mother Earth and knows all places and all people." The second part of this rite involves the songs sung on the journey. These include: a "Song to the Trees and Streams," a "Song When Crossing the Streams," a "Song to the Wind," and a "Song when Ascending Mountains." [90] The Pawnee sing songs to all the various parts of their particular *place* through which they travel, just as the mystae sang on the journey from Athens to Eleusis as they passed through and under the Mother Goddess forms of Mount Kerata.

The Pawnee rite is called "Many Children;" the similar Sioux rite is called "The Hako", after the two wands which represent earth and sky. Hartley Burr Alexander explains that these rites are concerned with "Permission that man *in his own kind* may continue to be, and after his manner flourish." [4, 101] Thus, these rites are related to the religion of reciprocity of the cave. A little child is important in these rites, just as Iacchos was in the Eleusinian Mysteries. Tahirussawichi said: "Upon this little child we are to put the signs of the promises which Mother Corn and Kawas bring, the promise of children, of increase."

The Pawnee rite involved a journey of one tribe, called "the Fathers", to the other tribe, called "the Children", with the purpose of establishing a friendly relationship. In the Eleusinian Mysteries the initiates traveled from Athens to Eleusis, thus fulfilling an old covenant of friendship. At Eleusis the wheat was important; in the Pawnee ritual the ear of corn, symbol of the Corn Mother, was sacred. According to Tahirussawichi, "The ear of corn represented the supernatural power that dwells in

---

*"The mixture" was called *kykeon* and was made from barley, water, and mint. The barley was probably roasted. Roasted barley in water produces malt and a drink which becomes alcoholic after a brief fermentation. After fasting on the journey to Eleusis from Athens even a slight amount of alcohol would have helped to induce visions. In analyzing the Greek name for the third ingredient used in the "mixture," Kerényi says it may have been some variety of the herb, pennyroyal. He quotes from a letter he received from a pharmacologist, Albert Hofmann of Switzerland, to the effect that the principal ingredient used in preparing an aromatic in southern Europe and "obtained by distilling the wild plant, is the aromatic substance pulegone . . . In large doses it induces delirium, loss of consciousness, and spasms." [151, 180] This refers to the distilled wild plant, while the form of the herb used in the *kykeon* was specifically described as being of fresh, tender leaves. The effect of the volatile oils from the fresh leaves, while not very strong, could have helped to "produce hallucinations in persons whose sensibility was heightened by fasting." [151, 180]

H'Uraru, the earth which brings forth the food that sustains life."*

When they arrive at the village of the other tribe, the sun has set and it is dark (as at Eleusis). The Hako are taken up and the singers perform the Invocation to the Visions:

> Holy visions!
> Hither come, we pray you, come unto us,
> Bringing with you joy;
> Come, oh, come to us, holy visions,
> Bringing with you joy.

Tahirussawichi says that the visions do come from above and "As we walk, the visions walk; they fill all the space within the lodge; they are everywhere, all about us . . . touching the Children . . . by their touch giving them dreams, which will bring them health, strength, happiness, and all good things . . ." At the end of the night devoted to rituals, when the morning light begins to come, they sing the Birth of the Dawn:

We call to Mother Earth, who is represented by the ear of corn. She has been asleep and resting during the night. We ask her to awake, to move, to arise, for the signs of the dawn are seen in the east and the breath of the new life is here . . .

With the rising of the Morning Star, for which a server has been on the watch, the second song is sung "slowly, with reverent feeling, for we are singing of very sacred things."

As Tahirussawichi finishes his account, he tells of the last ritual when a little child, representative of the tribe, is unveiled and dismissed to play and a song of blessing is sung over him. After Tahirussawichi finished singing this song for Alice Fletcher he said, "As I sing this song with you, I cannot help shedding tears. I have never sung it before except as I stood looking upon the little child and praying for it in my heart . . . This is a very solemn act." The depth of feeling brought about by recounting the ritual is reminiscent of the deep feelings of the Greeks and Romans when they referred to the events at Eleusis.

The central mystery of the Hako was the Holy Marriage of Heaven and Earth and the Birth of a Sacred Child. Tahirussawichi says "The life of man depends upon the Earth, the Mother. *Tirawa atius* works through it. The Kernel is planted within Mother Earth, and she brings forth the ear of corn, even as children are begotten and born of women." (All the quotations from the

Pawnee priest are from a Bureau of American Ethnology Report. See note 90.)

A similar rite among the Sioux has many features in common with the rite at Eleusis, as shown by Black Elk's account of the *Hunkapi*, "The Making of Relatives." Black Elk begins his account by telling of the culture hero, Matohoshila of the Lakota Sioux, who saw corn in a vision and later found just such a patch of corn and thus brought the concept of the growing of corn to his people. He did not know that the corn he found belonged to enemies of the Sioux, the Ree or Arikari. When the Ree asked for their corn back, Matohoshila went to the Ree and asked them to help him to establish a rite for the benefit of all the people, which had been given to him in a vision by the Great Spirit. He said, "He who is our Grandfather and Father has established a relationship with my people the Sioux; it is our duty to make a rite which should extend this relationship to the different people . . . May that which we do here be an example to others!" [41, 102]

During the rite, Matohoshila puts a stick through the ear of corn, which he equates with the tree of life reaching from Heaven to Earth and symbolizing all the people and things of the universe. "It is good to remember these things if we are to understand the rites which are to come." [41, 109] Later in the ritual there is a ritual battle and counting of coup, followed by an exchange of gifts of food and horses between the Sioux and the Ree. Then a procession is formed, led by the Ree, followed by the ritually captive Sioux. A small boy and girl are included. The procession stops four times at particular places in the journey and songs are sung.

At their destination of the sacred lodge, the people are painted. Black Elk explains, "By being painted, the people have been changed; they have undergone a new birth, and with this they have new responsibilities, new obligations, and new relationship. This transformation is so sacred that it must be undergone in darkness; it must be hidden . . ." [41, 111–112]

There is much more to the rite which is too complex for detailing here, but at the end of the rite the Sioux chant:

> We are all related;
> We are all one! [41, 112]

At the ritual feast of meat, Matohoshila says that they have done the will of the Great Spirit, and that "through

---

*Kerényi explains that the Persephone myth is related to a myth of the natives of the Indonesian island of Ceram, which has to do with the nourishment men derive from plants. He points out that an analysis of certain Greek words helps to explain this. The Greek word *zoë* means "not only the life of men and of all living creatures but also what is *eaten* . . . The same meaning attaches to *bios*, the characteristic life of men. Where men draw their nourishment chiefly from plants . . . are individually perishable, destructible, edible, but taken together, they are the eternal guarantee of human life." [151, xxv] Perhaps the best way to understand the underlying meaning of both the Pawnee's use of the ear of corn and the Greek use of the wheat in the Eleusinian Mysteries is to consider the meaning of corn in the life of the Indians of the southwest. "You simply cannot talk about Indian life without talking about the miracle that is corn," explains Frank Waters. In most of the mythologies they are synonymous. "The Navajos believe that man was created from an ear of corn . . . At birth every Pueblo child receives a perfect ear of corn as a Corn Mother. The Corn Mother gives them nourishment and is virtually synonymous with Mother Earth. The Indians use cornmeal in every ceremony. The Hopi elders said, 'Because we build its flesh into our own, corn is also our body. Hence when we offer cornmeal with our prayers, we are offering part of our bodies. But corn is also spirit, for it was divinely created. So we are also offering spiritual thanks to the Creator.'" [255]

this we have established a relationship and peace, not only among ourselves, but within ourselves and with all the Powers of the universe." [41, 114]

Black Elk sums up the ritual when he says, "Through these rites a threefold peace was established. The first peace, which is the most important, is that which comes within the souls of men when they realize their relationship, their oneness with the universe and all its Powers, and when they realize that at the center of the universe dwells Wakan-Tanka, and that this center is really everywhere, it is within each of us. This is the real Peace, and the others are but reflections of this." [41, 115] The second peace is that between individuals, and the third that between tribes or nations.

Otto, in his essay on "The Meaning of the Eleusinian Mysteries," tells us that the old myth handed down from ages past is not just remembered but relived during the cult rite. "The gods are at hand . . . not only as majestic figures demanding reverence, but as what they are: supreme realities of the here and now, primal phenomena of the movement of being, creating and suffering powers of the living moment which also encompasses death. Without death there can be no life; without dying, no fertility." [243, 29] This concept is called the pattern of initiation. The English word, *initiation*, "comes from a special use of the Latin word, 'inire' (enter) to signify 'ritual entry into the earth.'" [155, 176]

To understand why this pattern of initiation, which includes some sort of suffering, death, and resurrection, occurs in such different events as the Mysteries of the classical world of Greece and Rome, in puberty rites which give access to secret societies, and even in the personal lives of mystics, it is necessary to look at the underlying meaning. Eliade, in his essay, "Mystery and Spiritual Regeneration in Extra-European Religions," writes: "Above all, we understand this: the man of primitive societies endeavored to conquer death by according it such importance that it ultimately ceased to be a *stopping* and became a *rite of passage.*" The primitives felt that one died to something that was not essential, such as the profane life. "In short, death comes to be regarded as the supreme initiation, that is, as the beginning of a new spiritual existence. And, moreover, generation, death, and regeneration were understood as the three moments of one and the same mystery, and the entire spiritual effort of archaic man went to show that there must be no caesura between these moments. One cannot stop in one of the three moments, one cannot settle down in one of them, in death, for example, or in generation. The movement, the regeneration continues perpetually . . . Consequently, immortality must not be conceived as a survival after death, but as a situation which one creates continuously, for which one prepares oneself, and in which one even participates here and now, in this world." [77, 35–36] "Rites of passage" can be used to ease the transition through any of the changes of life such as puberty, marriage, birth of a child, etc.,

as well as the changes in the physical environment caused by the earth itself as it moves through the seasons.

In the ancient times, more primitive humans had lived in complete union with Mother Earth, but for the sophisticated philosophical writers of the latter days of the classical period, mystery rites such as that of Eleusis tended to re-establish the lost unity of human beings with the Mother Goddess, Earth herself, "whose body— no longer every day and night or for time everlasting, but only during the period of purposeful communion with her—was the complete refuge for men." [286, 49] It is now possible to see why the enactment of an ancient rite which gave the worshippers direct contact to the power of the earth through the Mother Goddess figure of Demeter was a liberating experience which they never ceased to recall with joy.

Eleusis was utterly destroyed in 396 by Alaric and his Gothic tribesmen, but we should recall that Alaric was a friend of the Christians who had achieved high office in late imperial Rome. John Holland Smith indicates that "Our suspicion must be that Alaric himself saw the raid confusedly as revenge on the Romans (in the widest sense) for the slights offered to his people . . . and some kind of extension of the religious war . . . for many in Greece clung to the old gods; the mysteries still survived there, and to Alaric and his clerical friends that country must have symbolized the whole past of the Helleno-Roman and pagan world." Smith goes on to report that at "the holy sanctuary of Eleusis, the home of the goddesses and their mystery . . . destruction was so complete that hardly a stone was left on another and Eleusis, one of the most evocative names in religion, has ever since been for the visitor one of the most barren of sites." [297, 188–189]

The powerful horns of Mount Kerata still mark the site of Eleusis, which many authorities believe is the famed "Gate of Horn," the controversial and pivotal point of Vergil's epic poem, *The Aeneid.*

Vergil's *Aeneid*

Vergil (70–19 B.C.), supposedly drawing on his own experiences of the Eleusinian Mysteries, used the symbolism of the cave for the climactic scene at the end of the Sixth Book of the *Aeneid*. In Knight's book, *Cumaean Gates,* concerning the implications of the Cumaean cave in Vergil, he states that it is thought that the Sixth book, which tells of the descent of Aeneas into the cave, is really a description of initiation into one part of the Eleusinian Mysteries. Near the end of the book, Knight writes, "Further, the community of principle in cave rites is clearer, so that the cave at Cumae can now be expected to recall the pattern belonging to other cave rites, from which the mysteries themselves besides much else were derived." [155, 226]

Furthermore, because Dante's inspiration was Vergil's *Aeneid* and Dante's work, in turn, has influenced literature down to the present time, the events in the Sixth Book are of prime importance. I will briefly recount the main events of the *Aeneid* so that the pivotal importance of the cave scene is clear, for what is at stake here is not only the importance of *place* vs. the glory of Empire, but also the futility of sacrificing human beings to Empire.

After Troy is taken by the Greeks and burned, Aeneas flees with his wife, his son, and his father, Anchises, intending to go to Italy, where the family originated. The wife is lost, Anchises dies on the way, but after many perils Aeneas and his son reach Italy. Latinus, the reigning king, receives the exiles hospitably and promises his daughter, Lavinia, in marriage to Aeneas. But Lavinia's mother has already promised her to Prince Turnus, who refuses to give her up. Latinus orders the rivals to settle the matter in battle. Turnus is killed, Aeneas marries Lavinia and thus begins Rome.

Vergil spent the last eleven years of his life working on his great epic poem and died before it was fully revised. Vergil's lifetime encompassed the time of Augustus, at the end of the Roman Republic and the beginning of the Empire. At the time the poem was taken—and sometimes still is today—to glorify the Roman Empire and Augustus. But other critics, more discerning, think as does Di Cesare: "The thought of this intelligent, sensitive, reflective poet, at the height of his powers and in the maturity of his later years, subscribing to a limited political program as the basis of his epic—surely, that is artificial and mind-boggling . . . to believe that Vergil clearly and persistently 'intended' to glorify Rome and Augustus is to degrade the poet." [71, ix]

Returning now to the crucial Sixth Book, Aeneas finally reaches the shores of Italy, landing at Cumae in Campania. Near Cumae was a temple dedicated to Apollo and Diana. Within this temple, a sibyl guards a cave which is supposedly the entrance to the underworld. In the beginning of Book Six, Aeneas stands outside the gate, which had been carved by Daedalus who came from Crete. Vergil thus uses the figure of Daedalus to connect Cumae directly with the old Minoan Mother Goddess religion of Crete. [155, 263] Aeneas is studying the labyrinthine forms of the gate when the sibyl finds him. She gives him instructions concerning the finding of the golden bough, which he must do to proceed further. Aeneas finds the golden bough and descends into the underworld carrying this lifeless symbol of splendor. He converses with his dead father, Anchises, who gives him a vision of the future glories of Rome which are to culminate in the reign of Augustus, the restorer of the Golden Age in Italy. The last verse of Book Six is the crucial one, the center of controversy.

"There are twin gates of dreaming (sleep): the one is said to be of horn, here is an easy exit for true visions (shades); the other is made of polished ivory, perfect, glittering, but through that way the Spirits send false dreams into the world above. And here Anchises, when he is done with words, accompanies the sibyl and his son, and he sends them through the gate of ivory."

Vergil patterned his epic on the Iliad and the Odyssey. This Sixth Book is so much more moving than its parallel in the Odyssey because we somehow gain the impression that not only has Aeneas gone into the underworld, but in some way his true self has died there. This effect is created first by the strange bough, which has the discoloured aura of gold. It glitters, but it is lifeless because it crackles in the wind. (Fraser wrote his monumental work, *The Golden Bough*, about the central theme of this bough, which is compared to mistletoe.) The mistletoe, a parasite, clings to the tree but has no living connection to it. "A powerful contrast," according to Parry [245] "to the culminating image of the Odyssey, that great hidden rooted tree from which the bed-chamber, the house and the kingship of Odysseus draw continuous and organic life." When Aeneas comes out of the strange gate, he is no longer a whole living man, but more an instrument for building the Roman Empire.

The crucial scene, that of Aeneas sped on his way by the gate of ivory, the gate of false dreams, has had many different interpretations throughout the centuries since Vergil wrote it; lately, more of the modern critics seem to favor the view that in portraying this gate of false dreams Vergil is in fact making an oblique attack on Augustus' Empire.

There are two gates, one of horn and one of ivory. The one of horn has the power to lead to true dreams. Concerning this gate, Scully remarks: "Eleusis is clearly that passage between worlds, that 'Gate of Horn,' celebrated in the Odyssey and by Vergil, about which Levy has written." [286, 75] (Levy's Gate of Horn was discussed earlier in the section on Eleusis.) The other gate, that of polished, glittering ivory, brings false dreams into the world above. Three of the recurring themes of this chapter provide further insight into the meaning of this "gate of horn." These are the power of the animals residing in the horn; the caves, deep in the earth, as places of rebirth; and religion as the maintenance of abiding relationship. By means of the "gate of horn," the human being continues in an abiding relationship, through the "old gods," to the earth itself, the source of all life. This relationship provides for the continuity of life: physically, through the death and birth of new individuals in the tribe and spiritually, through the rebirth of the individual. The gate of ivory, on the other hand, may refer to Augustus' attempt to establish himself as a god, to inaugurate a new era of worship of the Empire. To help him he had all the wealth of Empire—gold and ivory for embellishing statues. But these symbols of Augustus' wealth and the power have no relevance to the true life for either the land or the humans on it, which rests rather on the "abiding relationship" of the earth and human beings.

Allen Mandelbaum lends further support to this thesis when he writes about Book VII of the *Aeneid*, "This is more than a pastoral backward glance: Aeneas will defeat Turnus and the people of the 'old ways' but Vergil knows the price that is paid by the victory of the order of positive law over natural law." [195, 271] In a passage ostensibly to do with the death of Umbro, one of the Latin leaders, Vergil writes:

For you the grove of Angitia mourned, and Fucinus' glassy waters,
And the clear lakes . . .

Adam Parry tells us that the Latin words here have a liquid, mourning sound. He goes on to say, "If we could understand wholly the reasons for this lamentation, so elaborate within its brevity, and what makes it so poignant, and why it is so Vergilian, we should, I think, have grasped much of Vergil's art." [245] The place-names involved in this passage are from the Marsian hill country east of Rome. A few generations before Vergil the Marsi had lived in independence as Roman allies. In the Marsic war of 91–88 B.C., they had been defeated and lost their independence. For Vergil, the Marsi represented the original people and the true Roman spirit. Parry says "His feeling for them had something in common with what Americans have felt for the American Indian." [245] Explicitly, the Aeneid seems to claim that the Roman Empire was a happy reconciliation of the natural virtues of the local Italian people and the civilized Trojans, but the growing tragedy of the last books of the poem seems to say differently. The death of Umbro is not what is important in this passage, but "The real pathos is for the places that mourn him. They are the true victims of Aeneas' war . . ." [245] Commager, another authority on Vergil, agrees: "Historically, we may grant that the development from the huts of Evander to the marble buildings of the Forum marked a triumph of civilization over primitive simplicity, and the Eighth Book dwells upon the contrast between the two. Yet we feel not so much a sense of progress as one of loss; we are constant witnesses to the violation of the land. An extraordinary simile compares Aeneas in the final battle to a tempest bringing ruin to the crops and trees." [62, 10]

In the final battle, Aeneas' spear misses his chief enemy, Turnus, and hits an olive tree in a sacred grove, symbolizing the destruction of the pastoral civilization of old Italy.

On Caves and Human Consciousness Today

A recent experience, which reconfirms the power of caves, occurred in the United States and was narrated by Franklin Merrell-Wolff in his *Pathways Through to Space*. To understand his experience, a few preliminaries about the author's life are necessary. He graduated Phi Beta Kappa from Stanford University in 1911, having majored in mathematics, with philosophy and psychol-

ogy minors. He did graduate work at Harvard and taught mathematics at Stanford for a short time before he left the academic world to devote his time to a search for what he called "Fundamental Realization." He emerged twenty-four years later with a successful outcome, without benefit of a visible guru. Recently, Dr. John Lilly, who does research on dolphins, human consciousness and related topics, made a search and found Merrell-Wolff living at an altitude of 9,700 feet on the side of Mount Whitney, highest peak in the United States. It is important to understand that Merrell-Wolff followed a rigorous, almost "scientific" method in his search for fundamental realization and carefully documented the entire effort.

His first actual feelings of the "realized state" occurred after dinner following a day when he had been working underground in an old gold mine near the small town of Michigan Bluff, in the Mother Lode country of California. While working alone underground, he would often reflect on the work of Shankara, the ancient commentator on the Brahmasutras of India. After dinner, on the particular day, he passed into a state of contemplation characterized by an "elixir-like quality of the air . . . leaving throughout a quiet sense of delight." [216, 2] From events after this initial happening, he came to call it the true Ambrosia.

In recounting the physical events of that time he writes: "I did not know that it was a standard practice in the Orient to place candidates for the transformation inside caves at certain periods, and often for very long periods. It does, indeed, appear that there is some relation between the transformation of 'rebirth' and the entering into the earth." [217, 79] He goes on to relate that Indian and Tibetan Tantric literature and Western ritualism all are based on the concept that there is a "mysterious interconnection" between the physical actions and the state of consciousness one desires. He goes on to say, "As I, myself, have never been oriented to ritualism and have never sought from it a personal value, the conclusion forced upon me that it does have important transformative value is quite objective, all the more so as I find in retrospect that I actually performed an exercise, unconscious of what I was doing, which is a conscious practice in the Orient." [217, 79] Merrell-Wolff's time underground proved to be the culminating process necessary for him to reach the state he was searching for. He was about forty-nine years old at the time. John Lilly found him in 1972.

We find in the writings of Carl Jung a further elucidation of the cave as a symbol in the unconscious: "The cave or underworld represents a layer of the unconscious where there is no discrimination at all, not even a distinction between the male and the female." [137, 132]

Both limestone caves, created by the action of running water, and caves which have been created by slippage along fault lines, are the original of the labyrinthine passages found in the palaeolithic drawings and of the labyrinths and mazes of later times. The route of water and the fracture lines of rock are tortuous and labyrinthine. Upon first entering a cave, one experiences a feeling of shelter, but on going deeper this is some-

times followed by anxiety. My personal experience in caves is that just ahead, waiting to be found, is some incredible secret which seems to lure me ever deeper.

6. Death of the Gods

Roman religion for hundreds of years consisted of a great mass of local cults still connected with the land forms of a particular *place*. In later imperial times, as religion focused more on the power of the Roman emperor than the power of the land, the true religious hunger of the people was left unsatisfied. This contributed to the growth of the Oriental Mystery religions, which had been imported into Rome.

By the end of the classical period the Romans were city dwellers, but their roots remained in the earth roots provided by the ancient Mother Goddess religions because these religions formed the basis of the "mysteries." Mother Goddess characteristics were still connected to such figures as Demeter at Eleusis, Cybele in Rome, Isis, and even the male god, Dionysus. The two other main mystery religions were connected with Mithras (a sun and vegetable hero with origins in Persia) and Orpheus. These universal mystery cults weakened the relationship of the people to the local god of grove or cave, but what finally utterly severed the sacred relationship of man and nature was the growth of Christianity.

"From the beginning the Christians set out to destroy the gods of the classical world. They all but succeeded. And there can be no doubt that of all the crimes committed in Christ's name, this has been the most devastating in its consequences. During their attempt to murder the gods, the Christians destroyed the world of those who loved them." [297, 3] With these words, John Holland Smith begins his account of the *Death of Classical Paganism*.

The Christians, of course, thought that the destruction of the ancient gods was laudable because they believed that the gods were spawn of the devil. The Christians eventually gave the name *paganism* to the worship of Roman gods. The word was derived from *pagani,* which originally meant an unsophisticated boorish peasant who clung to the "old ways" of his ancestors.

The Christians further added to it the connotation—which soldiers had put upon it—of cowards, meaning those who would not fight in the army of Christ. [297, 81] There was not really any one thing which could be called Roman religion; there was only worship in many different ways, which established a relationship between the person, the divine powers, the *place* in which he lived, and the state itself.

In Roman Imperial times, with the coming together of many different races and cults, men of strong personality "who had heard the masters' names and some ear-catching sentences from their teaching" founded their own religions, cults, or schools that promised one or another kind of salvation. These men were called gnostics, "Men of Knowledge," whose doctrines were so eclectic and so esoteric that they could mean all or nothing. Another type of religion was *theurgy* (theurge means "god-power"). Originally it was based on magic, but later there were more sophisticated additions from philosophy. Its purpose was to bend divine power to human ends. Above all, it searched for the ultimate secret name of God. [297, 13] Traces of these eclectic systems can be found surviving in some of the occult movements in the United States today.

According to John Holland Smith, the most influential of these Roman cult leaders was probably Mani, who lived in the third century and was an important personage in the Persian empire but later was executed. He was a "sophisticated charlatan" and an eclectic, whose ideas "deeply influenced millions in later times down to the reign of Pope Innocent III and beyond." [297, 13] This dualistic system of Manicheanism, which viewed the world as evil and all of life consisting of a struggle between good and evil, played a significant part in turning human beings away from Nature.

As Christians gained political power and began occupying high civil offices, the pagan gods gradually lost their place and power. The last pagan public building was erected in Rome in about the year 340 A.D. Zealous Christians began destroying the pagan temples. In the consulate of Theodosius, a fanatical Christian, Cynegius, was appointed Prefect and began to destroy temples with great thoroughness. Libanius, a cultured, highly educated pagan, gave a speech before the Emperor in the year 386, "In Defence of the Temples," in which he pointed out that the first buildings built by early men were temples to the gods; and when towns began they were the first things built behind the walls, but now "men in black rush upon the temples, carrying baulks of timber, stones and fire . . . Roofs are knocked off, walls undermined, shrines thrown down, altars totally destroyed . . . So they rush through country places like flood waters—ravaging them by the very fact that it is the temples that they destroy. For every country place where they destroy a temple is a place made blind: a place knocked down, assassinated. For the temples, my Emperor, are the souls of the countryside . . .they have come down to us through the generations." [297, 166]

After a temple was destroyed, monks would often move onto the site to keep the people from trying to worship there. The local bishop would lead the Christian mob "with soldiers in reserve." In most cases the soldiers were not needed because the people remained loyal to the state and to the Roman officials who tolerated, or even ordered, the destruction; but when the local people resisted as at Alexandria, for instance, soldiers were sent in.

John of Chrysostom, who became a priest at Antioch in 386 A.D., was the most zealous Christian in the work of destruction and the *Ecclesiastical History* praises him for his work in the "total devastation to the temples of the devils which had survived." [297, 174] Alaric and his Gothic tribesmen sacked Greece and opened the sacred sites to the work of the "men in black," and "all sacred Greece was deliberately ruined and never recovered." [297, 190]

The famous sacking of Rome by Alaric in 410 not only finally destroyed the city but insured the supremacy of the Christians. Alaric issued an order that the Basilica of the Apostle Peter, established by Constantine the Great on Vatican Hill, should be spared. The Christian Sozomen's account said that Alaric gave his order "from reverence." At any rate, according to Sozomen, this prevented the city from being utterly destroyed, and what was "preserved there was used to rebuild the whole city." [297, 217]

Augustine's conception of the City of God, which he believed was destined to replace Rome, influenced European history for hundreds of years because "he saw his god as inexorably redeeming the world in spite of itself, and acceptance of this fundamental Augustinian tenet was what fastened the fetters upon mediaeval Europe." [297, 220] Augustine's ideas on sin and salvation, with his prayer to God to "Give me what you will," totally negated human freedom. Furthermore, because he was influenced by Manichean dualism, his ideas created an unbridgeable gulf between man and Nature, with Nature in the role of adversary and a hindrance to salvation.

The old gods were gone and no longer a threat to Christian imperialism, but they lingered on in secret places in the mountains and deserts and occasionally surfaced in organized groups such as the Cathars. The deeper rituals survived and were listed as the offenses of witches in the Fifteenth Century and even later, such as "the making of offerings at trees, rocks and springs, the blessing of fields, etc." [297, 293]

In the Pyrenees mountains and in northwestern Spain, for instance, the people, although supposedly Catholic, held onto the "old ways." But when Martin, Bishop of Braga, succeeded in converting the Arian king of the Suebians, who held the area, he discovered their heresies. He convened a council at Braga to tell the local bishops how to deal with these remnants of paganism. After the bishops had returned home, one wrote to him for further help. In his reply, it is clear that Martin saw evil everywhere. He said that the fallen angels, disciples of Lucifer, had adopted the names of "evil and wicked beings of the race of the Hellenes," the Greek gods, to deceive mankind. The letter goes on to list many of the old Roman gods as devils: "For many were the devils expelled from heaven. So some ruled in the seas, or rivers, or wells, or woods . . . and they were all malign devils and nefarious spirits, who hurt and troubled unbelieving people who did not know how to protect themselves with the [sign of the cross]." [297, 240]

Once again we see that beings called gods by one group were labelled devils by another, just as in Zoroaster's time. Only this time it is more specifically directed to Nature herself—thus cutting the people off from any sort of deep relationship with nature. But worse was yet to come. Until now, all the church did was threaten, condemn, and harass; but presently those who followed the "old ways" of real relationship with Nature paid with their lives. The little kingdom of Suebi was conquered by Visigothic Spain in 585, and later the King of the Visigoths became a Catholic. The Third Council of Toledo was held in 589 to provide for the rapid conversion of the whole nation. In the twenty-first canon adopted, the Council stated, ". . . the Holy Synod ordains the following: That every priest shall make most careful inquisition in his own area, together with one of the magistrates of the district, for survivals of the sacrileges, and shall not hesitate to destroy whatever may be found. And those people who have fallen into such errors shall be coerced from this danger to their souls by whatsoever warnings may be required." [297, 242] So began the dread Inquisition, which was to last, in one form or another, for well over a thousand years.

With every tree or rock or spring suspect as the abode of a devil and with death hanging over the heads of those who went to them for spiritual refreshment, it is no wonder that all wild places became feared and avoided. In Europe, mountains which had been thought sacred became places to be feared and often hated. On most early maps of the Alpine region, there were great blank spaces in the mountainous area. Early maps of Savoy, for instance, showed the area around Mount Blanc, the highest peak in the Alps, marked Mount Mallet (*maledictus* or accursed). Monsters and goblins were thought to live in the higher valleys. The meteorological phenomena, the glory, which Chinese monks thought to be a fortunate manifestation of the Bodhisattva's pleasure, was labelled the "spectre of the Brocken" by mountain peasants in Europe. The word spectre, according to the Oxford dictionary, means "an object or source of dread or terror." Another aspect of the Church's campaign to subvert the power of the old gods was the building of small churches and chapels dedicated to St. Michael on remote hilltops and on wild points along the seacoasts. [124, 241] St. Michael is the chief archangel and the foremost opponent of the devil. Here, in these wild places, the churches dedicated to him impressed upon the local population that, in fact, these places were filled with devils.

Although the authorities of the Christian Church made every effort to destroy all traces of the old sacred relationship to particular places, they never really succeeded. C. G. Jung traced the continuing importance of particular sacred wells and springs to the local country people. He explained certain aspects of wells and springs as follows: "The crypt at Chartres was previously an old sanctuary with a well, where the worship of a virgin was celebrated—not of the Virgin Mary, as is done now—but of a Celtic goddess. Under every Christian church of the Middle Ages there is a secret place where in old times the mysteries were celebrated . . ." [137, 129] Jung also pointed out that the main religious ceremony of Mithraism took place in a cave-like room half sunk into the earth, called a *Mithraeum*. These were always near a spring. "These sanctuaries were always a great scandal to the early Christians," Jung wrote, "They hated all these natural arrangements because they were no friends of nature. In Rome a Mithraeum has been discovered ten feet below the surface of the Church of San Clemente. It is still in good condition but filled with water, and when it is pumped it fills again . . . The spring has never been found." [137, 131]

The Christian destruction of the Roman temples did not cease until Gregory the Great (540-604) became pope and decided to convert the pagan temples into Christian churches. Blessed holy water was sprinkled over the temple, the relics of some saint or martyr put in the altar to preserve it from the influence of devils, and the pagan temple became a church. The first pagan temple actually converted into a church was dedicated by Pope Boniface IV, five years after Gregory's death. In this fortunate manner the impressive Pantheon (which means "all the gods") was saved. It had been erected in 27 B.C. in honor of the Olympian gods. Many exterior changes were made by the Christians, but the interior is essentially the same as it had been since its reconstruction by Emperor Hadrian (117-138 A.D.) after a fire. The great circular hall (42.75 meters in diameter) is roofed by a hemispherical vault, with an opening 9 meters in diameter in the center to let the smoke from sacrificial fires escape. Michelangelo said it was "the design not of a man but of an angel." [65, 48] There are no windows at all in the enormous interior, which has the same shape as a Pueblo Indian kiva. When I was in the Pantheon, the sun's rays slanted down into the great hall through the opening in the ceiling and moved across the floor as the sun moved. This, combined with the ancient circular sacred shape, created a feeling of connection with the powers of the earth and sky. Just as I began fully to realize this feeling, someone began to play the great pipe organ in thunderous tones, which brought the power of the wind into the experience.

For me, the experience in the Pantheon was more "religious" than any I had in the cathedrals of Europe; although these cathedrals, too, were inspired by Nature. They recreate the experience of the forest as the sunlight from the stained glass windows slants through the groves of columns embellished by leaves and flowers, carved into the stone. Paul Shepard, in *Man in the Landscape,* points out that "The great period of building cathedrals followed the peak of clearing forests in Europe . . . A metaphor of forms and spaces within suggests nostalgia and profound emotion linking cathedral and the post-Pleistocene primeval forest." [291, 172] The organ, intimately connected in the European mind to both the cathedral and religion, was also influenced by the forest. Oswald Spengler in *Decline of the West* writes, "The history of organ-building, one of the most profound and moving chapters in our musical history, is a history of longing for the forest, a longing to speak in that true temple of Western God-fearing." [304] For hundreds of years the cathedral and the organ, together, have evoked the heights of religious feeling for Europeans. Insight into the reasons for this evocation provides more information about the crucial step in European history, from reverence and awe for Nature, to "nature hating."

The organ can be considered as "calling up" the winds, which were considered as gods in most early cultures. For early European man, wind was connected with the forest deity, who provided him with all he needed—food, shelter, protection, and implements, "who surrounded him with the 'eternal song', the sound of trees in forests, which granted the intense feeling of holiness and the mood of being near god's hand." [343, 14]

The Sumerian wind god was Enlil, the "Lord of the Breeze." Vycinas explains:

Strength and dominance recur in Enlil's nickname, 'a huge mountain.' Mountains, as we know, resist mighty attacks of winds, and with this resistance they evoke the winds' far-sounding roar. On the other hand, a mountain breaks the force of the wind and provides a sheltering area at its foot for forests, plants, animals, and men. In the domain of the far-sounding roar of winds the reality of shelter or sheltering inseparably belongs and becomes meaningful.

Enlil contributed to the growth of plants by his fertilizing rain but also sometimes brought death to men and devastation to forests or fields by storms and floods. This power of life and death, along with protectiveness or sheltering, has the aspect of destiny; thus "Enlil was called the 'Ordinance of Destiny' and he was considered the possessor of 'the tables of destiny' according to which not only the destinies of men, animals, or things were executed, but even those of the gods. Wind is widely used in various mythical cultures to indicate the powers of destiny which sway the lives and happiness of all things . . . comparable to the wind which throws around a leaf and places it where it belongs." [343, 164–165]

In classical mythology, Aeolus was the god of the wind, which he kept imprisoned in a cave and let free as he wished. To aid the journey of the Greek hero, Ulysses, Aeolus gave him a leather bag, which contained all the ill winds, tied up so that they were harmless; but later, Ulysses' companions freed the winds. Boreas, the north wind, was Aeolus' son. As mentioned in Chapter 2, Abraham knew his god as El Shaddai, which means, "The One of the North." In Canaanite mythology, the god of the North was connected with the North Wind. *El* means power, which refers to the power of the wind. [212, 316] In Amerindian mythology, the Omaha tribe referred to the primal rock as standing "in the midst of the various paths of the coming winds—in the midst of the winds thou sittest." Alice Fletcher notes that this has to do with the "religious idea of the life-giving power of the wind." [90, 573]

In ancient China, the shamans "whistled for a wind," by means of humming-tubes or *lü*. They would call up a good wind in this way. Needham quotes from an ancient Chinese classic to the effect that "the eight winds obey the pitch-pipes." In Han times, notes on the pitch pipe were associated with each of the directional winds. The bamboo pitch-pipes were used in ancient music and set the pattern for the ritual dance. "Each wind, it was thought, could be induced by a particular type of dance, and each dance was controlled by a particular musical instrument." [231, 150–151] Needham suggests that, from etymological considerations, it might be deduced that steps for ritual dancing laid down by shamans might have been applied to the directions for conduct and other behavior laid down by a ruler. *Lü* is also the word for "statutes" or "regulations" in Chinese law. [231, 550–551] In this sense, the Chinese word for rules relates to the patterns of nature (the winds), with the intimations that human beings must somehow fit themselves into the greater patterns of nature.

The Chinese pitch-pipes were somewhat similar to the Greek "pipes of Pan." The Greek god, Pan, according to the legend, was chasing a water nymph. When he caught up with her and threw his arms around her, he found that he had embraced a tuft of reeds. As he sighed in disappointment, the air sounded through the reeds and produced a pleasing sound. The god took some of the reeds of unequal lengths and put them together, thus creating the "pipes of Pan."

In some cultures, such as the Zuni, the wind not only brings the life-giving rain but the very soil itself. In the spring there is the month of the "Lesser-sand-storms," followed by the month of the "Great-sand-storms," according to Cushing. [67, 154] Dust blown in by the wind creates the fertile soil, which the Zuni farm. Cushing states that "Zuni tradition will tell you that the 'Seeds of the Ancient were sown only by the Beloved,' which means that he (the Zuni) gathered the seed cultivated by winds and rains alone . . ." [67, 222] For those of us who consider wind only as an eroding agent, it is difficult to think of wind as a god who brings fertility. However, in Malta, according to March, the inhabitants drilled holes in the rock of the island to catch fragments of soil carried by the sirocco winds from Africa, and in fourteen years the holes accumulated enough dirt for cultivation. [202]

In Southwestern United States, it is a geologic fact that the main source of the erosion, which creates the fantastic rock arches and monuments, is the wind. This may be difficult to comprehend; but once I was camped on top of a red sandstone cliff, in a sheltering pothole, which had been scoured out by the force of the wind and blowing sand. This pothole was our only shelter from the wind of an approaching storm front. We could hear a great roaring in the distance. We crawled to the edge of a 1000-foot sheer drop to the canyon floor. When we stuck our heads over, we dropped flat to our stomachs. The sounds coming up out of the chasm were beyond anything I had ever imagined—high shrilling notes and low rumbling chords which shook the cliff from base to top, and our bodies resonated with the chords. We were utterly enthralled—that's the only way to explain the total ecstasy of sound which drew us into it until we felt almost compelled to throw ourselves into the sound. Wordlessly, we began to edge back, until we were out of the hypnotic sound and then crawled safely back to our sheltering pothole. I longed for a rope, so I could have tied myself to the single deeply-rooted juniper and gone to the edge of the precipice again and enjoy the orgy of sound free of the danger of throwing myself into it. I have been on hundreds of mountains and never before felt any wish to throw myself over the edge (as the Chinese did from their "throw-body precipices" on sacred mountains), but this sound was utterly compelling. It was an experience of the wind as an awesome power, which the ancients knew as a god.

ARCHES NATIONAL MONUMENT   (Photograph by Steve Meyers)

"The breath of the universe," said Tzu-Chhi, "is called wind. At times it is inactive. But when it rises, then from a myriad apertures there issues its excited noise. Have you never listened to its deafening roar? On a bluff in a mountain forest, in the huge trees, a hundred spans round, the apertures and orifices are like nostrils, mouths or ears, like beam-sockets, cups, mortars, or pools and puddles. And the wind goes rushing through them, like swirling torrents or singing arrows, bellowing, sousing, trilling, wailing, roaring, purling, whistling in front and echoing behind, now soft with cool breeze, now shrill with the whirlwind, till the tempest and the apertures are all empty (and still.)"

Chuang Tzu

The organ captures the power of the wind, so that when an organ thunders in a church human beings once again experience the age-old human awe of this power, surrounded by the carved representations of a primeval forest's tree columns, foliage, birds, and beasts. With the sunlight slanting through the colored windows, they re-experience the awe and reverence which man formerly held for Nature in past millenia. Thus the cathedral became the sacred place. The abode of Nature, especially wilderness, came to be considered "as a *person,* an extension of the Evil One, the Enemy opposed to the spread of the Kingdom of God." [218]

7. "The Mountains Are Calling Me, and I Must Go."

John Muir

Discovery of Mountain Beauty

The turning point in the European attitude toward mountains and wild nature came with the Italian poet and scholar, Petrarch (1304–1374). The nostalgia for wild nature, expressed by the erection of forest-inspired cathedrals, was still dominated by the church-instilled fear of wild places. With Petrarch, however, and the revival of the Latin language itself, interest began to replace the fear of the old gods. Petrarch and his pupils revived not only the use of the Latin language, but the study of Latin and Greek literature also, and initiated an interest in antiquities which led to the preservation of what remained of the buildings of pre-Christian antiquity. [297, 247]

Petrarch's interest in the classics led him to make his famous ascent of Mt. Ventoux in France in 1335. The historian Jacob Burkhardt says that Petrarch had "an indefinable longing for a distant panorama." This grew stronger in him "until at length the accidental sight of a passage in Livy, where King Philip, the enemy of Rome, ascends the Haemus, decided him." [45] He may also have been influenced by Dante's work.

The other famous early climber was Conrad Gesner, a professor of philosophy at Zurich University, who wrote:

I have determined, as long as God gives me life, to ascend one or more mountains every year when the plants are at their best—partly to study them, partly for exercise of body and joy of mind . . . I say then that he is no lover of nature who does not esteem high mountains very worthy of profound contemplation.   [99]

Gesner wrote a fine account of his ascent of Pilatus. "Everything delighted him, the discipline of hardship, the joys of remembered toil and danger, the summit panorama and the silence of the heights in which 'one catches echoes of the harmony of the celestial spheres.'" [99]

Gesner was one of the few who climbed mountains at this time. A genuine appreciation of mountains had been checked by the full flowering of the Renaissance period and its emphasis on the Classical Greek attitude that "man is the measure of all things." The writings of Gesner and other Europeans brought about a growth in the appreciation of mountain scenery some two hundred years before the English Romanticists turned to the subject of the beauties of mountains. Furthermore, the English were not the first climbers of the real peaks in the Alps, as is commonly thought. In 1492 Charles VIII of France ordered his Chamberlain, De Beaupré, to climb Mont Aiguille near Grenoble, which is still considered difficult enough to require the use of fixed ropes on it. Mt. Titlis (10,627 feet) was climbed by four peasants from Engelberg in 1744. Many of the early climbers were priests. The first of the higher Alpine peaks to be climbed was the Velan (12,251 feet) by a canon of the St. Bernard hospice. The Gross Glockner (12,461 feet) in Austria, was climbed in 1800 by the Bishop of Gurk. The most famous of these priestly mountaineers and the one whom Arnold Lunn regards as "the father of mountaineering" was Father Placidus, a monk of the Benedictine monastery of Disentis, in Switzerland. Between 1788 and 1824 he made the first ascents of five peaks over 11,000 feet. [191, 28] In 1804 an Austrian chamois hunter climbed the Ortler (12,802 feet), the highest peak in Austria.

Rousseau's political philosophy was greatly influenced by Albrecht von Haller's poem on the Alps, written in 1732, which praised the Alpine peasant, uncorrupted by ambition and greed. Despite Rousseau's love of mountain scenery, he never bothered to go near them. His mountains were ideal mountains, for, although born in Geneva, Rousseau never mentions Mt. Blanc, which stands out so impressively on the horizon of Geneva. Rousseau's book, *Nouvelle Heloise,* published in 1760, created great enthusiasm for the Alps, and people journeyed to the Alps looking for Rousseau's "idealized peasantry."

Mountains became fashionable in the early Nineteenth Century, largely owing to the romantic poems of Byron and Wordsworth, who were inspired by the mountains of the English Lake country, or, as in the case of Byron's dramatic poem *Manfred,* by his visit to the Swiss Oberland region in 1816.

Ruskin's influence on the appreciation of mountain scenery was enormous, but he never climbed them. Lunn suggests this is because he was self-indulgent. In his *Sesame and Lillies* he attacked the Alpine Club: "The French revolutionists made stables of the cathedrals of France; you have made racecourses of the cathedrals of the earth . . . the Alps themselves, which your own poets used to love so reverently." [191, 24]

The first of the "sporting" climbs was made in 1854, an ascent of the Wetterhorn by an Englishman. After this date, climbing became a true sport, and this led eventually to the ascent of practically every major peak in the world.*

Mysticism of Mountaineering

From the beginning of the era of mountain climbing in Europe up to the present time, there have been repeated references to the "something more" that is gained than the mere conquering of a peak. This "something more" can be appreciated by bringing together some insights, not only from climbers but from other widely differing sources, beginning with C.G. Jung, the Swiss psychiatrist.

As a child the Jung family lived along the Rhine. When Jung was fourteen, his father took him to the mountains, where they went by cogwheel railway up a peak named the Rigi. As Jung writes in *Memories, Dreams, Reflections,* "I was speechless with joy. Here

I was at the foot of this mighty mountain, higher than any I had ever seen." When the railway reached the top, he stood in the clear, high air and looked into the far distance. He was transported: "Yes, I thought, this is it, my world, the real world, the secret, where there are no teachers, no schools, no unanswerable questions, where one can *be* without having to ask anything." There was a felt need to "be polite and silent up here, for one was in God's world . . . This was the best and most precious gift my father had ever given me." [140, 77–78] Later, after decades of work in the field, Jung wrote that in the unconscious, "The mountain stands for the goal of the pilgrimage and ascent, hence it often has the psychological meaning of the Self." [144, 15] Self, in the sense Jung uses it here, means the great Self, of which our own experiencing self is a part.†

Fosco Maraini has written of this "something more" more clearly than most climbers. He is an Italian who first went to Japan to study the Ainu and remained there, throughout a great part of forty years, deeply involved with Japanese culture. In an introduction to a mountain climbing book, *On Top of the World,* he points out that once a peak has been climbed we know what is there so ". . . why do it again? Clearly it is not only a question of adventure and domination, but a question of love; we are dealing with a sort of magnetic, irrational, irresistible attraction emanating from the mountains themselves, a secret and deeply rewarding link which unites man and crag, man and stone, man and sky, man and wind." [197, xvi] He concludes his introduction thus: "One might also say that climbing is an act of religion—using this last word in a very wide sense, in senses, possibly to be defined by future developments. Only a religious component transcending the individual, with its roots in the whole aspirations of an age, can explain why a climber may feel willing to risk so much, life included, and consider himself, be considered by others, perfectly sane." [197, xx]

Maraini wrote this in 1966; some of those "future developments" were intimated by the poet Gary Snyder in 1977. When asked by an interviewer who his teachers were, Snyder answered, "My teachers are the mountains." Later, he remarked; "Another great teaching that I had came from some older men, all of whom were practitioners of a little-known indigenous Occidental school of mystical practice called mountaineering. It has its own rituals and initiations, which can be very severe. The intention of mountaineering is very detached —it's not necessarily to get to the top of a mountain

---

*The material in this account of early climbing came from a number of sources. The two most important are Lunn's *A Century of Mountaineering* and Lane's *The Story of Mountains.*

†According to June Singer, Jung's concept of the self is that "The self is the whole of psychic totality, incorporating both consciousness and the unconscious; it is also the center of this totality. The ego belongs to it and is part of it, the ego being the whole of consciousness at any given moment and also the organ that is capable of becoming conscious." [296, 280] Some writers have extended Jung's concept of the self to include the self as part of a greater whole, such as Self as part of the Godhead as in Eastern religions or the Self as the self-in-the-environment as a totality. In both these cases the word is capitalized.

or to be a solitary star. Mountaineering is done with team work. Part of its joy and delight is in working with two other people on a rope . . . in great harmony and with great care for each other, your motions related to what everyone else has to do and can do to the point of ascending. The real mysticism of mountaineering is the body/mind practice of moving on a vertical plane in a realm that is totally inhospitable to human beings." [57]

I would go a bit further than this. I agree that mountains can be totally inhospitable, in the ordinary sense, to human beings, but somehow it seems to me that in this very point lies the crux of the relationship between human beings and mountains/earth. Even in this most difficult and dangerous part of the earth, human life is not only possible but most often heightened or rather focused onto a deeper level of Being. Even when the worst happens, and one is overtaken by a raging storm, one is either unbelievably, quintessentially happy to be out of the raging wind in a makeshift shelter or one is drifting into the blissful state of freezing to death. The seduction of this latter state is beautifully explained in *The Magic Mountain,* where the hero, Hans Castorp, is caught in a storm and leans up against the wall of a hay shed for shelter. He drifts imperceptibly into a blissful dream from which he awakens himself with considerable difficulty and says to himself, "My dream world was a draught, better than port or ale, it streams through my veins like love and life, I tear myself from my dream and sleep, knowing as I do, perfectly well, that they are highly dangerous to my young life. Up, up! Open your eyes! These are your limbs, your legs here in the snow! Pull yourself together, and up! Look— fair weather!" And he rouses himself enough to finally ski down into the valley safely. [196, 497]

Sudden death is a constant danger, and below are accounts of three different aspects of death on the mountain. The first is that of former Supreme Court Justice William O. Douglas, writing of what he learned on his narrow escape while climbing Kloochman Rock when he was fourteen years old.

The thin ledge on which young Douglas was standing broke and left him hanging by his hands 200 feet in the air. He hung on until his friend got to him and helped his feet find the foothold eighteen inches higher up. Douglas wrote, "When a man knows how to live dangerously, he is not afraid to die. When he is not afraid to die, he is, strangely, free to live. When he is free to live, he can become bold, courageous, reliant." [74, 328]

The second account is from a letter written anonymously to a Seattle newspaper by a climber after the death of his friend:

Dan Raish, at the age of twenty-eight, is dead.
Wednesday, May tenth, he and a friend Barry Klettke, fell a thousand feet to the foot of a waterfall, into a ravine near Mt. Garfield.

I am trying to *see* that fall, I am not *looking* at it.

The Whiteman Castaneda asked the Indian shaman, Don Juan, what he experienced when his son died. Don Juan replied, 'When I came to the blasting area he was almost dead, but his body kept moving. I stood in front of him and told the boys in the road crew not to move him anymore; they obeyed me and stood there surrounding my son, looking at his body. I stood there too, but I did not *look*. I shifted my eyes so I would *see* his life disintegrating, expanding uncontrollably beyond its limits like a fog of crystals, for that is the way life and death mix and expand.

When I shift my eyes now I see what is real to me, the movement of all the days of his life that I knew.

He was vital. The motive music of life he made present as simply as walking.

I had felt him laugh. He was always laughing and I always felt it.

He loved himself. He listened to his body and he had stopped being afraid. I think that is why one would always feel his laughter. Sometimes he would dissolve you into glee.

I don't even know the facts. I know there was an avalanche. I know there was a totally random occurrence between two men alone and the earth. I know there are men who die dying and men who die living. I think that is all I need to know.

The tragedy is that he is so very young, but to fall, a thousand feet through the sun light, high on a mountain, is a *fine* death for a man who dies living. Let us then *see* the grace of that fall. [6]

The third account has to do with Devi Unsoeld and Nanda Devi (25,645 feet), a perfectly shaped Mother Goddess type mountain in the Himalayas. Myths have clustered about this mountain since long ago. According to legend, its name came from Princess Nanda, who was pursued by a prince of the clan who had slain her father. She took refuge on the summit of the peak, thus preserving her virginity, "and from that day she became one with the mountain which received her name —Nanda Devi, the Goddess Nanda." [312, 153] Early European climbers in the area linked the mountain with Artemis, Greek goddess of wild nature. Nanda Devi has the same outstretched arms or wings as the mountains in Greece associated with Artemis' shrines. Such mountains symbolize her role as mother of the wild beasts and guardian of untamed wild lands. Artemis is a deity of distant purity and clearness. According to Otto, she "dwells in the clear aether of the mountain summits . . . in the glitter and glare of ice crystals and snow flakes, in the silent astonishment of fields and forests when the moonlight illuminates them and sparklingly drops from the tree leaves . . . That is the divine spirit of sublime nature, the tall glimmering lady, the purity who overpowers everything with her enchantment . . . She is death-bringing when she draws her bow. Strange and inaccessible like wild nature, she is nonetheless all charm and fresh motion and lightning beauty. *It is Artemis.*" [242, 82-83] Virgin nature as typified by Artemis constantly eludes any attempt to possess it. It is real but always beyond reach.

Nanda Devi is protected by a great mountain wall of sheer rock and ice that almost completely surrounds it. The wall is seventy miles in circumference and no-

Nanda Devi (Photograph by Ad Carter)

where lower than 18,000 feet high. There is only one break through it, the Rishi Gorge, which was long thought to be impenetrable. Climbers first began attempting to get through the wall in 1883. In 1905 Dr. Longstaff, later president of the Alpine Club, gained a col on it and looked down into the Inner Sanctuary of the mountain, but he could not descend off the wall to get into the Sanctuary. Later he wrote, "The climbing of the beautiful and cloistered peak would be a sacrilege too horrible to contemplate." [312, 175] His words are typical of the depth of feeling which the mountain evokes and demonstrates the immense attraction Nanda Devi has held for many climbers. One senses the power which Mother-Goddess-shaped mountains have exerted through the ages. Nanda Devi is a consummate example of such mountains.

In 1934 two Englishmen, Shipton and Tilman, got through the wall and finally saw the full ten thousand feet of snow and ice which form the south face of Nanda Devi. The first ascent was finally made in 1936 by Tilman and Odell. It was the highest summit that had been reached at that time.

Willi Unsoeld, an American climber, first saw Nanda Devi in 1949. He writes that "The sheer beauty of the peak was such that I determined right then to name my first daughter after it—providing her mother had no objections." He was not married until two years later, and his daughter was not born until three years after that. But when she was, she was named Devi. In 1976, when Devi was in college, she joined her father and a group of other American and Indian climbers on an expedition to climb Nanda Devi. She had been in Nepal before and was very happy to be back in the Himalayas. She wrote, "It seemed in many ways a dream that I had never left." Devi told reporters in New Delhi shortly before leaving for the peak, "I feel a very close relationship with Nanda Devi. I can't describe it, but there is something within me about this mountain since I was born."

Devi died of acute abdominal complaints complicated by altitude on September 8, 1976, at the 24,000-foot level on Nanda Devi and her body was "left with the mountain she loved." Her family sent friends a memorial to Devi which contained this poem, which had been found in Devi's journal, dated Summer, 1971:

> In the end, it is the land
> that counts—be it dry or
> flooded, fertile or desert,
> sandy mountains or blue lake.
>
> The cricks of small-mouthed
> bass, the green seas, the red
> earth—these are the things
> that matter.
>
> For I have been given a love of
> this land, an insatiable thirst
> that can never be slaked.
>
> I wander among the foothills,
> across the marbled plains.

> I stand upon a wind-swept ridge
> at night with the stars bright
> above and I am no longer alone
>
> but I waver and merge with all
> the shadows that surround me.
>
> I am a part of the whole
> and am content.   [334]

The more frequent cause of death on mountains is falling to one's death. My experience while falling and the experiences of my close friends are that it is a timeless, heightened state of intense awareness (being) seldom equalled otherwise. Granted, we didn't die; but, while we were falling through the air, we were certain that death would be the outcome, so our emotions have some bearing on the case.

Whether one is caught in a dangerous storm or falling, the two greatest dangers on the mountains, one is not bored or anxious or alienated, the usual states of distress of modern humanity. But the earth *cares* for the human being in the ultimate sense, for the mountain allows one to *be* fully, if only one doesn't fight the experience but cooperates with the mountain. Not mere survival, but rather full *being* is the essence of living. This is most important of the lessons to be learned from our teachers, the mountains: The earth is not our enemy, or something we must outwit, but it is our source, our Mother, essentially good and to be trusted.

The last account comes from the sea. Although the sea is vastly different from a mountain, its immensity can provide much the same lesson and for many of the same reasons, as Robert Pirsig shows, writing on "cruising blues":

. . . But beyond this there seems to be an even deeper teaching of virtue that rises out of a slow process of self-discovery after one has gone through a number of waves of danger and depression and is no longer overwhelmingly concerned about them . . . As one lives on the surface of the empty ocean day after day after day and sees it sometimes huge and dangerous, sometimes relaxed and dull, but always, in each day and week, endless in every direction, a certain understanding of one's self begins slowly to break through, reflected from the sea, or perhaps derived from it. This is the understanding that whether you are bored or excited, depressed or elated, successful or unsuccessful, even whether you are alive or dead, all this is of *absolutely no consequence whatsoever*. The sea keeps telling you this with every sweep of every wave. And when you accept this understanding of yourself and agree with it and continue on anyway, then a real fullness of virtue and self-understanding arrives. And sometimes the moment of arrival is accompanied by hilarious laughter.   [261]

Understanding of our own being as human beings in relation to the *being* of the mountain or the *being* of the sea requires further clarification. We'll pursue that in the next section of the book. Part I delved into the "abiding relationship" of human beings and mountains; Part II will explore the further ramifications of this "abiding relationship" by examining the relationship of human beings to *Being* itself. This necessitates first an understanding of the possibilities involved in the concept of *mind*.

EAGLE'S NEST WILDERNESS AREA, Gore Range, Colorado   (Photograph by Steve Meyer)

"The art work opens up in its own way the Being of the beings . . . All things of earth, and the earth itself as a whole, flow together into a reciprocal accord. But this confluence is not a blurring of their outline . . ."

Martin Heidegger

Part II

8. Mind

"The relationship of mind to nature is the crucial question for man's ecology. If we deny that mind requires anything in its environment save other minds, we imply that the quality of natural surroundings is not very important and that, indeed, place is expendable."

Paul Shepard and Daniel McKinley
[293, 122]

My experiences with powder snow gave me the first glimmerings of the further possibilities of mind.

Because of a snowfall so heavy that I could not see the steep angle of the slope, I learned to ski powder snow quite suddenly, when I discovered that I was not turning the skis, but that the snow was — or rather the snow and gravity together were turning the skis. I then quit trying to control the skis and turned them over to these forces. Now, to begin a run all I need do is point the skis downhill. As they begin moving, I push down with my heels so that the tips can rise just enough for the snow to lift them. As I feel this lift, I respond as I come up by turning the tips ever so slightly out of the fall line to the right. Immediately I feel the snow turning them and then gravity takes over and finishes the turn. At a certain point in this process, I am totally airborne, but then, as I feel myself being pulled down, I cooperate with gravity and again push down on my heels and feel the snow lift the skis once again. This time I begin to move the skis to the left and once more the snow and gravity finish the turn. Once this rhythmic relationship to snow and gravity is established on a steep slope, there is no longer an "I" and snow and the mountain, but a continuous flowing interaction. I *know* this flowing process has no boundaries. My actions form a continuum with the actions of the snow and gravity. I cannot tell exactly where my actions end and the snow takes over, or where or when gravity takes over.

The more often I skied this kind of snow, the more intrigued I became. In those days there were few powder snow skiers, and we didn't talk about it much; but we learned a lot. We learned how easily we could destroy the complex interaction by consciously making demands or enforcing our wills.

Once this loss of ego boundary has been experienced, there is a radical shift in consciousness which gradually extends further and deeper. When I first began experiencing this relationship with the environment, it was only in the writings of mystics that I could recognize a similar experience; but, as the years went by, with the growing use of psychedelics in the sixties, more people began experiencing such states, and it became possible to write about them. In 1963, Alan Watts gave a lecture at Harvard University, later published in the *Psychedelic Review,* in which he argued that individuals have been taught by our culture to feel themselves as an individual within a skin, pitted against the environment. But biology, ecology, and physiology demonstrate that this simply isn't true. Watts stated:

If you will accurately describe what any individual organism is doing, you will take but a few steps before you are also describing what the environment is doing. To put it more simply, we can do without such expressions as 'what the individual is doing' or 'what the environment is doing,' as if the individual was one thing and the doing another. If we reduce the whole business simply to the process of doing, then the doing, which was called the behavior of the individual, is found to be *at the same time* the doing which is called the behavior of the environment . . .
We have the evidence (we are *staring* at it) to give us an entirely different conception of the individual than that which we ordinarily feel . . . a conception of the individual not, on the one hand, as an ego locked in the skin, nor, on the other, as a mere passive part of the machine, but as a reciprocal interaction between everything inside the skin and everything outside, it, neither one being prior to the other, but equals, like the front and back of a coin." [354]

If the individual is a particular relationship of all within the skin and the environment which is outside the

55

skin, what then is mind? Attempts to find answers to this question are the most exciting research of this era; furthermore, new breakthroughs occur at a staggering rate. In this chapter I can only begin to give a few indications of the direction in which events in this field are moving. Research on the effect of air ions on the human mind has been going on for the longest period of time, so I will begin with this field.

Effect of Air Ions on the Human Mind

Part I traced the beginnings of all the major prophetic religions to an experience of the founder on a mountain. For millenia, individuals seeking spiritual growth or "higher consciousness" have gone to live on mountains, by waterfalls, or near oceans. The ancient Greek physician, Hippocrates, noticed some 2300 years ago that his patients benefited from certain kinds of air. He ordered them to take long walks by the sea or in the mountains. [55, 349]

"I have heard that the Crystal Waters give rise to holy men," T'an Chung-yo succinctly remarks of the waters on Mt. Omei. [130] Baptism in "living water" marks the beginning of Christianity, when John the Baptist baptized Jesus in the Jordan River. Waterfalls in Japan are considered especially powerful *kami,* divine spirit. This intuitive knowledge of Shinto correctly mirrors the facts shown by modern research. Waterfalls do have the highest concentration of negative ions; furthermore, the presence of large concentrations of negative ions is the environmental factor which high mountains, rapidly moving water, and dense vegetation have in common.

In the late 1890's, it was found that atmospheric electricity depends upon the existence of gaseous ions in the air. The word *ion* is derived from the Greek word meaning "to go", "to move." An ion is an atom or group of atoms that is not electrically neutral, but instead carries a positive or negative electric charge. While I refer here to single atoms, the definitions apply to groups of atoms or molecules as well as to single atoms. An atom is electrically neutral when the number of electrons surrounding the nucleus (or nuclei) is equal to the atomic number. It becomes a positive ion if one or more electrons are missing; it becomes a negative ion if it has one or more extra electrons. In order to ionize an atom or a molecule, energy must be supplied to it in some way. This may come about as a result of kinetic energy; a collision with a rapidly moving molecule, ion, or electron; or by interaction with a quantum of radiation (a photon), as when solar energy acts on it. Ionization is also produced by cosmic rays and radioactivity.

Mountains rise higher into the atmosphere than the surrounding land and are subject to more solar energy and more cosmic ray energy from space. In the atmosphere, oxygen and nitrogen occur most often as molecules containing two atoms, O_2 and N_2. Cosmic rays easily ionize molecules, thus producing free ions. Even the light of the sun can excite the molecules enough so that the outer electrons break loose. Near a mountain top, positive ions, those which have lost an electron, are pulled towards the mountain by means of the earth's force fields and then move on down the mountain leaving the negative ions behind as they tend to move upward into the atmosphere. In general, then, mountain tops have a larger concentration of negative ions.

It is important to realize that the words, *negative* and *positive* when referring to ions have to do with the electrical charge of plus or minus, not with the effects on the human being. Negative electrical charges have good effects on humans; while positive, in general, often have bad effects.

According to Chizhevskii, a Russian research worker, the higher concentrations of air ions in the vicinity of vegetation are explained by the great mass of surface area of leaves giving off radioactive water from the soil through the foliage or herbage. "The leaf area of forests and meadows exceeds tens of times the soil area covered by the plants; in the grass meadows which we investigated it is, on the average, 25 times greater, and in the alfalfa fields, 85.5 times." [55, 384] So a forest with its millions of leaves gives off many more ions than grass. Areas of vegetation, including plants in houses, have a beneficial effect on human beings.

In the case of rapidly moving water, as in a waterfall, the kinetic energy of movement in the water strips off the loosely held outer valence electrons. The loose electrons easily combine with other molecules to produce negative ions. The remaining positive ions, being less dense, tend to disperse in the turbulent air flow surrounding the waterfall. Moving water, in general, will have more negative ions than positive; a waterfall will have even more negative ions.

For centuries the ill effect of the Foehn wind have been known in the Alpine regions of Europe. This wind flows up from the south, bringing with it warm air and positive ions which cause restlessness among animals and humans, as well as headaches, bad temper, depression, and inability to work. When I was in the Alps, I was delighted when I realized that such things were taken into account there and people could say, "I have a Foehn headache," and leave work early. Schools were sometimes let out, and everyone was more patient with one another at these times. In this country there are similar winds—Chinooks throughout the west and the Santa Ana in California—but we are not in a culture where continuing folk-wisdom has provided words for such effects on the human being. Thus people continue to suffer the effects; but, not knowing the cause, they can only blame themselves for the depression or bad temper. Weather-sensitive people are grateful when they are shown the correlation between such winds and their effects.

The ion balance of the atmosphere is also affected by an approaching storm front. The ions in a cloud behave in much the same way as the ions in a waterfall. The kinetic energy in the turbulent air strips off the electrons, leaving positive ions. These free electrons are easily picked up by other atoms and molecules to create negative ions, which results in a density difference, causing the negative ions to move down and the positive ions to move up; thus the cloud base is negatively charged. This negatively-charged cloud base induces a positive charge on the earth's surface, thus causing positive ions from a considerable area to move toward the point below the negatively-charged cloud base. This preponderance of positive ions below the area of the approaching storm front causes "headaches, general depression and lethargy . . . in weather-sensitive individuals," according to Beal. [22] Once the storm is well under way, the usual ion balance between the earth and the atmosphere returns, and people feel better.

In other parts of the world, these winds are called Sirocco, Zonda, Khamsin, and Mistral. Judges in France deal more leniently with crimes of passion committed when the Mistral is blowing. Surgeons postpone operations if possible.

In Jerusalem, researchers discovered that in weather-sensitive individuals, the levels of serotonin in the brain increased just before and during desert wind conditions bringing positive ions; but dropped significantly when these people were placed in negatively-ionized rooms. Symptoms included depression, tension, migraine, and asthma. [132]

Much research has been done in France, Germany, Italy, and especially Russia on the ions in the environment of health spas, particularly those situated near waterfalls. In Russia, according to Chizhevskii, such places are called "electrical resorts" and are known to have negative ions permanently outnumbering the positive ions. [55, 354]

Chizhevskii's research on negative ions and the erythrocytes—red blood cells that have to do with immunity and the absorption of toxins and drugs—showed that inhaling negative ions tended to stabilize the erythrocytic system and aid its function of preventing illness and promoting healing. [339] The Central Laboratory of Ionization was established in Moscow in 1931, and Chizhevskii described its research as "Medical investigations [that] corroborate the regenerating, strengthening, invigorating, preventative, and curative effect of negative ions." He claims that numerous illnesses can be successfully treated with negative ions in 85 per cent of cases. [55, 359]

The research on ionization of the past few decades provides a scientific basis for the intuitive belief of "holy men" from many ancient cultures who felt that mountains, waterfalls, and forests are conducive to good mental states. According to James Beal, the primitive shaman sensed these beneficial electrical effects "in the excited electrochemical processes in his own nervous system, and that these in turn triggered the neurons and synapses in the circuits of his brain. He sensed that a divine intuition, a revelation was upon him and that the gods were speaking to him—directly. And so the ancient holy places . . . were built." [22] Furthermore, all the evidence seems to indicate that negative ions may be the key to the importance of a particular quality of air held in common by the different spiritual disciplines of many cultures.

In *The Way of the White Clouds,* Lama Govinda explains the concept of *lung,* which developed in high-altitude Tibet. The word *lung* stands for both the air we breathe and "the subtle vital energy or psychic force (Sanskrit: *prana*)." He also points out that the Greek word *pneuma* signifies air as well as spirit. [103, 81]

Ornstein also believes that the prana of the Indian Yoga teachings has something to do with negative ions. [239, 214] In the Chinese moving meditation, Tai Chi, the Chi energy, which is associated with the breath, "must circulate freely through all the psychic pathways of energy." [131, 458] The 108 forms of Tai Chi are designed to help this circulation of Chi energy from the *tan tien* (abdominal area) through the body. The *ki* energy in Aikido from Japan is the same sort of energy system. All these disciplines have to do with achieving a special state of consciousness—commonly called enlightenment.

Franklin Merrell-Wolff, found that when he had begun to experience the state he describes as "consciousness without an object," he found it difficult to maintain this state down below. [216, 30 and 142] He was living at about 9000 feet altitude on the side of Mt. Whitney when John Lilly found him. Lilly himself stated in a workshop, in San Francisco in 1972, that he found he functioned best above 9000 feet.

Seekers in Tibet through the ages have commented on the exhilaration of the air. Marco Pallis writes in the *Way and the Mountain* ". . . The air is indescribably exhilarating to both body and mind . . . Tibet is a focus of spiritual influence in a particular and objective sense and apart from any power of one's own to respond or otherwise as the case may be." [244, 113] This same feeling occurs in other parts of the world at high altitude. Possibly, this particular feeling also has something to do with the preponderance of negative ions at high altitudes. Personally, I have noticed that the general feeling of the air at these altitudes is similar to the taste of the air after a quick thunderstorm at any altitude. Lightning ionizes the air, and there are many more free ions immediately after lightning. American Indians have reported many cases of visions connected with thunder and lightning.

Joel Kramer, one of the leading hatha yoga experts in the U.S. today, stated that as soon as one begins seriously working on yoga one finds it necessary to move where there is "good" air. He lives in Bolinas, California, just above the crashing waves at the foot of his cliff. [159] In general, human beings most concerned with the highest state of consciousness possible to humanity agree on the importance of the quality of the air, and this quality has something to do with the physical fact of the presence of negative ions. This, together with the evidence of modern science, provides incontrovertible proof that at least one aspect of Nature, air ions, is directly involved with the state of the human mind. How then can mind be limited to what is inside the skull? If not, where then is the boundary of mind?

The Boundaries of the Mind

I think perhaps the most interesting—though still incomplete—scientific discovery of the twentieth century is the discovery of the nature of *mind*.   Gregory Bateson [17]

I discovered Gregory Bateson's *Steps to an Ecology of the Mind* when I was just about to give up on my first book, *Earth Festivals*. It had begun as an explanation of how celebrating earth festivals helps children but was moving into a deeper level which necessitated radical assumptions about the relationship between human beings and the world. I decided that these assumptions were too radical at that time and that I might as well quit. I picked up Bateson's book at a friend's house and was elated. Here was what I was groping toward, and he had put it together. Wildly excited, I tried to get others to read it, but with no luck whatsoever. Later that fall, I read Stewart Brand's article in *Rolling Stone,* which began, "This book is important enough for me to come out of retirement to write about . . ." But I knew that even Stewart Brand would only convince a few. So then he wrote an entire book in his continuing efforts to get people to read Bateson. It's called *II Cybernetic Frontiers,* and on one of the first few pages, Brand reprints the entire table of contents of Bateson's book.

On the first page of the text Brand tells why he was so impressed with the book: "Cybernetics is the science of communication and control. It has little to do with machines . . . It has mostly to do with life, with maintaining circuit. I came into cybernetics from preoccupation with biology, world-saving, and mysticism. What I found missing was any clear conceptual bonding of cybernetic whole-systems thinking with religious whole-systems thinking . . ." Three years of his looking didn't turn up much of any way of doing it. "All I did was increase my conviction that systemic intellectual clarity and moral clarity must reconvene . . . and evoke a shareable self-enhancing ethic of what is sacred, what is right for life. Tall order. In the summer of '72 a book began to fill it for me: *Steps to an Ecology of Mind.*" [37, 9] I agree with everything Brand says here. I would add only that I have spent all my life, rather than three years, looking for a way to do it; now, having found Bateson's book and fully realizing the difficulties even

very intelligent people have reading it, I am going to make an attempt here to synthesize a few of Bateson's ideas most pertinent to this book, that is, the relationship of the human being and the earth. Before going further, I want to say that I believe the reason people find Bateson's book difficult reading is, first, because they have not asked the right questions yet; and secondly, Bateson is too much a maverick for most people. Throughout his life, he has refused to stay in any one discipline very long but goes on to whatever is necessary for his own further understanding. When he combines his insights from five or six of these disciplines in one long, rigorously exact sentence, it thoroughly destroys most readers' neat little boxes of categories in which they are used to operating, and they refuse to read further. It's too disturbing.

On the next page of Brand's book, he gives a few of his favorite quotations. The one which is particularly relevant to the subject of the mind is: "If Lake Erie is driven insane, its insanity is incorporated in the larger system of your thought and experience." [37, 10] Later, in Brand's book, in a taped conversation, Bateson explains why many important things concerned with human behavior cannot be studied in a laboratory. He states this is "because the experiment always puts a label on the context in which you are." It is even doubtful one can perform a valid experiment in the lab with dogs. "You cannot induce a Pavlovian nervous breakdown—what do they call it, 'experimental neurosis'—in an animal out in the field." Brand gleefully says, "I didn't know that." Bateson laughs and says "You've got to have a lab . . . Because the smell of the lab, the feel of the harness in which the animal stands, and all that, are context markers which say what sort of thing is going on in this situation; that you're supposed to be right or wrong, for example." Bateson tells of a hypothetical experiment which leads to the breakdown of the dog, and Brand then asks what happens in the field in this same kind of situation. Bateson answers, "None of this happens. For one thing, the stimuli don't count. Those electric shocks they use are about as powerful as what the animal would get if he pricked his leg on a bramble, pushing through.

"Suppose you've got an animal whose job in life is to turn over stones and eat the beetles under them. All right, one stone in ten is going to have a beetle under it. He cannot go into a nervous breakdown because the other nine stones don't have beetles under them. But the lab can make him do that, you see." And Brand asks "Do you think we're all in a lab of our own making, in which we drive each other crazy?" Bateson says, "You said it, not I, brother," chuckling, "Of course." [37, 25-26]

"Driving each other crazy" and "driving Lake Erie insane" are two aspects of the same problem. Bateson has been looking at this problem longer than almost anyone else. His book, *Naven* (1936), concerns his work with the Iatmul tribe in New Guinea where he observed the process which he labelled *schismogenesis* (split-producing). This has to do with situations which accelerate the differences between people. One example of a schismogenic pattern involves boasting. If a second man replies to the boasting of the first man with more boasting, each will drive the other one on to greater boasting. This ultimately leads to hostility and eventually, perhaps, to the total breakdown of that relationship. Another example of a schismogenic pattern is the ancient competition between dinosaurs leading to heavier and heavier body armor and body weapons, and the eventual destruction of dinosaurs as a species. The modern parallel in the arms race with one nation trying to build better weapons than the other nation is obvious.

Later, Bateson wrote, "The writing of *Naven* had brought me to the very edge of what became cybernetics, but I lacked the concept of negative feedback." [19, x] The famous Macy Conferences "that invented cybernetics" were held at Bateson's instigation between 1947 and 1953. [36]

Stewart Brand arranged for Margaret Mead and Gregory Bateson to meet with him in March, 1976, to tape a conversation about this beginning of cybernetics, which was printed in Brand's *Coevolution Quarterly*. This is a remarkable personal account by participants in one of the pivotal developments in human history. Just how important is shown by Bateson's remark in 1951 that Wiener's statement "marks the greatest single shift in human thinking since the days of Plato and Aristotle, because it unites the natural and social sciences and finally resolves the problems of teleology and the body-mind dichotomy which Occidental thought has inherited from classical Athens." [21, 177] Wiener, who wrote the book *Cybernetics* in 1948, had argued that the concept "information" and the concept "negative entropy" are synonymous.

In the conversation with Steward Brand in *Coevolution Quarterly*, Bateson said that the first cybernetic model was described in 1856. In that year, even before Darwin's *Origin of the Species*, Wallace "had a psychedelic spell following his malaria in which he invented the principle of natural selection." He wrote to Darwin saying that natural selection is like a steam engine with a governor. Bateson goes on to say that Wallace himself didn't know that "he'd really said probably the most powerful thing that'd been said in the 19th Century." Combined with this idea was that of Claude Bernard in 1890 about the internal matrix of the body which controls temperature, blood sugar, etc., which later became known as homeostasis. "But nobody put the stuff together to say these are the formal relations which go for natural selection, which go for internal physiology, which go for purpose, which go for a cat trying to catch a mouse, which go for me picking up the salt cellar. This was really done by Wiener, and Rosenblueth, McCulloch and Bigelow." And Bateson adds, "Wiener, without a biologist, wouldn't have done it." [36]

At the same time, most people saw cybernetics only in connection with machines; few saw what Bateson did because they had not asked the right questions. This is still true more than thirty years later.

Bateson's basic premise is that the mental world—the mind—the world of information processing—is not limited to the skin. The system which we ordinarily call "self" does not have a boundary which ends with the skin. The information coming to this self includes all the external pathways along which information travels such as other minds, light, sound, temperature, and all aspects of earth and sky.

What the individual who is called a self does is to select from this vast array of incoming bits of information a very small number relevant to that individual at that time. In explaining the full implications of this, Bateson talks of the infinite number of differences between a piece of chalk and the rest of the universe: differences between it and the sun and moon, between where it's molecules are and where they might have been. Out of all this vast number of differences a particular individual, which we label *self*, chooses a very small number which becomes information for that individual. "In fact, what we mean by information . . . is a difference *which makes a difference*." [12] Bateson later added "in some later event." [19, 381] Yet, this difference cannot be localized. "There is a difference between the color of this desk and the color of this pad. But this difference is not in the pad, it is not in the desk, and I cannot pinch it between them. The lines between man and environment are purely artificial, fictitious lines. They are lines *across* the pathways along which information or difference is transmitted. They are not boundaries of the thinking system. What thinks is the total system which engages in trial and error, which is man plus environment. [17]

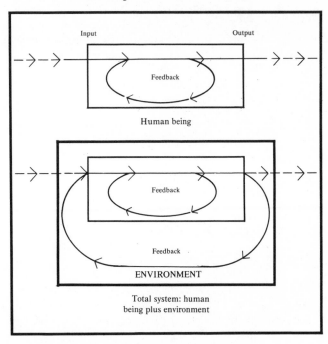

Total system: human
being plus environment

"An event here is reported by a sense organ of some kind, and effects something, that puts in here. Then you now cut off there and here, then you say there's an input and an output. Then you work on the box." [36] . . .That makes it all very simple. But you can't just remove the box from the whole picture because the circuits keep on going. There may be boxes of all sorts within the whole ecosystem but "essentially your ecosystem, your organism-plus-environment, is to be considered as a single circuit. And you're not really concerned with an input-output, but with the events within the bigger circuit, and you are *part of* the bigger circuit." [36] The arbitrary lines we draw between man and the environment are purely artificial, fictitious lines. They are lines drawn "*across* the pathways along which information or difference is transmitted. They are not boundaries of the thinking system. What thinks is the total system which engages in trial and error, which is man plus environment." [17] Bateson uses the analogy of a blind man walking down the street with his stick. "Where does the blind man's self begin? At the tip of the stick? At the handle of the stick? Or at some point halfway up the stick? These questions are nonsense, because the stick is a pathway along which differences are transmitted under transformation, so that to draw a delimiting line *across* this pathway is to cut off a part of the systemic circuit which determines the blind man's locomotion." [15]

I learned this same thing from skiing. Some persons can never learn to ski powder snow without exerting tremendous effort and strength because they allow their rational, left-brain hemisphere to control the entire situation. They not only cut off the pathways of information at their skin but cut off all possible information through their own internal pathways, depending solely on this one tiny part of the brain. The result is that when such a person begins a turn by pushing down on the skis, he does not know when to stop because there is no hard packed surface below him to force him to stop. His skis just keep dropping until he falls. If he had not cut off the mind-information circuits connecting him to the snow and gravity, at a certain point, co-determined by the depth and consistency of the snow and the force of gravity (connected to that particular angle of the slope), the snow would have picked up the tip of the ski and turned it for him. Cutting off all these interlocking circuits of mind limits the information available and, of necessity, leads to anxiety, which leads to further attempts to control with the rational brain that which is threatening to it. This particular schismogenic situation is a good analogy for the present technological disaster threatening the earth. The rational part of the mind alone, "is necessarily pathogenic and destructive of life, and . . . its virulence springs specifically from the circumstance that life depends upon interlocking *circuits* of contingency." The rational purposive brain "can see only such short arcs of such circuits as human purpose may direct." Having cut off the ongoing circuits of life at an arbitrary point and boxing them off into an object labelled "self," the rational brain tends toward hate because "seeing only the arcs of circuits, the individual is continually surprised and necessarily angered" when things don't work out as he thought they would. [20]

Cutting off the on-going circuits of environment-plus-organism and putting them in a box limited by your own interests, so that all you see are the arcs which fit your purpose, is an odd thing to do. To show just how odd, let's suppose that a rational minded, octopus-shaped organism from outer space lands on earth. This being sees a human being pick up a ball with its hand and thinks, "That's different. I can't do that in that way." So he arbitrarily cuts off the thumb from the human's hand and takes it along to study it. When he gets back to his laboratory on Arcturus, he wonders why the thumb won't/can't pick up the ball. The rational brain is always finding itself in a similar situation. Why won't/can't things work? Perhaps it's because our rational brain has been similarly cut off from the rest of the organism, the environment.

Bateson sums up this ongoing circuitry of mind in this way: "We get a picture, then, of mind as synonymous with cybernetic system—the relevant total information-processing, trial-and-error completing unit. And we know that within Mind in the widest sense there will be a hierarchy of sub-systems, any one of which we can call an individual mind . . . I now localize something which I am calling 'Mind' immanent in the large biological system—the ecosystem. Or, if I draw the system boundaries at a different level, then mind is immanent in the total evolutionary structure." Later on he says: "If I am right, the whole of our thinking about what we are and what other people are has got to be restructured . . . and I do not know how long we have to do it in." [12] The time is running out because modern man is finding that every battle he wins against the environment brings a threat of disaster. This is because the "unit of survival—either in ethics or in evolution—is not the organism or the species but the largest system or 'power' within which the creature lives. If the creature destroys its environment, it destroys itself." [15]

The question now is—how did we reach such a state of insanity? Can we honestly believe that the human being, the product of some three billion years of evolution, comes into this world totally cut off from that entire process? It doesn't seem likely; yet that baby grows up to be another alienated human being. In the next section I will look into the matter of what our culture does to this new human being so that it is forced to cut itself off from the whole.

The Mind of the Child

Alienation from nature begins as soon as the child is born in the hospital. Instead of remaining with the mother as all of nature designed it to do, the baby is removed and cleaned of its natural protective covering and sweetened up with powders and then returned some hours later to the mother, thus destroying the effectiveness of its first bonding with its mother. According to Joseph Chilton Pearce, in his book, *The Magical Child,* this is only the beginning. When he began to write the book he found that "Critical issues tumbled in: What is going so wrong in all technological countries today that infantile autism and brain damage are increasing at an epidemic rate, that childhood suicides are increasing yearly . . . that schooling is becoming increasingly unproductive, traumatic, even hazardous and improbable to maintain, and so on?" Pearce believes that what is at stake is the "nature of the child mind, human intelligence, and our biological connections with the earth system on which the development of the mind-brain depends." [250, xxi] His thesis is that, "Intelligence grows by moving from the known to the unknown and referring back to the known." The known he labels the *matrix,* from the Latin word for womb, and he points out that the womb provides three things for the new life therein: "a source of possibility, a source of energy to explore the possibility, and a safe place within which that exploration can take place." [250, 16] After the child is born, the mother becomes this "safe place" or matrix for further development of the newborn, but only if the child is bonded to the mother immediately after birth.

Pearce defines *bonding* as "a nonverbal form of psychological communication, an intuitive rapport that operates outside of or beyond ordinary rational, linear ways of thinking and perceiving." [250, 51] It involves what he calls "primary processing." He gives the infants in Uganda as an example of successful bonding. Marcelle Geber found the advanced development of these children to be astonishing. They smiled by the fourth day of life whereas American babies first smile from a month to six weeks old. General development of these Ugandan babies was months ahead of European children, and the superior intellectual development held for the first four years, until the child's bond with the mother was forcibly broken and transferred to the tribe.

Contrary to the usual belief, newborn infants can focus on and recognize a human face. Since this ability is stage-specific, it can occur only during a very short period after birth and must be continually stimulated. The baby should not be removed from the mother because, once lost, this ability will not be regained for weeks, thus seriously interfering with the growth of intelligence, because there is no safe mother matrix at the crucial time immediately following birth.

About the age of four the corpus callosum, the network of nerve cells connecting the two hemispheres of the brain, completes its growth so that by the age of seven the brain areas can begin to specialize: verbal and linear to the left hemisphere, and body-knowing and earth knowledge (primary process) to the right hemisphere. After this is accomplished, the mind can process information according to three different functions of consciousness which are separate but interdependent. One type of consciousness is that of the self as a unique individual and separate from the world; the second type is that of consciousness of one's body supported by and in interaction with the world (primary process); and the third type, which Jung called the collective unconscious and which others call mind-at-large or general field of awareness. [250, 122]

After the age of seven the child, who is securely bonded to the mother from birth, can easily move into the next matrix. The child will be bonded to the earth. During this stage, from about seven to eleven, *"nothing is important except physical interaction with the world."* [250, 104] Physical action *is* the child's thought process. "When the child is not acting, he is not thinking." [250, 111] As the child acts out new things, the brain patterns the action.

This shift of matrix at age seven, from mother to earth, is just as crucial as the one at birth, but due to the pressures in our culture, especially the abstract concept of death, it virtually never succeeds. The poet, Kenneth Rexroth, I believe, is one of the few who successfully made the shift of matrix to the earth while continuing to function on all of the three levels of consciousness mentioned above. In his autobiography, he wrote:

From earliest childhood I have had not rarely but habitually the kind of experiences that are called visionary . . . The first experience I remember clearly . . . I was about four or five years old sitting on the carriage stone at the curb in front of our house on Marion Street in Elkhart, Indiana. It was early summer. A wagon loaded high with new-mown hay passed close to me on the street. An awareness, not a feeling, of timeless, spaceless, total bliss occupied me or I occupied it completely. I do not want to use terms like "overwhelmed me" or "I was rapt away" or any other that would imply the possession of myself by anything external, much less abnormal. On the contrary, this seemed to be my normal and natural life which was going on all the time and my sudden acute consciousness of it only a matter of attention. This is a sophisticated description in the vocabulary of an adult but as a five-year-old child I had no vestige of doubt but what this was me—not the "real me" as distinguished from some illusory ego but just me . . . [273, 337]

Rexroth goes on to say that he has read of the same kind of experience in the works of authors as different as Richard Jeffries, H.G. Wells, and Rousseau, "including the new-mown hay." This latter factor is so often mentioned in such experiences that some have looked for a hypnogenetic principle among the esters and glucosides which occur in ripe grass. The hay may have merely been the natural element which allowed the consciousness of self as separate and self as part of the whole "mind-at-large" and earth to come together creating the state of "total bliss." Rexroth's incredible creativity is well-known. His total trust of the earth is fully demonstrated in one particular incident in his book, when roughly forty years ago he took his very young epileptic wife on a backpack trip through the wilds of the Cascade Mountains in Washington and down the west coast to California. There were no roads in the Cascades and very few along the coast at the time.

The crucial shift of matrix from mother to earth, beginning about four, is when children have experiences which we label ESP and psychic phenomena but which, as Pearce correctly points out, are neither occult nor psychological aberrations. These primary perceptions are "as biological as any other form of perception." [250, 130] But if not developed, they tend to disappear just as a muscle can atrophy. Because parents and teachers tend to dismiss anything children tell them in this realm and because their approval is so important, a child learns not to talk about them and thus these primary perceptions atrophy.

Children are completely absorbed in play. Parents and teachers continually force the child to do what they think is necessary, but "play serves survival," as Pearce puts it. Puppies play at fighting, and cats attack anything in their reach in order to learn their adult roles. Play in the human child is world plus mind-brain. In play, the child continually changes its own world. Imagination, fantasy, imitation, work, and play are merged together. The child learns best through play. When we force a child to learn by doing the *work* of learning we are going against his biological heritage and decreasing intelligence by inducing fear of failure and anxiety.

Fear is different from fright. "Fright is a natural response, a biological 'startle' effect. But fear is an intellectualized form of this 'startle' response . . . Fear is a learned response . . . Anxiety is fear over what might conceivably be done to us in the future." Anxiety's roots lie in the notion of a hostile universe. [249, 50, 51 and 56]

The culturally-induced fear in the child is much like the laboratory-induced neurosis of the dog which Bateson and Brand talked about. For a small child, learning to count in a classroom is a fearful, anxiety-producing thing. Recently a friend of mine, Beverly, was visited by a child of five. This child had been in kindergarten for three months. Because she has been raised in a free environment and was naturally bright, she was suffering. Beverly knew she was supposed to be learning to count. So she took some marbles and counted them out into the child's hand, counting aloud as she did so, "One, two, three, four, five." The child played and counted them over to herself for awhile. Then Beverly, who was cooking at the time, said, "Give me three of the marbles." The child tried to hand them all to her and Beverly said, "No, you count them." So the child counted out, "One, two, three." Beverly said, "Thank you for the three marbles." The child, very puzzled, said, "Is that all there is to it?" Beverly said "Yes," and the child was amazed. She could count. It was no big deal. The fear of failure instilled in the artificial environment of the classroom was gone because she was in a friend's house and in real life, so she was able to count easily.

When a child is forced to deal with abstract thought too soon, it prevents really intelligent abstract thinking later. The first ten years must be spent learning about the earth by dealing with it physically, with all five senses, not just seeing and hearing explanations. The child must be allowed to get down into the dirt of the earth and play with it, smear it around, even wallow in it. A very bright child of four once exclaimed delightedly, "I just found out that dirt and water make mud." This discovery is just as much his own and just as original as any scientific breakthrough.

Around the fifth or sixth year the child begins to "create *abstract* constructs, that is, synthesize possibilities 'in his head' that have *no* reference to objects or symbols." [249, 24] He can then interact with what he playfully creates. Nature designed the brain at this stage to interact creatively with nature, not to be cut off from it. "There is a vast difference between creatively interacting with the flow of nature—to transform it—that for which logic was developed by life—and creating a buffer to that nature out of fear. And yet logical thinking is used for both creative acts." [249, 25]

At seven years of age Balinese trance dancers are capable of dancing on red hot coals. When the small girl feels the power she gets up and, totally engrossed in imitating her models in the intricate dance, she moves across the coals, unburned—the dancing is the play. Afterwards she returns to her place and takes part in the feast, but she knows she could burn her hand if she touches the coals. This is a very powerful display of the powers of *reversibility thinking*. This concept is defined by Piaget as the ability to "hypothetically consider any state along a continuum of possibility as potentially equal to any other state, and return to the same state from which the proposed operation began." [257, 175] This highest form of all operational thinking becomes functionally possible at ages six to seven years. Piaget terms this the rarest form of our mental acts. It "generally atrophies as an open ended possibility through neglect and inhibition, somewhere around adolescence." [249, 26]

Around nine or ten the child begins to function according to cultural logic. In Piaget's terms this "reality adjustment" is the end of childish "magical thinking" and the beginning of true maturation. Piaget, however, was only interested in the development of left-brain, verbal, linear thinking. The fact that our culture forces children to abandon completely such primary process thinking causes the split of mind from earth because primary process is the connection with earth. Some children fight this splitting process on an unconscious level. This is probably the cause of poltergeist phenomena. The child does not consciously cause the bottles to break and the boards to split, but they do. Perhaps we could say that the child's primary process is demonstrating that the brain does not end with the skull.

It is no accident that Black Elk, the Sioux medicine man, had his famous vision when he was nine years old. This vision came after a period of intense weakness, when he couldn't move. In the vision he was taken up into the sky and saw the "sacred hoop of the world" intact—meaning all the people of the world are really one people. The Six Grandfathers, the powers of the four directions and the Above and Below spoke to him. Later, when he was grown, he realized he was to try to unify his people and the white people through this vision; but he died thinking he had failed. When Black Elk was a child, the railroad had split the great buffalo herds, and the last were being killed off. The last Indian battles were being fought. His world was splitting apart; but because his mind had not been split by his culture, he was not yet alienated from the wholeness of his relationship with the earth. A powerful vision was the result.

Paranormal experiences have always been baffling to the kind of science which defines the human brain as ending with the skull; but, lately the new theories in physics allow more leeway. Dr. Brian Josephson of the Cavendish Laboratories at Cambridge University, winner of the 1973 Nobel Prize in physics, did some of the studies on Matthew Manning, an English teenager who could bend metal, as Uri Geller does, since he was eleven. Pearce quotes Josephson: ". . . redefinition of Reality and Nonreality is needed now . . . We are on the verge of discoveries which may be extremely important for physics. We are dealing here with a new kind of energy." [250, 163] Dr. Joel Whitton of Toronto, in his work with Manning, discovered that the old brain, the cerebellum and brainstem, seemed to be involved in Manning's psychokinesis abilities. Whitton believes that such functions may be "an innate function and ability of homo sapiens that probably goes back to the earliest history of man." [250, 169] This hypothesis provides insight into the three billion year relationship of mind and earth.

In the same year that Pearce's *Magical Child* was published, in 1977, Edith Cobb's *The Ecology of Imagination in Childhood,* appeared, further documenting the relationship of the child's mind to the earth.

The Earth and the Child-mind

From Edith Cobb's study of three hundred autobiographies of creative thinkers—both those long dead and still living—she found that adult genius had its roots in the child's relations with the natural world. [59] For thirty years she was so involved in gathering

these volumes together, watching young children at play to discover new facts and other related research, that she had time to write only a few articles. Fortunately, Margaret Mead succeeded in gathering all her material together and editing it. The book was published the very year Edith Cobb died.

Edith Cobb considers that children "are born animals and mature biologically, but evolve culturally into human individuality." The difference, then, between animal and human nature is "the uniqueness of every human individual as a species in himself." [59] Pearce also agrees with Cobb's point here when he writes: "The reason for the long period of dependency is that the infant-child must structure his/her own knowledge of the world, and s/he must do this almost from scratch." [150, 9] An animal, on the other hand, is born with most of its behavior laid out by instinct.

The key point, bearing on later human genius in adulthood, is what Cobb calls "plasticity of response to environment and the child's primary aesthetic adaptation to environment." She notes that this original childhood experience may be "extended through memory into a lifelong renewal of the early power to learn and to evolve." This accounts for the ever-fresh joy in new discovery which certain persons of genius continue to exhibit into advanced old age, while ordinary people glumly settle for "nothing new under the sun." [58, 25] She further notes that genius does not result from an accumulation of information but from continued openness of the entire organism to new information and to the outer world.

Her findings agree totally with Pearce when she points out the importance of a special period, from five or six to eleven or twelve, where "the natural world is experienced in some highly evocative way, producing in the child a sense of some profound continuity with natural processes." [59] Recall Kenneth Rexroth's experience with the new-mown hay when he was five and his "awareness . . . of timeless, spaceless, total bliss occupied me . . . this seemed to be my normal and natural life which was going on all the time and my sudden acute consciousness of it only a matter of attention." In his autobiography, *Surprised by Joy,* C. S. Lewis uses similar terms in describing his experience of the currant bush: "As I stood beside a flowering currant bush on a summer day there suddenly arose in me without warning . . . a sensation . . ." He notes that it "is difficult to find words strong enough for the sensation which came over me; Milton's 'enormous bliss' of Eden . . . comes somewhere near it . . . It had taken only a moment of time; and in a certain sense everything else that had ever happened to me was insignificant in comparison." [181, 19] This is the very period in which, according to Pearce, the child develops its matrix with the earth. Furthermore, in Cobb's collection of autobiographies, she notes that it is to this particular period in their childhood that these creative thinkers "return in memory in order to renew the power and impulse to create at its very source." She summarized these early childhood experiences in much the same terms as those of Kenneth Rexroth when she wrote that the child seems to experience both "an awareness of his own unique separateness and identity, and also a continuity, a renewal of relationship with nature as process." [59]

From her analysis of the origins of the word, *genius,* she says that it refers to mental power of energy as well as giving life, "animating"; but of even more importance, in its earlier usage it referred most often to the spirit of place, the *genius loci,* "which we can now interpret to refer to a living ecological relationship between an observer and an environment, a person and a place." She further states "that genius consists in the continuing ability to recall and to utilize the child's primary perceptual intuition of time and space." [59] The autobiography of Giordano Bruno (1548–1600) not only provides an outstanding example of this "continuing ability," but furthermore it involves both mountains and the earliest example of European non-dualistic thinking. For all these reasons, I am going to give more details of his life here than are contained in Edith Cobb's article.

Bruno's home was in a small village outside Nola on the lower slopes of Cicada, a foothill of the Apenines about twenty miles east of Naples. In his autobiography, he tells of the beautiful fertile land where he lived and the seemingly bare slopes of Mount Vesuvius in the distance. Apparently he began to wonder one day if Vesuvius was really all that barren. He tells us that Mount Cicada assured him that "brother Vesuvius" was no less beautiful, so to satisfy himself he walked across the distance to Mount Vesuvius and truly found that it, too, was beautiful. "Thus did his parents [the two mountains] first teach the lad to doubt, and revealed to him how distance changes the face of things." [295, 6] This experience remained with him all his life and led him to continue "to relate 'depth of potentiality to the sublimity of action' and held him in a state of enchantment even to his death at the stake." [59]

Bruno not only accepted Copernicus' new conception of the sun (1543 A.D.) as the center of the solar system, but he went much further into the idea of a "completely new cosmological order." He anticipated Galileo and Kepler. His biographer, Dorothea W. Singer, gives a summary of his ideas: "The whole of Bruno's philosophy is based on his view of an infinite universe with an infinity of worlds. He conceived the universe as a vast interrelationship throughout space and time, comprehending all phenomena, material and spiritual. Thence he was led to contemplate the parts under the mode of relativity . . . Bruno conceived each of the infinitely numerous worlds to be moving on its course in relation to other worlds, impelled by its own two-fold nature as individual and as part of the whole. All estimates of direction, position and weight within the whole

must be relative." [295, 50] The influence of his two mountains can be seen in the relative viewpoint expressed here, as well as in his idea of the "coincidence of contraries." The latter was bound up with his conception of the identity of subject-object which was contrary to the duality implicit in almost all European thought. [295, 87]

The last and greatest of Bruno's works was published in Frankfurt in 1591, just before his return to Italy, where he was apprehended by Church authorities and imprisoned. In the *Dedicatory* to his patron, the Duke of Brunswick, he wrote: "So that the hindrance to natural knowledge and the main foundation of ignorance is the failure to perceive in things the harmony between substances, motions and qualities . . . It is these things, many of which when seen from afar may be deemed odious and absurd, but if observed more nearly they will be found beautiful and true, and when known very closely they will be wholly approved, most lovely and certain withal . . ." [295, 156] Here, in his last work, written when he was forty-three years old, we can still see the influence of his childhood relationship with the two mountains: Cicada and Vesuvius. Here we also see how obvious it was to him that things are seen differently from different viewpoints. He was so convinced that anyone would understand this if it was explained properly that he spent the eight years of his imprisonment repeatedly trying to explain these matters to his interrogators and jailers.

He returned to Italy, to a trial in Venice and eight years of imprisonment. At his trial, he quoted these words from Vergil's *Aeneid:* "Mind moveth the whole form and mixeth itself throughout the body." He had earlier used this quotation in one of his works on the "universal Intellect . . . a single whole which filleth the whole, illumineth the universe and directeth nature . . ." [295, 89] Finally, in 1599 the Pope in full Congregation declared his works heretical and that if he refused to admit they were heretical, he was to be "condemned . . . to the treatment usual for impenitent and pertinacious persons . . ." The judicial burning was held in the great Square of Flowers at Rome on February 19, 1600. A contemporary manuscript, the earliest form of newssheet, records that Bruno declared he died a willing martyr. [295, 178–179] An earlier writing shows why he was able to accept death with such equanimity: ". . . We shall discover that neither we ourselves nor any substance, but all things, wandering through infinite space, undergo change of aspect." [295, 72]

His works influenced the more unitary thinkers in Europe, such as Leibniz and Spinoza. Needham in his monumental *Science and Civilization in China* mentions those few early European thinkers "who revolted against the orthodoxy of the rational intellect . . . especially Giordano Bruno . . . whose writings abound in Taoist echoes." In Needham's opinion, Bruno's "world-conception approached almost more closely than that of any other European thinker to the 'organic causality' which we have seen was characteristic of classical Chinese thought." [229, 95 and 540] While affirming that Bruno cannot have had any direct Chinese influence, Needham does draw a parallel concerning the association between nature-mysticism and science as shown in both the Taoists and Bruno's work. [229, 95] I would specifically point out the direct influence of mountains in both Bruno's early life and Taoist thought in general, as shown in Chapter 2.

Turning now from the life of a sixteenth-century European to that of a modern American, Bernard Berenson, we find a similar on-going integration with nature. Berenson tells of one summer morning when he "climbed up a tree stump and felt suddenly immersed in Itness. I did not call it by that name, I had no need for words. It and I were one." This state of consciousness "was due not to me, but to the not-me, of which I was scarcely more than the subject in the grammatical sense." [26, 18] He adds that now, as an adult, "he seems to be the same in these respects as I remember being at the end of my sixth year . . ." He became aware non-verbally that, in Cobb's words, "the form-creating harmony of his perceiving body and the form-creating harmony of nature were one and the same process." [59]

Again, Berenson's feelings during this experience with the tree stump were similar to Kenneth Rexroth's with the new-mown hay. When I was a small child, just such an occurrence happened to me in connection with a field of meadow grass. I was lying in the grass watching the seed pods waving in the wind when I was suddenly enveloped in a feeling of complete happiness. I felt totally at one with everything yet totally myself—and infinitely important. In my experience, as in Rexroth's, it seemed that this was the reality which had existed all the time, and I had just suddenly happened to become aware of it. I never told anyone about it as I didn't know how to explain it; nor was I ever able to connect it with my Catholic religion, although I tried. It was not supernatural or occult or a vision; it was just the way things *really* are, I felt.

My own son had such an experience when he was four. We lived in Alta at the time. It was a clear, bright autumn day at 8700 feet altitude. He came in and told me of it with great excitement; but as a young mother locked into the Christian system, I felt I should link the experience with the concept of God and told him, "That's like God." I had forgotten this whole event until quite recently when Randy, now grown, reminded me of it. Instantly I recalled the entire episode and was stunned with the enormity of what I had done in verbalizing such an experience and trying to fit it in a box labelled "God." When I told him what I had just realized, he replied that it had caused great confusion in him for years, for he had tried to find such a feeling in religion, but had always failed. Eventually, he tried not to think

of it at all. The fact that I had forgotten such an important event indicates, of course, my own uncertainty over what I had done.

Cobb says that such an experience is an "acute sensory response to the natural world." *Sensory* is the key word, and a sensory response can only happen when a child is in direct physical contact with the world with *all* its senses. In most cases the child is alone at the time; or occasionally, with one or two others. Kazantzakis, the author of *Zorba the Greek*, in his autobiography tells of his sensual contact with the sea when he was very small.

I remember, a man with a thorny beard took me in his arms and brought me down to the harbor. As we approached, I heard a wild beast sighing and roaring as if wounded or uttering threats. Frightened, I jumped erect in the man's arms and shrieked like a bird; I wanted to go away. Suddenly—the bitter odor of carob beans, tar, and rotten citrons. My creaking vitals opened to receive it. I kept jumping and pitching about in the hairy arms that held me, until at a turn in the street—dark indigo, seething, all cries and smells . . . the entire sea poured into me frothingly. My tender temples collapsed, and my head filled with laughter, salt, and fear. [149, 42]

Kazantzakis had equally powerful first contacts with earth, woman, and the sky. In his old age, he wrote, "Even now, in the most profound moments of my life, I experience these four terrifying elements with exactly the same ardor as in my infancy . . . I thank God that this refreshing childhood vision still lives inside me in all its fullness of color and sound. This is what keeps my mind untouched by wastage, keeps it from withering and running dry . . ." [149, 43 and 49]

Life in the modern city prevents intimate, uncrowded contact with nature, and therefore any possibility of such an experience. The present tendency to push school and reading down to even younger ages—three and four —further discourages such whole brain/body learning. Reading type skills limit learning to the left hemisphere. Such school-type learning is accompanied by "fear and loathing." In whole brain/body learning the child is always "surprised by joy," as C. S. Lewis describes it. Edith Cobb explains, "The exaltation that the child feels is a passionate response to an awareness of his own psychological growth potential as a continuity of nature's behavior. This pattern of response is intimately connected with the needs of mental (*i.e.*, spiritual) health." [58, 33] The child desperately needs to interact with the whole world, while we demand that he limit himself to the narrow space of a school room. It's no wonder that children retreat into sullen apathy, and teachers go quietly insane trying to control that repressed energy.

Edith Cobb found similar experiences to those of Rexroth and Berenson in autobiographical recollections from Africa, Asia, Europe, and the Americas: "These vivid experiences, described retrospectively by adults, appear to be universal and suggest some universal link between mind and nature as yet uncodified but latent in consciousness in intuitive form." [58, 88] Further evidence of this "universal link" is repeatedly shown in the thinking which underlies many scientific breakthroughs. In his book, *Einstein—An Intimate Study of a Great Man,* Dmitri Marianoff, Einstein's son-in-law, tells how he was sitting with Einstein late one night when it was very quiet, and Einstein seemed unusually peaceful. Marianoff asked the question:

"How is it, Albert, that you arrived at your theory?"

"In vision," he answered.

He said that one night he had gone to bed with a discouragement of such black depths that no argument would pierce it. "When one's thought falls into despair, nothing serves him any longer, not his hours of work, not his past successes—nothing. All reassurance is gone. It is finished. I told myself, it is useless. There are no results. I must give it up."

Then this happened. With infinite precision the universe, with its underlying unity of size, structure, distance, time, space, slowly fell piece by piece, like a monolithic picture puzzle, into place in Albert Einstein's mind. Suddenly clear, like a giant die that made an indelible impress, a huge map of the universe outlined itself in one clarified vision.

And that is when peace came, and that is when conviction came, and with these things came an almighty calm that nothing could ever shake again, not while Albert Einstein lives . . . [200]

The most famous and often quoted example of this intuitive insight into nature is Friedrich Kekulé's "ring" theory of the constitution of benzene which, according to Encyclopedia Britannica, is the "most brilliant piece of prediction to be found in the whole range of organic chemistry." Furthermore, "three fourths of all modern organic chemistry depends on this discovery." Kekulé writes of his experience, which occurred during a bus ride while visiting London:

I fell into a reverie, and lo! the atoms were gambolling before my eyes! Whenever, hitherto, these diminutive beings had appeared to me, they had always been in motion, but up to that time, I had never been able to discover the nature of that motion. Now, however, I saw how, frequently, two smaller atoms united to form a pair; how a larger one embraced smaller ones; how still larger ones kept hold of three or even four of the smaller, whilst the whole kept whirling in a giddy dance. I saw how the larger ones formed a chain . . . [247]

That night Kekulé sketched his vision of the atoms, which evolved into a system of formulas to represent the structure of organic compounds. Later, in Ghent, he dreamed of chains of atoms in snake-like whirls. One of the 'snakes' bit its own tail; awaking, he developed what chemists now call the benzene ring. [247]

Edith Cobb agrees with Pearce on the importance of play in childhood. After summarizing research on child play, she states, "If, as I assume, all cultural innovation derives from the impulse that produces play during the period of growth and fulfillment of biological form in childhood, then Thorpe's words about 'true play' . . . can be placed within this context of cultural evolution." [58, 104] Thorpe's definition is as follows: "True play is to be expected where appetitive behavior becomes emancipated from the restriction imposed by the necessity of attaining a specific goal. Such play can lead (and in evolution appears to have led in birds and animals) to an enormous widening of perceptual horizons and thus to the development of exploratory drive. Thus the process of freeing appetitive behavior from the primary needs increases perception of and mastery over the environment, and must have been one of the first and perhaps the most important of the behavior changes which made possible the development of social life in the vertebrates, and indeed ultimately the mental and spiritual life of man himself." [321] I would suggest that in the case of human beings it is possible for "true play" to move beyond "mastery over the environment" towards a living relationship with the environment. As shown above, the child's playing relationship with its world is a prerequisite for adult creative thinking, but the problem for human beings is how to remain in the openness of this playing state and not fall prey to the demands of the rational hemisphere of the brain for control over the environment. Near the end of her book Edith Cobb summarizes the insights she has gained from her research: "In the creative perceptions of poet and child we are close to the biology of thought itself—close, in fact, to the ecology of imagination, in which the energies of the body and mind as a unit, an ecosystem, and the energies of nature combine in a mutual endeavor to adapt to nature, to culture, and to the societies devised by man to embody culture." [58, 109] The "mutual endeavor to adapt" has broken down in our culture. The insights of Pearce and Cobb clarify the stages of this culturally induced breakdown which occur in the individual's development during early childhood. In the next section I will review some of the new discoveries in brain research which are beginning to show *how* this occurs. More will be said on the future possibilities of the "mutual endeavor to adapt" in the next three chapters and in Part IV of this book.

Right and Left Hemispheres of the Brain

Something I owe to the soil that grew—
More to the life that fed—
But most to Allah Who gave me two
Separate sides to my head.

I would go without shirts or shoes,
Friends, tobacco or bread
Sooner than for an instant lose
Either side of my head.
Kim by Rudyard Kipling

In most human cultures throughout the earth there has been an awareness that there are two kinds of thinking. Various pairings of words have been used to contrast the two, such as rational *versus* intuitive and logical-analytic *versus* gestalt-synthetic. In fairly recent times, due to direct research on the brain, it is now possible to state the physiological basis of these two different types of thinking.

The brain of the higher animals, including man, is a double organ, consisting of right and left hemispheres connected by the corpus callosum, a narrow mass of nerve cells. The right side of the cortex controls the left side of the body and the left side of the cortex controls the right side of the body. In the early 1950s Myers and Sperry, through experiments on cats, discovered that when the corpus callosum was cut, each hemisphere could function independently as if it were a complete brain. "Working on a problem with one eye, the animal could respond normally and learn to perform a task; when that eye was covered and the same problem was presented to the other eye, the animal evinced no recognition of the problem and had to learn it again from the beginning with the other half of the brain." [96]

Some years later, as it became obvious that cutting the corpus callosum did not seriously impair mental facilities, J.E. Bogen and P.J. Vogel of the California College of Medicine developed a technique for cutting the corpus callosum of people with uncontrollable epilepsy. As Bogen pointed out, some of these people had up to forty scars from serious concussions from falling to the ground completely out of control with epileptic attacks and were desperate for some kind of help. It is a frightening situation never to know when you will lose all control of the muscles of the body. [31] The operations proved very successful: Bogen stated that "there is an almost total elimination of all attacks, including unilateral ones. It is as if the intact callosum had served in these patients to facilitate seizure activity." [96] The subsequent years of research proved that each of these two hemispheres can really be considered as a brain in itself, capable of mental functions.

As long ago as 1861, language was thought to belong to the left hemisphere, so there is much more known about how the brain processes language and linear thinking in general than about the right brain functions. [31] It is important to realize that the differences between the two brains are differences in the cognitive capacities, processes of thinking—not differences between such functions as thinking (intellect) and emotion (affect). Bogen clarifies this by pointing out that "each hemisphere has its own affective apparatus (which is, roughly speaking, its limbic lobe), one in each hemisphere." [35]

The best model I've found to show how each of these two hemispheres thinks was given by Ornstein in a lecture. He said that there is a vertical organization of thinking in the left hemisphere. Consciousness is located in a place and things come one at a time, in order. Language, logic, and scientific analysis depend on this type of thinking. In the right hemisphere, horizontal thinking takes place. Many different ideas can happen all at once. This kind of thinking is synthesis-oriented, non-verbal, and intuitional. Artistic activities, music, spatial activities in general, such as recognizing faces, are handled in the right hemisphere. [238] Pearce notes that right brain "thinking relates to the primary proc-

ess, the flow of things, and expresses itself through unity and bonding to the earth." [250, 178]

The two hemispheres deal with time differently.

We continually experience the immediate present passing by, the time that is always NOW. This is the time of our immediate contact with the world, a very short continually changing fading away, forever being replaced by a new NOW. . . . In the linear mode, time is directional, a duration carrying us from the past into the future; the present is always fleeting away behind us . . . In the nonlinear mode, however, the present exists, and is all that exists. [239, 82]

Mild doses of certain drugs such as marijuana and LSD may radically alter the "reducing valve" of the normal sensory systems. The increase in the contents of consciousness suggests more information is reaching the person, so that more is experienced during that interval than is normal. This is similar to dreaming, when many things are happening at once, but there is no durational order to it. The linear mode is really only "one possible construction" but is dominant in our culture. [239, 92] The nonlinear mode, the intuitive, wholistic is more dominant in such people as the Hopi, in mystical experiences, and in our own dreaming. Since things do not have to happen one-at-a-time and in order, much more information can be handled at once in gestalts or patterned wholes. Time does not seem as important in such cultures, and they are not always in a rush, for the all is present at any one moment. Bogen thinks that "what may well be the most important distinction between the left and right hemisphere modes is the extent to which a linear concept of time participates in the ordering of thought." [33]

A culture such as ours, which exposes children to early education in reading and writing, values left hemisphere thinking and covertly discourages thinking in the right mode. Thus left hemisphere thinking dominates even when dealing with problems where it is not appropriate. Children raised in a non-literate culture, such as the Hopi, receive training which enables them to think more readily in wholes, or intuitively. [84]

On the Street figure completion test, the Hopis have the highest scores—much higher than either whites or blacks. The test consists of unconnected bits of a figure such as a sailboat. The mind must be able to see the whole—the gestalt—to recognize the object. If it focuses only on the disconnected parts, it cannot see a figure at all. The Similarities test was used to test the left hemisphere. This test has questions such as, what is the similarity between an orange and a banana? The test is scored to reward abstraction. For example, the answer "both are fruit" gets a higher score than "both have peeling." The Whites scored much higher on this test than the Hopis; however, the scores on these two different types of test showed a more balanced ratio between right and left brain functions in the Hopi than in the Whites. [34] Bogen suggested that we need a term such as right brain non-literacy for our culture's neglect of right brain functions to correspond to the word *illiterate*, which in reality refers to only left brain function. [31]

In a Los Angeles conference, Bogen told of going with the Hopi leader, Banyaca, to see the rock drawings near Oraibi (often referred to as the Hopi Bible). Banyaca pointed out to him that the figures had two pairs of legs: one set for walking and one set for dancing, and two mouths: one for talking and one for singing. Hopi Kachinas are all two-sided. Thus the Hopis formally recognize the two different ways of processing information and are much more capable of seeing "the whole," which may contribute to their peacefulness. The Hopi, Bogen says, is almost incapable of individual aggression. [31]

The current problems in education, in Bogen's view, are partly caused by the almost complete emphasis on left brain thinking which helps students to be successful students, but not to *live* successfully. Students, Bogen says, "Are concerned not only with rationality but with sensitivity. They are concerned not so much with making a living as making a life. They see a world of warring elders, busily Becoming at the expense of Being, who want them to be unhappy in the same half-brained way. The fight with nature for survival is won, they feel; and it is time we learn to live within nature as bilaterally educated, whole persons." [35]

Bogen speculates that possibly the asymmetry of the cerebral hemispheres is process specific. "A geometric interpretation of process specificity is proposed—namely, that each hemisphere represents the other and the world in complementary mappings: the left mapping the self as a subset of the world and the right mapping the world as a subset of the self." [32] Obviously, if our right brain functions are underdeveloped we will have difficulty seeing ourselves as part of the world and find it much easier to destroy the environment, while for the Hopi it is clear that, in Bateson's words, "the organism which destroys its environment destroys itself."

The possibilities inherent in a more balanced development of both hemispheres are intriguing because the corpus callosum connecting the two hemispheres contains 200 million nerve fibers—more nerve fibers per square inch than any other part of the brain. Yet, people who have had this corpus callosum severed appear more or less normal and feel themselves to be normal, according to Bogen, who asks "So what do they *use* those 200 million nerve cells for ordinarily?" His answer is that we *don't* use them, but perhaps we could *learn* to use them. [31] It is possible that developing both hemispheres in a more balanced relationship, facilitated by a greater use of the connecting corpus callosum nerve cells, would provide access to two separate but complete information systems. Self and world could be seen as part of the same whole.

In an earlier book, *Crack in the Cosmic Egg,* Pearce exposed the limitations inherent in too much emphasis on left brain thinking:

Do you not see how logical thinking, in order to even function, must limit to a specific, and that this specific is then the only apparent reality—and how this fragmented form of thinking then orients quite naturally around the notion of *scarcity,* the idea that in order to have we must take from and deprive others, since only a limited amount can be seen? Do you not see that fragmented thinking turns all others into potential enemies . . . Can you not see that opening to the whole mind must open to a constant yield always sufficient, always ample? . . . Our universe is not a fixed and frozen machine grinding out in entropy. It can always be what we have need of it to be. The eternal mental life of God and Man has enough to go around—eternally round and round—by moving for and not against.   [248, 186]

In a footnote in *Magical Child,* Pearce discusses Michael Gazzaniga's speculations as to why the brain would make its most elaborate and difficult construction, language, in both hemispheres, as occurs in the young child, only to deconstruct this construction in the right hemisphere somewhere before age twelve. Gazzaniga had pointed out that nowhere else in nature do we find such a lapse of economy. Pearce writes that this separation should be only a "functional separation for an interacting relationship," but because of the way the child is conditioned by anxiety it becomes instead a "schism." "Certainly," says Pearce, "logical maturation and the growth of abstract thinking require a separation of word from thing and of self from world, but in the same sense as separation of infant from the womb—for a greater relationship, not isolation and abandonment." [250, 237] The old epithet, "You half-brained idiot!" turns out to be valid for our cultural emphasis on left hemispheric thinking, which effectively cuts us off from the rest of the earth.

The Holographic Model of Brain Function

More than twenty five years ago psychologist Karl Lashley found that 80 per cent or more of the visual cortex of a rat could be damaged without loss of its ability to correctly respond to patterns. (Recent research by others on cats gave similar negative results from severing 98 per cent.) [259] No matter where he cut, the engram or memory trace remained; it was only destroyed by cutting away most of the brain. No one could ever find this engram. Since about 1965, neuroscientist Karl Pribram has been working on research which suggests that perhaps one function of the brain may be similar to the holographic process in optical systems, so that memory is distributed throughout the brain. This could account for the persistence of memory despite great brain damage. Pribram states that this theory "addresses the interests of Gestalt, of existential concerns, of social encounter and transcendence. However, it is rooted in the disciplines of information, computer and systems analysis." [266] In the July 4, 1977 issue of the *Brain Mind Bulletin,* devoted entirely to the new theory, Marilyn Ferguson writes that Pribram's theories, combined with the theories of physicist David Bohm of the University of London, "appear to account for all transcendental experience, paranormal events, and even 'normal' perceptual oddities." [84]

Though it is certain that ideas behind this new theory of brain function will contribute to more understanding of the relationship between the human being's mind and the earth, the fact that the theory is so new means that it is all very tentative. At this time one can only present a few basic ideas and suggest some of the possibilities. There is no way to know just what further research will bring.

On the photographic film in a camera each part of the film records the scene arriving from the corresponding part in the visual field, so the film looks like the scene it photographs. In the holographic process, it is the wave field of light scattered by an object, not the object itself which is recorded. The light beam is split into two components by a half-silvered mirror. One part of the beam continues directly ahead undisturbed, while the other part is deflected to another mirror and then continues to the photographic plate. Because the undisturbed beam, called the reference beam, goes directly to the photographic plate while the deflected beam, called the working beam, is first deflected and then proceeds to the plate, it is out of phase with the reference beam because of the minute fraction of time longer that it takes to reach the plate. Later, when the photographic plate is illuminated by the laser, the pattern created by the interference of these two waves is what creates the hologram. The image seen is three-dimensional. If the hologram is cut into pieces each small piece can reproduce the entire scene.

The holographic brain theory does not say that the brain works just like a holographic process. Pribam explains, "What is to be taken seriously is the analogy between the *paths* taken by the energy, the interactions among these paths and the resulting organizations of 'information' that are produced." [266] Phase differential is the key point—the two "paths" of light are out of phase and the interrelationship or cross-correlation between these two phases is what produces the information. A further explanation comes from Paul Pietsch: "The reasons are mathematical. But, basically, the hologramic code depends on ratios established within the medium, not absolute values. Like an angle, the code is relationships . . ." [259] A right angle (such as the intersection of two streets) is still a right angle, whether it is carved out of wood or made by laying two bricks together at right angles to one another. The relationships between the two different beams established by the wavefronts of light are what makes up the reconstructed image in a hologram.

In the brain the different paths taken by the neuronal impulse travelling through the brain cells interconnect, thus producing a new bit of information.

If a single memory is distributed everywhere throughout the brain, how does the brain handle multiple memories? Holographers produce multiple holograms—the codes of many different scenes superimposed one on the other. They are kept straight "by manipulating such properties as color or the angle of the construction beam;" [259] then, during decoding, by making the necessary adjustments, the holographer can cause one whole scene to go off and another to go on.

According to Pribram, there is considerable evidence that in human beings the right hemisphere of the brain is concerned with images, and the left hemisphere is more compatible with program processing such as in a computer. Pribram cites evidence which shows that, "The visual system is sensitive to the spatial frequencies in patterns of light in much the same way as the auditory system is sensitive to the temporal frequencies in patterns of sound." [266] Until recently, neurophysiology has been mostly concerned with the transmission of signals from one part of the nervous system to another. This transmission is accomplished by nerve impulses travelling along axons, which can be likened to the interconnecting wires of electric circuits. The end axon divides into smaller branches, which make contact with the input terminals of a number of other neurons. The input terminals of a neuron consist of its dendrites and its cell body. The connection between an axon of one neuron and a dendrite of another cell is called a synapse. Transmission across these junctions is electrical. This type of brain action can be likened to that of a computer.

The image-making brain function, on the other hand, has to do with the slow potential microstructure surrounding these junctures. Both before and after the synapse itself, such slow potential waves can block or facilitate the movement of the electrical signal through the synapse. These interactions can occur because axons branch at the endings and become masses of tiny fibers. The endings of dendrites of the next cell also are a mass of small fibers. When electrical records are made "extracellularly from such fine fiber networks of interlacing branches of axons and dendrites, it is found that nerve impulses have decremented into small amplitude slow waves which propagate only short distances if at all." These slow waves are sensitive to all sorts of influences, giving them the potential for carrying out the computational work in the brain. Summing up, Pribram states that "the interactions among the slow potentials . . . are responsible for the distribution of information within the visual system . . . For brain function, we found structure to be in the form of program [computer-like] and distribution in the form of hologram. Is the rest of the physical universe built along these lines as well?" [266]

Optical information processing systems, such as the holographic process, construct images while a computer deals with programs. "Neither programs nor images reside as such in the information processing system—they are configurations made possible by the construction of the system." [266] When these images or programs are stored outside their processing systems, there is no resemblance between the way they are in storage and their image when shown. The marks on a computer tape bear no resemblance to the information contained in the computer program. The information is implicit; the way it is shown is explicit.

Pribram, basing his theory on Bertrand Russell's ideas, believes that scientific research as done today gives knowledge of the "*extrinsic* properties (the rules, structures, etc.) of the physical world." Although Russell thought that the "intrinsic properties" (which he defined as the stoneness of stones, e.g.) were unknowable, Pribram says that actually "they are the 'ground' in which the extrinsic properties are embedded in order to become realized." [266] Artists, craftsmen, and engineers make these intrinsic programs real by grounding them in a physical medium. In another article, "Proposal for a Structural Pragmatism: Some Neuropsychological Considerations of Problems in Philosophy," Pribram gives this example: "The Beethoven symphony to which I am at the moment listening is not in one sense reducible to the mechanics of the score, nor of the recording, receiver, amplifier, and speaker system which is emitting it; nor is it completely described by the contortions set up in my auditory apparatus by the describable wave patterns impinging on my ears. All these and more are components—but something more than this constitutes the symphony. This something more is not mystical. Musicians call it structure." [268, 495] The intrinsic properties of the symphony, the phrase of music, the mental structure could also be realized in such physical media as a living orchestra or a sheet of music. This *structure*, "hierarchically arranged by reference terms among levels . . . is what the biologist refers to as process or mechanism." The far-reaching implications of this for mind/earth relationship come with this statement by Pribram: "Once levels of discourse are recognized as such, and the potentialities and limitations of communication between them are accepted, the only recourse is to a truly monistic, seemingly pluralistic, multilevel *structural* mindbrain. As one scientist-philosopher aptly put it, to have mind there must be at least two brains." [268, 494]

Referring back to Pietsch's idea of an angle still being an angle no matter what it is made of—because an angle deals with relationship, not matter as such—we see now that the intrinsic properties of anything can be likened to a code of relationships. It is possible to transmit this information into other forms of matter—and the human physical brain is another form of matter.

The human being's brain can "apprehend the whole by the operations of coding and recoding. Languages, verbal (linguistic) and nonverbal (cultural), are constituted of these pieces." [267, 384] If these human languages lose real contact with the earth itself they begin to live separate lives, and become ends in themselves instead of means, and thus lead to neurosis, wars, and ecological disaster.

Too great a dependence on the linear left brain kind of knowledge, in either linguistic or cultural language, greatly limits the human being because nature is not linear. Our modern culture tends to link things together by lines. You start here and you go to that building on the corner, turn right and proceed ahead. Primitives, on the other hand, were multidimensional. They could visualize any spot in the region and tell all about it. The bushman of the Kalahari desert could locate a buried ostrich egg full of emergency water in a featureless desert of the Kalahri, walk right to it, and dig it up. He might have put it there three years ago. At a certain spot, at a certain time, is where the deer come to water. It's a sense of total pattern, holographic rather than linear. This involves total sensing—how the wind blows against the right cheek when you reach the ridge, how the cold of the valley hollow feels when you drop into it after dark from the warm up-country.

This sort of total sensing of the environment accounts for the fact that primitives seem to have far more than our limited five senses working for them. In my limited space, I cannot give further proof from anthropology, but I can tell of a particular personal incident to show the implications.

When I was a teen-ager, a group of us in Colorado were climbing all the 14,000-foot peaks in the state of Colorado. In the high mountains of Colorado in the summer there is a thunderstorm almost every afternoon around two o'clock, clearing off by four or five. We became very accustomed to lightning and thunder. Not knowing much about the scientific facts behind it, we had developed a theory that as long as we could get a buzzing discharge of electricity off our hands when we raised them in the air, the electricity was discharging harmlessly in small amounts; if it was absolutely quiet we would worry, thinking it was building up for a big one, and we would take shelter only then. This was, of course, totally wrong, and we could have been killed, I now know. From climbing each summer during these thunderstorms, we developed a particular sensitivity to the coming of thunderstorms and knew some time before they reached us that there was sufficient charge in the air. The way we felt it, this charge, resulted in a particular kind of deep headache, impossible to describe verbally, but very localized in a small area. When any of us felt this, we generally speeded up so as to cover as much ground as possible before the storm reached us. The conclusive proof that we had developed a specific sensory type of knowledge came years later. On very rare occasions, it is possible to have lightning and thunder in the winter. Most people have no warning this is about to happen. It is snowing, and they are amazed when the lightning and thunder occur. I always knew long before that it was coming and usually tried to hurry and get on the lift. I wanted to get one more ride before the lift was shut down, as is always done when lightning occurs. On this particular day, I was skiing with an old friend from our teen-age climbing days. We were on the chair lift. Just as we skied down the off-ramp, I noticed the headache, and just then my friend said to me, "I've got a lightning headache." And I answered, "So do I. Let's hurry down and get another ride before they shut the lift down." A man standing there looked at us as if we were crazy and shook his head. We had not skied very far down the mountain when there was a great crash of thunder, and it was upon us. We did not make another run up; they shut the lift down. We knew as plainly as if it was written on the sky that a thunderstorm was on the way while no other skiers that I know of can even feel it in the atmosphere before the first crash of thunder comes. If told in the proper occult language, this ability would be considered a paranormal event, but it is *not*. It is a perfectly normal human ability which humans have probably lost from nonuse. It is certain that primitives have a great many of the same senses—far more than we do. A man-made world such as ours is a limiting world—and many things atrophy for lack of use. The danger of living entirely in a man-made environment is that it contains only that knowledge which man already knows.

One other example comes from Monty West, an anthropologist who lived in Australia with the aborigines. He said that when an Aborigine is hunting he will use one eye to scan the entire horizon looking for anything which might be an animal. When he finds such a spot he will focus one eye on that spot so as to watch for movement or further clues as to what it is, while the other eye continues to move throughout the landscape. Thus the two eyes are being used for totally different functions. [355] According to authorities, human eyes do not operate in this way.

One great advantage of the holographic theory of the brain is that it provides a possible model for understanding other ways of knowing which until now have been considered paranormal, occult, or mystic. The following section on the "triune brain" gives some indications of the further dimensions of this kind of knowledge.

The "Triune Brain" and Ritual

Consciousness stretches up through time from the placid mass of cells on the drying mud, through reptiles browsing on the branches of trees and the little mammals peeping on them through the leaves, up to Proust in his exquisite, agonizing web . . . Consciousness must surely be traced back to the rocks—the rocks which have been here since life began and so make a meeting place for the roots of life in time and space, the earliest and the simplest.

Jacquetta Hawkes [114, 38]

There is growing knowledge of the right/left hemispheric functions of the cerebral cortex, the most recent evolutionary development of the brain. Less well-known is the relationship between the older brain and the new brain. Paul MacLean, neuroscientist and chief of the Laboratory of Brain Evolution and Behavior has been working on a theory of the "triune brain." If we think of the brain as an onion sitting on top of the spinal cord, the interior layer surrounding the top of the spinal cord is the reptilian brain, which probably evolved several hundred million years ago. Surrounding this oldest brain is the next layer, the limbic system (old mammalian), and the outermost layer of the onion is the neocortex, the newest brain. The word *limbic* means "pertaining to or having the character of a border," because it does form a border around the oldest brain.

MacLean's term, "triune," indicates that the three brains are part of one—and the sum is greater than the parts. He has concluded that the human brain "amounts to three interconnected biological computers," each with "its own special intelligence, its own subjectivity, its own sense of time and space, its own memory, motor, and other functions." [193] The three brains are different in structure and millions of years apart in evolutionary time. In effect, we experience the world through three different mentalities, "two of which lack the power of speech." The limbic brain and the reptilian brain have abundant connections with one another, but only indirect communication with the newest brain, the neocortex.

The oldest brain, the reptilian, according to MacLean, plays an important role in aggressive behavior, territoriality, ritual, and the establishment of social hierarchies. The idea of a reptilian brain seems repugnant to people of Western cultures; in India, however, there is the concept that by means of special yogic techniques the kundalini energy, "serpent power," can be made to rise from the base of the spinal cord into the brain producing powerful energy, and sometimes, instant enlightenment. In effect this "serpent power" would connect the sympathetic nervous system, the "abdominal brain" of Oriental cultures, with the triune brain in the skull. The special abdominal breathing of Taoism in China is supposed to rouse the "dragon power" lodged in the abdomen and send it up by means of the "Greater Heavenly Circulation" to the crown of the head.

The lower part of the limbic brain seems to be involved with basic concerns which keep the individual organism functioning; the upper part has to do with emotions. The master gland, the pituitary, which influences other glands, is in this limbic area. The beginnings of altruism and empathy can be traced to the limbic brain as well. This part of the brain is the source of mammalian interaction and, since to all mammals, humans included, relationship is more important than all else, [19, 412-413] it follows that the limbic brain seems to be the source of convictions as to what is true or important. The sense of smell is connected to the limbic system, as can be seen by the prominent place smell plays in the relationship patterns of dogs and, equally so, by the largely unrecognized importance of smell in sexual preferences.

71

These older brain structures are frequently in conflict with the demands of the new brain; and MacLean believes that psychoneurosis, some kinds of psychoses, and alcoholism may be traced to the more automatic processes of the reptilian brain.

Although the two older brains lack the power of speech in the usual sense, they obviously play an important part in the human mind. Bateson says that the unconscious, which may be equated to these older brains, operates in *primary process* modes. Primary process lacks negatives, lacks tense, and deals in metaphors. An example of the difficulties connected with the lack of negatives in *primary process* can be seen by watching two dogs who have not met before. The only way they can say they are not going to fight is by making the preliminary gestures of fighting, such as baring the teeth, laying back the ears, but then rolling over on the ground with feet in the air. This lack of negatives contributes to the difficulties involved in understanding dreams. Furthermore, in *primary process* the persons or things need not even be identified, as the communication is about the relationships between these entities and not about the entities as such, which would be the case in ordinary verbal communication. [20]

The mind as a whole is an integrated network of circuits, but what the conscious mind registers is only the bits and pieces of the on-going circuits which go through all three levels. In our culture, human beings tend to think that all of their consciousness can be found in that tiny arc of the circuit which is showing in the topmost brain, the neo-cortex. Concerning this fallacy, Bateson states, "that mere purposive rationality unaided by such phenomena as art, religion, dream, and the like, is necessarily pathogenic and destructive of life . . ." [20] Life depends on the interlocking whole.

It may be that the holographic theory of brain function can contribute some understanding to the possible relationships of these three brains. As stated in the previous section, Pribram said that, "What is to be taken seriously is the analogy between the *paths* taken by the energy, the interaction among these paths and the resulting organization of 'information' that are produced." [266]

Since there is communication of sorts between the three brains, the interaction of "paths of energy" between these three brains would produce the most profound impressions. Just for an example, Proust, mentioned above in the quotation from Jacquetta Hawkes, tasted a madeleine cake. Suddenly he was flooded with a vast interconnecting web of relationships and images—so much so that it took him years to write it down, and the finished book came to over two thousand pages. The smell of hawthorn blossoms also played a part in these recollections. It was the sense of smell and taste located in the limbic brain which triggered the experience. It seems to me that the peculiar power of rituals in the cultures of human beings resides in just this facilitation of communication between each of the parts of the triune brain. The drawings of the dancing masked medicine man in the Aurignacian cave of Trois Freres in France, dating from at least 15,000 years ago, show that human beings realized communication among these levels of mind through ritual dances, where they took on the appearance and mannerisms of the animal world (the old mammalian brain). By such rituals, the human being can get in touch with the information accumulated through millions of years of evolution of the human brain. Furthermore, perhaps by facilitating the expression of consciousness of these two older brains through rituals, the human being may be better able to communicate with the consciousness of other beings, such as animals and plants—perhaps even back to the rocks themselves.

This communication with other kinds of consciousness is shown in Amerindian rituals. Black Elk, in describing the ritual of the Sioux Sun Dance, tells how "one of the standing peoples has been chosen to be at our center; he is the *wagachun* (the rustling tree, or cottonwood) . . ." [41, 69] In the Hopi Indian Snake Dance, the reptilian mind is present in the close relationship developed between the human being and the snake in the days before the dance. In Pueblo Indian dances, certain human beings become seized by the spirit of the deer and dance as a deer would dance or the spirit of the squash blossom and speak as the squash life-giving form. The Ohama tribe in their Pebble Society ritual chanted,

Verily, one alone of all these was the greatest,
Inspiring to all mind,
The great white rock,
Standing and reaching as high as the heavens, enwrapped in
    mist . . .
He! This is the desire of the little ones
That of thy strength they shall partake . . .   [90, 572]

Frank Waters tells of this uniting of the three parts of the "triune brain" in ritual dancing of Indians in the Southwest, waving their spruce twigs, singing like the sighing of the wind through the trees, "stamping rhythmically as the beat of the drum, insistently as the pulse of the earth. No longer part man, part beast, part bird. But forces which sway the squatting mountains, which shape the cloud terraces building overhead . . . It is all one: the dancing gods; the pulsing cries and the singing drum; the whirling horizon; the mountains in the sky; the white clouds squatting on the plain. And no one . . . thinks it is all over, done, finished, for in this evocation of spaceless space and timeless time which obliterates the illusion of straight-lined progression from a distinguishable beginning to an ordered end, nothing ever is all over, done, finished . . . everything fuses in a whirling circle that encloses an undivided, undifferentiated, ever-living wholeness." [350, 162]

Jung on the Relationship Between Mind and Earth

Jung's investigations into the unconscious predated by decades modern theories of the "triune brain" and the holographic theory of brain function; yet some of his concepts such as "psychical energy," previously thought scientifically impossible, are just now beginning to be understood. Combining ideas from modern physics and brain research, physicists are finally beginning to deal with problems of human consciousness. In an interview in *Brain Mind Bulletin,* physicist David Bohm states: "Thought is a material process—not a statement about how things are, but an activity." [87] In another issue of *Brain Mind,* an article summarizing the increasing relevance of physics for psychology states, "By whatever means a mental event affects the physical body, sub-atomic exchanges of energy must occur . . . The relatively crude measurement of brain activity by the EEG has a basis in quantum physics." [86]

Jung's concept of psychical energy comprehends what Freud called the libido, but it is even broader in its implications. According to Jung, primitive man found the chanelling of psychical energy so concrete a thing that he felt the fatigue from work as a state of being "sucked dry" by the daemon of the field. All of the major activities of primitives such as tilling the soil, hunting, and wars were always entered into with ceremonies or chants, "which quite obviously have the psychological aim of canalizing libido into the necessary activity." Complex ceremonies of the Pueblo Indians show "how much is needed to divert the libido from its natural river-bed of everyday habit into some unaccustomed activity. The modern mind thinks this can be done by a mere decision of the will and that it can dispense with all magical ceremonies." [143, 44] But whenever an unusual event occurs that could exceed our powers or could easily go wrong, "then, with the blessing of the church, we solemnly lay the foundation-stone, or we 'baptize' a ship as she slips from the docks." [142, 50]

This special psychical energy or power has been given many different names by primitive groups: the Dakota Indians call it *wakanda*; the Iroquois, *obi*; the Algonquins, *manitu*. Lovejoy's classic definition of *wakanda* is the perception of "a universally extended, invisible, but usable and transferable life energy or universal power." The Huichol Indians of Mexico believe that a power circulates through men, ritual animals, and plants. The Melanesian concept of *mana* is similar. Jung quotes Condrington's definition of *mana*: "It is actually produced by persons, although it acts through the medium of water, or maybe through a stone, or a bone." In summing up his lengthy discussion of this psychical energy or power, Jung wrote: "The almost universal distribution of the primitive energy-concept is a clear expression of the fact that in earlier stages of human consciousness, the need was already felt to represent in a visible way, what man perceived of the dynamism of mental events. If, therefore in our psychology, we lay emphasis on the energic viewpoint, this is in agreement with the psychic facts which have been graven upon the mind of man since primordial times." [142, 75–76]

Jung explored the ideas involved in this energic viewpoint for more than twenty years; furthermore, it is closely involved with his ideas on synchronicity. His contact with the physicists Bohr and Pauli provided the impetus to formulate the details of his hypothesis in the essay on "Synchronicity as a Principle of Acausal Relationship," written when he was seventy-five years old. Many years before this he had written that "the psychic lies embedded in something that appears to be of a nonpsychic nature. Although we perceive the latter as a psychic datum only, there are sufficient reasons for believing in its objective reality." Jung goes on to discuss the underlying processes involved on the atomic level and sums it up by stating, "The existence of this remarkable correlation between consciousness and the phenomenal world, between subjective perception and objectively real processes, i.e., their energic effects, requires no further proof." [145, 438] Later on, in the same paper, he points out that his "concept of energy for the purpose of expressing the activity of the psyche" is not to be construed as a mathematical formula but "only as its analogy." He then notes that "this analogy is itself an older intuitive idea from which the concepts of physical energy originally developed." [145, 443] The primitive idea predated the modern physics. At the end of this paper he writes: "If these reflections are justified, they must have weighty consequences with regard to the nature of the psyche, since as an objective fact it would then be intimately connected, not only with physiological and biological phenomena, but with physical events, too—and, so it would appear, most intimately of all with those that pertain to the realm of atomic physics." [145, 444]

In 1927, in "Mind and the Earth," Jung pointed out that "The mind would then be understood to be a system of adaptation formed by the condition of an earthly environment . . . From the collective unconscious as a timeless and universal mind we should expect reactions to the most universal and constant conditions, whether psychological, physiological, or physical . . ." [141, 110–111] The collective unconscious and personal unconscious are two separate parts of the psyche. The personal unconscious contains that which at one time was conscious, but which was forgotten or repressed; the contents of the collective unconscious have never been in consciousness, and therefore, have never been individually acquired. The collective unconscious is made up of archetypes. "They are essentially the chthonic portion of the mind . . . that portion through which the mind is linked to nature, or in which, at least, its relatedness to the earth and the universe is most comprehensible. In these primordial images, the effect of the earth and its laws upon the mind is clearest to us." [139, 118] Jung says that we can recognize an archetype whenever a psychical reaction is out of proportion to its seeming cause.

As an example of the direct influence of the land upon the human beings, he refers to the colonization of the North American continent by the European race, "the greatest experiment in the transplantation of a race in modern times." The mixture with Indian blood is so slight that it can play no important part, yet the American unconscious definitely contains symbols connected with the Indian symbol system. "Thus the American presents a rare picture—a European . . . with an Indian soul! He shares the fate of all usurpers of foreign land, for in foreign soil live strange ancestor spirits, and therefore, the strange spirits will inhabit the newborn. There is a great psychological truth in this. The strange land assimilates the conqueror." [139, 138]

Jnana Yoga

We have been looking into some of the new dimensions of mind as revealed by current research. Despite all the evidence pointing toward mind-at-large, our culture continues to condition human beings to believe that *mind* is that tiny part of the whole brain labelled the *rational* mind. To give an idea of the dangers inherent in this fallacy, I want to retell here Joel Kramer's story of the cobra.

Suppose you find yourself in a room with no windows and only a faint shadowy glimmer of light which might indicate a door, but you're not really sure it's a door. The only other thing in this room is a giant cobra snake. What would you do? . . . Well, what would you do? There's no way out—what can you do? You'd watch it very, very carefully. You'd watch it when it was asleep and when it woke up. You'd watch every movement it made.

Joel Kramer begins his workshops with this story and then he goes on to explain that we do live in such a room with a deadly cobra. That cobra is our rational thought. This rational thought is out to kill us and is just as dangerous as a cobra. Why?

The answer to this question is what jnana yoga, sometimes called mind yoga, is all about. Patanjali's sutras, dating from the fifth century, are the oldest written source. The word, *yoga,* derives from the root *Yuj* which means *to join*—to join the individual and the *all.* Patanjali's second sutra is, "Yoga is the inhibition of the modifications of the mind." A later sutra states that the modifications of the mind are "right knowledge, wrong knowledge, fancy, sleep and memory." [314, 14] Notice that right knowledge is just as harmful as wrong knowledge. The reason for this is that if I think that I *know* something, I no longer *see* that object or that person in its real being. I have limited it. Krishnamurti, now in his eighties, for many years was the only teacher

of jnana yoga in the West. Just recently others have begun teaching. Joel Kramer came to jnana yoga through actual physical or hatha yoga and then went to Krishnamurti to learn more. The other main branch is called Vipassana or Insight Meditation, as taught by the Buddha and influenced by the ancient sutras.

A knowledge of Krishnamurti's early years is of the greatest importance for an understanding not only of jnana yoga, but for the insight into earth wisdom in his life. He was the child of a poor Brahman family in India. The Theosophist leader, Leadbeater, saw him playing on the beach and said that the boy had "the most wonderful aura he had ever seen." [192, 21] Leadbeater decided that the boy was to be the future avatar of the world and he, Leadbeater, was to train him for this. Thus, he formed the Order of the "Star in the East" in 1911 to prepare the world for the coming of the next great Teacher . . ." [192, 45] He was taken to England for education and from then on until he was thirty-two years old, he was under the complete supervision of Theosophists and indoctrinated with his supposed mission in the world. By all the usual standards he should have turned out to fulfill their expectations and taken over the leadership of the order. The fact that he did not take over his expected role, but instead devoted his life to showing others how to become more aware so that they followed no beliefs whatsoever, violates all the rules of psychological conditioning.

The book devoted to his early life, *Krishnamurti, Years of Awakening*, was compiled by Mary Lutyens, the daughter of one of the early Theosophists who was a close friend and almost a mother to the young Krishna. The book consists mostly of letters, journals, and printed material concerning his early years. Lutyens does not attempt to account for the events. However, the account of Krishnamurti's childhood years, together with a continuing theme in his later teaching, point to the crucial influence of his relationship to nature. Lutyens refers to Krishna's father's account of his childhood and says that due to frequent moving from city to city and Krishna's bouts with fever, he was far behind other boys of his age in his lessons. "Moreover, he hated book learning and was so dreamy as to appear at times mentally retarded. Nevertheless, he was keenly observant when his interest was aroused. He would stand for long stretches at a time watching trees and clouds, or squat on the ground gazing at plants and insects. This close observation of nature is another characteristic that he has retained." [192, 4]

Later she states that even Leadbeater was "exasperated at times by Krishna's apparent stupidity. Often during his lessons the boy would stand by the open window with his mouth open looking at nothing in particular. Over and over again he was told to shut his mouth; this he did, but then next moment it fell open again." [192, 26] In these two brief references, it is possible to note several things. Krishna directly observed nature at every opportunity and avoided and disliked school lessons, so was not damaged by too intensive an emphasis on left brain activity. Furthermore, the reports about his mouth always being open is important. The new body disciplines all agree that a tight jaw is very bad for the circulation of the blood to the head as it cuts off the blood in the arteries going up to the head in the area behind the jaw. With the emphasis in our culture of control, a tight jaw is a valued attribute, hence the insistence by the English Theosophist leaders on Krishna's firmly closing his mouth.

These insights into his early years alone would not be conclusive, but in the numerous books of Krishnamurti's taped lectures, in almost every other lecture, he refers his listeners directly to nature by saying such things as "The sun had gone down and the trees were dark and shapely against the darkening sky. The wide, strong river was peaceful and still. The moon was just visible on the horizon; she was coming up between two great trees . . ." [161, 17] These are not just poetic asides; again and again, from such references to nature, he proceeds to develop his thought directly. There is no doubt whatsoever that in Pearce's terms the young Krishna was bonded to the earth. Furthermore, his life validates Edith Cobb's idea that the "perception of wholeness has been a characteristic of all individuals who have thought more closely with the instrument of the body." [59] In all the years of his youth in Europe, Krishna's only pleasures were golf and his motor bicycle, both whole-body activities. Krishna learned directly from the earth itself how to think with the whole of the mind; so that later, he was able to see the trap of rational thought and refused to be caught in it.

A striking indication of his close ties with nature occurred at a very crucial moment in his life, in 1922, when he was twenty-seven and going through a psychic crisis accompanied by enormous pain for days. He was finally able to gain relief when someone suggested he go out and sit under a young pepper tree in blossom. During these days he had what he described as a "most extraordinary experience. There was a man mending the road; that man was myself; the pickaxe he held was myself; the very stone which he was breaking up was a part of me . . . the wind . . . the ant on the blade of grass . . . the birds, the dust," all was a part of him. "I was in everything, or rather everything was in me . . ." [192, 158]

For several more years he continued having frequent bouts with enormous pain connected with his psychic condition. Then finally, in 1927, at a Theosophist camp at Eerde in Holland, he spoke out, "You must become liberated not because of me but in spite of me." He said that all of his life, but especially the last few months, he had struggled to be free—"free of my friends, my books, my associations." He was not to be taken as an authority, no one can give liberation; one has to find it within. Liberation is not for the few, but for all. The problem is that most people "cling to this individuality, to this sense of I." [192, 244-245]

His talk created absolute consternation among the leading Theosophists, as it destroyed their very reason for existing. Krishnamurti, who was always considerate toward these Theosophical leaders, showed his concern and sympathy but remained quite sure of his decision. In a letter from Switzerland to Mrs. Besant, long-time head of the Theosophists, he wrote, "It's going to be difficult. It's all in the day's work. I am, more and more, certain in my vision of the Truth. These mountains and the clean air here are wonderful . . ." [192, 252]

The entire event was a sensation in many countries. Newspaper reporters interviewed Krishnamurti, trying to find out how he could so easily throw over the money, the power, and the prestige of such a role; but they could not understand. In 1929, in the presence of Mrs. Besant and more than three thousand Star members, he formally dissolved the Order of the Star. In part of his speech, broadcast over the Dutch radio, he said he did not want anyone to follow him or to create a religion. Rather, he wanted people to be "free from all fears— from the fear of religion, from the fear of salvation . . . from the fear of life itself." [192, 273] He ended the talk by saying that he had spent two years considering the matter, and he was now disbanding the Order. He was not concerned with what new organizations they wanted to form. "My only concern is to set men absolutely, unconditionally free." [192, 275] Mary Lutyens says that within a few years, he had ended the physical agony he had suffered all those years (since 1922) and attained an ecstasy that never left him.

All the years since Krishnamurti's break with the Theosophists have been spent in explaining to others how to really learn to see and how to be free of fear. Decades before research on right/left brain phenomena was to prove that rational, linear thinking is by its very nature fragmented, Krishnamurti had said that "all one's thinking is in fragments." Everything, he said, is broken up in bits—good and evil, hate and love, everything is viewed from a particular belief system. "So to see something totally, whether it is a tree, or a relationship or any activity that one has, the mind must be free from all fragmentation, and the very nature of fragmentation is the center from which one is looking . . . *whatever thought* investigates *must inevitably be fragmentary*." [163, 24, 25]

But how, then, can one learn to see totally? To show how this is possible Joel Kramer tells another story, which I will retell briefly here. I am walking alone in the woods very early in the morning. Suddenly I see a ray of the sun caught in a dew drop on a leaf. For a moment the gap between the observer and the observed is not there. There is no separation—just the experience. It is one thing. This is seeing totally. But, almost immediately thought comes in. I say to myself, "Wow! This is great." Or "I am going to tell my friends about this." Or, "I'm going to come down here every morning." You want to repeat the experience. This is pleasure. The experience itself just *is*, and you don't evaluate it. Evaluating it or wanting to repeat it is pleasure. This kind of pleasure is to be avoided, because it is not the reality. This tricky point was finally cleared up for us by Joel Kramer. Almost all Eastern disciplines condemn pleasure which is difficult to understand. The mistake is that we think that by *pleasure* is meant anything we enjoy doing. But not at all. To live intensely, to live in the moment, is the point of it all. But this intensity disappears the moment that thought comes in; then you have the memory of that intensity which is pleasure. But whenever you indulge in pleasure, you can be sure that its opposite, sorrow, will appear. We are continually seeking the one and avoiding the other, with all the conflict this brings.

Thinking, intellect, cannot solve anything. "It can invent theories; it can explain; it can see the fragmentation and create more fragments; but the intellect, being a fragment, cannot solve the whole problem of man's existence . . . Thought, the intellectual capacity to reason, however sanely, does not end sorrow." [164, 12 and 79]

But when you have no separation between the observer and the observed, as in the dew drop experience, there is no conflict. The problem is created by the conflict between what *is* and what we think about it. The problem, as Krishnamurti puts it, is this: "I realize my way of living is contradictory, double, divided, and I know I have lived that way, with all the pain and misery of it, and I say to myself: what am I to *do*? How am I to get out of it? The thing to do is look at it silently—in the 'quietness' some other activity takes place which may solve this problem." One of his listeners questioned Krishnamurti as to what he means by silence. Krishnamurti answers: "You know what physical silence is . . . You walk in the woods and everything in the evening is very still; you know the physical silence with all the beauty in it, the richness, the quietness, the immeasurable magnificence, the dignity of it—you know it. And apparently you don't know what psychological, inward silence is. So you say, 'Please tell me about it, put it into words.' Why should I? Why don't you find out for yourself if there is such a silence?" [164, 121, 122]

But the mind cannot be silent if there is any form of distortion. That is why every kind of conflict must be understood—even conflict within oneself—between what one wants to be and is, or between what one "should" do and "shouldn't" do. "To be completely concerned with 'what is' puts away every form of duality and, hence, there is no conflict." [164, 93]

When you are completely involved with something—putting your mind, your heart, everything into it—thought does not come into it at all. This is total awareness and does not happen very often, because if we try

to be aware, there is a duality: the way we are and the way we are trying to be, and this conflict breeds violence. "Violence is fragmenting the world into the internal and external and treating the other as external as 'other,' as 'not me.' We do this even with ourselves." [164, 121] So what do you do? Just be aware of inattention. Notice you are not paying attention, but watch it very carefully. Don't try to change it, just watch it.

Krishnamurti says that to observe the movement of your own mind you must have a free mind, not one that agrees and disagrees on values. This, he says, is "a very difficult thing to do because most of us don't know how to look at, or listen to, our own being any more than we know how to look at the beauty of a river or listen to the breeze among the trees." [162, 23] This listening to nature, to the earth, is something Krishnamurti comes back to again and again. He makes a direct reference to the way the sky looks or the river is moving or the trees are moving, and goes on from there, but he always returns to nature in an effort to help his listeners to get out of their rational mind and see the whole—to be aware. This is the idea behind the famous quotation: "Wildness is the state of complete awareness. That's why we need it." To further elucidate this point, I quote Gary Snyder, who points out that, "In the shaman's world, wilderness and the unconscious become analogous; he who knows and is at ease in one, will be at home in the other." [300, 12]

Kramer, also, is concerned with this problem of achieving a quiet mind. He goes into some of the ways we try to get rid of conflict by believing in something or some authority. This creates more conflict—conflict between what we want to do and what the authority or belief system requires of us. He says, "It's difficult to do away with all authority because it puts one in a rather frightening place. There is nothing to hold onto . . . Yet real learning . . . never occurs unless we do away with authority." [159, 5] Furthermore, "To believe anything at all is to be in a state of violence—external and internal violence." [159, 7] At one of his workshops he explained a simple technique to provide feedback to ourselves so that we know when we are involved in belief rather than a fact. He was sitting on a brown rug at the time. He said that "If I say to you that this rug is green, you'll maybe say, 'No, it's really brown.' If I insist it's green, you'll just think I'm color blind or crazy or putting you on, but you won't feel called upon to defend your knowledge that it's green. But if you know something from reading it in a book or from some belief system: Christian or any other, you find yourself defending it. When you see that happening, defending anything at all, you'll know it's a belief, not a fact. If you pay attention to this all the time, you find that arguing 'leaves you.'" [160]

Kramer's favorite term is "it leaves you." People are always asking him "How can I change?", "How can I get rid of that bad habit?" And he always tells them that such action is violence—violence to yourself. There's a separation between what you are and what you want to be, and that means violence. Somewhere I once read that yoga is not the effort of becoming but the discovery of being. You don't try to change, you just watch carefully what your thought is doing to you—watch it as you would the cobra. When over and over you see the results of what you are doing it eventually "leaves you."

"In the seeing is the movement," is another Kramer phrase. He explains that if you are walking through the woods and you hear a tree crack in the wind and begin falling, you don't stop to think which way should I move or what should I do—you move. In the same way, if you really see what something is doing to you, there's no conflict—you just move.

"There are moments in life that are marked by a quality of energy that does not live in time, wherein there is no fragmentation, no separation between the experiencer and the experienced. Bliss or serenity is what this is usually called." [159, 22] And, as was true of Krishnamurti, most of Kramer's examples are drawn from the earth. "As I get to know myself, I get to know that what I am is a being in relationship. Fundamentally, what we are is a part of an energy system. It is awareness, a moment to moment awareness that brings a seeing of the totality and connectedness of all things." [159, 103]

If these last few pages have been difficult to understand, it is not inherent in the ideas themselves, but in the conflict set up by the rational brain. One of the first things one learns when beginning jnana yoga is how much that tiny rational brain fights you—fights against any exposure to this kind of thinking, because it threatens the absolute control the rational brain exerts. So I would like to turn once more to a "primitive" for an example of Kramer's "seeing of the totality and connectedness of all things." Wilfred Pelletier is not a true primitive, which makes his testimony that much more valuable. He is a modern Odawa Indian who left his island reservation and became a financial success in the white man's world running a restaurant in a big city in Canada. But he didn't stop hunting and fishing every chance he got and through this awareness of nature he began to understand. He went back to the reservation and gave up game-playing—"It isn't that I'm not good at it—God knows I've had enough practice . . . I can't take it seriously anymore . . . The games were still going on and the movie was grinding away, but I wasn't there any more . . ."

"I" was there, but there was no longer an observer and an observed, no longer a "me" and "you," no "self" and "not-self," no separate and isolated individuals. There was only one inclusive totality which left nothing out. All those billions of polarized pieces of the movie somehow flowed together into one whole, and there was nothing left outside of that. It was all flowing . . . And it was all living. Nothing was dead. Pure life-energy, flowing uphill as well as down, piling up in crests, running down in troughs—clouds and rain, mountains and valleys, passions and peace. And it was nameless. In that flow there were no categories, no classifications, no races, no words; only the crystal-clear feeling of knowing. And if I tried to conceptualize any of that feeling, tried to qualify it with words like "reality" or "totality," I left the flow, I was out of it, *bang*, just like I'd flipped a switch. But so long as I remained in that flow, there wasn't anything I didn't know. That was the feeling—I knew everything. And none of it in the past or future, it was all right there. But nothing I could put a tag on, not one thing. There were no words and there were no errors. A mistake was not possible. Everything was exactly right. Perfect. Beautiful.

So that's how I came, finally, to know who I was . . .

[251, 195–196]

Gregory Bateson, coming from a completely different direction, from systems theory and information theory, has grasped the same concepts as those contained in jnana yoga in his final step, Learning III of the Logical Categories of Learning. Learning I may be summed up as "those items which are most commonly called 'learning' in the psychological laboratory." Learning II might be called "learning how to learn." It "determines much of the relational life of all human beings, (a) dates from early infancy, and (b) is unconscious." Some of the words used for the type of relationships involved are *dominant, submissive, succouring,* and *dependent,* and have to do with the roles of each person in the relationship. Bateson says that all we know of Learning II "indicates that Learning III is likely to be difficult and rare." This type of learning does sometimes happen in psychotherapy, religious conversion, and "in other sequences in which there is profound reorganization of character."

Learning III, learning about learning, leads to a freedom from the bondage of the habits of Learning II. "But any freedom from the bondage of habit must also denote a profound redefinition of the self. If I stop at the level of Learning II, 'I' am the aggregate of those characteristics which I call my 'character.' 'I' am my habits of acting in context and sharing and perceiving in terms of the context in which I act. Selfhood is a product or aggregate of Learning II. To the degree that a man achieves Learning III, and learns to perceive and act in terms of the contexts of contexts, his 'self' will take on a sort of irrelevance. The concept of 'self' will no longer function as a nodal argument in the punctuation of experience."

Bateson says "Even the attempt at level III can be dangerous and some fall by the wayside." Such people are sometimes labelled as psychotic by authorities, but for the more creative who achieve this level "the resolution of contraries reveals a world in which personal identity merges into all the processes of relationship in some vast ecology or aesthetics of cosmic interaction." [16]

Bateson says that even the attempt at Learning III is dangerous. This is true, but fully understanding why this is true only comes when one is part way along the path. Through powder snow skiing I had grasped some understanding of what was involved when there are "no boundaries" and there is "no separation between the observer and the observed." But somehow I thought that it only applied on such special occasions, that it was like an unlooked-for gift or blessing which comes but rarely. It never occurred to me to think of it as a way of actually living all the time. Now I know that it was fear which kept me from looking any further into it. Krishnamurti, too, spent years wrestling with the problem before he dissolved the Order of the Star and began living as he did. Joel Kramer, in one of his workshops, spoke of his early experiences. He had begun to see some of the implications of doing hatha yoga but didn't want to think about them. At a party he heard a tape of Krishnamurti and found that he couldn't listen to it. But the next day he was curious enough to wonder why he couldn't listen to it; so he went back, borrowed the tape and forced himself to listen. Then he knew. On the tape Krishnamurti was saying what he had been afraid to face and his conscious, rational mind was freaking out and refused to listen. [160]

What happens when one begins to understand? Robert Pirsig, in *Zen and the Art of Motorcycle Maintenance*, gives the best explanation. In the book, the protagonist and his son, Chris, are nearing the top of the mountain they are climbing. They hear a couple of small rockslides. Nothing to be worried about. It's usual on mountains. But then, quite suddenly, he's very worried. "If he's up there, some psychic entity, some ghost . . ." He's thinking of Phaedrus, the one who cracked-up mentally in his search for "Quality." He forces his reluctant son to turn around and they descend the mountain and Pirsig writes that we've gone far enough along Phaedrus' path now and it's time to leave it and develop my own ideas. Then he tells of the final steps in Phaedrus' breakdown. On a hunch, Phaedrus had picked up his old copy of the *Tao Te Ching* and began reading it, substituting the word *quality* for *tao* and realized suddenly that "he had broken the code."

Then his mind's eye looked up and caught his own image and realized where he was and what he was seeing and . . . I don't know what really happened . . . but now the slippage that Phaedrus had felt earlier, the internal parting of his mind, suddenly gathered momentum, as do the rocks at the top of a mountain. Before he could stop it, the sudden accumulated mass of awareness began to grow and grow into an avalanche of thought and awareness out of control; with each additional growth of the downward tearing mass loosening hundreds of times its volume, and then that mass uprooting hundreds of times its volume more, and then hundreds of times that; on and on, wider and broader; until there was nothing left to stand.
No more anything.
It all gave way from under him. [262, 254]

This is exactly what it feels like when the realization hits one that there really is no separation between the observer and the observed, that we really do create our world and *are* totally responsible. There are no more boundaries—"No more anything."

Usually, when reading mystical literature or accounts of nirvana, this state of consciousness comes through as total bliss. And it is total bliss, I'm sure, after you get through the realization and your rational brain quits fighting you; but in the interim there is a crumbling of all your structures and games and all that you thought held you together. For greater clarity on the actual meaning of nirvana, I return again to Franklin Merrill-Wolff, mentioned in Chapter 5, who managed to achieve "realization" without any teacher and through a rigorous scientific method.

Merrill-Wolff writes that "Etymologically, nirvana means 'blown-out,' and this, in turn, carries the popular connotation of annihilation . . . but it is the annihilation of a *phase* or *way* of consciousness, not of the principle of consciousness, as such. A careful study of the Buddhist canon reveals quite clearly that Buddha never meant by 'nirvana,' the destruction of the principle of consciousness, but only a consciousness operating in a certain way." [217, 198–199] He calls this nirvana-type of consciousness, which he realized, "consciousness without an object." In this state "the disjunction between the subject to consciousness and the object of consciousness is destroyed." To our ordinary consciousness "the complete balance of the perfect consciousness must seem like a void" and so seems to have no value. But once he reached this state it did not seem strange or other-worldly. In fact, he writes, "I have never known another state of consciousness that seemed so natural, normal, and proper. I seemed to know that this was the nature that Reality must possess, and somehow, I had always known it." [217, 24, 64, 70] These words are almost identical to Kenneth Rexroth's description of the state he experienced with the new-mown hay when he was five years old.

Summary

I have, rather hastily, covered a lot of territory in this chapter on Mind, in order to pull together many different strands pertaining to the relationship of the human mind and the environment. I began with scientific evidence concerning the effect on mind of positive vs. negative ions in the atmosphere. Full understanding of this effect leads to the question of just where the boundaries of the mind are. Bateson's work provides the necessary clues to reach a clearer appreciation of the fact that the unaided rational part of the mind is, in Bateson's words, "necessarily pathogenic and destructive of life." The next section, "The Mind of the Child," gives some clues as to how our culture forces such a destructive approach onto the child; furthermore, this section and the following one shows the importance of the child's direct interaction with the earth in preventing the imbalance brought about by too much emphasis on left-brain learning.

Next, a brief overview of right/left brain research and the recent holographic and triune brain theories shows how these areas of research are beginning steps toward regaining full use of *all* the brain; furthermore, the section on Jung gives evidence of how the earth itself acts on the unconscious mind. The final section, concerned with jnana yoga, shows how becoming aware of the fact that the human being is a being-in-relationship combats narrow, anthropocentric, left-brain thinking and leads to whole-body thinking and eventually, perhaps, to mind-at-large.

In 1927, the same year that C. G. Jung wrote his essay on *Mind and the Earth*, he wrote about "psychological compensation-processes" which have often recurred in the history of the world. The outstanding example which he gave was that of "the strange melancholy and longing for deliverance which characterized imperial Rome," which was, as he states, "a direct result of slave influence . . . The explosive spread of Christianity which, so to speak, sprang out of the sewers of Rome . . . was a sudden reaction that set the soul of the lowest slave side-by-side with that of the divine Caesar. Similar, though perhaps less momentous, psychological compensation-processes have often recurred in the history of the world. Whenever a psychic or social monstrosity is generated, a compensation comes along that overrides all legislation and disregards all expectations." [146, 173]

The Club of Rome, in *The Limits of Growth*, stated that a Copernican revolution of the mind is required to prevent the ecological catastrophe now looming. In this chapter on mind I have given some indications of the directions in which I think this Copernican revolution is moving—toward a recognition of mind-at-large or, as John Todd puts it, a relationship between mindscape and landscape.

Jnana yoga, as taught by men such as Krishnamurti and Joel Kramer, who have freed it from its age-old constrictions of conventional religion and the elitism of the "chosen few," is the most concrete tool available for freeing the individual mind. Its validity has been further reinforced by modern brain research, as I have shown; but it is a difficult process because the rational part of the brain puts too many obstacles in the way.

Facing the avalanche of understanding, which wipes away all your former limitations of structure, is terrifying if attempted alone; but if an entire group approaches the matter by means of day-to-day rituals, the growth of awareness is gradual and almost inevitable. This is the way culture operated through the millenia of human history. A basic restructuring of culture is necessary—from unawareness to awareness. Our present culture is based on unawareness, for it surrounds everybody with a surfeit of entertainments, distractions, and just plain noise, so that one can't be aware and, therefore, can be more easily *used* for such purposes as getting more money or greater power. On the other hand, according to Joel Kramer, "It is awareness, a moment-to-moment awareness, that brings a seeing of the totality and connectedness of all things." Furthermore, he states that, "As I get to know myself, I get to know that what I am is a being in relationship." [159, 103]

For an understanding of what it means to live as a "being-in-relationship," it is necessary to turn to Martin Heidegger, the only Western philosopher since before the time of Plato to investigate the meaning of Being and the relationship of beings; the only philosopher to explore the realm that is "completely other" to the subject-object polarity, which is so destructive in our culture. Truth is not located in the mind as the mind's response to something out there; neither is truth "out there" waiting for mind to discover it. It is neither subject nor object. It is world itself. Since the world, according to Heidegger's concepts "is the interrelation of earth, sky, gods and mortals, this interrelation, the mirror-play, is the primary revelation, the primary truth." [341, 235] Or, as Joel Kramer succinctly states, "Real meditation is a way of living, a way of seeing the world, because that's all there actually is—being in the world."

The next three chapters are devoted to Heidegger's ideas, to provide a few guidelines for the necessary "Copernican revolution of the mind," a culture of awareness.

9. Martin Heidegger and the Quest for Being

When the early morning light quietly
grows above the mountains . . .

The world's darkening never reaches
to the light of Being.

We are too late for the gods and too
early for Being. Being's poem,
just begun, is man.

Martin Heidegger   [117, 4]

Long before I had heard of Martin Heidegger, I now know I was experiencing what he calls the "round dance of appropriation," the interrelationship of the fourfold: earth, sky, gods, and mortals in *my* "world" of powder snow skiing—one of the few sub-cultures in modern industrial society still open to the fourfold.

The "worlding" of the powder skier's "world" begins with the mutual appropriation of the earth and the sky as moisture-laden clouds from the Pacific Ocean move in across the deserts from California meeting no barrier until the uplift of the Wasatch Mountains in Utah. Then, the mountains cause the sky-borne clouds to release their gift of snow down onto the high, steep slopes below, resulting in the highest delight of skiers—powder snow. But, according to Heidegger, the "worlding" of a "world" does not occur until the "thing" (in this case the skis) brings together the "united four, earth and sky, divinities and mortals." [117, 178] How is this done?

On a clear winter morning, just as the sun rises high enough for its slanting rays to shine horizontally through the trees, disclosing each branch and needle, backlit and rimmed with fire, each intricate facet of the snow crystals distinct and glittering with many-colored lights, each contour and dip of the land plainly outlined by the conforming snow, and every animal track sharp and clear, silently I lay my track through the snow—a silent listener awaiting Being. And Being responds. Because of the skis, I move so silently and swiftly that deer, rabbits, and weasels are surprised and caught in their inner lives; so swiftly and silently that they do not flee but stand out in their being. Each tree-being, aspen and fir, lit from within, stands out. The shape of the land is shown forth more clearly than in the summer, when its contours are masked and hidden by vegetation. The sky is bluer, more compelling against the contrasting white snow. The earth more present, the sky more present, I, the mortal, more present in total awareness, and thus these three of Heidegger's fourfold are completed by the almost tangible presence of the gods. "To dwell is to spare the earth, receive the sky, expect the gods, and have a capacity for death." [341, 15]

Don Juan says the warrior lives "with death over his left shoulder." Death itself, mortality, according to Heidegger, is necessary to let Being shine through as "world." The human being, man, breaks up the invisible white light of Being into its components of the colors of his world. Death, on the other hand, is the submergence into Being. [343, 239] Death is an ever-present possibility in the powder snow world as the snow, gift of the sky, when too deep or unstable, is drawn down by the gravity of the earth and this mutual appropriation of the one to the other is called *avalanche*. Having been in avalanches, I can grasp that impending fullness of Being itself—death.

In an authentic "world," the mortals are in togetherness not only with the others of the fourfold—the earth, the sky, and the gods; but mortals are together with one another. The freedom, grace, and joy of this togetherness in the powder "world" occurs in response to the gift of the sky: unbroken snow. This is most easily skied in direct response to the earth's gravity—down the fall line—but the dips and contours of the earth automatically lay out the "way" to follow; and for skillful skiers, there is only one best "way" for each, so all can ski together at top speed and still flow with one another and with the earth. "To be really free is to have no choice at all." [160] Just as in a flight of birds turning through the air, no *one* is the leader and none are the followers, yet all are together; so also the powder snow skiers are all together effortlessly, because they are appropriating, responsively conforming themselves to the earth and sky in their "world," thus there are no collisions. Each human *being* is free in his own path.

Now let's look at the same snow-covered world as experienced by an inauthentic being-in-the-world. This human being climbs onto the seat of his snowmobile, guns the motor, and roars out into the pristine white world. His track smashes the snow into a hard surface— "just as good as a road"—destroying not only the fragile snow crystals, which he never even saw, but the underlying plants which no one will ever see again as their living roots are crushed. The roar crashes through the still air, rebounds off the rocky cliff, and soon fills the entire valley. All beings flee. The vibration knocks the fragile crystals from nearby trees so he seldom sees the fire-lit needles glow. The sky is darkened by the fumes from the engine; the purity of the air destroyed. The earth recedes from him and is no longer earth, but a hard, icy track. The sky recedes and is no longer the blue source of all, and the gods can never appear. The world this mortal takes part in is inauthentic. All in it has been *used* by him. All beings in it are subordinated to his ends, forced to serve his desires, and thus Being retreats. All that is left is speed, noise, and a subjective feeling of power. There is no possibility of a flowing interaction of human beings together in such a world. The only possible interaction is competition—who can get there first or who can climb up the steeper hill with the machine ripping still deeper into the living beings beneath. Competition is the natural outcome of human will alone.

The machine lays out a *useful* track with no conforming regard for the earth. The consistency of the snow (gift of the sky) is unimportant. The machine can crush any snow down into a *useful* track. Without the living interaction with earth and sky, as gravity and snow, there is no possibility for this human being to move in total freedom and harmony with other human beings, gravity, and snow in a mutual flow through the "world." The "world" of this mortal is inauthentic. All is made to serve his purpose but—there is no Being. He is left in his loneliness and the resulting anxiety drives him forth for more experiences to escape the anxiety.

As I have discovered, even the solitary powder snow skier can, similarly, refuse to let Being be. The cause may be as simple a matter as a photographer asking to film the skier's next run. Although it's the same still morning, the same light crystalline snow, the mortal

involved has put it all to *use*, subordinated to the end of skiing well for a film; therefore, Being and beings retreat. The snow is no longer a gift from the sky but a medium for making a good film; the animal is no longer a hoped-for but undemanded appearance of being, but either a *something* which adds to the film or causes trouble by marring that perfect turn. Being retreats— the sky, the earth, and the gods all retreat—and all that remains is a technically perfect ski run down the hill, which looks fine on the screen and makes money for the photographer; but there is no Being, and the loss is felt in the hollow emptiness inside.

The difference between authentic and inauthentic being-in-the-world is the heart of the matter. Heidegger's word for man is *Dasein,* which is often translated as "There-being," whose manner of being in the world *is* "in such a way as to comprehend Being." To be a human being *is* to be "concerned about Being." [275, 35] The word being, with a capital letter, is the fullness of Being; in the lower case it refers to beings in the world. Man is also called the "being-withheld-in-Nothingness." [343, 127] This may seem negative but, actually, *nothing* here is the fullness of possibility, not emptiness. We can only know Being itself as showing forth in our world as individual beings. These individual beings must be recognized by us so that Being can *be* in our world. If man remains open to Being, which means maintaining a state of awareness to what Being is, then through the events and things in his daily life Being can speak to him. On the other hand, if man views them from a self-sufficient standpoint asking, "What is the *use* of this to me?", he can never even recognize beings as other than himself. All things become objects to him and the world is there for his *use,* to serve his survival, so that in the end he becomes an object himself.

Howard Hughes was the perfect example of an inauthentic being-in-the-world. Throughout his life there was a continual, growing effort to preserve his life and accumulate money to insure that he could close off all danger—not only physical danger, but mental discomfort as well—so that in the end he lived in one small hotel room, "protected" from all disturbance by his "bodyguards," thereby also guarded from all possibility of being. Death, for him, was utterly terrifying because it meant the end of his being—the only being in his entire world. There was truly *nothing* else.

Being can only show itself to us as beings in our world. We cannot know Being as such in our mortal world, but in death, the being that we are returns into the fullness of Being. Rilke, the poet, compared this situation to the moon—which always has a side turned away from us—"that is not its opposite but its completion to perfection, to plenitude, to the real, whole, and full sphere and globe of being." [117, 124] It is important not to give this statement a too-narrow Christian interpretation. It does *not* mean that only life after death is real. On the contrary, it means that life in our mortal world is real, but in it we have not yet reached our total, full being. To reach this we die and return to the fullness of Being itself. This is why mortality is important to us. Mortals are necessary in the "world" to experience ever new facets of being, ever new possibilities of being.

The human being's difference from an animal does not consist specifically in his having a rational mind or in his being a tool-using animal. Animals have reason and animals use tools. The essential difference consists in this: "As an animal man is still unborn." Arnold Gehlen, a well-known German anthropologist, in his book, *Der Mensch,* "sees man's trait of possibilities or openness in his being unspecialized as regards his living milieu, and thus unprepared for it and unequipped for a certain direction in life." Man is not firmly set in a certain "way" or "path" as animals are. Man is really in an embryonic state and therefore open to possibilities. "Amid these possibilities man himself is, or can be, active in completing himself or in giving birth to himself." [343, 127] Man is continually in a process of completion without reaching it. "Self-completion would mean the cessation of man's being man: it would mean his death." [343, 139] Man is continually proceeding toward completion so he is continually dying. According to Vycinas, this means that man in his cultural life, in his "cults," makes a dip into Nature's source, Being, "rises from it in order to make another dip, and then does so over and over again." [343, 145] An authentic culture is this openness toward Being; such a culture provides ritual occasions during festivals which allow for the manifesting of new modes of being.

To live authentically is to "dwell," according to Heidegger. This is concisely defined by Hart and Maraldo: "Dwelling is not primarily inhabiting but taking care of (*schonen*) and creating that space within which something comes into its own and flourishes. Dwelling is primarily saving (*retten*), in the older sense of setting something free to become itself, what it essentially is . . . Dwelling is that which cares for things so that they essentially presence and come into their own . . ." [118, 131] However, to fully understand Heidegger's concept, *dwelling,* necessitates some knowledge of his own way of dwelling during his lifetime.

Martin Heidegger's Relationship to His *Place*

When through a rent in the rain-clouded
sky a ray of the sun suddenly glides
over the gloom of the meadows . . .

> We never come to thoughts. They come
>   to us.

> That is the proper hour of discourse.
>   Martin Heidegger   [117, 6]

For those human beings who are trying to find their way back into the earth family by trying to live authen-tically on the earth and who are searching out the paths of Being so they can once again learn from the earth, it is well to listen for awhile to this stubborn descendant of peasants who was born in the German Black Forest. Although he was later an academic philosopher, he always retained his ties to the earth; and at a crucial time in his life he returned to the forest to live in a small cottage and rethink Being. This crucial time in Heidegger's thinking is called the "step back" or "reversal" or "turn around."

Martin Heidegger was born in 1889 into a Catholic family, joined the Jesuits as a novice after high school, and studied Catholic theology at the University of Freiburg. Heidegger states that ". . . the first philosophical text through which I worked my way, again and again from 1907 on, was Franz Brentano's dissertation: *On the Manifold Sense of Being in Aristotle* (1862)." A quotation from Aristotle was on the title page: "A being becomes manifest in many ways." Heidegger says that behind this phrase is the "question that determined the way of my thought: what is the pervasive, simple, unified determination of Being that permeates all of its multiple meanings? . . . What, then, does Being mean?" [119, x] Since that time Heidegger kept to his own way—the "path of thinking" on Being—and it led him far from his Catholic beginnings and farther still from the suppositions of our culture; yet curiously enough, his "path of thinking" had all along been inspired by his ties to his native *place*, the Black Forest region of southwestern Germany, where he lived for most of his life as a professor at the University of Freiburg, except for six years at the University of Marburg. During the early 1930's he was twice offered a more prestigious professorship in Berlin, "but he declined, preferring to remain in home territory." [115]

In 1928 the cottage Todtnauberg in the mountains near Freiburg was built. Throughout most of his life he spent a great deal of time at Todtnauberg, his own *place,* living there continuously after the war and during his later retirement. According to *The New York Times* article, written at the time of his death, he was "an avid hiker and an accomplished skier* who used to hold seminars on the way up mountains and then ski back down with his students . . . He was at home among villagers and uneasy in the midst of academic pretension . . . He remained open to poetry when this was not in style, and he never abandoned the conviction that man is tied to history and the earth on which he walks." [91] He died May 26, 1976, at the age of 86.

An indication of the depth of Heidegger's relationship to his *place* is given in one of his later works, *Erläuterungen zu Hölderline Dichtung*, where he investigates a poem by Hölderlin in which the poet is shown as the one who is returning home to the "place of proximity to the primeval source." He has been far away in the

---

*In *Martin Heidegger, An Illustrated Study* by Walter Biemel, there is a photo of Heidegger and his wife on skis, taken in 1959 on the evening before his seventieth birthday (photo 38). Photo 26 is of his snow-covered cottage at Todtnauberg.

high Alps, snowy sublime mountains, but having experienced Being there, he can now return home and tell his own people what Being is as manifested in their own *place*: "Now *our* flowers and *our* woodlands bestow upon him the joy that consists essentially in sheltering what is true . . ." This translation is by Richardson who explains, "Letting beings appear as what they are means exposing them in their truth, their beauty in the Beon [Being] which they are." [275, 457] Further insights into Heidegger's concept of Being are given below in the section, "The Path of Thinking," which is not an attempt to describe Heidegger's work, which would be a formidable task, for volumes have been devoted to it; but merely a brief dipping far enough into his thought to comprehend some of his terms useful for all of us who are heirs of European thought, with its long neglect of thinking on Being. Perhaps only now, in the late seventies, with the growth of ecological consciousness, will this late phase of Heidegger's work become more known. This phase has been called the "step back" or "turn around," where he turned from preoccupation with the human being toward a consideration of Being itself.

The Path of Thinking

When the mountain brook in night's
stillness tells of its plunging
over the boulders . . .

> The oldest of the old follows behind
> us in our thinking and yet it
> comes to meet us.

> That is why thinking holds to the
> coming of what has been, and
> is remembrance.

. . .

> We may venture the step back out
> of philosophy into the thinking of
> Being as soon as we have grown
> familiar with the provenance of
> thinking.

Martin Heidegger   [117, 10]

Heidegger did not consider himself a philosopher but a thinker on Being. He has been called an existentialist, which he adamantly denied; and a phenomenologist, which he said he had either passed beyond or that he was the only one who remained true. He's been called mystifying, obscure, and suffering from chronic hyphenitis. All of which is true, in a way, but necessary because all of our language has been based upon a subject-object relationship; however, in the chapter on Mind, we began to see that consciousness may very well transcend this duality. Such a consciousness cannot be truly represented through language built upon a dualistic base. The only way to express Heidegger's concepts of mutual interrelationship, which are completely other than the subject-object polarity, is to use hyphens in order to show

that the interaction is more complex than simple subject-object. Other cultures, such as the Hopi, do have such a language.

Fortunately, when I first encountered Heidegger, I was in a *place* where it was possible to listen for Being: a rock outcrop 8,700 feet high, surrounded by the ice and snow of the Blue Glacier on Mr. Olympus, in the very center of the Olympic National Park Wilderness area. I was doing the cooking for the crew of a glacier project. Realizing that I would have ample time between chores to read and being curious about Heidegger, I had brought along *Martin Heidegger and the Pre-Socratics* by George J. Seidel. [288] When I began reading it, I discovered that the very sections where the author admitted finding difficulties in Heidegger's thinking, I found the most clear. Seidel had a Christian orientation, and it seemed to me that his difficulties came from trying to fit Heidegger into the Christian system. Since I was in a location far from the academic or the Christian world, I was much closer to Being and saw more clearly what Heidegger was attempting in his thinking.

Heidegger himself, during his quest for Being, spent a great deal of time at Todtnauberg, his retreat on a mountain. I have since found that the best introduction to Heidegger is Vincent Vycinas' *Earth and Gods*. Vycinas is also a man close to the earth. His grandfather, although a Christian, was like a Lithuanian *krivis* priest in the old Lithuanian cult of nature gods. While writing *Earth and Gods* and other books on Heidegger, Vycinas lived in the British Columbia forest in an attempt to start what we would call a commune, but it was actually a transplanted, Nature-cult, Lithuanian village. Later, when this failed, he lived on Salt Spring Island in a salt water inlet on Vancouver Island.

In the present chapter, I have quoted a few lines in three different places from Heidegger's work: *From the Experience of Thought*—a series of epigrams in poetic style—because, as Richardson points out, these pages concern Heidegger's reflections upon the experience of Being "made presumably, in the mountain haunts of Todtnauberg." Richardson goes on to say, "By reason of the poetic description, we have some knowledge of the beings about him through which Being came." [275, 553] In other words, this work provides insight into the manner in which thoughts came to Heidegger from Nature, from his *place*, Todtnauberg.

As the quotation from Heidegger's work at the opening of this section indicates, he begins by going back to the ancient Greek thinkers. "Thinking on Being," as Heidegger understood this term, has not been attempted since the time of the pre-Socratics. The early Greek mind had a sense of the wholeness of things—the modern mind takes things apart to analyze. The Greeks did not split the human being into a body/mind duality until the time of Socrates and Plato. [153, 173] Thales of Miletus was considered the first philosopher, and Anaximander was his successor. These men were "practical" men, as they worked with things in the world. Anaximander made the first map and guided people to a new colony. [153, 180] It has been suggested that later Greek thought lost this unity because of the increase of slaves, with the result that the intellectuals were divorced from physical interaction with the earth.

Before Plato, truth was concerned with "the universal presence which is the presence of nature." [344, 49] After Plato this was replaced by truth as an idea. "For Plato . . . ideas were more fundamentally being than nature itself." [341, 143] Vycinas goes on: "When physics (Nature) is no longer breaking forward, governing, and holding everything in order, it becomes the field of matter which can be formed and exploited," [341, 144] "while for the early Greeks, the truth was *aletheia*, the disclosure of Being itself, in our world as beings." [343, 143] Or, as Sallis notes, "Heidegger reads Western history as a choice dating from Socrates and Plato, to regard man as the decisive factor in being. This decision remained for a long time more or less implicit until it emerged as the cogito in the philosophy of Descartes, as the I-principle (the 'I Think . . .') of Kant, and as the Romantic belief in the infinite productiveness and self-creativeness of the ego." [280, 61]

Western thinking from the time of Plato became anthropocentric—man was the focus. All things in the actual world, according to Plato, are formed or shaped by the ideas of the ideal world, thus limiting Being. The final blow to the thinking on Being came with the rise of Christianity and its "attempt to murder the gods." [297, 3] All Being was locked into one Being called God, and all access to *this* Being was through the Church alone. And Being retreated, hid, and became increasingly inaccessible.

The best way to begin to understand Heidegger's thought is with his analysis of a fragment from the pre-Socratic Greek philosopher, Anaximander, which—in loose translation, compiled from many sources—reads: "*Apeiron* (Being or The Unlimited) is the coming forth and arriving at the condition of being non-concealed . . . and it is that into which they return when they perish . . ." In other words, Being is that which comes forth and is non-concealed and then leaves and passes again into the concealed state. Being comes to presence in our world as individual beings, and these individual beings go back into the fullness of Being (death), but this does not mean that we can understand Being itself. "Being is the constant coming into openness, the constant breaking into the world . . . That which enables everything to appear; itself appears merely as that which constantly remains in concealment." [341, 114 and 141] Being could be defined as "that which gives possibilities." [280, 39]

Vycinas helps us to understand how the event of reality occurs in the world of the human being. Of all the commentators on Heidegger, Vycinas most succinctly explains the human being as *part of* the fourfold:

. . . the event of . . . reality, Nature's play, is the transcendental movement in the sense of arranging or breaking-open trails (*Bewegung*—Heidegger) or ways for beings or entities . . . Human language is a response to the cosmic language of Nature's spatio-temporal play. Man does not respond to cosmic language as it is in itself; he can only respond to it as reflected in or assembled by things or entities. Entities reflect or assemble space always as earth-bound—time as sky-bound, and movement or play as brought into the human *Dasein* by gods and received or responded to by men in their mortality. Earth, sky, gods and mortals are not entities: they are transcendental realities. Consequently, human language is rendered possible by a complex cluster of transcendental powers (we often for brevity's sake call them gods!). None of these transcendental realities is known to us unless in or through the entities or phenomena of our world.   [343, 178-9]

As an analogy to the relationship of Being and beings in our world, Vycinas uses Eugen Fink's idea that we never see light itself. We only see it at various angles or reflected by specific things.

In spite of the distortions or "impurities" of the transcendental powers in man's world, these are disclosed or come to light only in it—in man's world—and they are so disclosed by man's responsiveness, by his language . . . Language is the bringing to light and the guarding, within itself, of the transcendental powers of reality which are anterior to things and which render things meaningful and substantial.

Things become meaningful and substantial by being set on the way or trails . . . assigned to them. Spatio-temporal play—the language of Nature or of Being—sets things on their ways or trails. This is why Heidegger understands Nature's play or movement (*Bewegung*) as "trail-breaking" (*Be-wegung*). This interrelation is much more clear in German than it is in English, since the word "motion" in German is *Bewegung* and the word "way" or "trail" is "*Weg*." When Heidegger says that "language is the world-moving relay . . . the interrelation of all relations," he uses the word "moving" in the sense of "trail-making" or "trail-breaking." [343, 254-256]

Heidegger himself said: "To break a way, for instance, through a snow-covered field, means even today in the Alemmanic-Swabian dialect, *wegen*. This transitively used verb means: to make a way, to hold it ready while making it. *Be-wegen* (*Be-wegung*) means, thought of in this manner, no longer to carry something back and forth on an already existing road, but to bring a way itself forward, and to be this way." [121, 261]

The way that thought must follow is not a well-laid out road which each can follow in his turn. Instead it is a path, a way that each must step-by-step break open for himself, "the thinker must let every step of the way come to him as he proceeds." [275, 616] Being is not a given way laid out like a road, but is shown forth by the relationship discovered anew at every step as he moves along the path.

In order to fully understand this important concept, *Be-wegung*, it is necessary to consider the environment in which Heidegger did most of his later thinking—the snow-covered mountains of Todtnauberg. As mentioned earlier, Heidegger would hold seminars on the way up the mountain and then ski back down with his students.

Climbing up mountains on skis necessitates breaking open the way through the unbroken snow. This activity would provide Heidegger with an excellent metaphor for the "opening of a way" for Being's appearance in the human world. Furthermore, while skiing down with his students, it would be clear that each human being was making his own path, "breaking open the way," each slightly differently, because the combined effect of terrain, snow, and gravity would differ for each person. Thus another metaphor was provided for the human being's response to Being, which sets him on his way as a being in his "world." The fourfold of Heidegger is concretely present in the act of skiing down a mountain, because of the mutual appropriating or fitting one to the other of the earth (gravity and terrain), the sky (snow or weather), and the almost tangible presence of the gods. Thus awaiting the action or reaction of Nature, not forcing Nature, letting "every step of the way come to him as he proceeds," is the essence of skiing in unbroken snow. It is also the essence of the mutual appropriation of the fourfold which permits the many manifestations of Being as beings in the human's world.

Vycinas provides more help here when he writes concerning Nature's movement (*Be-wegung*) as trail-breaking. "Trail-breaking provides things with temporal-spatial trails, on which, first of all, all four transcendental powers acquire mutual nearness of interbelonging, and secondly, man encounters his things as real in his living environment." [343, 177] Heidegger's explanation is that this ". . . 'spacing-in' breaks trails for the encounter of the four milieus of the world: of earth and sky, god and man. This encounter is the world's play." [121, 138]

In Heidegger's concept of *Be-wegung*, the *trails* or *ways* "must be thought of in the way Lao-tze thought of his *Tao*, which means *logos* or ordering cosmic wisdom anchored in Nature herself." [343, 256] There has been discussion among scholars as to whether Heidegger was influenced by the Chinese concept of Tao. [275, 571] It seems to me, on the contrary, that both the Chinese concept of the Tao and Heidegger's concepts came directly from Nature. In the case of the old Taoist sages, they came from walking on mountains, and in Heidegger's case by his skiing and hiking in the mountains near his retreat, Todtnauberg. Of further interest is the fact that (as seen in Chapter 2) the Chinese character for *tao* shows a step and a halt, and then another step. In a similar fashion to "break a way . . . through a snow-covered field" on skis is done by pushing one ski forward and putting one's weight on it. Then a slight halt is made at this point while the other ski is brought up and in turn pushed forward, weighted, etc.

The connotations of Heidegger's *way* shed light on Don Juan's paths. Don Juan said, "Today I am neither a warrior nor a diablero. For me there is only the travelling on the paths that have a heart, on any path that may have a heart . . . And there I travel — looking, looking, breathlessly." [53, 195] This "looking breathlessly" is the awaiting of Being.

All three of these ways of knowing depend on whole-body thinking, not just left-brain thinking: The Taoist sages *walked* over the mountains as they thought; Heidegger *skied* down a slope. Throughout all the books in the series, Don Juan tries to get Castaneda to quit thinking only within his head and begin to learn how to use *whole-body* knowledge. Whole-body thinking provides some understanding of the possibilities inherent in the interaction between mind-within-the-skull and mind-at-large, the environment. Or, as Edith Cobb explains it, "In the creative perceptions of poet and child we are close to the biology of thought itself — close, in fact, to the ecology of imagination, in which the energies of the body and mind as a unit, an ecosystem, and the energies of nature combine in a mutual endeavor to adapt to nature, to culture, and to the societies devised by man to embody culture." [58, 109]

Whole-body thinking must take into account the things in the environment as well as the environment itself; hence the importance of the "art work" and the "thing" in Heidegger's thinking. In an important passage in *The Thing* [*Das Ding*], Heidegger is concerned to describe the world and its presencing, its "worlding." "This [passage] is decisive," according to Hofstadter, the translator of Heidegger's works, "because, if Heidegger gets close to saying what the Being of beings is, taking them all together, in their world, it is in and through this description of the world's being as such, the true and sole dimension of which is 'nearing' . . ." In this passage Heidegger defines the world as ". . . the *ereignende* mirror-play of the simple onefold of earth and sky, divinities and mortals." [117, xix] Briefly, *ereignung* (the verb being *ereignen*) can be translated as mutual appropriation or mutual fit, one to the other; but to understand the deeper meanings, it is necessary to investigate the "thing" in Heidegger's writing.

In an earlier work, *Der Ursprung des Kunstwerkes*, based on a lecture given in 1935, Heidegger discussed the work of art as the assembler of the fourfold, while by 1950, in *Das Ding*, his thought had broadened in the sense that the very "thingness" of a thing assembles the world through its bringing together the fourfold. Heidegger's example is a pitcher or jug. The essence of a jug consists in the pouring of liquid from it — water or wine.

The jug brings together the water from the deep rock of the earth, the water which is the marriage of sky and earth. The outpouring of the jug is what makes it a jug. The outpouring of the jug quenches the thirst of mortals on ordinary days; on festival days, however, the jug is used in a "libation poured out for the immortal gods." Heidegger goes on to point out that the word "gush" comes from the Middle English and is related to Greek and Indo-European words, which all have the meaning of "to offer in sacrifice." A further explanation of this concept is contained in the discussion earlier of the Greek Eleusinian Mysteries. Recall the unstable jugs which stood in the cave and which were tipped over so that the liquid within flowed out or "gushed" out into the earth. Heidegger continues:

> To pour a gush, when it is achieved in its essence, thought through with sufficient generosity, and genuinely uttered, is to donate, to offer in sacrifice, and hence to give . . . In the gift of the outpouring that is a libation, the divinities stay in their own way, they who receive back the gift of giving as the gift of the donation. In the gift of the outpouring, mortals and divinities each dwell in their different ways. Earth and sky dwell in the gift of the outpouring. In the gift of the outpouring earth and sky, divinities and mortals dwell *together all at once* . . .
>
> The gift of the outpouring is a gift because it stays earth and sky, divinities and mortals . . . Staying appropriates. It brings the four into the light of their mutual belonging . . .
>
> The jug's essential nature, its presencing, so experienced and thought of in these terms, is what we call *thing*. We are now thinking this word by way of the gathering-appropriating staying of the fourfold. [117, 173–174]

This way of thinking at first seems strange to us. Here it is necessary to remember our Western predicament of not having thought on Being since Plato's time. For a similar view of the world, it is helpful to turn to the Sioux medicine man, Black Elk, and his mythic view of life. In describing the rite of the sweat lodge, *Inipi*, he points out that the rocks used in the sweat lodge are the earth, the steam is the meeting of the rocks (the earth) and the gift of the sky (water). When the sacred pipe is lit, it is offered to Heaven, Earth, and the four directions, and it is then passed around the circle. "As it passes around, each man mentions his relationship to the person next to him, and after everybody has smoked, they all say together: '*mitakuye oyasin*!' (we are all relatives!) . . . The door of the lodge is closed, and the holy man at the east begins to pray in the darkness: 'Behold! All that moves in the universe is here!' [41, 53] Furthermore, the "sacred pipe" itself is the "thing" which "things the world" in another rite, when Black Elk says, "Behold this pipe which we—with the Earth, the four Powers, and with all things—have offered to You. We know that we are related and are one with all things of the heavens and the earth, and we know that all things that move are a people as we. We all wish to live and increase in a holy manner. The Morning Star and the dawn which comes with it, the moon of the night, and the stars of the heavens are all brought together here . . ." [41, 97–98]

Joseph Brown, who recorded Black Elk's teachings, explains: "In filling a pipe, all space (represented by the offerings to the powers of the six directions) and all things (represented by the grains of tobacco) are contracted within a single point (the bowl or heart of the pipe), so that the pipe contains, or really *is*, the universe." [41, 21]

This account of Black Elk's relationship to Being underlines further why there is required, as Heidegger states, an "overcoming of the history of metaphysics in its entirety from Plato to Nietzsche." [203, xxi] We must return to the very beginning of Western tradition, "to the basic words which have preserved the most basic experiences of Being which the pre-Socratics had." But we cannot simply go back to the beginning; we must create a new and different beginning of thinking on Being, "by re-trieving it in its originality more originally," in Heidegger's words. [203, xxi] Heidegger's continual attempt is to re-think or retrieve the authentic sense of Being, as conceived by the early Greeks, whether he focuses on a "thing" such as the wine jug or on Indo-Germanic root words or on poetry itself. We have seen above how this kind of thinking is not limited to the mind-within-the-skull of the human being but extends to mind-at-large. Heidegger explains further: "The beginning must be begun again, more originally, with all the strangeness, darkness, and insecurity that a true beginning brings with it. Retrieve as we understand it is anything but a better way of continuing the past by the methods of the past." [203, xxi] According to Richardson, "It is worth-while insisting that this is not so much a step back from the 'present' and into the 'past,' as through the past and into the future, . . . [into Being] in continual ad-vent. But this spring into man's Origin is a return to the element that he has never left and cannot leave, for it is that by which he is." [275, 612] The further implications of this position, as implied in Gorsline and House's "future primitive," are explored in Part IV of this book.

Heidegger's work occurs "within the long evening of the spirit which intervenes between the time of the departure of the gods and the time of those not yet come." [10, ix] At a symposium held in 1966, on the occasion of Heidegger's eightieth birthday, Heidegger wrote a letter which made it clear that he did not want his books to be made the source of any kind of exact scholarship in the usual sense, but that he intended them to be a way to lead each person to investigate and to experience on his own the same questioning which inspired Heidegger's own quest for Being. The letter ended with, "I thank all participants for the interest which they show in my efforts in the dangerous field of thinking." [280, 11]

Nowhere is this kind of thinking more dangerous than when it comes to the subject of gods. By now the other three aspects of the fourfold: earth, sky, and mortals have become a little clearer. For preliminary help in this difficult matter of thinking on the gods, I am going to devote a few pages to the Japanese "way of the gods." Japan is the only modern nation which, due to fortuitous circumstances, has been able to carry its ancestral primitive relationship to the gods down to modern times as the root of its living culture.

10. The Way of the Gods

I was privileged to live in Japan for a few months in the winter of 1971-72. My husband, an expert in the field of snow research, was asked by Professor Kuroiwa of the Japanese Institute for Low Temperature Science to come to Hokkaido, Japan's northernmost island, to work with them during the time of the 1972 Olympics. I arrived in Sapporo, capital of Hokkaido, in early January of 1972, knowing no Japanese whatsoever except for the word for mountain, *yama*, and practicing no spiritual discipline except for mountain climbing, skiing, and Tai Chi (which is, of course, Chinese, not Japanese). Fortunately, my basic approach of learning from Nature and my accumulated knowledge of American Indian ritual, provided me with a sufficient background to begin to understand Japanese culture. Furthermore, because I had the discipline of Tai Chi, I had no urgent need to rush out and join a Zen center as many Americans do. This left me more open and aware of other influences in Japan.

So I did Tai Chi facing the mountains around Sapporo and watched the incredible Japanese snow and, later, began skiing and watched the relationship between snow and the Japanese people. As I met more Japanese who spoke English, I began asking a few tentative questions. Gradually, a whole world opened up, which is there on every side in Japan, but hidden.

I noticed early in my stay that in every neighborhood in Sapporo and in every valley we went through on the ubiquitous Japanese National Railroad, there was a Shinto shrine with its *torii*, a curved archway; but in all of Sapporo I could find only one Buddhist temple. When I asked our new Japanese friends in the academic circle of the Institute about Zen, they told me that Buddhism was "for dying in"; Shinto was "for living."

Then came the opening day of the Olympics. As a learned Western guest, my husband was given ringside seats at the opening ceremony. Just above us was the Emperor's box. The day was incredibly cold and remained cloudy until the Emperor (descended from the sun) stepped into his box. When he arrived, the sun immediately broke through. (Jung calls this syncronocity.). The sun stayed out until the end of the Olympic ceremony and then promptly disappeared again. For the opening ritual, a young maiden skated in carrying the Olympic torch, which had been delivered to Sapporo by relays of runners. She was truly beautiful and remote in her concentration and seriousness. There was not a sound from the crowd as she ceremoniously made her circuit of the huge amphitheater. She reverently handed the fire to a young man who ran up an enormous flight of steps to the top of the stadium and lit the perpetual fire, which would burn there through the Olympics. The breathless hush of the crowd lasted until the main torch was lit and then was released in joy at this successful conclusion. This entire opening was truly sacred in the ancient sense. Fire is important as a purifying element in the *way of the gods*. It was ritually correct that the woman, who has the *power*, delivered the fire to the man who then carried it aloft.

Of course, this was followed by the usual Olympic parade of athletes in their nationalistic competition, but the opening was truly Japanese and truly a rite of human beings meeting with their gods. This, of course, was the original meaning of the ancient Greek games. This was my first glimpse of the Japanese relationship to the sacred.

My next glimpse came deep inside the Kurobe gorge, the hydroelectric complex which furnishes power for Tokyo and Osaka. It is built in the midst of vertical mountains. We visited the site where, during construction in the 1930's, one of the most spectacular avalanches of modern times occurred. During the construction, men slept in a two-story concrete bunkhouse, on a rock promontory, which was reached by tunnel. When the day shift came off work and headed out through this opening toward their bunkhouse—there was no building. Nothing at all. It had vanished. There had been an avalanche, but even an avalanche leaves some traces, and there were none. Not until later that Spring was it finally discovered what had happened. An avalanche of major proportions had roared down several gullies. When it hit the bottom it rebounded into the air with such force that it picked up the two-story concrete bunkhouse, carried it further up into the air and across an intervening ridge and smashed it up against a vertical rock wall. All eighty men sleeping in it were killed and the wreckage found at the bottom of the cliff. Then it was realized that a gap in the trees lining the ridge was the very place where the building had gone over the ridge before slamming into the cliff. Even some forty years later, when we were there, this gaping hole in the tree line on the ridge was still visible, but standing there and looking at it—far above us—there really isn't any way you can believe that a concrete building could be lifted that high into the air. Since then the entire complex has been put underground.

We were heading in an electric train deep into the heart of this underground complex when our train had to pull out to let a work train by. Our Japanese guides led us into a little way station to get warm. Here, in a rough workingman's way station, the only decoration was a tiny bonsai tree with a scroll behind it—living nature enshrined, in the midst of a vertical world of rock and avalanches.

In Japan, nature is powerful and capricious. I have never seen it snow as hard as in the streets of Sapporo—even harder than at Alta where it may snow an inch an hour. Walking through the streets one day, the snow piled up on my arm to a depth of four inches in only three blocks. I went into a shop thinking, "This is the end of the world. Don't they know it? No city can survive snow at this rate." I came out fifteen minutes later and the sky was bright blue. Sapporo is off the coast of Siberia and when the ocean air meets the Siberian cold, the weather is totally unpredictable. But this is not unusual in Japan, where typhoons routinely kill hundreds and earthquakes occur frequently! Surrounded by totally powerful and capricious nature, the Japanese had two choices: gloomy despair (as in some parts of Asia) or all-embracing joy in *life* in all its aspects. The Japanese chose joy.

From the wife of one of the professors, I learned that gathering wild vegetables in the spring is of such importance that the Emperor and Empress are the first Japanese out in the Spring to engage in the ritual. Again, as in primitive groups, a very important early Spring ritual is the gathering and eating of the first greens in a kind of thanksgiving to the returning life of nature.

Travelling through northern Honshu, visiting avalanche sites, I noticed that in every single tiny valley or hamlet, everywhere that the Japanese National Railroad took us, was a Shinto shrine surrounded by massive old trees—long gone from all the surrounding countryside. On this journey I began asking questions of the young Japanese scientists who met us or travelled with us. I got nowhere. Then on two separate occasions, I happened to be alone with each of these men. Then, rather than being diffident and polite in cautious English, the response was quite different. We plunged into fractured English. Each had a chance to ask dozens of questions important to him, and I had a chance to ask my questions. On each occasion the man quite openly wanted to help and it was obvious these things were important to him but, as each said, he had never ever thought of these things in English and had no words to express them.

We climbed Mt. Yotei, the Fuji of the North, a perfectly symmetrical volcano, with a retired Japanese professor of geology, Dr. Hashimoto. Long ago, when he was still a student, all of his close friends had been killed in an avalanche while climbing in the Japanese Alps, but he had gone on climbing, including the Himalayas. He had built a little cottage at the foot of Mt. Yotei and climbed it often. He was probably seventy, yet we could barely keep up with him—he never stopped moving up and up the mountain. His actions, together with his brief answers to my questions, taught me more about the deep relationship to nature which is inherent in Japanese culture.

The real breakthrough came the evening we left Sapporo on our way back to the States. Professor Higashi and his wife had been gone from Sapporo and returned just in time to invite us to dinner. Both of them had lived abroad a great deal and so they knew English words in many different fields. This was my last chance, so I plunged in unceremoniously and found I was on the right track. Even more important, he showed me a book, just published, which could help me. By this time, he was as excited as I because he had never met another American who had ever asked him these questions. On our way through Tokyo we bought Fosco Mariani's *Japan, Patterns of Continuity*. Mariani is an Italian who has been involved with Japan for more than thirty years. He came originally to do research on the Ainu for his doctorate in anthropology and was a lecturer at Kyoto University. He was interned during the war and almost starved to death. Mariani survived and returned to Japan later to make films, still an ardent admirer of Japanese culture.

In his preface, he refers to how confusing modern Japan is to a foreigner. "But deep down, one detects a monolithic something that functions like a structural frame holding all parts of the complicated machinery together. Shocks, blows, bumps are absorbed and eventually converted into stimulants to further progress." [198, 8] This something is the underlying *way of the gods* or Shinto. Our preconceived Western ideas of what constitutes progress are shaken by Japan, says Mariani. When "We find that this pagan entity is not only civilized but advanced, prosperous, disciplined, industrious, and progressive, then the situation becomes absurd, ludicrous, blasphemous . . ." [198, 12] Even worse for the closed Western mind, Japan isn't even pagan in the sense of Greek or Roman paganism, which we have come to tolerate. Japan is pagan in the ancient primitive sense. There man is one with his natural environment. Trees, stones, and mountains are as much real beings as man, and all these are divine—a truly outrageous view to the average European; but possibly of the utmost importance for those who are trying to find their way back to living in harmony with the earth. "In Nature is the Piccadilly Circus, the Times Square . . . the Place de la Concorde—a point from which all avenues of thought depart, and to which they finally return." [198, 14] When Mariani first went to Japan he was told that Buddhism was by far the most important spiritual influence but "after a war, an Olympiad, a world Expo, and thirty years of loving study and familiarity with Japan, I have come to a different conclusion . . . Shinto, often unrecognizable, is all around us, an invisible fluid running throughout Japanese society." [198, 20 and 21]

The word Shinto has unfortunate connotations to Americans because of state Shintoism, emphasized during the war; so, in general, I will continue to use the translation, *way of the gods*, so our minds can be freed from the negative connotations attached to its Japanese equivalent.

On three separate occasions throughout its history Japan went through intense cultural growth spurts: The first one began about A.D. 400—Japan achieved political unity and was at the end of the bronze age; thus it was about 1,500 years behind China at that time. But in the next two centuries, through its contacts with China, it had accelerated its progress to the point where it had caught up with China. It thus achieved a growth almost unique in world history before the industrial revolution.

Fourteen centuries later, in 1854, Commodore Perry visited Japan, and the Japanese again decided to catch up—this time with the West. And they did so. The third surge followed Japan's defeat in 1945. The Japanese caught up so well that Herman Kahn predicted in *The Emerging Japanese Superstate* that Japan has "just begun its climb" and will become "the first truly post-industrial culture." [147, 182–82]

Each time Japan decided to move in a new direction, it moved successfully. But between these epochs of change, Japan achieved even more momentous results. Japan had an uninterrupted period of 300 years of peace—longer than any other country has ever had—during the years 794–1185. Kyoto, enclosed within a ring of mountains, was then the capital, the center of a flourishing, sophisticated, richly aesthetic culture, which involved probably no more than 3,000 persons—the rest were servants. Much of Japan's future culture was shaped during this era. Mariani sums it up: "It was a period of rarefied search for perfection, both in poetry and in doctrine . . ." [198, 242] The source of this creativity, which is reflected in all of Japanese culture, lies in Japan's *way of the gods*.

Kami is the word for god, divine spirit, "personalized individualistically." After contact with the Chinese mainland, the Japanese developed a word for their religion, and it was called Kami Nagara. Nagara means "natural" or "the same as," so Kami Nagara means "whatever is, is Kami," or divine spirit. Only later did the Chinese-based word, *Shinto*, come into use. The syllable *to* comes from the Chinese *tao*, or "way," and *Shin* means "divine spirit," hence *way of the gods*. [208, 58 and 59] Divine spirit in Shinto is the universe in every aspect, seeking self-creative growth. It is important to remember that sacred forms such as mountains, fire, and rivers do not have spirits dwelling *in* them, but everything *is* divine spirit itself.

According to Motoori (1730–1801), the great historian and a leader in the movement to restore the pure, original *way of the gods*, following a prolonged Buddhist influence: "The term *kami* is applied in the first place to the various deities of heaven and earth mentioned in the ancient records, as well as to their spirits which reside in the shrines where they are worshipped. Moreover, not only human beings, but birds, beasts, plants and trees, seas and mountains, and all other things whatsoever which deserve to be dreaded and revered for the extraordinary and pre-eminent powers which they possess, are called *kami* . . . It is not their spirits which are meant. The word applied directly to the seas or mountains themselves . . ." [9, 8 and 9]

The reason that Japan's *way of the gods* is so important to us is because it has come down to us uncontaminated by self-conscious analyzing and thinking. Fosco Mariani explains: "Over the centuries they have resisted first the huge cultural pressure of China and Buddhism, and then that of Europe and the West, and have maintained intact their own primary, original form of worship, linking them with nature and the gods." [199, 132] Actually, the coming of Buddhist ideas into Japan helped preserve the continuity of the *way of the gods*. Buddhist religious dogmas furnished the rationalizations which some required for peace of mind, while leaving undisturbed the living primitive religion, which has continued in a relatively undiluted form to the present time. Thus, Japanese culture has never been cut off from its roots in the living relationship of early man and nature, while our Western culture had its living continuity cut at the time of Plato. By the year 712 the Japanese were using Chinese ideograms, and it was then that the first written account of the myths was compiled, the *Kojiki*. Only much later, in the early 1700's, did the Japanese engage in any kind of metaphysical speculation. Unfortunately, those Japanese who did so were all too anxious to prove things in Christian terms. These distortions can be avoided by reference to Joseph W.T. Mason's *The Meaning of Shinto*. Mason spent most of his last years writing this book. Following his retirement from *The London Daily Express* in 1931, he went to Japan specifically to study Shinto.

He had written his first philosophical work, *Creative Freedom*, in 1926 at the suggestion of Henri Bergson. His Shinto studies late in life were a direct outgrowth of this earlier work, for he had discovered in Shinto a living tradition aimed specifically at creative evolution. Mason spent most of the last years of his life in Japan studying Shinto in the firm belief that it held the best hope for the creative evolution of mankind. His book appeared as the U.S. and Japan were heading for war, and in such a climate it met with no success. There is as yet no better popular work on Shinto. [136]

In the *way of the gods* "there is no separation between the universe and divine creative spirit. The universe is divine creative spirit extending itself as matter and life. Matter and life are divine spirit self-creating itself in different manifestations, but always divine spirit." [208, 44] There is no omnipotent mechanism such as the Christian God, as we can see in the *Kojiki's* account of creation: "Now when Chaos had begun to condense, but force and form were not yet manifest, and there was nought named, nought done, who could know its shape?" [208, 49] Mariani tells us that "this world is not an image, a shadow, a reflection of something more perfect or more significant, but rather it represents the ultimate and final reality . . . The world is good; 'man is a *kami*'—Motoori Norinaga; 'Man is the *kami* stuff of the world'—K. Chikafusa; work is good; wealth is good; fruits are good; sex is good . . ." [198, 22-23]

Chaos began to condense and Heaven and Earth first separated, the three *kamis* "performed the commencement of creation, and then vanished." The first *kami*, the "Center of Heaven Kami" never comes back into the records: "In him; the emphasis falls . . . on the idea of 'commencement,' as the creative impetus, initiating itself and thereafter self-developing, not being subjected to an omnipotent center of Heaven mechanism . . . directing the course of the universe. The universe itself is Heaven, objectified and self-creating its future." [208, 50] The Center of Heaven Kami can be likened to the original Tao. Far Eastern peoples generally conceive of the universe as developing from the Tao by means of the "ceaseless interplay" of yin and yang. "But it must be pointed out that the underlying principle in nature's unique law between the pair of opposites—Yin and Yang—is harmony, balance or equilibrium, or more exactly, the Vital Centre . . . Extremism is not correct because there exists no axis around which the bipolar whole harmoniously revolves." [131, 421]

Other *kami* appear and finally, after a time, the first Heavenly *kami* who procreate sexually: the "Male-who-invites," Izanagi, and the "Female-who-invites," Izanami. Through sexual intercourse they produce the islands of Japan. For brevity we must skip over many events and come to the time when Amaterasu, the sun goddess, hides in a cave and leaves the world in darkness because she is offended by the roughness of her brother, Susano. Many attempts are made to get her to come out, but she refuses. Then one of the *kami* performs a dance which causes the other gods to laugh so loudly that Amaterasu becomes curious and comes out. Thus light comes to the world again. Eventually Ninigi, Divine Grandchild (of Amaterasu), comes down from the Plain of High Heaven to a mountain in Kyushu to rule men. Jimmu, traditionally considered the founder of the line of emperors in Japan, is supposed to be descended from Ninigi. Before contact with the mainland, the Japanese did not differentiate between the human and the divine. Their way of life was thought of as the way of *kami*—the heavenly divine spirit manifested on earth. Man was not considered to have been condemned or victimized by being born on this earth. "Earthly life . . . is a desired satisfaction for divine spirit." [208, 70]

There is no dualism because human beings are *kami*, divine spirit on earth, "self-developing and making its own way by creative action." [208, 89] Divine spirit on earth can make mistakes and become involved in impurities which retard divine spirit's "earthly self-development," for which purification ceremonies are held. Purity and brightness are therefore important in shrine architecture: unadorned wood showing the original grain, rock, straw, and other natural materials.

The *kami* way naturally acknowledges evil, but it is not an independent spirit luring human beings into sin; instead, evil results from difficulties encountered by divine spirit's creativity in "venturing upon new ways of life." [208, 112] For example, Susano, "the impetuous male," is a personification of storms, and his sister, Amaterasu, is the sun. To grow crops it is necessary to have both sun and storms. Storms are necessary but at times can be fierce enough to ruin the crops. Rough Divine Spirit and Gentle Divine Spirit exist in the same *kami*. Susano was punished when Rough Divine Spirit got out of control and caused Amaterasu to hide in the cave. Mason explains, "Life struggling against itself is Divine Spirit sacrificing itself to itself, so that from the standpoint of divine spirit as a whole, there is really no sacrifice nor any evil." [208, 115] A much better sense of this process is to be found in the *give-away* of the Plains Indians. The word sacrifice entails loss or deprivation of one for another; while *give-away* implies a chain of continuous giving. If an individual human being manifests too much Rough Divine Spirit, recourse to purification rites restores purity. As a result of this flexible and creative approach to evil, according to Mason, delusions of a religious nature with the overwhelming sense of guilt usual in Western countries are practically absent in Japan. If a human being fails at something, it is not because he is evil; it is simply because he has upset the balance, and this can be restored by ritual.

In the *way of the gods* there is little speculation about happenings after the individual's life on earth, because the most important thing is "divine spirit's objective self-development in the universe. The body's decay is the mark of divine spirit's failure to hold itself in personalized material form for earthly activities; and is also a clearing of the ground for life's renewed experiments in progressive evolution when the body can no longer retain sufficient vitality for creative action." [208, 95] In other words, the way is cleared for other manifestations of Being in this world.

Every part of Japan has its Shinto shrine. In every shrine there are at least one or two very old trees—usually an entire grove—and all shrines have either a fresh flowing stream or a small pond. The fundamental impression is one of the continuity of heavenly *kami* and earthly *kami* divine spirit manifesting itself on earth as man, tree, or rock. In many Shinto shrines, there is no building at all; instead the shrine *is* the natural feature of the land—the mountain, the tree, a rock, or a waterfall.

The Nachi Waterfall pours down from such a great height that when the water hits the rocks it vaporizes. It is called *Hiryu* Shrine, the Shrine of the Flying Waterfall. The Flying Waterfall *is kami*, divine spirit. Mason inveighs against the "modern" view that to term this waterfall *kami* is simply a primitive superstition, and he states, "To confine spirituality on earth to the human soul is to move in the dark of spiritual ignorance where the Flying Waterfall's divine nature becomes obliterated in the materialism of the self-conscious mind. The universality of divine spirit, if it be accepted, must follow the Shinto conception, and must admit Nature within the spiritual realm side by side with man, attributing Heavenly origin to both. If the universe is monistic, then the Flying Waterfall has divine origin, and man rightly pays it spiritual respect and feels his own soul broadening toward universality as he does so." [208, 207]

At a shrine there is no worship in the usual sense because man and the divine spirit are the same. Instead the human being shows respect and gratitude to all the powers of life. There are no prayers; the Shinto priest recites *norito*, ritual ways to pay respect and gratitude for "heavenly divine spirit's" help to earthly divine spirit—human beings. In other words, the shrines are places for "spiritual refreshment where man renews the primeval intuition that humanity and divine spirit are the same . . ." [208, 109]

Ninigi came down from the Plain of High Heaven in possession of the three treasures of Shinto: the mirror, the sword, and the jewel. When Amaterasu, the sun goddess, gave him the mirror, she told him: "Worship this sacred mirror as my own soul." (The *Kojiki*) Each shrine contains a mirror, and when the human being looks into this mirror he sees earthly divine spirit (himself) reflecting heavenly divine spirit. Stiskin explains this further: "In our accustomed way of thinking, infinity and finitude, macrocosm and microcosm, God and man are all mutually distinct. Nevertheless, Shinto

and the Orient treat them as mirror images of each other and therefore as fundamentally identical . . . The universe is, then, the mirror reflection of Infinity. The mirror, however, has reversed the nature of that Infinity. The latter is undifferentiated unity; the imaged universe is finite and endless differentiation. These two are, then, front and back, and creation is a glance in a mirror." [310, 121 and 123]

Here we can see another aspect of Heidegger's idea that the mutual mirroring appropriation of the fourfold —earth, sky, gods, and man—*is* the world.

When a Japanese visits a shrine, the first thing he does is take hold of the bell rope and pull it vigorously. This is to announce to the *kami* that he is there. According to Stiskin, pulling on this helix-shaped rope connects the human being to the womb-shaped bell. Within this shape lie two small solid spheres, which might represent the testes. The bell itself is the feminine, the yin, and the spheres, the yang. The two together create life. The rope represents the entire created universe. "He connects himself to it, his origin, by grasping the helical rope extended to him . . . for it is from the universe that man draws his physical and spiritual nourishment and creates his life." [310, 142] Stiskin says, "The entire materialized universe is a great umbilical cord through which the life-giving energy of Infinity flows to man." When the human being grasps this rope and vigorously shakes it, "He creates vibration and *increases* Infinity through an act of self-expression." [310, 143] After ringing the bell, the visitor claps his hands twice and then, with the hands still clasped, gazes into the sacred mirror. "By means of its self-reflection, the unity of Deity transforms itself into differentiation; by means of his self-reflection, man transforms differentiation into oneness, himself into Deity . . . They are not separate processes but the mirror-image halves of one continuum. They constitute the front and back of the process of human existence." [310, 144] Again, using Heidegger's terms, we can say that Being comes forth into our world as beings and then returns into the completion of Being at death.

The entire visit to the shrine is a cheerful on-going relationship between man and heavenly divine *kami*. There is no trace of gloomy, pious worship. In fact, laughter is the more usual emotion. In a footnote, Aston points out that at the festival of Nifu Miōjin, "when the procession bearing offerings arrives before the shrine, the village chief calls out in a loud voice, 'According to our annual custom, let us all laugh,' to which a hearty response is given." [9, 6]

According to Tsunetsugu, ". . . the principal object of a festival (matsuri), in the strict sense, was to appease a Kami by: arranging a festival at some time or place; inviting the Kami spirit; making offerings of clothing, food, and other objects; having music and dancing; and feasting for days and nights." [329, 75]

The idea of death is not a morbid matter in Japan. What fascinates the Japanese imagination is action pursued so intently that it completely disregards and is indifferent to death. [208, 198] Intense living—venturing all on being—is what matters, rather than merely surviving. This is the main theme of the film, *The Man Who Skied Everest*. Of particular importance for this theme is the scene following the accidental deaths of several of the Sherpa porters. The Japanese try to talk the porters into continuing despite the deaths. Unfortunately, due to a fundamental philosophical error in the translation, unless the Western viewer knows something about Shinto, this scene and, in fact, the entire film comes through as an ego-centered, almost maniacal, desire to ski Everest. This is regrettable, for the film could have been a fruitful exposition of Shinto, but it failed utterly in this. While true Shinto meaning is in every filmed scene, the excerpts from Miura's diary used in the soundtrack were translated into dualistic Christian spiritual terms—the result being total con-fusion. The average viewer has no recourse but to think that Miura is an egocentric maniac out to prove how good he is. Actually, Miura's grandfather was a Shinto priest [254], and this Shinto background is present in the film. If one does not listen to the soundtrack, but instead closely watches Miura's action, the film proves to be a pilgrimage into sacred Nature herself—"Mother Goddess of the Snows."

In 1972, years before the release of the film, Yuichiro Miura was interviewed in a Seattle newspaper and gave a truly Shinto account of his relationship to Everest: "I was alone on the South Col saddle, a tiny speck amidst the white expanse . . . dissolved the essence of my Self into the void of Himalayan sky . . . The Mountain . . . taught me the real identity of a man named Yuichiro Miura . . . The sole meaning of one's existence—whether on the highest peak or in the lowliest of pursuits—is not to understand life, or mold it, or change it, or even really love it . . . but rather to drink deep of its undying essence." [222]

11. "The Gods are Talking Still"

In Japan, from primitive times to modern times, nature has been considered as "divine creative spirit," extending itself as matter and life in this world. In Europe, on the other hand, there was, as we have seen, a break in this continuity with the "death of the gods," caused by the rise of Christianity. John Holland Smith, referring to a quotation from the Iliad, "While the gods were talking, the sun went down," notes that fifteen centuries have passed since the attempted "murder of the gods" by the Christians in the last days of Rome. Many are beginning to realize that after the battle, the gods did not die. They are the immortals.

"They went on talking, as they had talked in the hills above Troy, long after the sun had set. They are talking still. They let themselves be heard in beauty, in nature, in dreams, in imaginings, in the researches of psychologists and the explorations of mystics. And as time passes, more and more are listening to them—and being surprised by what they hear." [297, 248]

I first heard the gods talking when I was climbing many years ago in the wildest part of the Canadian Rockies, on first ascents to the summits of mountains on which no human being had ever stood before. I could feel them but we didn't talk of them because the "reality" of a two-week climbing expedition and the setting of our "world" at the time did not provide the cultural milieu required to live "in expectation of the gods."

Vycinas, in his *Search for Gods*, based on Heidegger's thinking, writes that "it is not man who is the primordial ground of the gods of his world, but Nature. Gods are Nature's transcendental powers which, when colliding with the responsive openness of man, become disclosed *in man's world* with its situations . . . The birth of a god means his being brought forward to revelation or appearance on the grounds of certain conditions or historical living situations in man's cultural world." [343, 36] It takes a living and working together of human beings in contact with the earth and sky to bring about the fourth aspect of Heidegger's fourfold, the gods.

The first culture which I found that was intensely involved in a relationship with earth and sky was the powder snow skier's "world" of Alta. The workers at Alta—ski instructors, ski patrol, lift crew, and others—

were directly, physically, and emotionally involved with nature each day. Vycinas clarifies this further when he writes, "Man enters the way of his search for gods by being responsive to the movement (play) of Nature; to the movement in the sense of 'trail-breaking' (*Be-wegung*) carried by Nature and in no wise by man . . . alone." [343, 263] According to Heidegger it is language, the naming, which invokes the god. This naming in our skier's world occurred toward the end of a day of heavy storm; and, as happens in primitive cultures, the naming occurred at a crucial, tension-filled time. Nearly two feet of snow had already fallen that day on top of the three feet of the day before. If it continued to snow as hard the area would be shut down because of avalanche danger. We had just skied off the ski lift at 10,000 feet and were standing looking out at the seething blackness of the next storm front coming in from the west. Someone, in the intensity of the moment, said, "GAD, *please* don't give us any more snow. We've got enough." Immediately, this naming of GAD (Great American Desert) caused all the realities we had been experiencing to cluster around that name: thankfulness for snow, fear and anxiety about too much, longing and hope when there had been no snow. For the powder snow world of Alta, the Great American Desert is the reality—that unknown "out there" who carries the snow-laden winds to us which can, at any time, withhold or bring too much snow, as the gods capriciously play in man's world.

In the human world, according to Vycinas, "Nature's playing powers [are] mutually and harmoniously inter-related *on the ground of Nature*." They are not supernatural entities. "They are no entities!" [343, 45] We cannot know these "playing powers" of Nature in their own milieu, but only in our own world. In the skiing sub-culture, the ski is the "thing" which assembles the earth, the sky, the mortals, and the gods. In pre-Christian northern Europe, as well, the ski allowed human beings access to the snow-covered world, so there was a ski god named Ulla, who had taught the humans to make skis.

This importance of the "thing" in assembling a "world" is comprehensively documented in a discussion on the *tuhunga*, the master craftsman, in Marquesan society: "A part of the *tuhunga's* training was the learning of chants that accompanied the creation of an object. A food bowl made without the proper magic ritual would be just a bowl. It would have no real place in the universe and consequently no value . . . The magic chants were, in part, a formula for the work, so that if a man knew the charm he could not forget the process, but the ritual was also part of an actual creation, beginning with the genealogy of the universe, building step by step, and finally calling upon the essence of the things to make their contribution to the art of creation, which was regarded as a sexual act." [187, 146]

The cultural history of ancient Greece provides another example of this disclosure of gods. In the time before the Indo-European invasions, Mother Earth was the goddess with many local manifestations. When the Indo-European sky god, Zeus, was imposed, these mother goddesses were not killed, as the later prophetic religions demanded. Instead, their on-going myths became part of the new cults. Hera, an ancient mother goddess, was married to Zeus and became the head of the Olympic pantheon. Leto, another mother goddess, had two children by Zeus: Artemis and Apollo. Artemis is Nature in "its innocent purity and its strange darkness —nature as seen in the moonlight." Apollo is Nature showing forth itself to the mind of man—bright and glaring as the sun. Artemis "is the divine spirit of sublime nature, the tall glimmering lady, the purity who overpowers everything with her enchantment . . .Strange and inaccessible like wild nature, she is nonetheless all charm and fresh motion and lightning beauty." [242, 83] To the Romans she was known as Diana, surrounded by wild animals, but death-bringing when she drew her bow. She is virgin nature, which eludes all attempts to possess it and is always beyond reach. The "thing" which assembles the fourfold of the world of Artemis is the hunting bow. The sea-faring Greek ships cause Poseidon, the sea-god, to appear for them. Poseidon, who was associated with horses when the Aryan invaders first arrived, was later associated with the foaming sea-horses, the white crests of breaking waves which dash up against ships and rocks.

Vycinas turns to his own Lithuanian heritage in describing the forest world of the northern Europeans. "Mythical man observed the presence of a sheltering power in his world. In the Lithuanian myths Dimste, the goddess of settlement or homestead, was also the goddess, Nature's transcendental power, which had granted to animals the ability to establish their 'homes', to shelter themselves." [341, 143] Dimste was the daughter of Mother Earth, Zemyna, and sister of Medeine. Women's work such as making bread and preserving fruits and vegetables was the teaching of Dimste. Medeine gave the oak for making benches and tables, and maple for spinning wheels and looms. [342, 107–108]

This openness to the coming of gods, shown in the cults of primitive human beings, ended with the coming of the "prophetic" religions. Although Zoroaster's vision on a mountain was of the earth itself, appealing to him for help; and Abraham was confronted by El Shaddai, who, in his manifestation to the previous inhabitants of that *place* was "The One of the Mountain;" [212, 620 and 316] the development of these prophetic religions by their followers succeeded in destroying contact with *place* and making the religious structure itself central. Interaction with the sacredness of earth was possible only through the religions' priesthood, and all Being was concentrated in one monolithic God. This is why it is said that Christianity murdered the gods; but so also did the other prophetic religions.

Hölderlin, the poet whose works had such a profound effect on Heidegger, considered nature as the "all-living" and "all-present." Nature is above men and even above gods. Modern men find this strange and, according to Otto, in his book, *Gestalt*, this is because "we do not let it (Nature) be what it is; but we violate it or rather—since it does not let itself be violated—by our technical thinking and mechanization, we erect between it and us a second, dead nature as a partition. How then, according to Hölderlin's words, could the divinity dwell between the two?" [341, 172] Jung's answer to this is that divinity cannot manifest itself in such a situation, but instead gods are:

called phobias, compulsions and so forth, or in a word, neurotic symptoms. The gods have become diseases: Zeus no longer rules Olympus, but the solar plexus, and creates specimens for the physician's consulting room, or disturbs the brains of the politicians and journalists who then unwittingly unleash mental epidemics . . . It is completely forgotten that the reason mankind believes in the 'daemon' . . . is due to simple perception of the powerful inner effect of the autonomous fragmentary systems. This effect is not nullified by criticizing its name intellectually, nor by describing it as false. The effect is collectively always present; the autonomous systems are always at work, because the fundamental structure of the unconscious is not touched by the fluctuations of a transitory consciousness . . . Insanity is possession by an unconscious content which, as such, is not assimilated to consciousness; nor can it be assimilated, since the conscious mind has denied the existence of such contents. Expressed in terms of religion, the attitude is equivalent to saying: 'We no longer have any fear of God and believe that everything is to be judged by human standards.' This *hybris*, that is, this narrowness of consciousness, is always the shortest way to the insane asylum. [137, 112–113]

Jung clarifies this further when he writes that

within our own unconscious psyche those powers are still active which men have always projected into space as gods . . . With this knowledge it might be shown that all the manifold practices and convictions, which from the remotest times have played so great a part in human history, do not rest upon arbitrary discoveries and opinions of individual men, but owe their origin far more to the existence of strong, unconscious powers which we cannot neglect without distrubing the psychic balance. [139, 161]

A modern psychotherapist, Sheldon Kopp, states even more forcefully, "The Unconscious which all men share . . . is a source of primordial powers, sometimes more awesome than a man can bear to face." [158, 17]

Gods are immortal or eternal as "they do not start in the cultural world; they merely are disclosed there as powers which are imbedded in the eternal play of Nature." [343, 151] The human being's response to the gods, created by cult, allows them to come forward into this world. Cult is the response to myth. "Gods approach man with their word, the *mythos*. Such an approach is powerful and overwhelming. It tears man from his familiar everydayness, and carries him into the enthusiasm of gods . . ." [341, 223]

Frank Waters demonstrates this cultic response when he writes of a Zuni kachina ceremonial, the *Shalako*:

The crowds outside now wait in darkness, cold, and silence . . . They wait as one must wait for the gods: in hope and patient humility, facing the dark slope, the freezing river and its new causeway of stones and sticks.

In a breathless moment they appear again at last.

The *Shalako* come! It is the incoming of the gods to Zuni . . . Sound the drums. Let the gourds be shaken, the deer bones and the turtle shell rattles. We have waited long enough . . . There is only the timeless flow of the divine through all, a quickening perception of the spiritual essence in all things . . . Palely the tall spectral shapes come gliding across the causeway . . . Magnificent figures, their breasts top the heads of the retreating crowd, their eagle feather head-dresses reach above the roof beams . . .

In the tremendous resurgence one knew now that this was prayer. But not prayer as we know it. It was not a collective supplication, not even communal in the sense that it was merely participated in by every unit of the whole. It was a unification and release of psychic forces of all creation. These were not men humbly beseeching the gifts of life. They were the forces of life made manifest in man as in earth, demanding by the laws that governed both an interchange of the energies potential in each. [350, 271, 290 and 291]

Heidegger, in "What is Called Thinking?", wrote, "It is the prejudice of history and philology, founded in Platonism and taken over by modern rationalism, to imagine that *mythos* was destroyed by *logos*. Nothing religious is ever destroyed by logic; it is destroyed only by the god's withdrawal." [118, 180]

Cult is essentially the naming of the god. The responder to the myth, the one who tells of the gods, for the Greeks as well as for Hölderlin, is the poet. The poet for our times, the one who first spoke of allowing other "beings" into our community is Gary Snyder.

One of the most religious cult-events of my life occurred during a poetry reading by Gary Snyder in May of 1976. The audience of almost 800, Gary told me later, was the largest he had ever read to. Most of them were hardworking men in overalls. Not until months later did I find out who they were—cooperative workers in the forests. They were a real sub-culture, unified in their efforts to save and promote the growth of trees; they lived and worked in the deep northwest woods, so that when Gary Snyder read his poem "By Frazier Creek Falls"—

Standing up on lifted, folded rock
looking out and down—

The creek falls to a far valley.
hills beyond that
facing, half-forested, dry
—clear sky
strong wind in the
stiff glittering needle clusters
of the pine—their brown
round trunk bodies
straight, still;
rustling trembling limbs and twigs

listen.

When he said, "listen," there was not a sound from the hundreds of human beings, who in utter stillness felt the nearness of the gods' presence—there, with us mortals in the fourfold of the northwest woods culture. He went on—

> This living flowing land
> is all there is, forever
>
> We *are* it
> it sings through us—
>
> We could live on this Earth
> without clothes or tools!
>
> [302, 41]

followed by the *total* response of those who suddenly find they are together—a true culture—together as mortals underneath the heavy, waterfilled sky, the fertile forest-covered earth of the Northwest; and, by virtue of the togetherness of these mortals, the gods are near and in the mutual give-away of this earth, this sky, these mortals and their gods, our "world" *is*.

No matter that we had to leave the magic room where this happened and go out into the destructiveness of the modern city of Seattle. Having once felt Nature's playing powers, the gods, near us even in the midst of the destruction we, who often *know* Earth's wisdom out on the mountains and woods now *know* it can also manifest in man's own "world." It happened once. It can happen again. It *is* happening in isolated creek bottoms and mountain towns—people in this wasted land, now, like the forest workers who spent that evening with Gary Snyder, are learning again how to dwell on this earth. Heidegger says, "Dwelling is the manner in which mortals are on this earth." He points out that the Old Saxon word, *wuon* and the Gothic *wunian* and the old High German word, *bauen* all mean "to remain, to stay in a place." The Gothic *wunian* most explicitly defines how this remaining is experienced:

Wunian means: to be at peace, to be brought to peace, to remain in peace. The word for peace, *Friede*, means the free, *das Frye*, and *fry* means: preserved from harm and danger . . . safeguarded. To free really means to spare . . . Real sparing is something *positive* and takes place when we leave something beforehand in its own nature. *The fundamental character of dwelling is this sparing and preserving*. It pervades dwelling in its whole range. That range reveals itself to us as soon as we reflect that human being consists in dwelling and, indeed, dwelling in the sense of the stay of mortals on the earth.

But "on the earth" already means "under the sky." Both of these *also* mean "remaining before the divinities" and include a "belonging to man's being with one another." By a *primal* oneness the four—earth and sky, divinities and mortals—belong together in one.

Earth is the serving bearer, blossoming and fruiting, spreading out in rock and water, rising up into plant and animal. When we say earth, we are already thinking of the other three along with it, but we give no thought to the simple oneness of the four.

The sky is the vaulting path of the sun, the course of the changing moon, the wandering glitter of the stars, the year's seasons and their changes, the light and dusk of day, the gloom and glow of night, the clemency and inclemency of the weather, the drifting clouds and blue depth of the ether. When we say sky, we are already thinking of the other three along with it, but we give no thought to the simple oneness of the four.

The divinities are the beckoning messengers of the godhead. Out of the holy sway of the godhead, the god appears in his presence or withdraws into his concealment. When we speak of the divinities, we are already thinking of the other three along with them, but we give no thought to the simple oneness of the four.

The mortals are the human beings. They are called mortals because they can die. To die means to be capable of death *as* death. Only man dies, and indeed continually, as long as he remains on earth, under the sky, before the divinities. When we speak of mortals, we are already thinking of the other three along with them, but we give no thought to the simple oneness of the four.

This simple oneness of the four we call *the fourfold*. Mortals *are* in the fourfold by *dwelling* . . . Mortals dwell in that they save the earth . . . To save really means to set something free into its own presencing. To save the earth is more than to exploit it or even wear it out. Saving the earth does not master the earth and does not subjugate it, which is merely one step from spoliation . . .   [117, 149–150]

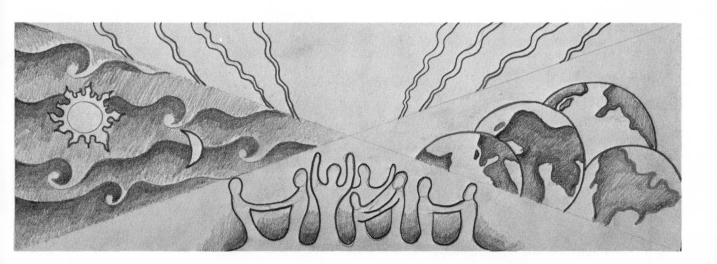

But modern technological culture, instead of "sparing" the earth, subjects the earth and all its beings to technology's own *use* and thus violates each *place* formerly held sacred by primitive human beings. Thomas Sanchez tells of a modern Washo Indian moving through his *place*, the Sierra Mountains, and his awareness of what the Whiteman had done to it.

He crossed the red dirt of logging roads that were broken with chuckholes bigger than a man's head and studded with the furred carcasses of gray squirrels run into Earth under truckloads of slaughtered trees. He travelled in forests of ghost trees cut through the heart. The Whiteman had come with the power of his chainsaw, he could tear the hide off a tree as old as the rivers and slice through its flesh in minutes. He stood on the spur of a mesa and looked down to where the Whiteman had cut the river. A band of concrete across the full current robbed the power of great waters. Everywhere now he saw the mark of the White beast on the mountain heart of the land . . . He tore the scalps off the high mountains, blasting with stolen water for gold metal. He was blind to the Earth and blasted great peaks to stone rubble, he choked the life from breathing streams with mud and silt. He moved mountains for bags of gold dust. He left his mark everywhere.   [281, 483-484]

And Heidegger:

Mortals dwell in that they receive the sky as sky. They leave to the sun and the moon their journey, to the stars their courses, to the seasons their blessing and their inclemency; they do not turn night into day nor day into a harassed unrest.
[117, 150]

But technological culture does just that. The doctor, part of Edward Abbey's *Monkey Wrench Gang*, tells of what happened to his *place*, the southwest desert, in order to turn night into day in another *place*, thousands of miles away.

All this fantastic effort—giant machines, road networks, strip mines, conveyor belts, pipelines, slurry lines, loading towers, railway and electric train, hundred-million-dollar coal-burning power plant; ten thousand miles of high-tension towers and high-voltage power lines; the devastation of the landscape, the destruction of Indian homes and Indian grazing lands, Indian shrines and Indian burial grounds; the poisoning of the last big clean-air reservoir on the forty-eight contiguous United States, the exhaustion of precious water supplies—all that ball-breaking insult to land and sky and human heart, for what? All that for what? Why, to light the lamps of Phoenix suburbs not yet built, to run the air conditioners of San Diego and Los Angeles, to illuminate the shopping-center parking lots at two in the morning . . . to charge the neon tubing that makes the meaning (all the meaning there is) of Las Vegas, Albuquerque, Tucson, Salt Lake City, the amalgamated *metropoli* of southern California, to keep alive the phosphorescent putrefying glory (all the glory there is left) called Down Town, Night Time, Wonderville, U.S.A.   [1, 153–4]

And Heidegger again:

Mortals dwell in that they await the divinities as divinities. In hope they hold up to the divinities what is unhoped for. They wait for the intimations of their coming . . .
[117, 149–150]

And Gary Snyder, the poet for our time, proclaims:

> listen.
>
> . . .
>
> This living flowing land
> is all there is, forever
>
> We *are* it
> it sings through us—

97

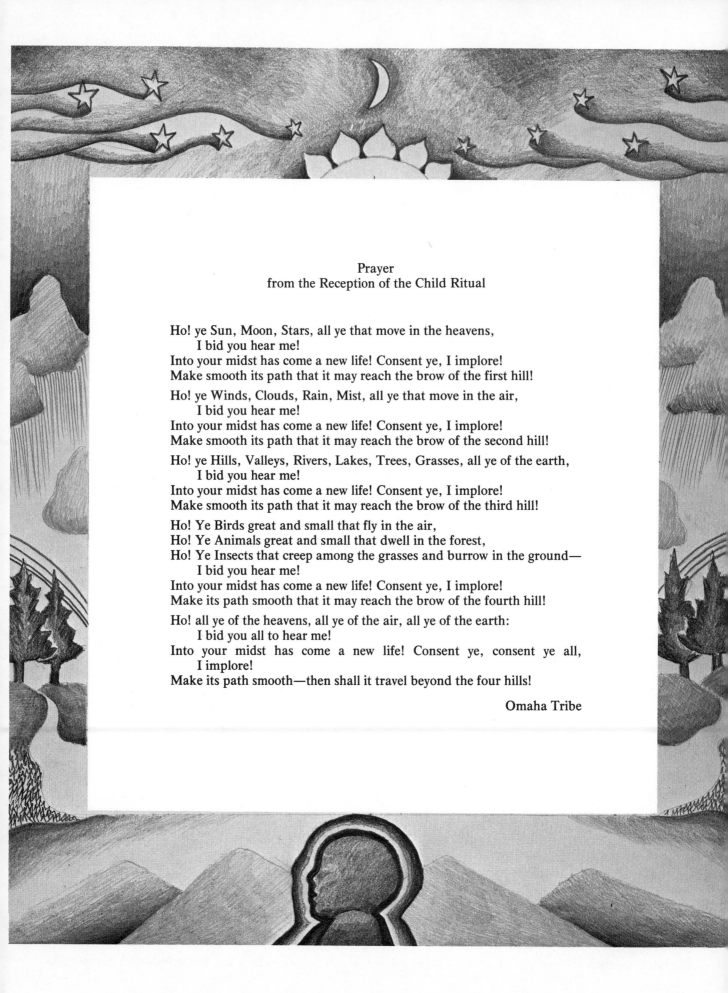

Prayer
from the Reception of the Child Ritual

Ho! ye Sun, Moon, Stars, all ye that move in the heavens,
    I bid you hear me!
Into your midst has come a new life! Consent ye, I implore!
Make smooth its path that it may reach the brow of the first hill!

Ho! ye Winds, Clouds, Rain, Mist, all ye that move in the air,
    I bid you hear me!
Into your midst has come a new life! Consent ye, I implore!
Make smooth its path that it may reach the brow of the second hill!

Ho! ye Hills, Valleys, Rivers, Lakes, Trees, Grasses, all ye of the earth,
    I bid you hear me!
Into your midst has come a new life! Consent ye, I implore!
Make smooth its path that it may reach the brow of the third hill!

Ho! Ye Birds great and small that fly in the air,
Ho! Ye Animals great and small that dwell in the forest,
Ho! Ye Insects that creep among the grasses and burrow in the ground—
    I bid you hear me!
Into your midst has come a new life! Consent ye, I implore!
Make its path smooth that it may reach the brow of the fourth hill!

Ho! all ye of the heavens, all ye of the air, all ye of the earth:
    I bid you all to hear me!
Into your midst has come a new life! Consent ye, consent ye all,
    I implore!
Make its path smooth—then shall it travel beyond the four hills!

                              Omaha Tribe

Part III

The Hills of Life:
An Introduction

In the Omaha tribe, according to a report by Alice Fletcher in 1911, "When a child was born it was not regarded as a member of its gens or of the tribe but simply as a living being coming forth into the universe, whose advent must be ceremoniously announced in order to secure it an accepted place among the already existing forces." [90] Alice Fletcher not only studied the Omaha tribe for thirty years, her co-author and friend was Francis LaFlesche, a member of the tribe and son of a former chief of the tribe in the early part of the last century, when the culture was still intact. Here, then, we have a valid written account of a "world" in which the human being lived in responsible relationship with the earth, the sky, and the gods.

The Plains Indians were hunters, as were all of our ancestors, and it is to the hunting-gathering cultures we must look for examples of an "aware culture." "Cultural man has been on Earth for some two million years: for over 99 percent of this period he has lived as a hunter-gatherer. Only in the last 10,000 years has man begun to domesticate plants and animals . . ." [172] Ten thousand years is only four hundred generations, "too few to allow for any notable genetic changes . . . We and our ancestors are the same people." According to the anthropologist Carleton Coon, who drew upon a lifetime of study and field work for his book, *The Hunting Peoples*, the same physiological and psychological structures make up our behavior patterns, so it is to the hunting cultures we must turn to learn how "nature intended us to live." [63, xvii, 393]

Paul Shepard, in *The Tender Carnivore and the Sacred Game*, tells about the needs of the human being based on the body/mind of the hunter-gatherer. First of all, the human body is not designed for heavy continuous work such as farm labor, but for short, intense activity such as running after game. In hunting societies this brief, strenuous effort was followed by long spells of leisure. Even today the !Kung Bushmen of the Kalahari Desert work an average of only twenty hours a week to hunt and gather enough food to live in one of the most inhospitable environments in the world. [172]

The same activities have been popular with leisured human beings throughout history, from the primitives to the wealthy nobility of Europe. These activities are hunting, dancing, racing, and conversation. [292, 150] In the New World, the staple crop was corn, which depends on summer rains, such as occur in Pueblo Indian country. But California's Mediterranean-type climate has winter rains, which produce plentiful supplies of acorns and grass seeds. As a result, the California Indians never cultivated corn and were spared the blight of agriculture. They lived on the plentiful acorns and grass seeds. After collecting and caching the mature acorns, they went visiting other tribes, using desert trails (memorized in songs), socialized, danced, and sang. [166] This immense leisure horrified the early Spanish invaders. Jose Espinosa y Tello described the life of the Indians of Monterey:

Men and women go feeding in the fields like brute beasts, or gathering seeds for the winter and engaging also in hunting and fishing. Although some of these natives have now been *reduced to obedience* [italics added] and form part of the Mission of San Carlos, they still preserve their former disposition and customs. Among other habits which they retain, it has been noticed that in their leisure moments they will lie on the ground face downwards for whole hours with the greatest content. [189]

Some ten thousand years ago, agriculture began with the domestication of plants and animals. According to Coon, "Agriculture brings with it a whole new system of human relationships that offer no easily understood advantages, and disturbs an age-old balance between man and nature and among the people who live together." [63, 3] Contrary to the usual historical assumptions "primitives" do not stay primitives because they haven't the intelligence to change. This is shown by hunting-gathering groups now alive who have techniques "every bit as complex and ingenious" as ours. In fact, they are far more efficient than we are. According to Rappaport, "South African bushmen and Australian aborigines are able to support a person on 1/75 to 1/100 of what it takes to support an American. That is, from the standpoint of the ratio of energy flux per unit of standing biomass, hunters and gatherers are 75 to 100 times more efficient than we are." [271] The reasons they haven't changed is that they were lucky enough to live in such far-away places that agriculture didn't reach them, or they lived in such severe climates, such as the Eskimo, that food-growing didn't work. "The third reason is that they did not want to change. The hunter's life gave them all the food they needed and an eminently satisfactory way of living together in small, intimate groups. The hunter is free from tedious routine, and his daily activities are more exciting." [63, 3]

On the other hand, the agricultural disasters now facing us are not new. They are just a "continuation of an earth trauma that began ten thousand years ago . . . A civilizing, progressive commitment to conflict with the natural world and with ourselves," according to Paul Shepard. [292, 34] The on-going extermination of races, such as happened in North America, as well as other parts of the world, really has little to do with the color of skin, as is usually thought; actually it's part of "the ten thousand years of eradication of hunters by farmers." [292, 30] The two things that stand out over this long time-span of civilization are "war and environmental crisis." [292, 34] Actually, "in both the state of war and peace man is waging an incessant war upon nature . . . Whether one pollutes water resources in a single bombing or does so over a twenty-year period is essentially the same; the only difference is the matter of time." [227, 135] Famine is not new either. It has been an ever-recurring threat since the beginning of monoculture and the end of the hunter-gatherer culture which kept the population in balance with the environment.

The hunter was aware of every part of his environment. His awareness was not limited to what was useful for him, as the farmer is concerned only with what is good for his crop. "The hunter's look and attention are completely opposite to this," according to Ortega y Gasset, in *Meditations on Hunting.*

The hunter does not look tranquilly in one determined direction, sure beforehand that the game will pass in front of him. The hunter knows that he does not know what is going to happen, and this is one of the greatest attractions of his occupation. Thus he needs to prepare an attention of a different and superior style—an attention which does not consist in riveting itself on the presumed but consists precisely in not presuming anything and avoiding inattentiveness. It is a "universal" attention, which does not inscribe itself on any point and tries to be on all points. There is a magnificent term for

this, one that still conserves all its zest of vivacity and imminence: alertness. The hunter is the alert man.   [240, 150]

There seems to be very little difference between the state of the "alert" hunter and the "total awareness" of jnana yoga. In fact, Lama Govinda, in *Way of the White Clouds*, says that the discipline of "meditation" in India had its origin among the primitive hunters in the lower reaches of the Himalayas. But it is not limited to the Himalayas of long ago; true hunters the world over throughout the ages hunt in this fashion. The purpose of those beautifully drawn animals on the walls of paleolithic caves was the same as the American Indian fasting and chanting before the hunt, the same as the practices of the Australian aborigine to this very day. The greatest hunter in any of these cultures becomes so identified with the consciousness of the animal that the animal comes to him as a give-away. The great hunters seemed to work magic, but the magic involved was the intensity of the relationship between human and animal and place, the ecosystem itself.

In a hunting-gathering culture the human being, the game animals, the plants, and the place are inextricably bound together. Old Moke, one of the elders of the Pygmy people who live in the Ituri forest in the Congo in Africa, told Colin Turnbull when he came to study them, "You will see things you have never seen before. You will understand why we are called People of the Forest . . . When the Forest dies, we shall die." [331, 278] This is true community, but most parts of the earth have seen the progressive destruction of such community by successive waves of empire-building, until even the idea of such community was lost. Only in the last century has the concept begun to come back, although narrowly, through scientific studies. It was not until 1947, with Aldo Leopold's famous "land ethic," that such community was redefined.

After thirty-eight years of experience in game management and conservation, Leopold had gradually come to realize that the community included the "soils, the waters, the plants and animals," as well as people. Several times in the last decade of his life he had tried to put down on paper his conception of an ecological ethic and "finally succeeded some time in late 1947 or early 1948." [88, 34] In his most important essay, "The Land Ethic," he wrote, "A thing is right when it tends to preserve the integrity, stability and beauty of the biotic community. It is wrong when it tends otherwise." [178, 224–25] This is a truly revolutionary statement, for, as Leopold himself wrote earlier, "To change ideas about what land is for, is to change ideas about what anything is for." [88, 33] In addition, his "land ethic" clearly takes ethics out of the miasma of "human" rights, privileges, and manipulations and puts them where they belong—in the network of relationships between all the beings of any particular *place.* And it can only be a "particular" *place,* because the needs of a *particular* soil, say a heavy clay soil saturated with rain as in the Pacific Northwest, are going to be totally different than the needs of a sandy soil on a steep slope in southwestern Colorado. Such an ethic strives for a balance in the relationship between all the beings of the *place,* so that all beings may flourish. This is Heidegger's "letting be" of Being, rather than *using* beings.

Modern technological man, convinced that all beings on earth are for his *use*, is destroying more and more beings in order to produce more useful objects and in the process is destroying the air he breathes and the water he drinks. As Gregory Bateson says, "The organism which destroys its environment destroys itself." [17] Now we arrive at the next and probably final stage of insanity: more technology to alleviate the damage already done by technology. For example, if your farmland has been ruined by monoculture of wheat, the cure is more heavy machinery to plow deeper, more chemical fertilizers which take more fuel. The insatiable demand for fuel leads to strip mining coal in places such as Wyoming and Montana, thus utterly destroying other wheat fields. What has been accomplished? Certainly neither an increase in wheat nor an increase in fertile soil, but somewhere along the line someone has got an increase in money (green frog skins, as the Sioux medicine man, Lame Deer calls it). That someone who made the money will probably never see the devastated farmland or the ravaged strip-mined land. Such behavior is clearly unethical from the point of view of Leopold's "land ethic"; but then, human beings have been unethical in this sense ever since the rise of the first large civilizations.

Until these large civilizations devloped, all human beings were "ecosystem people," as Raymond Dasmann calls them. "They lived within one ecosystem or, at most, a few closely related ecosystems, and depended entirely on the continued functioning of those ecosystems for their survival." They didn't destroy the soil, kill off the game, or devastate the forests. Biosphere people, on the other hand, conquered other ecosystems and appropriated their resources. As Gary Snyder puts it, "Biosphere cultures . . . are cultures that spread their economic support system out far enough that they can afford to wreck one ecosystem and keep moving on. Well, that's Rome, that's Babylon"—and most of the big civilizations since. [300, 21]

Primitives, ecosystem people, *knew* they were part of the earth because they could see the results of their actions in diminished game and other changes in their immediate environment. Over millenia the wise ones of the tribe developed rituals and the gods came to harmonize them with their land. These early human beings watched the environment around them and learned directly from it, applying its principles to their own relationships within the tribe. This was called totomism. The next step was animism, in which early man felt that mountains, rivers, and rocks had mind and personality like himself. There was still relationship —mind was something in common. With the rise of civilizations and empires came the further step, that of separating mind from the natural world and the gods from their local *place.* The aggressors took their own "god of place" with them in their conquering marches across other lands. The power of their gods was corrupted when they were no longer tied to place and were *used* as an excuse for further aggression. For instance, the god was no longer "The lord of the mountain of the North" but Jehovah, the god who leads his people forward to do battle with others so that his people can have the "Promised Land." At this stage mind is separated "from the structure in which it is immanent," human relationship from the ecosystem. This is the root cause of the present destruction of the earth. Gregory Bateson explains it:

If you put God outside and set him vis-à-vis his creation and if you have the idea that you are created in his image, you will logically and naturally see yourself as outside and against the things around you. And as you arrogate all mind to yourself, you will see the world around you as mindless and therefore not entitled to moral or ethical consideration. The environment will seem to be yours to exploit. Your survival unit will be you and your folks or conspecifics against the environment of other social units, other races and the brutes and vegetables.

If this is your estimate of your relation to nature *and you have an advanced technology,* your likelihood of survival will be that of a snowball in hell. You will die either of the toxic by-products of your own hate, or simply of over-population and overgrazing. The raw materials of the world are finite.

[12]

To stop this insanity it is only necessary to cultivate an awareness of the totality of the self in the environment; in other words, to become, like the primitive hunter, an *alert* human being. But, as Joel Kramer points out, this is not popular: "People don't want it. Civilization certainly doesn't want it. Society has no use for it at all. Awareness is a wild thing, not a tame beast; it is not respectable, which means, of course, it doesn't respond to the usual pushing of buttons of conditioning that are used to control us. There is then great pressure not to see." [159, 116] But by seeing other beings in the environment, not simply as things to be *used* by humanity but as beings in their own right, the human being becomes free. "Freedom reveals itself as the letting-be of being," [341, 157] Heidegger tells us. This is not to be understood as mere indifference but rather as similar to the Taoist *wu wei,* "non-action," which was explained in Chapter 3 as "refraining from activity contrary to Nature" or the whole. Only here, in the midst of the beings of his world, can the human being begin to grasp the meaning of Being itself. As we noted in Chapter 9, Heidegger calls man "the being-withheld-in-Nothingness." This Nothingness out of which man comes is the fullness of Being. The human being on this earth can never know this fullness of Being but can only know Being as it is shown forth in the beings of our world. It is possible though, by analogy, to consider some attributes of Being.

Some possibilities concerning Being were set forth in a remarkable science fantasy book in 1937. Just before the Second World War, a British philosopher, Olaf Stapledon, clearly seeing the coming apocalypse, wrote *Star Maker,* conceived in a sort of vision while sitting on a hill watching the stars. The narrator, a contemporary Earthman, eventually joins a community of cosmic explorers who range among the multiple intelligences of past and future to the farthest reaches of the cosmos seeking for traces of Intelligence itself. Stars are born and die; forms of life merge, mature, manipulate their environments, and perish.

John Lilly, in his lectures, often refers to *Star Maker* as a book which puts one in another state of consciousness. In an interview at New Dimensions Foundation in San Francisco, he was asked, "Do you think it's possible for human beings to be in touch in some way with the Starmaker God?" Lilly answered, "I doubt it. I think we are parts of his/her/its body and we may be just viruses on one part of that body, or electrons in one atom of that body. I am part of a much greater whole, and if that whole is greater than the sum of its parts, which if there is feedback, is inevitable, then I, as one individual of many, many linked individuals, interconnected parts of a larger whole, can't possibly conceive of the thoughts of that larger whole. That's like asking one of the neurons in my brain to account for the way I think. It can't do it." [184]

Gregory Bateson, considering the problem which religions have with the question of whether God is transcendent or immanent, suggested a new approach based on cybernetic epistemology: "The individual mind is immanent but not only in the body. It is immanent also in pathways and messages outside the body; and there is a larger Mind of which the individual mind is only a sub-system. This larger Mind is comparable to God and is perhaps what some people mean by 'God,' but it is still immanent in the total interconnected social system and planetary ecology." [12]

The approach of the Plains Indians to the ultimate Being was given by Tahirussawichi, the Pawnee priest, when he was explaining the ritual, "Many Children." "The white man speaks of a heavenly Father; we say Tirawa atius, the Father above, but we do not think of Tirawa as a person. We think of Tirawa as in everything, as the Power which has arranged and thrown down from above everything that man needs. What the Power above, Tirawa atius, is like, no one knows; no one has been there." [89] At each stage of the individual's life the Plains Indians had special rituals, "rites of passage," for getting in touch with this Power. They conceived of life as surmounting the "four hills" of Infancy, Youth, Maturity, and Old Age. Each ritual marking entrance to the next hill focused on "total awareness"—concentrated attention both within the human being and on that human being's *relationships* within the tribe and with nature and "the Powers."

In Part III, which sets forth some preliminary ideas on living in a culture of awareness, I have used the Plains Indians' "four hills of life" as chapter headings.

12. The First Hill of Life

Infancy and Childhood

In the poem beginning this section of the book, the Omaha priest asked permission of all the other beings in his *place* for the child to come into that *place,* thus ensuring that all beings flourished, not only the human beings. In primitive cultures such as the Omaha Indian culture, the individual human being had no claim on the right to be born. This allowed all beings to flourish; thus the human beings had plenty of buffalo for food

and sufficient leisure for rituals and festivals in order to continue "living in harmony" with the earth. Awareness, in such cultures, begins even before the birth of a child.

In contrast, in our modern world, we have a scarcity of food and little leisure because we have *used* up the resources of the earth. Human overpopulation has destroyed the topsoil, the very basis of life, in large areas of the earth, to say nothing of the myriad species of plants and animals which have been forced into extinction. And, as Garrett Hardin has pointed out, more human beings suffer and die because of over-population today than from any other cause. [108] It is a recent development, for a million years ago the estimated world population was 125,000, according to Hardin. If those humans had "multiplied steadily at the *present* rate of 2.03 percent per year, how long would it have taken them to produce the present population of some three-and-a-half-billion?" The answer is only 512 years, and the time would still be nearly 1,000,000 B.C. [109, 169] It was not only war, disease, and famine which kept population down. From his analysis of life expectancies and populations from Paleolithic times, Deevey states that "some degree of voluntary birth control has always prevailed." [69]

"Most primitive populations practiced spacing of children," according to James V. Neel, professor of Human Genetics at the University of Wisconsin Medical School, whose statement rests on a multi-disciplinary study of three of the most primitive tribes of Indians in South America in which he took part. These Indians were thought to be living very nearly under conditions like those out of which human evolution in early life and human variability arose. Intercourse taboos during special times, for instance before hunting, was one method used to space children. Other methods were prolonged nursing, abortion, and infanticide. Infanticide is used whenever a baby is born before the older sibling is thought ready for weaning, which usually occurs about three years of age. "I conclude . . . that perhaps the most significant of the many milestones in the transition from higher primate to man—on a par with speech and tool-making—occurred when human social organization and parental care permitted the survival of a higher proportion of infants than the culture and economy could absorb in each generation and when population control, including abortion and infanticide, was therefore adopted as the only practical recourse available." [233]

The deliberate killing of a grossly deformed child who cannot hope for a full participation in his tribal society or of the second child when it endangers the first-born's nutritional status would generally be viewed as morally repugnant in our culture. Neel, however, points out that "we have condoned in ourselves a reproductive pattern which (through weanling diarrhea and malnutrition) has contributed, for large numbers of children to a much more agonizing 'natural' demise than that resulting from infanticide. Moreover, this reproductive pattern has condemned many of the surviving children to a marginal diet inconsistent with full physical and mental development . . . I find it increasingly difficult to see in the recent reproductive history of the civilized world a greater respect for the quality of human existence than was manifested by our remote 'primitive' ancestors."

In his summary, Neel states that "Civilized man . . . each year is departing farther and farther from the population structure that obtained throughout most of human evolution and that was presumably of some importance to the evolutionary process." Furthermore, it is obvious that humankind is living beyond a reasonable energy balance and so is destroying the very base for all life in the future. He says this calls for "a philosophical readjustment which has the impact of a religious conversion." [233] In these times we don't have to resort to infanticide. Neel recommends voluntary sterilization after the third child.

The !Kung people of Africa are just now in the process of making the change of the Neolithic Revolution, when people forsook hunting-gathering and began to grow food and keep domestic animals. The !Kung have lived as hunters and gatherers in the Kalahari Desert of South Africa for at least eleven thousand years—since the Pleistocene—but recently have begun to live in farming villages of the Bantu. Investigators find that the settled !Kung women are losing their equal status, children are learning to act aggressively, and the population, once stable, is rapidly increasing.

The astonishing thing about this tribe throughout the past millenia has been their balanced use of the land. Artifacts from Late Stone Age hunter-gatherers, of about eleven thousand years ago, are to be found at the same water holes where the modern !Kung set up camp. They even hunt the same animals as their prehistoric ancestors did, such as the nocturnal springhare. When you consider the numbers of animals now extinct in the world because of the activities of man, the way of the !Kung is direct proof of the balanced life of their ecosystem, all the more remarkable for the fact that the Kalahari Desert is one of the most barren parts of the world—seemingly furnishing so little food that a modern "civilized" man would starve or die of thirst there.

The !Kung population achieved a long-term stability without either contraception or abortion, owing to a number of factors. The average age of the beginning of menstruation is fifteen-and-a-half years. The !Kung marry at puberty but a woman does not have her first child until she is about nineteen years old. Furthermore, the women have a low fertility rate. The average length of time between births is four years. The babies are nursed for four years and during this time the women rarely conceive. According to Howell and Rose Frisch of the Harvard Center for Population Studies, the late age of menarche and the long time between births may both be due to the fact that the amount of body fat must be above a certain minimum for the onset of menstruation and for its maintenance. The !Kung are thin, although well-nourished, and have been described as "exceedingly healthy." When these women nurse, they need about 1000 extra calories a day; thus, a woman nursing a baby would have too little fat for ovulation to take place. Among the !Kung who have become sedentary, menstruation begins at an earlier age and the intervals between births are shorter. Sedentary !Kung nurse their babies a shorter time and also have more body fat so ovulation is more probable. The nomadic !Kung live on nuts, vegetables, and meat, but consume neither grain nor milk, while the settled !Kung consume a great deal of cow's milk and grain. Although further research is required to prove the Frisch thesis, they conclude that "the settled !Kung seem to have lost a natural check on their fertility rates." [156] Do not the !Kung show that possibly in primitive times it was not even necessary to resort to abortion or infanticide if the tribe lived totally in harmony with their *place*?

This "balance" of hunter-gatherers with their environment was destroyed when human beings became agriculturalists, with their "lust for more children and more production." [292, 244] The loss of this balance has brought recurrent famines, soil destruction, and other earth traumas.

For those human beings today who have begun to move toward "reinhabitation," forging once again the close relationship of humanity and *place,* the decision to bring their child into their "world" is made only after consulting the other living beings of their *place.* Such a child is truly wanted. It has a place from the beginning and is thus freed from the modern curse of children, "anxiety."

From the beginning of its time in the womb, the child interacts with the earth. "The fetus," Gasell tells us, "is a growing action system . . . Its first and foremost function is to adjust to the ceaseless pull of gravity." [98] The other omnipresent force, while the child is in the womb, is syncopated sound. The amniotic fluid in the uterus conducts sound much better than air. The fetus heartbeat is twice as fast as that of the mother. Both heartbeats, together, provide the sound of a syncopated drum beat. For the newborn baby, syncopated sound and movement in response to gravity has been its natural state for some months prior to birth. It is no wonder that the drum is the heart of rituals in most cultures. The combination of dance (continuing the basic relationship to gravity) begun in the womb, and the drum beat (also continuing the womb) are the powerful centers of life. Indian dancing furthers this contact of person and earth. As Jaime de Angulo explains its, "The foot is raised flat from the ground, put down again flat, and then, as it were, pushed down into the earth by a bending at the knee." [68, 242]

The child is born perfect. It comes into the world with all the gifts of a "three-billion-year experiment in genetic coding." [250, 35] It is ready to interact with the living earth—*knowing* all it needs to know to begin life on earth. Nikos Kazantzakis, the author of *Zorba the Greek,* is one of the few people able to remember with frightening intensity his early contacts with the world. In his autobiography, *Report to Greco,* he writes: "The

child's brain is soft, his flesh tender. Sun, moon, rain, wind, and silence all descend on him. He is frothy batter and they knead him. The child gulps the world down greedily, receives it in his entrails, assimilates it, and turns it into child." [149, 44] He writes vividly of his earliest memory in life:

Still unable to stand, I crept on all fours to the threshhold and fearfully, longingly, extended my tender head into the open air of the courtyard. Until then I had looked through the windowpane but had seen nothing. Now I not only looked, I actually saw the world for the first time. And what an astonishing sight that was! Our little courtyard-garden seemed without limits. There was buzzing from thousands of invisible bees, an intoxicating aroma, a warm sun as thick as honey. The air flashed as though armed with swords, and, between the swords, erect, angel-like insects with colorful, motionless wings advanced straight for me. I screamed from fright, my eyes filled with tears, and the world vanished.   [149, 42]

Kazantzakis' earliest experience with the sea was quoted in Chapter 8 and ended with these words, ". . . the entire sea poured into me frothingly. My tender temples collapsed, and my head filled with laughter, salt, and fear." Both these experiences show the total interpenetration of world and child. He says that even in his adult life he experiences his first contacts with earth, sea, woman, and the star-filled sky—"experiencing them with the same astonishment, fright and joy" which they gave him as an infant. He says "This is what keeps my mind untouched by wastage, keeps it from withering and running dry." [149, 49] He further clearly remembers when the culturally-induced (Greek Orthodox) split between the world and him happened, "It stood on one side, I on the other, and the battle began." [149, 45] This battle continued unabated until he died.

Others without such a fierce cultural inheritance managed to remain intact, in spite of the modern world. Rexroth never lost the experience he had, when he was four, of "timeless, spaceless, total bliss" and the energy given him by this relationship to the earth.

Another important childhood experience was Jung's remembrance of the stone which he sat on: "Am I the one who is sitting on the stone, or am I the stone on which *he* is sitting?" [140, 20] His close relationship to rocks continued through his life. At about ten years of age, Jung's state was one of "disunion with myself and uncertainty in the world at large" when he carved a little mannikin on the end of a wooden ruler and put him together with a smooth, oblong black stone from the Rhine. He hid these on one of the beams under the roof and felt safe from all harrassment and tormenting. He writes that this secret had a powerful influence on his character: "I consider it the essential factor of my boyhood." He says, although he was nominally Christian, that when religious teachings were pumped into him he would think to himself "Yes, but it is not so certain as all that!" . . . "Yes, but there is something else, something very secret . . ." thinking of his mannikin and what it meant to him. [140, 22]

All such experiences fit Edith Cobb's definition of genius as "an involuntary phenomenon, at biocultural levels, beginning with the natural genius of childhood and the 'spirit of place.'" [58, 44] It is only in early childhood that these crucial events can happen. Never again is the human being as open to the whole. Above all else a small child must be allowed time alone in nature—even if only under a tree in a backyard. If this unity with the earth is not cemented, it won't happen later. Just as there is only one time in a human's life which is the specific stage for learning language, there is only one specific time in life for building this total trust relationship with the earth.

During the first few of years in my life I spent a great deal of time hanging in aspen trees. My father was allergic to certain types of pollen so my family spent considerable time in the mountains, where lowland weeds did not grow. I was put into a canvas seat, suspended from a spring, which was hooked onto a tree limb. In this way I was imprinted on aspen leaves. To this day, when autumn begins I have a compelling urge to be among the aspen and silently watch the play of golden light and shadow among the constantly flickering leaves. The stems of aspen leaves have a unique shape of four flat sides so that the slightest whisper of a breeze sets them to quivering. I have seen babies become completely fascinated by the constantly moving aspen leaves for an hour or more. The power of this movement of light and shadow caused by moving leaves comes from the long span of time in our evolutionary history when the higher primates, and later our hunter-gatherer ancestors, lived and hunted among flickering leaves in the forest.

Amerindians frequently hung their infants in cradle-boards among the trees. They knew what moving leaves do for a baby. In fact, all the gimmicks and toys strung on elastic cords across baby's crib are merely a modern mechanized substitute for real leaves.

The baby comes into the world with all it needs to become the being it was meant to be. It's not up to parents to mold it; they need only furnish the necessary food, shelter, and love so that its own being may flourish. Parents cannot know what this baby is meant to *be*. A baby has its own ways of fighting for the right to be. Childhood autism is one way—just giving up and withdrawing so they can't reach you. Edith Cobb hints at the depth of this need to *be* when she writes: "I believe, however, that the child's purpose and attitude are to a large extent directed toward preserving the self as separate—a species in himself." [58, 56] Wilfred Pelletier wrote of the fundamental difference between the white man's world and his Amerindian reservation: "I guess what I've learned—and it's taken me a long time—is that if you live in white society the most difficult thing to do is simply be yourself . . . And that's because in white society just being born is a putdown . . . that infant, as he grows up, learns he's under pressure to

become somebody. And so he begins inhabiting all kinds of identities . . ." [251, 156] And there's no more being.

As modern society becomes more relentless in its demands that the human person "fit" into its forms, the demands parents put on the child become more violent. The growing problem of child abuse has many facets, but this is one of them. "Each year, more children under the age of 5 die because of child abuse than die of disease. Figures vary from 50,000 to 100,000 deaths." [194] Erik Erikkson states, "It is well to remember that the majority of men have never invented the device of beating children into submission. Some of the American Plains Indian tribes were . . . deeply shocked when they first saw white people beat their children. In their bewilderment they could only explain such behavior as part of an overall missionary scheme . . . It all must mean, so they thought, a well-calculated wish to impress white children with the idea that this world is not a good place to linger in, and that it is better to look to the other world where perfect happiness is to be had at the price of having sacrificed this world." [81, 69]

It is of utmost importance that parents keep in mind the strength of the drive built into a child to be himself or herself by nature. This applies especially to mind and emotions, because it is rare indeed that parents will be determined to stop a child from walking. Yet these other drives are just as strongly present as the drive to walk.

For most parents in ordinary civilized surroundings, the drive to walk is not fully experienced as the child has flat, level, smooth floors or the flat ground to experiment with. When our son was small we had the unique opportunity to see this "drive" in full action. He began to walk shortly after his first birthday in October. We lived at the time in the mountains of Utah, at Alta. Before he was able to walk very far it snowed and continued to snow. So he walked in the house—busily and devotedly, as small children do. Then, in early December we went to town for a day of Christmas shopping and he was, for the first time, on a level space that stretched forever. And he walked and walked and walked and never stopped. We understood his need to walk, we thought at first. He tugged us along as fast as he could as he walked; we thought that he would soon be exhausted and then we would carry him, but he never gave up. At four that afternoon he was still walking. This child of fourteen months walked for more than seven hours continuously.

Further proof of this intense drive to walk came a little later in his life. He was nearly two years old, and we were on the Blue Glacier in the Olympic Peninsula for snow research. We lived in two tents pitched among the rocks of the moraine. A moraine is just about the most unstable bit of earth one can imagine. It is composed of all the loose rocks the glacier has picked up or gouged out and then left behind when the glacier shrank back from its greatest expansion. This moraine was long and narrow and composed of totally unconsolidated rocks. For a two-year-old it was one continuous climb after another to merely go from one side of the moraine to the other. There was no place at all for him to walk. His greatest fun was throwing rocks down the side of the mountain. One beautiful day I decided to hike down to a nearby lake and spend the day with him so he could play in the water. We left very early so he could walk the three miles down to the lake, as I knew he would like the walking after all the climbing over boulders. We spent the day floating on logs and lying in the sun. Late in the afternoon, I put him in the baby carrier on my back and started up, thinking he was tired. He would have none of it and demanded to be let down. Then he walked back up—all three miles. I hadn't allowed for this and it grew late. The sun went down and still he forged his way on, although by this time he was exhausted and stumbling. Then his father came down the trail looking for us and met us just a few hundred feet below the moraine. It was cold then, so he allowed us to put him in the carrier and he immediately fell asleep. Most people do not know that a two-year-old can walk six miles in one day down and up a steep mountain trail. A three-year-old or a four-year-old will complain and complain and may or may not do it, but a two-year-old, deprived for a month of walking, will joyfully do it because he's still in the drive to walk and it's his total purpose and joy.

This is a very vital "critical-period learning," and it's important to remember. Keep it in mind as we talk of other critical periods which are important for a child's development of awareness. Regarding childhood fantasy and imagination, Pearce says, "The whole crux of human intelligence hinges on this ability of mind." Yet, few parents are able to stand aside and let this happen to its full extent. We too often impose our adult view of reality on the child—with the best of intentions, of course. Actually, our adult view is really *world plus our idea*. It is *not* reality, and we find this hard to admit. We think it is for the child's self-preservation that we do certain restrictive things. But if we clearly have in mind that self-unfolding to the greatest potential is the goal, not self-preservation, we will give the child fewer fears; and the child will be enabled to be more aware and thus more intelligent in the true sense.

From ages one to seven "nature programs the child to do two things"—get concrete knowledge from all its senses of the world and at the same time play with that world. Play is the most important thing a child can do. [250, 92]

At about the age of four, primary process becomes noticeable—extrasensory perceptions, telepathy, etc. These are not occult, but normal processes available to human beings, but which our culture has lost. If these "primary perceptions" are not developed, they tend to disappear, just as a muscle atrophies when it is not used. These primary perceptions draw on nature's body of knowledge. [250, 137] But almost as soon as the child of four achieves these primary perceptions, our culture tries to force him to abandon it. Adults at this age can do the most for the child by encouraging all ventures into "other states of consciousness"—storytelling, fantasy, and play of all sorts.

Middle Childhood

"This is . . . the little-understood, prepubertal, halcyon, middle age of childhood, approximately from five or six to eleven or twelve . . . when the natural world is experienced in some highly evocative way, producing in the child a sense of some profound continuity with natural processes . . ." [59]

Pearce is adamant when he says that "*nothing is important* except physical interaction with the world." The child's physical actions *are* his thought processes. He cannot think in any other way.

Play is how he learns. This is why the child is so determined to play in spite of all the adults forcing him to do otherwise. Remember the determination of two-year-old Randy to walk. The drive to play is just as strong and just as necessary. If adults could only see that they are up against a genetically coded *need* for play perhaps they could relax and let it happen. As Pearce says, play serves survival. In animals the young play at fighting or hunting. The human child plays with the world—*world plus mind-brain*. The child plays in imagination, fantasy, and imitation, and in this play all the non-conscious procedures of learning take place. "Awareness is the end result." [250, 143]

As we have seen, 99 per cent of the human beings on this earth have lived as hunter-gatherers, thus what their children do must be valid for children, and what they do is play. The !Kung of the Kalahari live in such an inhospitable desert that we would expect everyone in the tribe to be hunting for food, but their children play. We cannot afford to let our children play. They must work hard and learn all that they need know to become successes in our world. Who is wiser? Because the desert bands contain small numbers of people, the play groups consist of many ages and both sexes, which discourages developing distinct games for boys and girls. They do not play competitive games, because of the wide range of ages involved; and because there are always adults around, the adults quickly stop aggressive behavior, with the result that Kalahari Bushmen simply are not aggressive. When these people become sedentary, aggression develops. [156]

Based on the needs of the body and brain system, which we inherited from our hunter-gatherer ancestors, there are three ecological needs of children under ten, according to Paul Shepard: "architecturally complex play space shared with companions; a cumulative and increasingly diverse experience of non-human forms, animate and inanimate, whose taxonomic names and generic relationships he must learn; and occasional and progressively more strenuous excursions into the wild world where he may, in a limited way, confront the non-human." [292, 267] If the child is interacting with the earth in a total manner, the still plastic brain can register many different patterns learned from non-human life without going through verbal explanations and rote learning. The patterns learned in this fashion may not be used for years, and the child may not even be consciously aware of them, but they are ready for use when needed.

Play, including ritualized play, is widespread among mammals. Shepard explains that "Ritual is always a signal that condenses (or symbolizes) information about a relationship. [Furthermore] . . . the 'as if' of play is the heart of ritual and, eventually, formal religious activity." [292, 196 and 199] Later, in formal ceremonies involving rituals "one moves between bases as in a game, now remembering that it is really Joe Smith behind the mask in the ceremony and now suspending that knowledge in transcendental experience. Play and worship are the two human activities removed from commonplace life. One is necessary for the other . . . It began with ancient hunters' recognition of formal and sacred rules for 'playing the game' [of hunting in balance with the environment]." [292, 199–200] The play of childhood is a necessary biological prerequisite to adult cultural rituals where human beings take their part in the fourfold relationship along with the earth, sky, and the "playing gods."

If the child has been allowed natural development, it has a "period of intensive and ecstatic play in which varying the possibilities of one's survival tools are explored." [250, 176] This is the joyous, yet peril-filled time of childhood—the time for walking limbs high above the ground in follow-the-leader, for jumping off garage roofs, and other such activities. Have you ever noticed how many of the dare-devil escapades of childhood have to do with balance? Concerning balance, it is interesting to note that the group which has most successfully preserved their culture against the encroaching white world, the Balinese, call the time before the Whiteman came, "When the world was steady." Furthermore, according to Bateson, their culture is structured around physical balance. They extend attitudes based upon this bodily balance to human relations; furthermore, they consider that motion is essential to maintaining balance in physical, social, and spiritual affairs. [13] The Balinese provide an excellent example of the mirroring interplay among earth, sky, gods, and man.

Children play with earth's gravity in many ways. As mentioned earlier, Gesell says, "The first and foremost function of the embryo is to adjust to the ceaseless pull of gravity." In childhood this seems to continue in their play with gravity. Perhaps they are learning just how much they *can* trust the earth. The present craze for skateboards seems to have opened up whole new areas for fundamental play with gravity. A boy careening down a city street, lying almost horizontally to the side of his board and yet steady and sure, is learning something of the utmost importance which no amount of pressure and force from adults is ever going to erase. The balance sports of skiing and surfing have had enormous influence on the lives of those adults devoted to them. These people say that it's the only thing that balances them out so they can stay sane in our insane world. Few people have been able to devote enough time to such sports to grasp their full implications—partly because of the seasonal nature of such sports and partly because of the distances involved to reach mountains or ocean. Realizing that today's children can skateboard every chance they get in cities throughout the country, I can't help feeling that there's some sort of breakthrough going on here. These children are not going to be as ready to believe all the culturally induced fear and anxiety thrown at them by schools and parents when they *know* they can trust the earth. The more they trust the earth, the less they can be reached by the weapon of fear which our culture uses to force people to conform.

Some skateboarders are killed, of course, but far more are killed by automobiles than by gravity. Furthermore, as Pearce points out, if the culture does not purposely induce anxiety because of the knowledge of death as ours does, "Awareness of death acts as a catalyst on all the child's knowledge . . . and brings alertness to his/her acts." It provides an exciting challenge rather than a source of anxiety and dread. "Child play becomes the deep play of late preadolescence and adolescence, play in which the young person is aware of how high the stakes are and so desires to increase his/her skills and up the ante." [250, 190] This is analogous to Heidegger's philosophical concept of the importance of mortality in human life. Only a mortal being can live to the fullest. Don Juan's idea of living with total attention because "death is over the left shoulder" is similar.

In our culture, however, this important play stage is suddenly shattered in the midst of childhood by our culturally-induced anxiety concerning death, which breaks the bond with the earth and forces the child into our premise that the best way to succeed is through success within our institutions. [250, 173]

To go further into the matter of death and parental concern, Pearce, in another book says that "parents' fear of social condemnation for 'irresponsibility' is projected as 'concern' for the child," which has led to extreme overprotection of children. Every aspect of the child's life is supervised. "Buffering the child against danger throughout his formative years, we then, somewhere around his sixteenth year, put him behind the wheel of two or three hundred horsepower, turn him loose on the freeways, and wonder why the vast majority of automobile accidents occur with young drivers." [249, 64] This is the first chance most kids have to get out and *do* without adults hanging around advising and controlling. Some years ago I knew a woman, so protective of her children that her younger son wouldn't go into a low marshy area with us to see the frogs because he might "get his shoes muddy." Her older son tried various ways of breaking away, but his mother successfully thwarted him each time. When he was sixteen and driving, he was killed—racing another car.

It is important to realize the difference between sudden fright, which is a biological "startle" affect occurring when a danger threatens so that the body can get ready or flee, and fear, which is a learned response. According to Joel Kramer's jnana yoga, fear lives in memories of the past and it lives in the future, which is past memories projected forward. But it is 'literally not possible to be afraid of anything that is happening. If I point a gun at you, you are not afraid that I'm pointing a gun at you. You're afraid I'm going to shoot you. If I have shot you, you're not afraid of being shot; you're already shot. You're afraid that I will shoot you again or that you will bleed to death, etc. So fear is never a response to what is, but rather what will be out of memories of what was." [159, 40] Anxiety is fear of something which might be done to us in the future. Fear and anxiety are our main weapons against our children. Our culture uses anxiety to motivate all of us to do that which we don't want to do naturally or willingly. The more we use fear and anxiety as a weapon on children, the less *being* they have. They learn they cannot trust their own being. We negate their bond with the earth so they learn not to trust the earth wisdom given them by this bond.

American Indian cultures, in general, permit and encourage their children to turn to the earth whenever there is a crisis in their life by sending them out when they are small to meditate in nature. Later, in adolescence, this culminates in the Vision Quest. Abraham Maslow provides a good example when he tells of an incident which happened during his early years in his profession, when he was on the Blackfoot reservation:

He was about seven or eight years old, and I found by looking very close that he was a kind of rich kid, in a Blackfoot way. He had several horses and cattle in his name, and he owned a medicine bundle of particular value. Someone, a grownup, turned up who wanted to buy the medicine bundle, which was the most valuable thing that he had. I learned from his father that what little Teddy did when he was made this offer—remember he was only seven years old—was to go into the wilderness by himself to meditate. He went away for about two or three days and nights, camping out, thinking for himself. He did not ask his father or his mother for advice, and they didn't tell him anything. He came back and announced his decision. I can just see us doing that with a seven-year-old kid.   [204, 231]

What is our seven or eight-year-old doing? He's sitting in school. Our culture is so fear-ridden our parents don't think a child has any time to waste out there in nature—he's got to be in school, learning to read and acquiring the tools for "success" in our competitive world. He can't waste time out there in nature, walking along between the two volcanoes like Giordano Bruno, or sitting there watching a current bush like C. S. Lewis, or sitting on a rock like Jung. In other words, he can't just *be*, he's got to perform, prove, and compete. Modern parents want their child to have a "superior mind" so the child had better do what they say, study hard, and perform well. Never mind that Edith Cobb documented the fact that three hundred creative human beings from the sixteenth century to the present discovered their "superior minds" in nature [59] and the fact that, as Pearce says, "Forcing the early child to deal prematurely with adult abstract thought can cripple the child's ability to think abstractly later on." [250, 27]

Ordinarily school is thought of as a place where a child becomes educated but, instead, the school is actually performing a kind of split-brain surgery. Dr. Bogen, the surgeon who performs split-brain operations to help epileptics, explains that, "Since education is effective only insofar as it affects the working of the brain, we can see that an elementary school program, narrowly restricted to reading, writing, and arithmetic, will educate mainly one hemisphere, leaving half of an individual's high-level potential unschooled." [35] There is far more involved than specific difficulties for individuals, since "the entire student body is being educated lopsidedly." School is forcing children to function "half-brained."

We hear a lot about our high rate of left-brain literacy in this country. We never hear a word about our right-brain non-literacy, as contrasted to the high levels of such people as the Hopi in right-brain functions. Right-brain non-literacy is much more fundamental because it really means an inability to read the earth itself, because learning from the earth comes to us through the spatial, sensuous, relational, gestalt-making right brain.

Were you thinking that those were the words;
Those upright lines, those curves, angles, dots!
No, those are not the words, the substantial words are in the ground and sea,
They are in the air, they are in you . . .
The workmanship of souls is by those inaudible words of the Earth.
                        A Song of the Rolling Earth by Walt Whitman

Or, as Conrad Aiken, influenced by ancient Chinese poets, wrote:

The landscape and the language are the same
For we ourselves are landscape and are land.   [3]

Yes, a child does have to learn to read books, but this is a fairly easy matter. John Holt and other authorities have frequently said that if you leave a child absolutely alone with no schooling at all, and—providing he isn't brain-damaged—he'll learn to read sometime around the age of nine. He can't avoid it in our world filled with signs and written instructions. The difficulties in learning to read come from culture-induced fear and anxiety.

Nine is a crucial age for much more important matters than reading. It is the age for finishing the development of the important bonding to the earth and for developing primary process thinking.

Bruner, referring to the impact of literacy on children in the Belgian Congo, wrote: "School seems to promote the self-consciousness born of a distinction between human processes and physical phenomena." Pearce quotes Bruner, but says this is not what we want in the years from seven to eleven, when "such premature separation breaks up the functional unity between individual and world system" and limits primary process thinking. [250, 189] He says this leads to the alienation that contributes to the concept of death around age nine. What happens is that the primary process in the brain cannot do what it is supposed to do and, at the same time, filter its own function through our cultural death-concept, which classifies the flow of primary process as dangerous and says the only safe space is the culture's body of knowledge. The result is a splitting of the brain. The primary process is pitted against the rest of the brain. The child feels isolated from the world and even its own body. This is the beginning of the split from the earth. As mentioned earlier, around the age of nine and through eleven is the most usual time of poltergeist activity. There is usually such a sub-teenager in the household where bottles break with no one touching them and furniture cracks. It seems most likely this is an unconscious protest of the child's primary process, which is connected with the life flow of the earth. It is a protest against being cut off from the flow.

"The stage-specific period for bonding to the earth" begins to fade at around eleven and disappears about fourteen or fifteen. And with it the ability for "reversibility thinking," true creative thinking. It's only by fortuitous circumstances that the adult ever recovers this ability. Drugs can do it occasionally, reprogramming your mind by jnana yoga or some other discipline might help, but it would be much more simple to let it develop through Nature when it is meant to.

Now we can begin to see some of the fear involved in schooling. "Real learning does not live when there is fear," according to Joel Kramer. [159, 38] A fearful child cannot simply go ahead and learn. He has to figure out first if it's safe to learn, and what it is the teacher wants him to learn. You can begin to see the maze he's confronted with. This is not what school is supposed to be about. The word "school" according to

Richards means "the leisure to learn . . . Its root means 'a holding back': wait, there is something here to pay attention to, to be mindful of." [274, 177]

The word *education* comes from the root word "educare," which means to draw out—not pour in or force, but a mindful drawing out. It's all in the child or rather in the *child-plus-earth* together. One further word will help us here, *academy*, "the Greek school of philosophy founded by Plato, so-called from a garden planted by Academus where Plato taught his followers." [25, 5] To the Greeks, it was inconceivable to learn without paying attention to Nature. It was just as inconceivable to the hunter-gatherers. To them the earth was the greatest teacher. Mindfulness, awareness of the earth, drew out the secrets of Nature for their life. Learning was done all the time in the context of living within the tribe and its relationship to the *place*. How else did primitive people discover every type of food we eat today and most of our medicines?

Our children, from elementary school through college, are telling us in both violent and non-violent ways that schooling just isn't working. It's irrelevant. "They are concerned not so much with making a living as making a life." Dr. Bogen says, "They see a world of warring elders, busily Becoming at the expense of Being, who want them to be unhappy in the same half-brained way. The fight with nature for survival is won, they feel; and it is time we learn to live within nature as bilaterally educated, whole persons." [35]

Standing Bear, an Oglala Indian, succinctly explains Indian education in nature: "Children were taught to sit still—and look when apparently there was nothing to see, and to listen intently when all seemingly was quiet." [206, 171] In other words, they learned total awareness. Paul Shepard gives us a few more details of how our children can once again begin to learn from Nature: "The strategies for the authentic life are blueprinted in the genes." Those very activities which most attract children are how they learn: "In those crucial experiences of childhood play and exploration, in the impulse to name and classify and anatomize, in the yearning for skill tests, heroes, and the 'other,' in ceremonial revelation or workable myth . . . are the moments when the perception of nature is fixed and the heart of the hunter-gatherer comes to the surface." [292] In fact, *the* major learning situations for both children and adults, for the vast majority of those humans who have inhabited this earth, have been the great seasonal festivals where story-telling, dance, music, and chanting combine in a total, synesthetic learning experience of the earth, the sky, the mortals, and the gods.

Even in modern times, a profound early experience in nature can lead to a conscious choice to learn from nature rather than from school. Austin Post became one of the top experts in the United States Geological Survey as a direct result of such an early experience.

Austin grew up on an apple farm near Lake Chelan in Eastern Washington during the depression. The land is arid and must be irrigated, but he could see snow on the distant mountains. The first time he actually saw a big snow peak up close was on a trip to Seattle with a youth group, the Future Farmers of America. The group stopped at the top of Chinook Pass to let the boys see the view. In Austin's own words, "Someone said, 'There's Mount Rainier!' And so I raise my eyes from all the wild flowers and green meadows and such as a desert dweller is feasting on hungrily, looking for a regular mountain, like all those about, only bigger, of course—seeing first Governor's Ridge—and impressed by the lofty pinnacles rising into a sky curiously mottled and hazy. Then looking closer at this curious sky and realizing it wasn't sky, it was snow, crevassed and broken and glistening in the hazy light! The eye going up by degrees from crevasse to yawning crevasse, to the clouds, looking at the crevasses in awe at the height and then suddenly aware that these clouds, too, are snow! The eye then non-plussed, rising higher and higher and it's *still* snow —until, impossibly high in the sky and incredibly grand, a tiny rim of soil against the pale blue of the sky itself. [The summit] What a way to first see a great mountain! Many's the time I've been there since on a clear day and nothing of the sort is to be seen. Conditions that day were a real set-up with the soft haze and afternoon lighting. So Mount Rainier appeared in my first view— immense beyond the faintest glimmering of imagination! Beautiful, too, in all its sublime, pristine unearthiness— a case, too of 'love at first sight'—a love which will never dim or become commonplace. Each time I fly around that great mountain doing glacier photography, I always make one close-in pass (generally at Willis Wall) in order to recapture some of the feeling of immensity, and believe me, flying close enough does it!" [265]

As with Edith Cobb's three hundred autobiographies, this nature experience shaped Austin's life. He had no time for school when he could learn from the mountains and snow. He dropped out of high school early and went to work on the old Forest Service trail crews and as fire lookout, but all the time learning from the earth. His total awareness of the shapes and forms of the mountains gave him what one might call a "body knowledge" of the ancient glacier which formed them and a working knowledge of modern glaciers. As his knowledge grew, more interesting jobs opened up, in which he came into even closer contact with glaciers, until finally he was asked to work for the United States Geological Survey office in Tacoma as a research hydrologist. But there was only one problem: The government requirements for the salary they wanted to pay him demanded a high school diploma which, of course, he didn't have. So they wrote to his high school back in Chelan, Washington and got an honorary diploma, because by this time he was famous in his field. His articles appear in scholarly journals, such as the *Journal of Glaciology*. In fact, he is frequently referred to as Dr. Post. After all, such an authority must have at least one Ph.D. Austin just laughs and goes ahead learning and suffering with his glaciers in a bad year (when there's not much snow and the glaciers shrink), and rejoicing in a good year when the rain and snow is worse than usual in Washington and his beloved glaciers are healthy and growing.

13. The Second Hill of Life

Youth

Among the tribes of the eastern forests and the Great Plains the Youth's Vigil, also called the Vision Quest, marked the second hill in the Indian's life. All males and some females followed the custom. The age at which this occurred varied from as young as seven or eight to sixteen or seventeen. It was a solitary time of "total awareness" and total receptivity, of awaiting word from the earth itself as to the direction of that life. The messenger which brought this word was perhaps an eagle or a lowly mammal or even a plant or tree, but the word it brought gave the youth insight into the particular manner in which he would "walk in balance" with the earth through the remainder of life.

The great Indian prophets, Tecumseh, Keokuk, Smohalla, and Wavoka received their revelations from Vision Quests. Many details of major Indian rituals came from Vision Quests. If a youth was granted such a gift for his tribe, he achieved great prestige for his contribution to the tribe. The Plains Indians had the Vision Quest, the Australian natives had the "walkabout," the early Christian cultures had a valid confirmation sacrament in the Church, and the Jewish have "Bar Mitzvah." All of the "rites of passage" deal with youth at the crucial stage of becoming adults. For millenia, in most human cultures, boys around the age of twelve have been separated from their families and given special instruction for periods varying from a few days to years, which culminated in a ritual proclaiming that they were adults.

The changes taking place in adolescence prepare the youth for moving from the limited personal family to the realization of a greater, "cosmic" family. To the extent that the human beings of a particular culture have clarified their relationship with the earth, the sky and the gods of their *place*, the adolescents' task is made easy or difficult. Occasionally, as in the modern world, it is nearly impossible. Margaret Mead's book, *Coming of Age in Samoa*, showed that the Samoan teenager was calm and free from trauma, proving that adolescence is not necessarily a specially difficult period in a young person's life. [213] In *The Forest People*, Colin Turnbull tells that the forest pygmies have such a close relationship to their forest and such faith that it will provide for them, that they don't even need any kind of initiation for their youths. They permit their boys to go through the initiation rites of the neighboring village, but only so that their boys will be considered adults by the neighbors. [331, 217-227]

In hunting-gathering cultures, the long period of taxonomic learning which took place in middle childhood now bears fruit, as the knowledge of species of plants and animals, which had formerly helped develop cognitive thought, is now used for an extension of thought into other realms—even into that area commonly labelled religious. The root meaning of religion is "a binding together." Accomplishing this binding together, this relationship with his cosmic family, is the task of youth. Paul Shepard states that the basic taxonomic knowledge of primitive peoples "repeatedly astonishes" scientists. "One group of Columbian Indians knows two hundred species of a single genus of plants by sight, name, medical, nutritive, ecological, utilitarian, and symbolic use. As many as two thousand plants are recognized by many groups . . . Apparently the absence of writing, of man-made landscapes, and of an elaborate political state has not impaired the development of individual capacity. As Lévi-Strauss has observed, the most primitive people on earth today, the Australian aborigines, are unequalled in their intellectual sophistication, 'in their taste for erudition and speculation.'" [292, 202]

At about the age of twelve, the child develops a poetic mood and a predilection for punning. "The formal, ceremonial part of developing the initiate's disciplined devotion is based squarely on his newly felt capacity for poetic dualism." [292, 207] Ceremonies for the initiate depend on words that are linked with the deepest experiences in the child's life—those that are related to experiences of the mother matrix and the earth matrix. All of space and all of time are inseparably linked with the particular *place* and actual events in the life of this young human being, so that every act of daily life can become a cosmic ritual.

This "cosmic taxonomy," as Shepard puts it, is brought about by bringing the language brain of the left hemisphere together with the spatial, artistic function of the right hemisphere. Without this, there cannot be full self-realization for the person. This gives us a clue why youth find modern schooling, with its emphasis on left-hemisphere intellectuality, so irrelevant.

Species behavior is determined by evolution, not culture. "Ceremonial initiation based on myth and trial is biological, a specialized activity of all human minds, while the content of any particular ceremony is a cultural matter and varies among different peoples." [292, 219] Myth-making is a part of this. Throughout man's entire history as a hunter, at the end of the hunt the young boys joined with the older hunters as they recounted the events of the hunt. With time, the repetition of particular events became myths. Because the particular events of the hunt are related to landmarks, gradually the entire locality or *place* becomes the setting of a continuing myth-drama. Bushmen and Australian aborigines do this even today. In our own culture the mechanism is still there. At the age of fourteen and fifteen, boys spend a lot of time at the end of the day talking over the events of the day—what happened to whom—who got a new job—who got hurt on the corner of 14th and Elm. All sports involve this same talking over—in skiing, how so-and-so did that gelande off the cornice or how Kim broke a leg on the headwall. What is happening is that the daily events are being linked to a "mythology of places". Shepard says that for youth, "their most solemn and formal group activity is this ritual review." [292, 219] Shepard goes on to explain that among the Bushmen of the Kalahari Desert, the whole clan still gathers to hear the hunter tell, sing, and re-enact the events of the hunt. Events happening at particular places are gone over both powerfully and lightly, so that new experiences "are woven—primarily through local geography—into an eternal tapestry, continuous with the myths of creation." The wisdom of the older men makes the connections. It is just at this point that the whole thing collapses for modern boys. "Like zoo-born lions trying to bury their uneaten leftovers in the cement floor, young men gather at the end of the day to spin out the eternal from the day's events—except that, once the spinning is done, there is no one else there to do the winding." [292, 220-221] They have to try to do the winding up themselves; but since all they have is a limited experience with no continuity to the past, their "clan mythology" cannot fill the need and it only leads to eventual disillusion. The continuous "shucking and jiving" of our present street youth and drug subcultures is a twisted version of this necessary activity. The very places where their events happen can vanish tomorrow with the wrecking of an old building and the rise of a new one in its place. When we know the deep ties to *place* of modern kibbutz youth (see below), we can perhaps appreciate the psychological damage done to our young people by wrenching their landmarks from them almost overnight.

Even today, in the retelling of events among youth there spontaneously develops at times a sort of chanting —mostly in answer to the teller of the "myth." It is easy to see how traditional chanting developed as a learning process. The older person repeated the lore of the tribe and was answered by the youths over and over until it became a part of them. Words and rhythm together link the right and left hemispheres of the brain and provide total learning.

Youths of hunting-gathering cultures were initiated into a new family, the clan. Clans are named after animals, as nature is the model for culture. The different plant and animal totems are not only religious, they also define relationships in the human cultural system and between human beings and Nature. Totemism extends to the land itself. All the features of *place* of the tribe, such as rivers and mountains, have proper names with appropriate myths. The "walkabout" of Australian youth is a "grand tour of the ancestral past." [292, 204] California Indians had long song cycles which not only held the locations of watering holes and such in the Indians' mind, but also the cultural relevance of each important rock or mountain. [166]

Part I of this book showed how "sacred" mountains are a part of every early culture. But not only mountains are sacred; many other features of the landscape may be accounted sacred and so become involved in the youth's initiation time. As a result initiation is "a series of environmental feedbacks [culminating] in maturity and the young adult's capacity for fidelity." [292, 206] Erik Erikson has defined fidelity "as that virtue and quality of adolescent ego strength which belongs to man's evolutionary heritage, but which—like all the basic virtues—can arise only in the interplay of a life stage with the individuals and the social forces of a true community." Youth is the time of a "search for something and somebody to be true." [82] When Erikson wrote this some years ago, I know he did not have in mind the full definition of community provided in Aldo Leopold's "land ethic," where he defines community as including the soils, the waters, the plants, and animals, as well as human beings. [178] It is just this total community, however, which was present in the hunting-gathering cultures, which comprise most of humanity's history.

The largest-scale attempt at true community in modern times, the Israeli kibbutz movement, has brought many individuals into intense involvement with the land. Bettelheim, in his book, *Children of the Dream*, seems puzzled by the phenomenon. "Usually it was not nature in general a kibbutznik would speak of, but a particular feature of his kibbutz: a place by the lake; the view from (or at) a hill; a glen; or some other small place which, by loving, he had made his own. The romantic attachment of their parents to Israel-as-idea has been translated by their children into a fierce love for a particular landscape, which will keep many at the kibbutz, despite strong pulls to leave." He mentions two examples. "One young man spent fourteen and more hours a day, often seven days a week, tending sheep, because it allowed him to be out in his beloved landscape all by himself. Another had a wife who wanted desperately to leave the kibbutz so that their children could live with them at home. But though a good father and husband (by the wife's account), he could not bear to leave behind him the small lake where he spent nearly all his time as a fisherman—not for the fishing, but because of the beauty of the lake." In his attempt to account for this "odd" aberration, Bettelheim goes on: "Theirs is not a farmer's love for his land; it is a true love relation with nature. Since nature does not disappoint them, in relation to it they can let themselves feel deeply . . . Virtually every person I interviewed who had grown up in the kibbutz and then left it spoke with deepest longing for the natural beauty of his kibbutz, though none wanted to return." [28, 266–267]

The lack of what Erikson terms "true community" is at the root of most of the adolescent difficulties of our day. It is not basically the adolescent-parent conflict at all. Shepard is very outspoken when he writes: "The idea that conflict between adolescent and parent is due to individual faults and personal attitudes must surely be one of the most dangerous misconceptions of modern man." He enumerates the repressions and useless entreaties involved in this misunderstanding of the roots of the conflict and attributes to them "a fair share of unnecessary human suffering." [292, 215] Unnecessary, because the trauma of the adolescent in our time goes deeper than family. It is the culture itself that is at fault, and the family alone cannot cure it. "Derangements of human behavior of this magnitude have their roots in the evolution of human intelligence and nervous systems," the heritage of our hunter ancestors. The high degree of specialization in human intelligence, a result of the hunting-gathering life, may not be able to survive dense populations and our unstable environment of today. What is needed is "drastic ecological revampment . . . and a revival of the lineaments of tribal society." [292, 227–228]

The theme of tribal man recurs again and again in modern times as an ideal. Marshall McLuhan's "tribal man," immersed in the group, linked by instant media, is one example. The many variation of experiments in communal living is another example. A third, relatively little-known example is the exciting living and learning of all ages involved in scientific field work. John Platt writes: "Good living is with a tribe. At the Marine Biological Laboratories at Woods Hole, Massachusetts, where I have spent several summers, the boundaries between the generations seem to disappear, as well as the boundaries between work and play, and between indoors and outdoors and between man and environment. Children and students and teachers walk barefoot in and out of the laboratories, arguing science and studying the odd creatures brought up from the sea. All night they watch the fish embryos developing in the dishes, and they go out before dawn together to catch the big striped bass. The four-year-olds solemnly examine frogs, and ten-year-olds sell their catch of dogfish to the labs, the fifteen-year-olds listen to the DNA arguments on the beach or play savage tennis with the senior scientists." [263] In my own experience we found similar conditions even on such a small project as the snow research on the Blue Glacier in the Olympics. Our son, Randy, even when a child, was a valued member of the station, doing his share of the necessary work to keep it going, such as carrying buckets of snow to melt for drinking water. As soon as he was old enough to stay up long enough he played cards with the graduate students. With this new equality he was able to enter into the discussions with no put-down, engage in the exciting sport of pack-rat trapping or trying to outwit the field mice with incredible new traps. Learning and playing and working were inextricably mixed for him.

Merely trying to live as a tribe on an experimental commune is not enough for genuine community. "No one can live on empty function," according to Paul Shepard. "There must also be a content, passionately believed in, that relates man to nature, centering all human experience." [292, 228]

Not only is a real relationship to the land necessary for youth, but also contact with animals as beings who are both like and unlike human beings and "who evoke the mystery of creation and the continuity of a life that is shared . . . As beings with their own purposes, they are the planet's rebuke to human self-worship." [292, 230] This contact must be with animals in the wild—not in zoos or as domesticated animals—but wild with their own life, which human beings can never wholly understand.

Aldo Leopold began his career in Wildlife Management in the Southwest, where at first his sole interest and purpose was to see that there were plenty of deer for hunting. In pursuit of these, he one day shot a wolf and watched it die:

We reached the old wolf in time to watch a fierce green fire dying in her eyes. I realized then, and have known ever since, that there was something new to me in those eyes—something known only to her and to the mountain. I was young then, and full of trigger-itch; I thought that because fewer wolves meant more deer, that no wolves would mean

hunters' paradise. But after seeing the green fire die, I sensed that neither the wolf nor the mountain agreed with such a view."   [178, 130]

Susan Flader, Leopold's biographer, continues: "The deer, the coyote, the cowman, the hunter, in each the call [of a wolf] instilled some immediate, personal fear or hope: 'Only the mountain has lived long enough to listen objectively to the howl of a wolf.'" [88, 1] Leopold began to try to "think like a mountain." As he began to see more clearly, he became more aware and his thinking changed. He saw that too many deer ruined the plant growth and eventually led to starving deer; that wolves were necessary for healthy deer; and then, eventually, he saw that land health was at the heart of it all. After many more years of "thinking like a mountain," Leopold finally wrote down his "land ethic": "A thing is right when it tends to preserve the integrity, stability and beauty of the biotic community. It is wrong when it tends otherwise." [178] Aldo Leopold was a hunter all his life, yet he actually killed only two deer. The first one, shot in 1909, was for meat for the men in a Forest Service camp, and the second was shot in 1923 on a hunting trip. He loved to hunt, but he did not need to kill any more deer; he was a true hunter—not a trigger-happy hunter.

Most of the youth activities derived from our hunting past have to do with males. Females had a vastly different role. As Shepard succinctly put it, "The gathering activities of women, and their parental, sexual, and social roles are too basic and important to society to trust to the hazard and arbitrariness of learned performance [as in hunting]." [292, 210] Women's initiations were usually shorter and less intense. The Apache tribe had a special ceremony for girls which took place not at the precise time of first menstruation "but on some fine summer day that could be appointed before hand so that hundreds might attend."

The girl spent four days in a special tipi. But this was ceremonially built and known as "the home of White Painted Woman," the divine mother of the Apache Culture Hero. The girl herself was White Painted Woman for four days and able to give blessing like her namesake. She was painted and dressed by a woman who must be industrious and good and has perhaps had a vision from the White Painted Woman. A male singer "cared for her" daily with sacred songs.

At the end of this seclusion, the girl scattered pollen over the people, especially children, who were brought for her blessing. At night, there was an imposing dance of masked men, representing the spirits of the four directions, come to bring blessing as they did on all crucial occasions. Then there was feasting and dancing. No wonder a girl who was maturing was known to these Apaches as "she through whom we shall all have a good time."

Ruth Underhill [333, 58]

The Washo Indians who lived around Lake Tahoe and in the Sierras had a very powerful ceremony for a girl when she had her first menstruation. She fasted for four days and late in the fourth day she climbed to the top of a nearby mountain carrying a basket of live coals. When she arrived at the top she lit the four piles of cut fir branches arranged there. The straighter the smoke went up into the sky, the better her life would be and the more blessings she would bring on her people. Then, carrying a sacred painted stick she raced down the mountain to her people and was welcomed by the Dance of the Woman, which lasted all night. At dawn she washed herself in the stream, and a great feast was held. [281, 103–119] In the Mescalero Apache puberty rite, the young girl ran down the mountain carrying a burning torch from the fire which she had lit.

Such rituals as these caused the young Indian girl to be proud of the special "woman power" which came to her with her first menstruation. The entire tribe honored the "woman power" she brought to them. Nowadays we dismiss this power and instead call it "the curse."

The young girl in primitive tribes had a further advantage over modern women in that her first husband was likely to be twenty years her senior, so she profited by his maturity for he was a better hunter than a young man. Her second husband was usually nearer her own age and often her third husband was much younger than she. "Indeed, it seems probable," according to Paul Shepard, "that the absence of a parental Oedipal barrier between daughter and father equivalent to the paternal threat separating mother and son and the presence of widespread father-daughter incest (even today) are indications that natural selection in the evolution of human society has worked toward the imprinting of a dominant male image and the mating and bond of the adolescent girl to the mature man." [292, 210] This helps the more rapid advance of maturity in the young female without the need of the long periods of trial and error necessary for boys.

Sex is not the problem in traditional cultures that it is in ours. Wilfred Pelletier tells of the differences between sex on the Indian reserve in Canada and sex in the white world:

My own introduction to sex was provided by a relative. I still look on that as one of the greatest and happiest experiences of my life. From that time on, it seems to me that I screwed all the time, without letup. Not just my relatives, who were not always available, but anywhere I could find it, and it always seemed to be there. I was always running into some girl or some woman, and our relationship was a sex relationship. That doesn't mean that that's all we did. These were people I had a social relationship with. I saw them lots of places and we did all kinds of things together, but during that period in my life the thing that was foremost, always in my blood and in my brain, was sex . . . Everybody was completely relaxed about it because it always just worked out. You always seemed to end up with whoever you wanted and you did whatever the two of you wanted to do . . . It all just happened . . . I have the impression that in white society, at least for those of my generation, sex and relating to girls was really rough. It was sinful and immoral, stuff like that. There was a whole ritualistic courtship attached to it, and "honorable" intentions. And all that seemed hypocritical and dishonorable to me, because there was no trust there, only

anxiety and fear. The girls were afraid of getting knocked up and the boys were afraid of being found out. It also seemed to me that screwing always had to be tied to what I would call romance, which pretty well removed the chance of a young boy being introduced to sex by an older woman.

[251, 76–77]

Now that it is clear how our culture thwarts the biologically programmed development of youth, it is no wonder that there are such traumas and breakdowns at young ages. A few statistics: Dr. Moritz Chafetz, director of the National Institute of Alcohol and Alcohol Abuse, Washington, D.C., states, "Our study shows that more than 1.3 million kids between the ages of twelve and seventeen get drunk at least once a week . . . The 1.3 million are only those who are detected. It says nothing about how many more are drinking without being detected . . . What is equally horrible is that by the time the students reach the tenth grade, about fifty percent of them are drinking regularly." [348] In the same article, the superintendent of schools in a suburb of Philadelphia, where the school board had just bought a breath-analyzer kit to use on students, is quoted: "Our school system has no more of a drinking problem than any other. We just decided to do something about it. Too many were coming to school drunk and passing out or getting sick."

The continually increasing drug abuse in this country is even better known. But the underlying cause of both phenomena is not so well-known. Tom Pinkson, who was formerly with the San Marin (California) County Drug Abuse program and now gives healing workshops in Nature based on Vision Quests, writes of his own experience in therapy work in the "world of the heroin addict, juvenile and adult 'criminal offenders,' junior and senior high school students." All this has "provided me an empirical base which postulates a powerful and distinct relationship between alienation, destructive patterns of drug abuse and the diseased condition of the environment." He further points out "that success in future therapeutic and educational endeavors to ameliorate the crisis situations of youth will prove fruitful *only* when we return to a holistic perspective that recognizes and understands the complex interaction between the world of the individual psyche and the physical environment. Healing will occur only when we realize that separateness between the human brain and the world 'outside' is an illusion and this illusion is both self-destructive and environmentally destructive." [260, 3]

Pinkson makes it very clear that "the heroin addict, the self-polluter *extraordinaire*, is merely a more public manifestation of a toxic pattern that involves us all." [260, 19] When he began to realize that getting heroin addicts out into Nature might be a clue to healing, he sent some of his Marin County drug-abuse kids on an Outward Bound course. But these "sophisticated members of the heroin sub-culture" were too smart for the

Outward Bound people and manipulated their way out of every real confrontation. So he realized it would have to be set up differently, so that each heroin kid had to confront Nature directly, with no intervention. "The Natural world provides physical-level feedback that manipulative verbal skills will not suffice to avoid. Try setting up a shelter with a cord and a poncho in a driving rainstorm and you'll see what I mean." [260, 60]

Pinkson actually cured heroin addicts. In his summation of his success with these addicts, he wrote that ". . . something is working, consistently, with a wide range of personality disorders and with effects of some duration as evidenced by the findings emanating from my own research efforts." [260, 263]

That Tom Pinkson has cured addicts is a fact, but as he emphasizes repeatedly, he needs total wilderness to do it—not campgrounds with other people in them or areas where the kids can walk out and get a hamburger at the local drive-in—but true wilderness. How many acres of wilderness does it take to cure each heroin addict? We can't really compute this. But one thing is certain—if we had more wilderness and our youth had access to it and knew how to live in and with it, we wouldn't even have heroin addicts, drug abusers, or alcohol abusers among our youth. Here is one example, in an ex-addict's own words, of what happens in a wilderness cure. A young woman who had been on methadone and, since the experience, is now off all drugs and a counselor at the Marin Open House, had her experience on a river trip. "I had to go with it, with its turns and rocks and all, just like life with its obstacles and rocks in our path. I had to learn to flow with it and deal with those things that spring up, and most of all, to get high from it! God, did I get high! No drugs, oh no, I wanted to be so alert and so aware, it would have been crazy to be stoned. Like life, we need to be alert and aware so we can be ready to deal with the unexpected." [260, 181] This is how nature intended us to live—alert and aware, as human beings lived in hunting-gathering cultures.

Pinkson found that mountain climbing was the experience which produced the most startling curative results, and he mentions Dr. Charles Houston's studies in this field. Houston, a psychologist and mountain climber, writes: "Mountaineering is one of the few human activities where stress is clear, apparent and freely sought. The goal is sharp and visible. There is no doubt when one has succeeded or failed. Mountaineering is more a quest for self-fulfillment than a victory over others or over nature. Climbers court and control risk, they seek stress but avoid uncontrollable dangers. By their repeated self-testing, capacity grows. By such expansion of capacity, man finds that he has wider limits than we know." [154] This kind of learning experience is what the poet, Gary Snyder, had in mind when he said, "Another great teaching that I had came from some older men, all of whom were practitioners of a little-known indigenous Occidental school of mystical practice called mountaineering." [56]

Gaston Rébuffat, one of the most famous climbing guides in the Alps, can certainly be called one of the teachers in this "school of mystical practice." He tells of his careful efforts in providing for the encounter of a fifteen-year-old youth with the mountains. The father of the boy was a long-time client of Rébuffat who knew his son needed help in growing at this time. In his book, *Between Heaven and Earth*, Rébuffat writes:

From now on, I was to introduce to Jean-Francois the loveliest thing between earth and sky. For him, I should compose, high up in the mountains, a "manly poem," a poem which should be beautiful and which would grip him. And, as he followed me silently, I delved deep into my thoughts. Mine is a wonderful job, but sometimes I find it very difficult to reach the heart of an adolescent.

I did not say a word. I was afraid to shatter the silence with some clumsy or meaningless remark. I knew that a youth is not to be won over with words, and that words will not gain his confidence or his friendship. Rather as a gardener shows a visitor his grounds, I was showing Jean-Francois this world of rock and ice in which his father and I had so often journeyed . . . His father had warned me: Jean-Francois gives no outward expression of joy; he ruminates in silence and if he goes on, you can take it that he has been won over. This confrontation between Jean-Francois and the mountain world around him, then his captivation, had a certain quiet dignity. The mountains were indeed beautiful but for this moment they were more than that. For Jean-Francois this was a moment of Truth and it is Truth which helps a young boy to become a man . . . It is not a question of enjoying danger; that is easy and somehow corrupt. It was not a question of foolishly risking life. Face to face with danger one learns little . . . But it is in face of difficulty or an obstacle that one stretches oneself and shows what one is capable of. Mountaineers love beauty, friendship and life; these they respect. They have no liking for foolish risks.

Moving from serac to crevasse, from a wall of ice to a slab of rock, from a bridge of stone to a ridge of snow, Jean-Francois and I built our mountain, composed our poem.

[272]

"A human life, so often likened to a spectacle upon a stage, is more justly a ritual. The ancient values of dignity, beauty, and poetry which sustain it are of Nature's inspiration; they are born of the mystery and beauty of the world. Do no dishonour to the earth lest you dishonour the spirit of man. Hold your hands out over the earth as over a flame. To all who love her, who open to her the doors of their veins, she gives of her strength, sustaining them with her own measureless tremor of dark life. Touch the earth, love the earth, honour the earth, her plains, her valleys, her hills, and her seas; rest your spirit in her solitary places. For the gifts of life are the earth's and they are given to all . . ."

Henry Beston

BLACK CANYON OF THE GUNNISON

(Photograph by Steve Meyers)

14. The Third Hill of Life

Maturity

The word, *maturity*, means "the state of being complete, perfect or ready" according to the Oxford dictionary. In a hunting-gathering culture such as the Amerindian, maturity marked a coming into the fullness of skill as a hunter or gatherer. From childhood on, these human beings had learned from the earth and its animals so that by the time of maturity, according to the anthropologist, Hartley Burr Alexander, the hunter's "sincerest vital prejudice is for a kind of sympathy with wildlife itself, which, while he slays for need, is nonetheless cherished and felt even in its humblest forms to be participant with man in nature's rights . . . He feels himself, along with other creatures, to exist by the sufferance of powers not all of whom are human in form or spirit, and to deserve to live he must show his quality." [4, 183-184] Instead of the prime motive of most mature humans in modern civilized cultures, that of acquiring more money and more material possessions, the Indian had "the cult and pursuit of wisdom, both of the body and of the mind . . . It is this wisdom—of conduct, lore, ritual, song and dance—which is the treasure of life as the Indian understands it." [4, 185-186] The Indian's total reliance on nature as teacher, that which gives wisdom, is based on the three billion years of "research and development behind every living thing." [260, 13]

This surety of the Indian is in marked contrast to the frantic efforts to succeed in modern technological society, where every "solution" breeds a bigger problem. For example, "our agricultural economy has destroyed more than half of our soil energy reserves in less than two hundred years." [23, 34] Such ruined topsoil can no longer grow healthy crops. The solution was more chemical fertilizer and more insecticides which, in turn, poisoned the soil and the water we drink. The solution to that, of course, is more technology which requires even more machines which use still more oil; until now humanity has not only ruined the land, it has succeeded in polluting the entire ocean. The magnitude of this disaster was shown by Thor Heyerdahl. In 1947, when he crossed 4,300 miles of the Pacific Ocean in his balsa raft, *Kon-Tiki*, the ocean was clean and crystal clear. In 1970 when he crossed 3,270 miles of the Atlantic Ocean in a papyrus raft, the *Ra,* he found sporadic oil clots floating by within reach of his dipnets during 43 days of the 57-day crossing. [123, 59] And so the never-ending spiral of destruction grows bigger and bigger.

"Things are hopeless, so quit trying," says Greg Brodsky. [40] Far from being pessimistic, this is the beginning of wisdom. Brodsky says that hope is a dangerous word. If you have hopes for some particular thing, you are trying to make things go the way your tiny bit of rational brain thinks it *ought* to be done, instead of relying on your total relationship to Nature as a whole, including your million-year programming by Nature. Things seem to be getting worse and worse—personally, nationally, and globally. Nothing works. It's because I'm not good enough. I don't know enough. I've got to work harder. *Forget all that*. It's never worked, so let's quit trying and go back to the life that nature intended for human beings.

We must again call to mind that cultural man has been on Earth for some two million years and that he has lived over 99 per cent of this period as a hunter-gatherer. Only in the last 10,000 years have humans been agriculturalists. [172] Compared to this time span the present destructive technological era is "an inconsequential ripple." [300, 82] As shown earlier, the hunter's life makes him aware of the continuum of life and death—that all life is interconnected. The hunter came to maturity, "the state of being complete, perfect or ready," as a culmination of living in relationship with all the beings of his community, not merely the human beings, just as fruit reaches true maturity only because of the complex interrelationships of its entire community. The peach requires the leaves of the tree to provide it with the energy from the sun by photosynthesis; it requires the trunk of the tree to hold the branches high in the sky to enable it to get the sun which ripens it;

it requires the rain from the sky to provide the water it needs; it requires trace minerals from the soil brought to it by the capillary action of the root hairs and, most important of all, it requires soil which supports the tree. In short, an entire community of interrelated organisms is required to bring one single individual peach to the fullness of maturity. There is a radical difference, however, between a tree-ripened peach and those picked green for easy shipping, then boxed and sold in a supermarket. The peach, picked green and arbitrarily, cut off from its living community, will eventually look mature but will always remain somewhat bitter and unfulfilled. In a similar manner, to attain true maturity —not merely a slightly bitter travesty of maturity—the individual human being needs the entire community: "the soils, the waters, the plants, and animals" of a particular *place*; not just the presence of other human beings.

Since the nonhuman beings in the environment were considered a part of the community, they had an effect on the hunters' decisions. We have seen, throughout the earlier parts of this book, how our culture lost this sense of true community; but we return again to Aldo Leopold redefinition of true community in his "land ethic": "A thing is right when it tends to preserve the integrity, stability and beauty of the biotic community." [178, 224–5] This definition of community both broadens and narrows the usual idea of community. Community is broadened because it includes other species than man; it is narrowed, or rather, localized in space, however, because it is concerned with the biotic pyramid and the "fountain of energy, flowing through a circuit of soil, plants, and animals" in a particular *place*. [178, 216]

Sacred mountains, holy springs, and sacred groves of trees are found all over the earth. These places became sacred because of the intensity of the relationship between the human beings of that *place* and the other beings, both great (mountains) and small (micro-organisms in the soil). "Modern science looks superficial and invasive beside the ancient learning born of generations of attention to a single place." [189, 19]

Real community must include this on-going relationship to Nature. I discovered this fact because I was fortunate enough to live for brief periods of time in true communities, those which included non-human beings of nature. It began when I was a teenager and joined the Junior Colorado Mountain Club, which was unique among climbing clubs for teenagers. Because of the dedication of one man, George Kelly, the Juniors had permission to learn directly from the mountains with no adult intermediaries—they had control of planning and leading their own trips and suffering the full consequences of their mistakes.

When I was older, I went on Canadian Alpine Club outings. At the time these were true expeditions, often into areas where there wasn't even a trail. The Canadian government cooperated with the Club in opening up these wilderness areas. In such a total wilderness for these two or three week spans, we had wise elders, competent teachers, newcomers, and frightened beginners. Because many different ages were represented and all ranges of experience were present, it was tribal living. Leading a rope with beginners on it was tiring, but their exultation at reaching their first summit was so gratifying it made the effort worthwhile. When skilled climbers made first ascents, everyone felt exalted. We had ceremonies and liturgies. We always had afternoon tea, very British, but over the strong, hot tea everyone exchanged stories of their varied experiences on the nearby mountains, so that the moods and personalities of these mountains developed. At night we had singing around a fire with northern lights overhead and wild animals lurking in the forest. It was not much different from primitive life except we did not dare acknowledge the proper gods. Now climbing groups have it organized so there are climbing outings for real climbers and family outings for families. But the older type of outing was where I first learned about tribal living: how one learns to care for even the most incompetent person, because that person is trying and the two of you can share the joy of accomplishment together; and how the skilled experience of an old-timer climber, his assurance, can almost literally hold one together under very adverse circumstances; and above all, I learned that group living in the daily rhythms of the natural environment clarified human relationships. In my "hunter's heart" I knew this was what life was all about. But then the culture of our "real" world doesn't accept this kind of life. One must get out and make a living. So I did.

I went through college as fast as I could, getting my "ticket to success," as John Holt puts it. The idea of relevance in a college class never even occurred to me. I did what I was "supposed" to do and got out to live and teach in a Colorado mountain town so I could ski all winter and have summers off to climb. The town was Aspen, long before it was "discovered," and this provided my second exposure to tribal living. The time was long before skiing became fashionable; even before it was known that one could make a living from it. Aspen was full of men who had been in the mountain troops during the war, and they were taking a few years off to do what they wanted to do before they had to "go to work." Skiing was what we were there for, and that was our life. All else came second in those first years—work, the daily hassles of getting along, sex, and material possessions except for skis. Practically, what this meant was that it was much easier to live together. There were no long discussions over inner feelings; we just shared the work and shared the bills and skied. If you didn't fulfill your share, you were dropped because any time or money wasted meant that much less skiing. Of course, this was simplistic and couldn't have lasted for long. It didn't. It was discovered that money *could* be made in skiing, and it was all over.

The lasting lesson I learned wasn't clear to me until the commune movement began in the sixties. Many of my friends were involved in communes and it was a *lot* of work—meetings and long sessions, holding someone's hand who had had feelings hurt. The flaw was that people were living together for the sake of living together, and it was work all the way. When we lived together for the sake of skiing, we had a clear, visible goal which had to do with nonhuman factors in the environment—terrain, weather, and the snow. This automatically clarifies human relationships because you can't manipulate the weather or the snow. I am not saying that skiing is *necessarily* a valid goal. But living is. Living in a particular *place* in a real relationship with the earth and the sky and the living beings around you—the fourfold of Heidegger—is a valid goal, as this relationship contributes to more *being*.

Community is sharing a particular physical place, an environment, not only with other people but the other beings of the place and fully realizing that the needs of *all* the beings of that place affect how you live your life. Such an awareness of relationships *is* a culture of awareness. The Pygmies of the Congo forest recognize the rights of the forest even in personal disputes among the people. When an argument got too violent, an elder, Moke, gave a low whistle, such as is given on hunting trips, and then said "in a very deliberate, quiet voice, 'You are making too much noise—you are killing the forest, you are killing the hunt.'" [331, 119] There is increasing evidence from anthropologists such as Robert Redfield, Stanley Diamond, and Roy Rappaport that the "social 'morality' of past tribal societies, built into their customs and everyday habits, puts modern man to shame." [46] Furthermore, the very word *Utopia*, according to the meaning given in dictionaries: "a place of ideal perfection," refers ultimately to the life of a tribal people. According to Arthur Morgan in his book, *Nowhere Was Somewhere*, Thomas More's book, *Utopia*, was largely based on the order established by the Inca Indians. [46] Such primitive cultures were "synergistic."

Synergistic Culture

Anthropoligist Ruth Benedict developed the concept of synergy in cultures as a result of her dissatisfaction with certain interpretations of her book, *Patterns of Culture*. The book was often used as proof of cultural relativism—that no culture can claim moral superiority over any other. The two basic patterns in *Patterns of Culture* were Apollonian and Dionysian; however, these two classifications did not imply that one culture was better for human beings than the other. "The Dionysian Kwakiutl were meanest to each other in the heights of ecstasy. The Apollonian Dobu never flipped out, but were cruel and prudish in their constant sobriety." [110] Cultural relativism distressed Benedict, so she began a lengthy search for the concept which all "good" cultures had in common. Abraham Maslow tells of how she listed the cultural characteristics of eight primitive peoples on huge sheets of newsprint hung on her wall. She had divided them into two groups: one type were like the Dobu and the other like the Zuni. She came up with the concept of synergy: "Drawn from medicine, it described a combined action of chemicals and cells that produces a benign result greater than the sum of the separate actions." [110]

Maslow went off to live among the Blackfeet, a high-synergy culture, to check out her idea. He found that private possessions were accumulated only because they could be given to others. Maslow reported one instance where a man owned a car which he never used. He walked, but left the keys in the car so all the others could use it when needed.

Benedict actually developed the concept of synergy during a series of lectures which she gave at Bryn Mawr College in 1941. Because of her failing health, Maslow persuaded her to give him the only copy of the sixty-page manuscript so that it wouldn't be lost. Then Maslow himself had a heart attack. He sent the manuscript back to Benedict just before her final heart attack, and the paper was lost. Maslow spoke of it often in the intervening years in lectures. Oddly enough, as Harris points out in the article, "About Ruth Benedict and Her Lost Manuscript," [110] The idea of synergy first caught on among idealistic young businessmen and so it became a managerial word, corrupting the basic concept. In 1970 it was discovered that John Honigmann, a graduate student under Maslow in 1941, had seen the paper while it was in Maslow's possession and had copied long sections of it. Maslow and Honigmann, now a professor in anthropology at Chapel Hill, edited the long-lost paper for publication in 1970. It was entitled, "Patterns of the Good Culture," [24] and in it Benedict summarized her ideas on synergy. She began with aggression—"behavior in which the aim is to injure another person or something that stands for him." Is there any sociological condition that correlates with much aggression or little agression? was her question. She found that low aggression correlates with societies which "provide areas of mutual advantage and eliminate acts and goals that are at the expense of others in the group." Nonaggression is high in societies where "the individual by the same act and at the same time serves his own advantage and that of the group . . . Nonaggression occurs not because people are unselfish and put social obligations above personal desires, but when social arrangements make these two identical." A conspicuous sign of a high-synergy culture is what Benedict calls the "syphon system." Wealth is continually channeled away from any single point of concentration and spread through the group. This makes for very fluid wealth. She states that in such a culture, ". . . if a man has meat or garden produce or horses or cattle, these give him no standing except as they pass through his hands to the tribe at large." The Plains Indians' Sun Dance, with its *give-away*, is an example. Maslow writes that Ruth Benedict defined synergy as "social-institutional conditions which fuse selfishness and unselfishness, by arranging it so that when I pursue 'selfish' gratifications, I automatically help others, and when I try to be altruistic, I automatically reward and gratify myself." [204, 140]

Non-human beings in the community also fit into a synergistic culture, and we learn how by turning to a primitive tribe. In *Stone Age Economics*, Marshall Sahlins devotes a chapter to the "spirit of the gift," based on Marcel Mauss' famous essay. Tamati Rana-piri, a Maori wiseman, spoke of the concept of the *hau*, but as this is quite detailed I will merely quote Sahlins' explanation: "The *mauri* that holds the increase-power (*hau*) is placed in the forest by the priests (*tohunga*); the *mauri* causes game birds to abound; accordingly, some of the captured birds should be ceremoniously returned to the priests who placed the *mauri*; the consumption of these birds by the priests in effect restores the fertility (*hau*) of the forest . . ." [279, 158] The *hau* has to do not only with human beings but also the animals and the forest. Sahlins quotes from *Maori Forest Lore*: "Thus the *hau* or vitality, or productiveness, of a forest has to be very carefully protected by means of certain very peculiar rites . . . For fecundity cannot exist without the essential *hau*." Sahlins then goes on to say that "the benefits taken by man ought to be returned to their source, that it may be maintained as a source." The further extension of this concept to human beings is gone into by Mauss near the end of his essay. He "recapitulated his thesis by two Melanesian examples of tenuous relations between villages and peoples: of how, menaced always by deterioration into war, primitive groups are nevertheless reconciled by festival and exchange." Amplifying this, Lévi-Strauss wrote, "There is a link, a continuity, between hostile relations and the provision of reciprocal prestations. Exchanges are peacefully resolved wars and wars are the result of unsuccessful transactions." [279, 182]

Hyemeyohsts Storm, of Cheyenne Indian descent, in his *Seven Arrows* deals with ideas similar to the concepts of synergy and *hau*, "the gift." According to Storm, all of life is involved in the *give-away*—the land, the animals, plants, and human beings. [311] This idea can be seen in Heidegger's concept of the fourfold, as well as in Leopold's "land ethic." Ruth Benedict's concept of synergy in connection with human communities was drawn from medicine, where it is used to refer to a combined action of separate parts that produce a "benign result greater than the sum of the separate actions." Extending this concept to the total community, the soils, the plants, animals, and human beings of a particular *place*, results in a totally new relationship between humans and environment—one

in which all beings can flourish. Certainly the land will then no longer be destroyed, for the land has been abused because we regard it as a commodity which belongs to us. "When we see land as a community to which we belong, we may begin to use it with love and respect." [178, viii] By freeing the land, human beings will free themselves from destructive use because the system, which exploits the land to secure more power and wealth for a few, does not stop there but subordinates *all* beings to the same ends.

"Man demonstrates *in his own nature* a pressure toward fuller and fuller Being, more and more perfect actualization of his humanness in exactly the same naturalistic, scientific sense that an acorn may be said to be 'pressing toward' being an oak tree," according to Maslow's psychology of being. [206, 130] He further explains that the ultimate of being for a person is the coming together of what "I must do" with what "I want to do." Such a person is "being his own kind of person, or being himself, or actualizing his real self." In this state of being, a person's "work is his play and his play is his work . . . The self has enlarged to include aspects of the world and . . . therefore the distinction between self and not-self (outside, other) has been transcended." Maslow calls such values B-values, B for being.

Maslow proved that "The value-life (spiritual, religious, philosophical, axiological, etc.) is an aspect of human biology and is on the same continuum with the 'lower' animal life." [205] Self-actualization is a continuous process or growth toward more and greater being. In this process human beings achieve a better understanding of themselves and the world, of the being that they are and of the greater being of the world. Maslow sums it up when he says, ". . . if you love something or someone enough at the level of Being, then you can enjoy its actualization of itself, which means that you will not want to interfere with it, since you will love it as it is in itself . . . if you love something the way it is . . . you may then see it (or him) as it is in its own nature, untouched, unspoiled."

The being of the world in Heidegger's fourfold concept depends on the mutual appropriation—the mutual fit—of the earth, the gods, and the human beings, and therefore the humans cannot *be* fully without allowing all the other components of the fourfold to *be* fully. Mutual appropriation means literally "to fit one another." Not just one of these components decides what kind of being will occur, but the mutual interaction of all. If the fullest possible being of the soil is not permitted, I am diminished by the resultant lack. Thus, if the soil is not completely healthy, it will be lacking in trace minerals and my own being will not be able to reach its full potential. For *my* fullest being I must allow the fullest expression of all the other beings of my world. In this kind of relationship with the environment there is a "flow" of being. I first became conscious of this flow while skiing powder snow. Gradually I learned that the more I could duplicate this flow in daily life, the better it was not only for me but for those around me.

Through play one begins to sense this flow. In fact, "Play was in its first beginning accounted a sacred thing, something dedicated to the Divinity." [270] In an earlier section of this book, play was seen to be crucial for children's development; a recent study shows that true play is equally important for the mature adult.

Mihaly Csikszentmihalyi, of the Behavioral Science Department at the University of Chicago, studied a variety of people who had "invested a great deal of time and energy in play activities." [66] After preliminary interviews, the study was narrowed to specific fields and administered to thirty people in several fields, including rock climbers, modern dancers, basketball players, and chess players. Csikszentmihalyi found that "There is a common experiential state which is present in various forms of play, and also under certain conditions in other activities which are not normally thought of as play." He calls this condition "flow." "It is the state in which action follows upon action according to an internal logic which seems to need no conscious intervention on our part. We experience it as a unified flowing from one moment to the next, in which we feel in control of our actions, and in which there is little distinction between self and environment; between stimulus and response; or between past, present, and future." He stresses that this flow experience "seems to occur only when a person is actively engaged in some form of clearly specified interaction with the environment." A clear sign of flow is "merging action and awareness," which is reminiscent of jnana yoga's no separation between the observer and the observed. Another important component is that the experience "usually contains coherent, noncontradictory demands for action, and provides clear unambiguous feedback to a person's actions." This is possible because of total attention to a restricted field of possibilities. Csikszentmihalyi further states that the flow model has interesting implications for human motivation and suggests that "As long as we continue to motivate people mainly through extrinsic rewards like money and status, we rely on zero-sum payoffs that result in inequalities as well as the depletion of scarce resources. It is therefore vital to know more about the possible effects of intrinsically rewarding processes."

Csikszentmihalyi refers only to the possibilities of restructuring jobs, schools, and neighborhoods to increase the flow experience, but I suggest that Czikszentmihalyi's insights into play pull together a number of ongoing themes in this book: the importance of mountains in religions; nature's "playing gods" in Heidegger's fourfold and the resulting implications for Being; Maslow's B-values and "peak experiences"; and the importance of *place*. These converging themes show that living on this earth is its own intrinsic reward when one decides to live in one *place* and cultivate a lasting relationship to the other beings of that *place*: soil, animals, plants, beings in the sky; clouds, rain, snow, thunder, and the gods of the *place*. As Gary Snyder said of his Northern California *place*, "Because we are together in the same part of the world and expect to be together there for the next two or three thousand years, we hope to co-evolve our strengths and help each other learn." [57] In such a relationship there is no longer a separation between work and play, or things done for self and things done for the "greater self," that is, for others, including non-human beings. It all becomes part of the mirroring play of the fourfold. The more deeply involved one is, the more one learns, and the more one learns, the more deeply involved until there is a total on-going flow—no longer even limited to this time, as one's actions extend into the future as part of the love of *place*.

In such a relationship to *place*, there are always clear demands for action and clear unambiguous feedback on these actions. You know when you have hurt the land. You can see topsoil bleeding down the hillside in the next rain. You know when you've done the right thing for the land. You can see the spiral of complexity and diversity grow out from the soil you have helped to recover. There is no boundary between work and play as what starts out to be work—such as cutting wood for the fire—develops into play as you smell the clear, sharp pine smell, feel the rhythm of the chopping interaction with the wood in your body. What begins as play—a hike up the hill to see the new spring flowers—turns into work as you automatically gather brush to plug up a tiny gulley which the melting snows have disclosed. Or on another day, a particular combination of light after a sudden thundershower on distant rocks and you are "transformed by a ceremony residing in the land itself." [102] All is part of the on-going flow when one lives and learns together with all the other non-human beings of the place.

Wilfred Pelletier left the reservation and tried to "make it" in the white man's world. He tells of one of these non-human beings he encountered and of what he learned. He had been doing all he was "supposed" to do—church meetings, political meetings, and lectures, but he found that he was lost, "before I was thirty years old . . ."

Then one day I came bang smack into reality. I suppose it sounds silly, but what happened was that I saw a dandelion. Here I was, a middle-aged man surrounded with dandelions all my life. Then I saw one. But there was nothing that stood between me and that dandelion, that's what I mean: no classifications, no categories, no words, not even the word "dandelion." Nothing. And that dandelion was not just a thing, one of a million yellow things that were bright and pretty and very common. That dandelion was a being, a living being that accepted and included me totally. I felt like I was standing in the center of the sun with those cool yellow petals going out from my feet and away into the distance forever.

I said I saw a dandelion for the first time. But it really wasn't the first time. I learned that too because there was a flash of remembrance in that experience—no when or where, just a flash—but enough so I knew that when I was a very young child I lived in that reality all the time . . . Perhaps that is a way of saying what had happened. "I" was there, but there was no longer an observer and an observed . . . no separate and isolated individuals. There was only one inclusive totality which left nothing out . . . It was all flowing . . .

I'm not really dependable any more by white standards. But I'm getting freer and freer. [Others are finding out, both Indians and whites.] They're going back to the land, more and more of them. And that's the only real seat of learning there has ever been. They'll learn from the land, all they need to know, all there is to know. If they stay there long enough, they'll learn that they *are* the land . . .

Wherever you are is home. And the earth is paradise and wherever you set your feet is holy land . . . You don't live off it like a parasite. You live in it, and it in you, or you don't survive. And that is the only worship of God there is.

Wilfred Pelletier   [251, 191, 195, 208–210]

Since maturity means the "state of being complete," the human being cannot achieve full maturity without religion. As Wilfred Pelletier's remarks on the worship of God shows, religion in a complete culture such as that of the Amerindian is so intimately connected with the land and so closely bound up with daily life that it cannot be separated from it; therefore, further insight into religion in a culture of awareness will be found in the chapter on "Rituals for a Sacred Ecology" in Part IV of this book; there is, however, one further aspect of community to look into and that is the family.

In a recent interview, Margaret Mead was asked what she thought of the future of the nuclear family. She answered, "The nuclear family never was strong! A nuclear family all by itself is an exposed, endangered, inadequate form of social organization. It is the easiest social grouping for those who must move from one place to another . . . So in a period of colonization and migration all over the world, the nuclear family is the most suitable and the most exploitable—that's where industrialization comes in. Get your young men and their young wives to go to work in the city. Then we have a housing situation where you build boxes like egg crates, and families move into the egg crates. These isolated families don't form a community." [336] Long ago, in 1927, Robert Briffault, who spent years of research in preparation for his book, *The Mothers*, wrote: "Since individual men and women differ profoundly in their fitness for one or another form of sexual association, marriage may have to take varying new forms . . . Lifelong monogamy . . . calls for special qualifications . . . The belief that it is a 'natural' relation, founded on biological functions . . . is one of the commonest causes of its failure. It is, on the contrary, a social product and a compromise." [39, 443] But it was not until the landmark conference in Chicago in 1966 on "Man the Hunter," which began the surge of interest in the hunter's life, that sufficient knowledge became readily available as to the general role of sex throughout most of human history.

For millions of years, in both human and protohuman scocieties, the tribe and its *place*—not the sexual bond—provided the stability in an individual's life. Marriage bonds were quite flexible. Divorce was simple. Among some tribes that is still the case today: the woman merely puts the man's belongings outside the door, and the whole thing is over. There are few solitary women because polygamy is common. The rigid rules and traumas associated with marriage in our culture developed recently, with the rise of agricultural societies, where the transfer of land and property became the underlying cause of marriage.

The large, interlocking clan structure of the tribe is stable because the individual is born or initiated into a group as "durable as the plant or animal species taken by it as a totemic emblem," [292, 132] Sharing of the hunter's kill leads to sharing in other areas of tribal life. On the Indian reserve where Wilfred Pelletier grew up, "All the resources of that community were available to whoever needed them; sex was not excluded. Sex was a recognized need, so nobody went without it. It was as simple as that." [251, 78]

For our primate ancestors, sex was not merely a reproductive process but served also as a bonding agent for the group. Female primates do not all come into heat at the same time, as do some species of animals; they have a peak season of births, but the mating game and sexual activity continue throughout the year, thus freeing sexual energy for new social uses. One or another female is in heat at any given time. The continuing courtship and copulation in primate groups acts as a sort of bonding mechanism throughout the tribe. In general this bonding action of sex continued in the cultures of human beings.

Satisfying sexual intercourse is one of the few experiences in modern life which involve both hemispheres of the brain and all levels of the triune brain, which accounts for its importance as a bonding mechanism. According to Erik Erikson, a satisfying sexual act is "a supreme experience of the mutual regulation of two beings [that] in some way breaks the point off the hostilities and potential rages caused by the oppositeness of male and female, of fact and fancy, of love and hate. Satisfactory sex relations thus make sex less obsessive, over-compensation less necessary, sadistic control superfluous." [80] Occasionally there is such a pronounced receptive-mode state that there is decrease in self-other boundaries, which results in mystical states. [169] The decrease in self-other boundaries is probably one of the reasons why in most traditional cultures, down to quite modern times, sexual orgies were connected with religion. In agricultural societies, such orgies were connected to the fertility of the soil. When the entire group is open to the "power," such sexual encounters release pent-up anxieties, and fears and hostilities are erased, thus reaffirming the close bonds of the group. The very absence of such a mechanism in isolated small-town life was one of the causes of the gradual accumulation of hatred and feuds during the last century in this country.

The Ute Indians had a particularly graceful method of providing a ritual situation where new choices and changes of sexual partners could take place. The Utes were a hunting tribe who spent most of the year in small kin groups hunting in widely separated parts throughout the high Rocky Mountains. Once a year the entire tribe came together for the annual spring Bear Dance. "It was a quiet time, with spring moving slowly into their valleys; for the People were listening. They were waiting and listening for the first thunder, which would awaken the sleepy bear in his winter den and awaken the spirit of the bear in the People. Awaken their feet and their hearts and bring music among them. This was the time for Bear Dance." A great cave of branches, the *avin-kwep*, was built with the opening facing the afternoon sun. At one end of the cave a round hole was dug to make an entrance into a small underground cave. Covering this entrance was an upside-down basket.

The main instrument for the music of the Bear Dance was a long stick, notched on one side and shaped like the jawbone of an animal. One end of this stick was placed on top of the basket covering the hole, and it was rubbed along the notches by a smaller stick. The sound was amplified by the cave and basket and "the little thunder sounded deep in the cave, spreading out over the awakening land and rumbling in the spring air. The song of the other singers closed around the first thunder, and the first song of the Bear Dance was made."

As the female bear chooses her mate, the woman chose which man she would dance with by plucking his sleeve. The men and women danced opposite one another in a long line. For three days the dance continued. By the third night the couples danced together. By this time the bears were considered to be awake in the forests and "the spirit of the bear filled the night inside the *avinkwep*." From time to time a couple would leave the dance and "take their blankets up into the brush on the hillside to let out the spirit of the bear and the thunder of spring that had grown too strong in them to be held back any longer."

There were many healings during the three days by means of the spirit of the bear in the *w'ni thokunup* [the notched stick]." At noon the dance ended with a great feast. Then gradually, over a period of days, the big camp broke up as the small hunting groups went off into the hills. A woman who plucked the sleeve of a man during the Bear Dance might visit the bushes with him for an hour, or for the entire night or might stay with him for the entire year's hunting until the next Bear Dance, or even for 'many snows.'" [78, 29 and 35–38]

In such a culture there is no rape. In fact, rape, as we know it now, may be another cultural disease. Pearce,

in a very enlightening part of his book, provides information that links rape with the fact that a male, who was bonded neither to his mother nor to the earth, cannot have a satisfactory relationship with a woman and that this growing frustration may erupt in total anger at the mother/earth/woman matrix, so he uses his strength to rape. He rapes either crudely or with sophistication, that is, bodily, or intellectually, raping the earth matrix with technology. [250, 218]

In the last few decades, human beings have begun to try to function sexually more in accord with the way nature intended them to, as programmed in the genes for the last 40,000 years; but the way will be difficult and long. There is a grave danger for the earth in some of the experimental sexual relationships because some women feel they want a child by every man they love. Any woman who cares for the earth must very firmly vow to have only two children and no more, so it behooves her to be very careful about whose child she has. The most creative solution to this problem I've learned of was one given by Garrett Hardin in his book, *Exploring New Ethics for Survival*. [109] Because it is women who bear children, and since we are close to being able to determine the sex of the child at conception, Hardin suggests making it a law that every woman can have only one girl child. She can have as many boys as she wishes—a dozen or more if she wants a big family, but only one girl. Such a law, of course, would very quickly change the structure of our society. Women would become important beings. They might marry a whole group of men, as in Tibet long ago. At any rate, because women might come into control through this power, it is doubtful whether our culture would ever adopt such a solution!

Until the concept of "fatherhood" came into being with the patriarchal tribes, the woman in primitive times did have complete control of her own body and could make the decision on childbearing. In a beautiful retelling of the ancient Welsh *Mabinogion* in modern fantasy style, Evangeline Walton deals with the wrenching change caused by the coming, with the patriarchal invaders, of the idea of fatherhood. Math, the ancient venerable king, is speaking of Arianrod:

Hers are ill deeds; and an unloving mother violates the Ancient Harmonies. Yet you have made her a mother against her will. And that is a thing that has seldom happened in the world before, but will happen often again in the ages that begin. You have done it for love's sake, in pure longing for a child. But many of those men who are to come will do it for pride's sake and lust's; and this breeding of her like a beast will lower the rank and degrade the ancient dignity of women . . . For the recognition of fatherhood will enslave women. It will no longer leave her absolute ownership of her own body, that it will place at one man's pleasure, this to demand rather than hers to give or withhold as her heart bids . . . And the end of it all will be that there will be no free women left in the world, to love for love alone as women did aforetime.
[347, 202–203]

15. The Fourth Hill of Life

There are souls, he thought, whose umbilicus has never been cut. They never got weaned from the universe. They do not understand death as an enemy; they look forward to rotting and turning into humus.

Shevek [174, 150]

In Ursula K. LeGuin's novel, *The Dispossessed*, Shevek is musing on his wife's love relationship to nature, a love much broader than mere "love of nature." For those fortunate few who have developed this continuity of life and death and nature in their thinking, the heritage of our hunter-gatherer ancestors still lives in them. For others of us, more numerous, who have succumbed to the tyranny of the separative, rational mind, death is an enemy. For the hunter, "ecologically, death leads to life, not in a hazy and obscure way but in the eating of the prey." [292, 153] Conversely, the hunter knows he may become prey of the animal he hunts, but he also knows that by his death he will contribute to the life of the animal. Livingstone, the early African explorer, was attacked by a lion which bit into his shoulder and thigh. Although he could see his thigh in the jaws of the lion, rather than terror, he related, he felt a sort of acceptance. For Livingstone, this was the most impressive event of his life. "He knew, after that, the *concept* of death, with its prestructurings and imaginations, has no actuality in life. The concept is the tragedy, not the event. He spoke of knowing that within nature life gives itself to life in ways our thinking doesn't grasp." [249, 57]

In all hunting societies, after the kill is made, there is a ritual connected with the first eating of the flesh. American Indians, in their ritual prayer to the animal, often used the phrase "that we may live." This ritual eating has come down into every religion in the actual eating of some food—bread or fruit or flesh—as a communion with the gods. It is the validation of a relationship between animal, human, and god. This ritual communion meal is used at the present time by Elisabeth Kubler-Ross, the world's leading authority on death and dying, as the culminating ritual at the end of her week-long workshops for terminally-ill persons and their close relatives. Briefly, as she describes the experience, the workshop starts off with "Baloney Day," when all tell about their roles. Everyone takes it very seriously.

This goes on throughout the day until someone, usually a dying person who gets just sick and tired of the baloney says, "Listen, we only have five days, and I may have only two months to live, and I'm sick and tired of this crap." [316] Then everybody begins to share experiences, and this continues through the second day. The third day is "Angry Day," when everyone deals with old angers. Thursday night they talk of life and death, and everyone must find a pinecone into which they are to put "that negative part of themselves which they're willing to give up permanently." The last night they have a big fire outdoors, sit around it in a circle, and sing all night. As each person is ready, each gets up and throws the pinecone into the fire. Then they have a party. "We have wine and we bake our own bread, and we make a whole ritual with bread and wine." All the ancient rites are here: fire and music and the ritual meal. What Kubler-Ross provides in these five days is a sort of ritual crash program to help people see that everything is interconnected—that the real self is part of the whole and thus does not end with death.

As we saw earlier, in the chapter on Mind, it is becoming clear that the poets and artists and shamans were correct all along: Our mind does not end with the boundary of our skull. It is partly the separation of right and left brain and the emphasis on left-brain activities in this culture (which can only split up and take apart and never put things together), which initiates our fear of death. As Bateson says, "I suggest that it is equally monstrous—and dangerous—to attempt to separate the external mind from the internal. Or to separate mind from body . . . It is understandable that, in a civilization which separates mind from body, we should either try to forget death or to make mythologies about the survival of transcendent mind. But if mind is immanent not only in those pathways of information which are located inside the body but also in external pathways, then death takes on a different aspect. The individual nexus of pathways which I call 'me' is no longer so precious because that nexus is only part of a larger mind." [12]

Wilder Penfield, who spent fifty years in brain research, decided in his later years that, although the mind and brain share the same organizational processes, they are not the same entity: ". . . the brain is a place for newly acquired automatic mechanisms, it is a computer . . . the mind . . . directs the programming of all the mechanisms within the brain." If we say that the human being's mind is the person, then we can say, "He walks about the world, depending always upon his private computer, which he programs continuously to suit his every-changing purposes and intent." [252, 60–61] He further states that the mind develops and matures independently throughout an individual's life, and as the person grows older the mind "comes to depend more and more on the memory and the automatic patterns of action stored away in the brain's computer." This gives the mind more free time "to explore the world of the intellect, its own and that of others." [252, 86] The body and brain reach their top development in the twenties or thirties and in the forties begin to level off and then to fall in older ages. However, "the mind seems to have no peculiar or inevitable pathology. Late in life, it moves to its own fulfillment." As the mind "arrives at clearer understanding and better balanced judgment," the brain computer begins to fail in strength and speed." [252, 87]

Referring back to the holographic model of the brain mentioned in Chapter 8, Pribram explained that the analogy between the brain and the holographic process has to do with the "*paths* taken by the energy, the interactions among the paths and the resulting organizations of 'information' that are produced." With this in mind, it is possible to say that in the human being who has actively interacted with the earth throughout most of life, the mind has many patterns of earth/mind interrelationships and, by a sort of geometrical progression, the more patterns of interrelationships already there, the more interrelationships there can be. Rational knowledge alone, mere accumulating of facts, is of no consequence here; it takes whole-brain learning to create relationships. The linear, rational left-hemisphere brain can only take apart to analyze, it cannot think in wholes. Whole-brain activity by its very nature involves interacting with the earth. People who have interacted with the earth become more centered the older they are—everything comes together more and more. There can be no fear of death because they *know* there is no boundary between mind-inside-the-skull and mind-outside. Those who have not actively interacted with the earth tend to have fewer patterns of earth/mind, so that when the computer begins to go, the whole thing goes and they are locked into a disintegrating pattern where nothing holds together. Their senility gets worse and worse, until frequently all that remains are the very earliest childhood memories. Most of the

people of advanced age whom I know and who are functioning well, both physically and mentally, are still deeply involved with nature.

George Kelly, the man who was responsible for the group I climbed with as a teenager, is now eighty-four years old, yet he leads visitors on a rock-scrambling tour of the sandstone rimrock near his home to see the Indian ruins. Once when we arrived with some college students at his *place,* George was working inside in moccasins. He dropped his work and set off up a sandstone draw, guiding us to some new ruins he had found. A rather unathletic young women in the group had to be pulled up a rock wall which George had just bounded up in his moccasins. All his life he has climbed mountains, including all the peaks over 14,000 feet high in Colorado. As far as I know, he is the only man who has walked the entire boundary of Colorado. When he was seventy-three, he "retired" and he and his wife, Sue, built their own adobe house, planted a huge apple orchard, began a new experiment to see what food plants would grow with no watering in the desert-like climate, found undiscovered Indian ruins on his land, and dug out a flawless little kiva and other ruins. When I last visited him a year ago, he was eighty-three; I found him down at the bottom of a huge new kiva he had found. He was throwing the dirt higher than his head to the next level. From this level he would then throw it out over his head onto the ground level.

George Kelly's lifelong work is in horticulture, and he is an authority on native Colorado plants and shrubs. He is in the process of identifying all the plants on his desert-like land along McElmo Creek in southwestern Colorado. He has already found some three hundred species. As George grows older, he seems to spin a web of more and more intricate connections with more people and beings of nature; he is continuous with a larger and larger environment although centered in his *place,* his beloved canyon. George Kelly's viewpoint contrasts with that of many older people who begin to fragment their world, viewing everything from the point of view of their own comfort and needs. They become more and more isolated; fewer people and things have any meaning to them. Their world becomes smaller, until nothing is left because they have so seldom lived. George's world becomes always larger and larger. The older person who continues to form more connections with the earth continues to grow until the "self" in the skin becomes no different from the "self" outside the skin—until the "self" becomes as big as the earth. Death is no ending for such a person, so it is not feared.

When I was just beginning climbing as a teenager, there was an old woman in her eighties who was still climbing 14,000-foot peaks. All her climbing friends were gone, but she still went up the easier ones. She was found dead one day sitting in the trail with a smile on her face. She had sat down to rest and never got up.

In Washington state, Edith Ellexson, 81 years old, received her degree from Central Washington State College in June of 1977. Two years before she had climbed Mount Kilimanjaro. Amanda B. Gaverick is 85 years old, and each winter she still takes to the hills with her 79-year-old sister-in-law, on their sleds. Mrs. Gaverick said, "I love cold weather. It's healthier than 'tis to stay in the house. My mother had three ribs broke ridin' down hills when she was in her seventies." Mrs. Gaverick has lived nearly all her life in the same *place*, called *The Horn*, in the north-central Pennsylvania hills. [253] Lowell Thomas is still skiing in his eighties. Buckminster Fuller is now 83 and has been around the world forty-three times. Scott Nearing began to build a stone house at 93, sure that he had all the time he needed to finish it.

A predilection for working with stone is fairly common among active older people. Jung's experience is worth recounting; he had the knowledge of the unconscious necessary to understand it. In his autobiography, *Memories, Dreams and Reflections*, he says that as he grew older words and paper "did not seem real enough to me. I had to achieve a kind of representation in stone of my innermost thoughts and of the knowledge I had acquired." [140, 223] He began to build a structure in stone called "The Tower." The *place* he chose on the upper lake of Zurich was what one could term a "sacred" place. It had been land belonging to the ancient monastery of St. Gall and, as is often the case, it was a Christian monastery built on land which had had particular importance to the pagans in the area. Jung's first stone building was a small round hut-like edifice which, when finished, showed itself as a round tower. He later built more stone buildings—four sections altogether. But the Tower was always central. He felt that "the Tower was in some way a place of maturation—a maternal womb or a maternal figure in which I could become what I was, what I am and will be. It gave me a feeling as if I were being reborn in stone." As he was building the stone tower, he did not know all these things but, as the years went by, he realized more and more what unconscious needs the building had fulfilled. Concerning Bollingen, the name of his *place*, he wrote: "At times I feel as if I am spread out over the landscape and inside things, and am myself living in every tree, in the plashing of the waves, in the clouds and the animals that come and go, in the procession of the seasons. There is nothing in the Tower that has not grown into its own form over the decades, nothing with which I am not linked. Here everything has its history, and mine; here is space for the spaceless kingdom of the world's and the psyche's hinterland." [54, 225–226]

Jung kept it all very simple, without electricity, chopping his own wood for fuel and pumping his water by hand. "Silence surrounds me almost audibly, and I live 'in modest harmony with nature.' Thoughts rise to the surface which reach back into the centuries, and accord-

ingly anticipate a remote future." [140, 226] Heidegger, too, in his later years, withdrew into a simple life in the Bavarian mountains and chopped his own wood.

In all the examples above, the "self" grows to encompass all the beings in the *place* until there is no boundary between the self and world; the human self has no need to fear death. *Place* becomes crucially important for the older human being. In primitive cultures the aged were revered for their wisdom. They had lived so long in their *place* that they had knowledge which was impossible to acquire in any other way, and they were valued for it. Today, in most cultures, the aged no longer are repositories of wisdom, gleaned from long interaction with a particular *place*: No one stays in any one place over the long time necessary to acquire such knowledge. Even worse is the fact that places themselves are not permitted to endure but are bulldozed over, ripped up for strip mines, or otherwise destroyed. Mankind is impoverished because invaluable wisdom, which can be acquired in no other way, is lost when human beings do not, or are not permitted to dwell in one place for most of their lives. Such knowledge cannot be acquired by research, in laboratories, or by scholars trying to dig up the past. It can be acquired only by living in relationships with all the beings of the earth and the sky in the *place*.

In rural Japan, where people still live their lives out in one place, it is astonishing to see joy in the faces of the old people. Due to my husband's work in avalanche research, we spent considerable time in back country rural areas looking at avalanche defenses, so we saw many fine old people. One day particularly stands out. We were on one of the branch lines of the Japan National Railway in northern Honshu. There were three old people ahead of us in the car. They were laughing and talking in total abandon. We stopped at the next station. A very tiny, bent little woman got on with a huge bamboo basket on her back loaded with firewood. She saw her friends and the already deep smile lines of her face broke into canyons of joy as she joined them. In a ski resort in Hokkaido, the northernmost island, I saw three old women squatting on their heels around a big bucket, peeling potatoes. Their eyes were glowing and their faces beaming. We saw this phenomenon all over Japan—even in Tokyo, the largest city in the world. Women with huge straw hats and big baskets were weeding the public parks by hand. They were outside working with the earth—doing good for the earth and for themselves. Because Japan has never completely cut its ties with the primitive past, old age is a treasured time. Young children and old people are considered to have more "kaminess" than other people—more "creative divine spirit"—and they are revered by all, even in this modern age.

A further insight into the status of the aged in primitive cultures comes from the !Kung bushmen in Africa. The old people have no deficiencies in B vitamins and show few signs of degenerative diseases; most live to sixty and some to eighty. The !Kung are one of only about a dozen groups of people in the world whose blood pressure does not increase as they grow older. This is due to the natural diet and exercise, as well as their culture. [156] By contrast, thousands of Americans die each year from heart disease, although in 1912 when Paul Dudley White first set up practice he saw only three or four coronary patients. "Until this century, heart disease, which is directly related to crowding, stress, and anxiety, was virtually unknown anywhere in the world." [283] In a hunting-gathering culture such as the !Kung, death in old age is not a stressful situation such as a heart attack, but a time of fulfillment—a rejoining of "the ancestors," another moment in the ongoing continuity of the tribe.

The advantage of mortality is that it permits ever new manifestations of Being to occur. For example, the components (atoms, cells, etc.) which go to make up the temporary organism which is my self at this moment, have been contained in many other beings in the past and will be part of many new, as yet unknown beings in the future. But the parts which go to make up my self have always been around and always will be as long as there is life on Earth. What changes is the relationships involved. This can be clarified by referring back to an incident, mentioned by Joel Kramer, in the section on jnana yoga in Chapter 8. This was the moment of real living, when one saw the sunlight in a dewdrop and there was total awareness with no separation between the observer and the observed. In his book, *The Passionate Mind*, Joel Kramer asks a question about such moments: "In the moments when there isn't any gap or space between the seer and the seen, is there a personality living at that time, or is there not simply a living relationship, which is always something new, fresh, and vital?" This is real living and it involves a constant dying—to the past, to preconceptions. Every moment of our life we are constantly dying—cells are being replaced. Within a few years there is no cell within me that was there before. "Life *is* death. There is no difference . . . The very thing I fear [in the fear of death]—losing my personality—is necessary if I'm actually to be in contact with the living moment." [159, 49]

In contrast to the concept of death commonly held in our technological society, that it is somehow repugnant, human beings who never severed their close ties to nature view death very differently. John Muir, who throughout his entire life was "tormented with soul hunger" whenever he was away from his beloved mountains, spent most of the latter part of his life trying to save nature from man in California. He managed to save such places as Mount Tamalpais and large areas of redwoods. He wrote of death in this manner: "Pollution, defilement, squalor are words that never would have been created had man lived conformably to Nature. Birds, insects, bears die as cleanly and are disposed of as beautifully . . . The woods are full of dead and dying trees, yet needed for their beauty to complete the beauty of the living . . . How beautiful is all Death!" [352, 61] And Annie Dillard became so enamored and fascinated by all the beings of Shadow Creek, her *place*, that her "self" expanded to fill the whole of it and she lived joyfully, transformed by her *place*. Near the end of her book, *Pilgrim at Tinker Creek*, she wrote:

The world is wilder than that in all directions, more dangerous and bitter, more extravagant and bright. We are making hay when we should be making whoopee; we are raising tomatoes when we should be raising Cain, or Lazarus.

Ezekiel excoriates false prophets as those who have "not gone up into the gap." The gaps are the things. The gaps are the spirit's one home, the altitudes and latitudes so dazzlingly spare and clean that the spirit can discover itself for the first time like a once-blind man unbound . . . Go up into the gaps. If you can find them . . . aloft, up to any gap at all, and you'll come back, for you will come back, transformed in a way you may not have bargained for . . . Did you think, before you were caught, that you needed, say life? . . . You see the creatures die, and you know you will die. And one day it occurs to you that you must not need life. Obviously . . . I think that the dying pray at the last not "please," but "thank you," as a guest thanks his host at the door . . . And like Billy Bray I go my way, and my left foot says "Glory," and my right foot says "Amen": in and out of Shadow Creek, upstream and down, exultant, in a daze dancing, to the twin silver trumpets of praise. [73, 277–279]

CANYONLANDS

(Photograph by Steve Meyers)

"Within and around the earth, within and around the hills, within and around the mountains, your authority returns to you.

A Tewa Prayer

Part IV

16. Reinhabiting Your Place

The first thing to do
is to choose a sacred place to live in . . .

Tahirussawichi, Pawnee tribe   [49, 63]

I'll say this real clearly, because it seems that it has to be said over and over again: There is no place to flee to in the U.S. There is no "country" that you can go and lay back in. There is no quiet place in the woods . . . The surveyors are there with their orange plastic tape, the bulldozers are down the road warming up their engines, the real estate developers have got it all on the wall with pins in it, the county supervisors are in the back room drinking coffee with the real estate subdividers . . . and the forest service is just about to let out a big logging contract to some logging company.   Gary Snyder [56]

Athens in the Classical Age had a population of 120,000; Florence at the height of its culture in the Medici era was so small that one could walk from one end to the other in less than half an hour. Great cultures do not require large human populations. The quality of a culture depends on the depth of the relationship of the human beings to their *place*. The Pueblo Indian communities provide an outstanding example of depth of relationship between the human being, the earth, the sky, and the gods.

John Collier, onetime head of the Bureau of Indian Affairs, explained how the Pueblos happened to be spared by the encroaching white man: "The years since 1540, when Coronado had entered New Granada, had established as a stark fact that the Pueblo societies could not be broken down by any means short of killing all the Indians. And Spain absolutely required the Pueblos; they were the barrier against the wild tribes, Apaches, Comanches, Cheyennes, Navajos. They were also the granary on which local colonization depended." [61, 139] When the United States took over these former possessions of Spain, they generally followed the Spanish precedent in their relations with the Indians of the Pueblos. Then, in 1922, the Interior Department "launched an all-out, final attack against the Pueblos." Collier, in his efforts to help the Pueblos, was in contact with each of the twenty-one New Mexico Pueblos through 1922 and the eight critical years following. The Pueblos revived their Union, latent since 1680, and fought the

government legally for eleven years, becoming the leaders for all the Indian people. In 1933, owing to their efforts, the old Indian Bureau was overturned and the government stopped the plan to liquidate the tribes. All this was accomplished by a total Pueblo population about equal to the number of free citizens in Athens, according to Collier.

Collier writes of the long series of meetings during the crucial year of 1922 at Tesuque Pueblo. "As our meetings progressed . . . I came to realize that I had entered a time dimension . . . These men and women were living in a time a thousand years ago. An event of many thousand years of group volition, no part of it lapsed into a dead past, was travelling across the present into a future of unknown thousands of years . . . So intense was the reality of this effort of flight between the 'twin eternities' of past and future, that all minor aspects fell into oblivion. Personal contingency, personal fate, simply did not figure at all." [61, 17]

Yet, when Acoma Pueblo decided to use modern technologies, it caused them no conflict. White men cannot understand this way of thinking; to them modern technology should doom the traditional way of life to extinction. Collier points out, "The Pueblo Indian silently repudiates that assumption. The livingness of the earth, the reality of the two-way flow between earth and man, the deeply religious character of that relationship, are the fundamental premise of Pueblo life. New technologies, including the mathematical and

130

quantitative operations of science, *if they be ecologically relevant and true within the Pueblo environment* are brought into the ancient ecological enterprise . . . without collision or contradiction." [61, 111] This is an example of Leopold's "land ethic" at work: a thing is right when it tends to preserve the integrity and stability of the biotic community; it is wrong otherwise. Such questions are not impossible to solve if the needs of the entire community are taken into consideration.

Culture depends on the level of consciousness, not on overall knowledge. Consciousness is awareness of more and more interrelationships. It is possible to travel the entire world and into outer space collecting facts and have no understanding; for understanding comes only from a lived relationship with the earth, and relationship takes time. Time spent in one place is required to grasp the interconnections. Aldo Leopold, in 1927, wrote, "This land is too complex for its inhabitants to understand . . ." [88] And in 1977 John Todd, speaking of the origin of the New Alchemists, said that he and Bill McLarney were teaching in California when they decided to go off and start a commune in a place which was mostly boulders and chaparral. "We wanted to make it partially self-sufficient; in fact, we just wanted to make it work. We discovered to our horror that, even with our collective boatload of degrees, we weren't able to make that little piece of land work. We didn't know what was going on." [325, 176] Man's consciousness is limited to the purposes man can conceive of. The natural world has forms of consciousness with different purposes than those of man; that's why human beings need the complexity of the natural world. Interaction with these alien forms of consciousness can expand man's own consciousness.

The study of all the organisms (beings) of a particular place, an ecosystem, is called ecology. Paul Sears explains this relationship:

Natural communities . . . operate on a current budget of solar energy, deploying it so as to keep the system itself in operating condition, maintaining or even enhancing the capacity of habitat to sustain life. Through variety and complexity, niches are afforded to organisms, visible and invisible, each of which plays its part in sustaining activity. Organic materials produced by green plants out of the raw substances of air, water and earth are broken down step by step, in elaborate food chains until their components are returned whence they came, once more in usable form. [375]

As long as the necessary balance is maintained, the ecosystem is eternally viable. To live in balance with Nature means to keep in balance with the way the pattern of energy use moves through your own *place*. What is at stake here is a question of means and ends. We cannot use the means provided us by Nature and ignore the ends of Nature. Nature's goal is *not* the survival of human beings; it is the survival of life itself— greater diversity of life. This provides a standard for us. Whatever values we decide upon in a particular place must conform to the overall concept of the balance of Nature, which means whatever we do which uses energy from Nature must return energy to Nature. This is Storm's *give-away*. This is inherent in the rituals of all ancient cultures: returning energy to nature.

Conforming to Nature's law is not like conforming to an arbitrary man-made law which restricts freedom— "Do such-and-such because you are told to do it"; instead it's more like a group of experts skiing a powder snow slope in perfect freedom. No one is being pushed around or forced. It's merely that by mutual interaction of the human being, the gravity, the snow, and the angle of the slope, there is only one best way to ski down the mountain in any particular line; so if all conform to the mutual interaction there is perfect freedom for all. There is no way they can collide; yet all are moving in perfect freedom. In this sense, the greater the knowledge, the awareness of all the other factors involved, the greater the freedom. Knowing becomes a matter of finding out how organisms and natural forces relate one to the other and how human beings can fit themselves into this relationship so that all continue to function with greatest freedom.

The highest good is the optimally functioning ecosystem as a whole, not the immediate purposes of any one being in the ecosystem—man included. Again to use an analogy from skiing, if it so happens that a strong, determined, egocentric packed-slope skier happens to venture onto a back-country powder slope just as a number of good powder skiers are moving down it— the result can be catastrophic. This one man can instantly disrupt the fall line route of any number of skiers and ultimately collide with one or more, simply because he is not aware of the interaction of the whole ecosystem—snow, gravity, angle, etc., and insists on inflicting his will on the whole—in this case, to show off as a fancy skier.

But this example is exactly how human beings act within an ecosystem. Instead of living in balance with the rest of the beings in that ecosystem so that all flourish, human beings behave as the egocentric packed-slope skier—taking up the entire slope for his ski run, so that where before fifty organisms flourished, only five still do. The more sudden changes humans inflict on an ecosystem, the more diversity is destroyed, until all that is left are the few pioneer species which can take such disruption, those which we usually label as weeds. In fact, human beings have generally behaved just like weeds, surviving by destroying all competition. Our much vaunted "pioneer" is a perfect example. According to Charles Russell, the painter of western scenes, "A pioneer is a man who comes to virgin country, traps off all the fur, kills off the wild meat, cuts down all the trees, grazes off all the grass, plows the roots up and strings ten million miles of wire. A pioneer destroys things and calls it civilization." Unfortunately this country has had the pioneer mentality far too long. "Reinhabitation" is beginning to reverse this process.

According to Peter Berg, of *Planet Drum*, "Reinhabitation refers to the spirit of living-in-place within a region that has been disrupted and injured through generations of exploitation. It means becoming native to places by developing awareness of their special life continuities and undertaking activities and evolving social forms that tend to maintain and restore them . . . It is simply becoming fully alive in and with a place." [349] As Wendell Berry says, a human being cannot really own a place; he can only learn to belong to it. "And I began to understand that so long as I did not know the place fully or even adequately, I belonged to it only partially . . ." He began to dimly see that he wanted "to belong fully to this place, to belong as the thrushes and the herons and the muskrats belonged, to be altogether at home here. That is still my ambition . . ." [27, 150] But now, years later, he knows the depth and extent of this ambition.

Wendell Berry comes from a family which has lived in the same part of Kentucky for generations. He consciously made the decision to go back to this land after university studies and travel abroad. He has lived there ever since as poet, teacher, farmer, and reclaimer of ruined land.

When Berry left New York for his Kentucky land, his friends thought that returning to the land would be intellectual death. Their certainty caused him some doubts at first, but what happened was that "far from being bored and diminished and obscured to myself by my life here, I had grown more alive and more conscious than I had ever been." [27, 176] He writes that once a person "is joined to the earth with any permanence of expectation and interest, his concerns ramify in proportion to his understanding of his dependence on the earth and his consequent responsibility toward it. He realizes, because the demands of the place make it specific and inescapable, that his responsibility is not merely that of an underling, a worker at a job, but also moral, historical, political, aesthetic, ecological, domestic, educational, and so on." [27, 86]

Reinhabitation means learning from the *place* what its needs are. Primitive traditional cultures learned from their *place* by totemism. Linn House defines totemism as a "method of perceiving power, goodness and mutuality in *locale* through the recognition of and respect for the vitality, spirit and interdependence of other species." Linn House goes on to say, "Salmon is the totem animal of the North Pacific Range. Only salmon, as a species, informs us humans, as a species, of the vastness and unity of the North Pacific Ocean and its rim . . ." [128]

The buffalo was the totem animal for the Great Plains. In 1830 about 75 million buffalo roamed the Great Plains; in 1850 there were close to 50 million left, but by 1883 there were none to be found there. The last few remaining buffalo were discovered in 1886 when the National Museum of Washington sent out a taxidermist to find six specimens. He searched for a year and a half and finally, in a rugged area of Montana where no horse could penetrate, he found eight survivors. [79, 170] We have largely destroyed the soil of the Great Plains in a similar fashion. Restoring respect for the buffalo as a totem animal would teach us a great deal about restoring the health of the Great Plains.

Each place has a particular species of animal or bird, which in Amerindian lore, was especially identified with that place. Find out what species is identified with your *place* in Indian lore, and then find out what habitat it needs. Begin to provide that habitat on any piece of land you have access to. In this small way, you will begin to restore the health of the land. Remember that Aldo Leopold began to learn to "think like a mountain" after looking into the green eyes of a dying wolf.

There has been considerable controversy concerning the Sacred Blue Lake of the Taos Indians. This is the source of the water that comes down to their land. It is their watershed. "Watershed is a whole, defines what is upriver/downriver, what the space is we roam in, in our own bodies of water . . . When you follow a watershed, it teaches, leads you on in. When you cut a watershed with roads, dams and ditches, it bleeds, erodes, floods. Watershed defines place, wind, food, pathways, ceremonies and chants. Enter into that flowing moment of watershed living, in this place, celebrate the return of salmon and herring, dream of waters merging, enlarge the watershed with your own self, until you are in it, totally, until you are it.

"Watershed is a living organism: rivers and streams and underground flows are veins and arteries; marshes are the pollution-removing kidneys; water to drink; water is the cosmic sense organ of the earth . . ." [189]

Not only the Taos Indians' Blue Lake, but all watersheds are sacred, because they define the flow of the life-giving gift of water to all the beings of that *place*. Follow your local creek or river up to its source and downstream as far as possible. Become aware of its life as an organism, what is good for it and what is destructive to it. I am not talking here about political action, I am talking about increasing your own awareness, so you learn from the land itself what its needs are. When you are sufficiently aware, you will begin to work with the land, probably in small ways at first, but it will grow. A change of consciousness from land as a thing we own and can buy and sell, to land as a living being will take many years—perhaps many lifetimes. After all, there have been ten thousand years of ever-increasing land trauma, ever since human beings turned to farming.

A change of consciousness in only one person can do much for the land. The most powerful example I know of is the story of the shepherd, Elzeard Bouffier, who began planting trees in the barren, desolate foothills of Provence—in land which had been ruined by overgrazing probably as long ago as Roman times. When Jean

Giono, author of "The Man Who Planted Hope and Grew Happiness," first saw Bouffier, the man was 55 years old and had successfully planted 20,000 trees, of which he thought half would live. This was in 1913. He went on planting trees. The last time Giono saw him, in 1945, he was 87, and the entire area had been transformed: "Instead of the harsh dry winds . . . a gentle breeze was blowing, laden with scents. A sound like water came from the mountains; it was the wind in the forest; most amazing of all, I heard the actual sound of water falling into a pool." The old streams were flowing again because they are fed by the rains and snows which Bouffier's forest conserves, the villages have been rebuilt, small farms are there. "More than 10,000 people owe their happiness to Elzeard Bouffier." [367] He died in 1947.

So, don't worry about organizations or governments or laws; begin now to become aware of the needs of your *place* and work with it.

As we saw in Part I of this book, every great culture of the past had its sacred mountain. One way to begin the reinhabitation of a *place* is to set aside a tiny bit of the ruined land as a "Nature shrine." Replant it with native vegetation, which will in turn lead to native small animals and birds returning. From this small beginning, others in the locality will realize the diversity of plants they have lost. This can even be done in a city. For instance, in San Francisco there is a hill, Corona Heights, along State Street, an area topped by red rocks on which nothing grows because the land has been beaten to death by trampling of generations of feet. Fencing off one tiny area, returning it to native vegetation, and caring for it on a shared basis by various people among the surrounding thousands is a beginning.

Probably the next step will be to guard it because some misguided, destroyed human being will not tolerate this natural beauty. This leads to the idea of a youth corps as guardians of the earth. They will have to be entrusted with actual police power for the area. Such responsibility is important learning for young people. When caught, the culprit should be treated in a fashion similar to Finland's treatment of drunken drivers. Every single person, without exception, including government leaders, caught driving while drunk, has to put in time working on the highways in Finland. This cuts down drunken driving immediately. In a nature shrine, every single person caught destroying the area must work so many hours at restoring the land. Such work instills care for the earth.

Russell Lord, in *Care of the Earth*, presents a somewhat similar idea. During the depression, the Civilian Conservation Corps enrolled upward of 400,000 young men. Lord suggests some of the problems: "It will take a nice sense of distinction, in drafting the measure proposing such a corps, to separate the idea of prison camps for juvenile delinquents and the idea of an honored and vital service to the State, and so ignite in the public mind the ardor and admiration for such an 'army without banners' in a 'battle without guns' to save the environment." [369, 257]

Such a Nature shrine will not be a "park" in the usual sense whatsoever. It will not be for recreation in the usual mindless sense but for "re-creation" both of ourselves and the natural environment. It will not be for looking at but for working in. The "people's parks" of the sixties were a somewhat similar attempt, but without any clear vision of the needs of the land itself. Places were merely "prettied up" for the enjoyment of human beings.

Such a youth corps may seem Utopian but, actually, it could well prove to be the salvation of many. Some young men have deep within them a love for the non-human, which our culture forces them to disown; and, as a result they become unnecessarily brutal toward animals or the environment as some kind of measure of self-defense. I can give two examples here. One was an Englishman who came to Canada in the early years of this century, passed as an Indian and took up trapping. His Indian name was Grey Owl. He had loved animals as a child and loved the wild. When he got back to his part of Canada after the First World War, he found destruction where there had been an Indian-based trapping industry. He knew this exploitation of the woods would "tear the heart out of it, mock its silence with their explosions, burn its woods, slaughter the animals, poison the fish and seduce the Indians." [72, 115] He went back to trapping but "filled with self-disgust . . . he . . . skinned them ferociously and quickly because the action went against something instinctive in him which could not and never would be suppressed." [72, 113] He began drinking heavily and was involved in almost lethal fights. Eventually, his young Indian wife talked him into letting her keep the two kits of a mother beaver who had been killed. Living in the same cabin with these young ones changed the man's life. All the love for animals, which he had hidden all the years, came to the surface. He began to write about them. The stories were published. Eventually, with the support of the Canadian government, he started a beaver shelter and spent the rest of his life writing and speaking to raise money to help the beaver. After he died, it was discovered he was really an Englishman, not an Indian, which discredited him with some people. The only remnant of memory of him in this country is the Grey Owl Trading Post, in New York state, which sells Indian craft materials to Boy Scouts.

The other example is from a novel, *When the Legends Die*, by Hal Borland, concerning a young Ute Indian who through force of circumstances becomes a rodeo rider and develops a terrible love-hate relationship with horses, which becomes worse as he gets more entangled in the brutal rodeo game. He tries to ride every horse to death and kills seven of them, until he is almost killed by one. While recuperating, he takes a job as a sheepherder and is drawn back to his own country. He leaves the white man's world and returns to his real love of nature. I was told by a Ute Indian that this book presents the truest picture of his people of any book yet published. [364]

Further insight into this same complex love-hate relationship with animals comes from Dr. Karl Menninger, writing of the beginnings of the Society for the Prevention of Cruelty to Animals: "When Bergh's own large fortune had become practically exhausted in the fight for the prevention of cruelty to animals, he was suddenly given $115,000 by Bonnard, a dying French trapper, who had made his money by securing animal pelts." [215, 58-59] Menninger also notes that the charter of this organization bore the signature of John Jacob Astor, whose family fortune, started by his grandfather, was founded on trapping animals for furs.

In his book, *The Nonhuman Environment in Normal Development and in Schizophrenia*, Harold F. Searles says that far too little attention is paid to the significance of the nonhuman environment in man's psychological life. It is a source of ambivalent feelings to man, but "if he tries to ignore its importance to himself, he does so at peril to his psychological well-being." [287, 6] Relation to the nonhuman environment is of special importance in the life of an adolescent, Searles goes on to say:

It may not be so much that the adolescent's predominant emotional orientation shifts *from* the nonhuman environment *toward* the world of human beings, but rather that from his loving relatedness to Nature and to other elements of his nonhuman environment there *emerges* a loving relatedness, now the primary focus of his emotional life, to other human beings.   [287, 94]

As mentioned earlier, the Norwegian philosopher, Arne Naess, points out that we cannot have full self-realization without granting self-realization to all the beings in the environment. Martin Heidegger said that for human beings to live authentically they must "spare the earth, receive the sky, [and] expect the gods."

Vine Deloria, in his book, *God is Red*, writes, "American Indians hold their land—places—as having the highest possible meaning, and all their statements are made with this reference point in mind . . . Revelation becomes a particular experience at a particular place . . ." [365, 75 and 80] Deloria goes on to say that economics cannot be the sole determinant of land use. "Unless the sacred places are discovered and used as religious places, there is no possibility of a nation ever coming to grips with the land itself. Without this basic relationship, national psychic stability is impossible." [365, 294] Vine Deloria wrote this in 1973; recently, a Sioux Indian, George Barta spoke out even more strongly at a conference at Black Lake, Michigan: "We believe that land and people are one. We believe that only people with an integral relationship to the land can survive. We consider the land as our church, thus the destruction of the land is equal to the destruction of the cathedrals of Europe and the temples of Asia. We view this preservation of our natural land as our right to freedom of religion and our right to freedom of worship." [377]

It is time for all of us who are trying to reinhabit the land to stand up for the sacred rights of the land. A necessary first step is a reevaluation of agriculture. "The myth of the return to rural life has been mentioned. It's baloney; we've destroyed our soils. The industrialization of agriculture will not permit us, without a lot of agony, the luxury of going back to 1850," according to John Todd of the New Alchemists. [325, 180] Sahlins points out that in fact this soil depletion and destruction has been going on for ten thousand years, since the beginnings of monoculture and the end of the hunter-gatherer culture, when population was kept in balance with environment. [279]

There *are* alternatives: humans *can* continue to eat without destroying Mother Earth. The vegetables needed by each person can be grown individually with little damage to the soil. Protein is the real problem. Paul Shepard suggests that we learn to cultivate the microbes. They can easily be grown in very small areas; furthermore, microbes can make all the amino acids known to be essential to humans. Some photosynthesize just as plants do; others live directly on wastes of all sorts, including human wastes.

In the New Alchemy Institute, phytoplankton (little green microscopic organisms) act as solar absorbers, causing the tanks of water to warm and heat the greenhouses. [325, 181] Tropical fish, which can be fed all sorts of refuse, live in the tanks and provide the essential protein needed by humans; and the combined heat of the sun on the plastic dome and from the phytoplankton in the tanks permits the growth of vegetables. [325, 181-183]

Yeast can produce one ton of protein from each two tons of the petroleum on which it is grown. Thus, as Paul Shepard explains, "The oil burned to operate the machines of the present industrial farms would feed more people when channeled through yeasts than the farms now feed, and free the earth's skin from us parasites." [292, 261-262]

Immediately some people rebel at the thought of eating microbes and other invisible beings, forgetting that the bread we bake and the beer we drink depends on them. This dislike of microbes is peculiar, when you think of all they have done, and do, for us. For over three billion years they have been working to make this earth habitable for us. They gave us the oxygen we breathe and keep the earth at a reasonable temperature for us. According to Margulis and Lovelock, in their Gaia hypothesis, microbes can perform nearly all the chemical transformations of larger organisms, such as the photosynthesis of plants. [370] (*Gaia* is a Greek word, more or less equivalent to Mother Earth.)

Furthermore, microbes are necessary for many of our own internal processes. We can't do without them; it's about time we learned to appreciate and work with them instead of against them.

One of the best foods known to man depends on microbes—miso, used in Japan for millenia. It is made by allowing fermentation of soybeans over a period of two years. It then keeps indefinitely without refrigeration. It contains all the amino acids that are in meat; it is used as a medicine and is said to have prevented radiation sickness in Japan near Hiroshima and Nagasaki.

One of the problems with agriculture, as it is practiced now, is that farmers plant the most succulent species possible for humans to eat. And these are the very species which attract the most pests. Then ever new chemical poisons are developed to get rid of the pests, and the soil and environment are poisoned. Odum suggests that the reverse strategy should be practiced, "Why not select plants which are essentially unpalatable, or which produce their own systemic insecticides while they are growing, and then convert the net production into edible products by microbial and chemical enrichment in food factories? We could then devote our biochemical genius to the enrichment process instead of fouling up our living space with chemical poisons." [236]

The other frequently destructive aspect of agricultural life is farm animals. Henry Bailey Stevens, in the *Recovery of Culture*, explains that it was "the breeding of animals that made the difference. So long as man hunted them, he was simply another beast of prey—a part of the natural balance keeping animal life in check. But when he bred and protected vast hordes of livestock he threw an intolerable burden upon the soil resources of the earth and has been paying for it with war ever since." [309]

Bailey's basic idea is that we must return to the use of tree crops. The California Indians long ago lived easily off a staple diet of acorns; farther east in the United States, Indians had access to enormous amounts of beech nuts from the trees. In Douglas' *Forest Farming* a summary states:

Of the world's surface, only eight to ten per cent is at present used for food production. Pioneer agriculturists and scientists have demonstrated the feasibility of growing food-yielding trees in the most unlikely locations—rocky mountainsides and deserts with an annual rainfall of only two to four inches. With the aid of trees, at least three quarters of the earth could supply human needs, not only of food but of clothing, fuel, shelter and other basic products. At the same time wild-life could be conserved, pollution decreased, and the beauty of many landscapes enhanced, with consequent moral, spiritual and cultural benefits. [366]

Henry Bailey Stevens states that human beings used arboreal and horticultural methods of food-raising as long ago as 15,000 B.C. in southwestern Asia, and in Northern India and China as long ago as 12,000 B.C. [309]

These alternatives can let us live in peace with the land. We can then begin to live whole lives and not continually be split between the way we know we should live, coded in our genes from our three-billion-year heritage of earth's wisdom, and the way we are forced to live by our present culture. Never have I seen this dichotomy put so forcefully as in a poem by Gary Snyder. He was up on Mt. Baker, alone in a glorious snow gully; but—

> I must turn and go back:
>   caught on a snowpack
>   between heaven and earth
> And stand in lines in Seattle
> Looking for work.
>
> [301]

To understand the peace which can come from a commitment to *place*, I turn again to Wendell Berry, poet and reclaimer of land:

The great change and the great possibility of change in my life has been in my sense of this place. The major difference is perhaps only that I have grown able to be wholeheartedly present here. I am able to sit and be quiet at the foot of some tree there in the woods along Camp Branch, and feel a deep peace, both in the place and in my awareness of it, that not too long ago I was not conscious of the possibility of. This peace is partly in being free of the suspicion that pursued me for most of my life, no matter where I was, that there was perhaps another place I *should* be, or would be happier or better in; it is partly in the increasingly articulate consciousness of being here, and of the significance and importance of being here. [27, 198]

Throughout this book, we have seen that many of the evils that plague us have resulted from our misuse of the land. But, as Wendell Berry says in *The Long-Legged House*:

To make public protest against an evil, and yet live in dependence on and in support of the way of life that is the source of the evil, is an obvious contradiction and a dangerous one. If one disagrees with the nomadism and violence of our society, then one is under an obligation to take up some permanent dwelling place and cultivate the possibility of peace and harmlessness in it . . .

But isn't this merely a quaint affectation? And isn't it a retreat from the "modern world" and its demands, a way of "dropping out"? I don't think so. At the very least, it is a way of dropping *in* to a concern for the health of the earth . . . when one undertakes to live fully on and from the land the prevailing values are inverted: one's home becomes an occupation, a center of interest, not just a place to stay when there is no other place to go; work becomes a pleasure; the most menial task is dignified by its relation to a plan and a desire; one is less dependent on artificial pleasures, less eager to participate in the sterile nervous excitement of movement for its own sake; the elemental realities of seasons and weather effect one directly, and become a source of interest in themselves; the realation of one's life to the life of the world is no longer taken for granted or ignored, but becomes an immediate and complex concern.

[27, 87-88]

Wendell Berry speaks for the fertile lowlands of Kentucky. Ian Thompson, a fourth generation resident, speaks for my own *place*, the Colorado Plateau country, in a letter he wrote for the *Colorado Plateau Rendezvous* and published in the *Telluride Deep Creek Review*:

I grew up believing, as each of us raised in these Plateau villages believed, that to emigrate to the coastal cities was, itself, to succeed. No one ever put it to us in quite that way but we all knew emigration to be a mark of success, of worth. I have tried to leave. I have not been able to stay away for long. That is my first clue. My soul cannot travel with me, my soul remains here in the west-sloping mesas, in the aspen groves, in the sculpted side canyons along the desert rivers, in the banners of snow whipped from the peaks, in the wildness, in the fields, in the towns. Now I hear the wistfulness in the voices of my people, I see the pain in the faces of my people.

Now I know that after a century here the sacredness is at last seeping into our very genes.

There are places where this land talks to us in a silent voice . . . I cannot yet write of them. We all know where those sacred places are.

There are consonants and vowels tumbling through our own arteries to match those spoken by the rivers, mountains and woods of the Plateau waiting to become the sacred phrases.

Now I know that we do not have to leave here to feel pain. We are brought to agony with each dynamite blast in the crust of the Plateau and in the ether of our souls, with each mouthful of the scattered fragments consumed by the draglines and furnaces, with each new five acre tract, with each newly arrived saviour who promises to stay if he can just find a woodsy crash pad.

We have, for a century, erred in many ways, not always willfully. The land speaks, is worthy of our worship. It makes us whole. We have not stopped to listen, to worship. We are just beginning.

Let us resist the preservation of our "traditional values" as surely as we must resist the draglines. Let us resist learning our colorful lines as surely as we must resist the destruction of the Colorado Plateau in a last brief, desperate doomed attempt to save our fossil fuel addiction from its last agony.

Let us sit in the aspen grove, the canyon, on the peak, by the river until the sacredness wells up irrevocably within us and begins speaking. Let us, then, speak it to one another. And when we can bring to Reason, Policy and the Pursuit of Happiness a dimension of Sacredness we will have begun the revolution.

Forever yours,

Ian (Sandy) Thompson
Durango, Colorado Plateau   [320]

17. Rituals for a Sacred Ecology

But there's more than just solving the how-to problems. I've often said that if we're going to have a real rural renaissance I'd just take the solving of the how-to problems for granted. The first thing *I'd* provide would be festivals.

Ralph Borsodi   [264]

A newborn animal is a member of a particular species, but the human child is essentially a specieless being. An animal has a definite path laid out for it; the plasticity of the newborn human being allows it to be molded to fit any kind of culture. In some cultures, the individual is enabled to be truly born again; in others, "misbirths" occur, which Joseph Campbell calls neuroses and psychoses. According to Campbell, "Myth is everywhere the womb of man's specifically human birth . . . Rites, then, together with the mythologies that support them, constitute the second womb, the matrix of the postnatal gestation of the placental *Homo sapiens*." [47] Jean Wahl goes even further: "Festivity is the origin of all civilization and all culture." [344]

The purpose of culture is not to overcome Nature but to be open to the play of Nature's powers. The underlying meaning of festivals and rituals is a communing with the gods; the human being temporarily leaves his daily involvement and purposely assumes an openness to Being itself. "To celebrate a festival means: to live out, for some special occasion and in an uncommon manner, the universal assent to the world as a whole," according to Josef Pieper's succinct definition in his book, *In Tune with the World*. [258, 23] When a festive occasion goes well, human beings receive something that it is not in human power to give. This is the real reason for the custom of wishing one another well on great festival days. Pieper explains that the real thing we are wishing for is the success of the festive occasion itself and "the gift that is meant to be the true fruit of the festival: renewal, transformation, rebirth." [258, 31] That's the real meaning behind the trite "happy holidays." It is also the reason for the desperate attempts at merry-making at holiday times; a desperation forced

to fail, because no matter how much willful effort is put into it, no one can force festivity "to yield up its essence." All that can be done is to prepare for the hoped-for *give-away*, to remain in a receptive but aware state so that one can take part in the mirroring interrelationship of the fourfold for that particular season and in that particular *place*.

In ordinary daily life, centered as it is on human affairs, we tend to over-depend on the rational left-hemisphere brain, thus becoming oblivious to communication from the remainder of our own mind, as well as from the natural environment which surrounds us. A true festival effectively limits control of the left-hemisphere brain and allows communication to occur between the right and left hemispheres and throughout the entire triune brain—the reptilian, the limbic, and the neo-cortex. As was seen in Chapter 8, the oldest brain, the reptilian, plays an important role in ritual and the establishment of social hierarchies, as well as in aggressive behavior. The limbic brain has to do with emotions, mammalian interaction, and the beginnings of altruism and empathy. These two older brains have abundant connections with one another but only indirect communication with the newest brain, the neo-cortex. Through rituals, as well as art and poetry, the knowledge of these older brains can be integrated with the conscious brain. [20] Ritual also facilitates interaction between mind-within-the-skull and mind-outside-the-skull, the environment.

By returning to the earth itself for the basis of our festivals, we include all the manifestations of Being wherever we live. The natural world becomes an intimate part of our community. As we celebrate a ritual, we begin to move toward a relationship with our *place*—

that in which we live right now (with all its shortcomings and glories). Once begun, this relationship deepens with the result that true festivity again becomes possible.

Ritual and festival balance all the factors of the community. In primitive cultures, the very function of the shaman and his rituals is "to be the living circuit connecting opposing forces," according to Barbara Meyerhoff in her article, "Balancing Between Worlds: The Shaman's Calling." [219] He maintains equilibrium and balances the conscious and unconscious processes of each person, the individual with the group, the human beings and the beings of the natural world, and occasionally, acts as mediator between the tribe and the town.

As was shown in Part I of this book, rituals in the past grew out of a particular people's relationship with particular aspects of their land. For example, Greek rituals began in groves of trees; later, perhaps as a result of the progressive deforestation of the land, they set up groups of wooden columns taking the place of the trees. Still later, these became carved stone. But, always, the columns were arranged to focus on particular Mother Goddess forms of the landscape. As a first step toward regaining a living relationship with the earth, all rituals should be either outdoors or in a setting where the outdoors can be easily admitted. The Japanese provide an example here. Their tea houses and shrines are set so as to provide particular views of nature.

Rudolf Arnheim tells of visiting a tearoom in Kyoto. The monk opened one of the paper windows, sliding it aside, and said, "'See out there.' I looked and there was a small maple tree about twenty feet from the window. The monk continued, 'In September when the leaves turn red, the reflection of the red leaves are going to show on this paper window. That will happen at a particular time every year, and it will be seen every year.'" [373] This continual seasonal change of focus in their rituals goes along with the idea in Shinto of "creative divine spirit" on earth continually evolving and changing. Change is built into their culture.

Specific Aids in Beginning Nature Rituals

Any group planning to begin developing nature rituals should subdivide into what could be called clans. Each of these clans is given responsibility for one of the main seasonal festivals or for a particular type of ritual. According to Cushing, the Zuni tribe is divided into people of the north, people of the south, the west, and the east, as well as people of the zenith and the underworld or nadir. Each direction has its own color, but there is a center or middle which contains all the colors of the other directions. The leadership for any undertaking automatically shifts from one group to another depending on the season and other factors. [61, 179] Another system which can be used is Hyemeyohsts Storm's four directions based on type of personality as

he described it in *Seven Arrows*: north—wisdom, buffalo; south—sees near, mouse; west—looks within, bear; and east—eagle, sees-far. [311] You can use Storm's colors or assign the colors which are typical of that direction in your own *place*. For instance, if there are red rocks to the north, the north is red; a forest to the south, the color is green. The midmost point, where all meet (if you use this concept), is the color of the rainbow and is used for meditation or to settle difficulties.

The Tewa Indian world is surrounded by its four sacred mountains but in the middle is "earth mother earth navel middle place," the sacred center of the village, which both concentrates the energy from all the four directions and is the source of energy in itself. [241]

Without adequate care in the preparation, ritual will fail. Somehow, modern people feel that rituals should be spur-of-the moment affairs; the Hopis, with their thousands of years of experience, know better. Their preparation "includes announcing and getting ready for events well beforehand, elaborate precautions to insure persistence of desired conditions, and stress on good will," according to Thompson's book, *Culture in Crisis*. [376, 166] They have inner preparation, prayer, meditation, and good will from all concerned, as well as outer preparation. Outer preparation involves meticulous preparation of ritual objects, which can take several weeks for a ritual of a few hours duration. The time spent in ritual preparation *is* part of the ritual—part of the action of getting both the human consciousness in tune with the purpose and the objects prepared. Rituals done over and over again, sometimes in the same day, are not just useless repetition, as we tend to believe. "To the Hopi, for whom time is not a motion but a 'getting later' of everything that has ever been done, unvarying repetition is not wasted but accumulated. It is storing up an invisible change that holds over into later events." [376, 169]

The terms, which we can roughly translate as "manifest" and "unmanifest," allow the Hopi to take into consideration many aspects which our culture tends to ignore. The manifest comprises all things and events that are or have been accessible to the senses: trees, rocks, sunsets, etc. The unmanifest refers to all that appears or exists in the mind, or as the Hopi say "in the heart." The unmanifest realm includes hopes, desires, and wishes. The unmanifest also includes what is in the inner heart of animals, plants, and other things. In the growth of corn or the condensation of clouds into rain, the Hopi see the unmanifest becoming manifest. Things which are hoped for or strived for ritually are considered *already present* in some way but not yet manifest. What actually becomes real or manifest is the result of the covert desires of the whole community, so to speak, if we think of the community as the fourfold of earth, sky, gods, and human beings. As Heidegger explained, the worlding of the world *is* the mutual interrelationship, mutual fitting of one to the other of the fourfold. [356, 57-64] To a much greater extent than our culture, the Hopi world view allows for the participation of the older levels of human mind as well as mind-at-large in the environment of nature.

Seasonal Festivals in General

We generally think of the Middle Ages as a time of oppression for the peasants; in fact, they had as many as one hundred fifty festivals a year, according to Ralph Borsodi. [264] On these days they danced and feasted and celebrated the seasonal festivals. Now we try to cram all that into one holiday—Christmas—and then wonder why things go so wrong.

Usually the important festivals in most cultures have to do with seasonal changes because human beings are affected by the changing relationship of the sun and the earth on these crucial "balance days": solstices and equinoxes. When it is fully realized that these great "balance days" do indeed involve the relationship of the sun and the earth in a particular place, it becomes obvious that the only way to celebrate these festivals is to be in your own *place*—no other will do. Not even a peasant could have celebrated these days away from his own fields and animals, much less could primitive peoples. For them, these days were of crucial importance for renewing the energy of the land and the sun as well as the people. Today, on holidays people flee their ugly homes in cities to seek beauty and inspiration by ravaging and destroying the last outposts of nature—high mountains or the ocean. In the process neither the weary, exhausted traveller nor the land is re-created.

One of the first steps in learning how to reinhabit your *place* is to understand how the ancient earth festival days were taken over by church holidays during the first few hundred years of Christianity, in order to transfer the power and customs associated with those festival days to the new Christian Church. In late Roman times, there were still a few men who understood the importance of the relationship between the temple of the local god, the land of that place and the people. In the year 386 A.D., Libanius, a highly educated Roman pagan, spoke out to the emperor against the Christians, who were ruthlessly destroying pagan shrines and temples. I have already quoted from his speech earlier, but I will do so again: Libanius begins by telling the emperor that after "the first men who inhabited this world" found shelter for themselves, they built temples as best they could for their gods. He goes on to tell how the Christians are utterly destroying the temples, and he ends his speech with these words: "So they rush through the country places like flood waters—ravaging them by the very fact that it is the temples that they destroy. For every country place where they destroy a temple is a place made blind: a place knocked down, assassinated. For the temples, my Emperor, are the souls of the countryside . . . [297, 166] He was absolutely correct. If the sacred relationship of human being and Nature in a particular *place* is ruptured and the energy diverted into an organized, structured system, such as Christianity or any nationalism, or any other such system, the *place is* assassinated, as Libanius said. The Pueblo Indians know this. The Tewa Indians know this. That is the meaning of the Tewa prayer: "Within and around the earth . . . within and around the mountains your authority returns to you." This "power circle" is the consciousness of a people reacting with the energy of the *place*, building up the energy, circulating it through the system again and again with each seasonal "earth festival," getting higher each time around. Black Elk, the Sioux, called this the "sacred hoop of the world."

Seasonal festivals are based on the sun passing through the solstices and equinoxes. (For full explanation of solstices and equinoxes and a table of dates for future years, see page 181 in *Earth Festivals*.) Although these particular days mark the beginning of the seasons in the temperate climates of the earth, it takes several weeks for the temperature to change enough to show the full effects of the difference in the sun's relationship to the earth. In many cultures these intermediate dates were celebrated, too. Evangeline Walton calls them "quarterdays" [347, 163]; others call them "cross quarterdays." In the ancient Celtic culture fires were lit not only on the four main "balance days" but also on the four other nights which came halfway between each of the main "balance days," thus dividing the year into eight parts. Certain modern Christian feast days still occur on dates near to these ancient "quarterdays."

Earth Festival Day (approximate dates given)	Christian Feast Day
1. Winter solstice (December 22)	Christmas
2. Winter quarterday	February 6, Candlemas (Feast of the Purification of Mary)
3. Spring equinox (March 21)	March 25, Feast of the Annunciation (Mary). Also Easter is set for the Sunday nearest to the full moon after spring equinox.
4. Spring quarterday	Mayday rites associated with Mary—always held in early May
5. Summer solstice (June 21)	Vigil of the Feast of John the Baptist
6. Summer quarterday	August 15, Assumption of the Blessed Virgin Mary
7. Fall equinox (September 22)	Michaelmas harvest festival
8. Fall quarterday	October 31, Vigil of the Feast of All Saints

Four of the quarterdays are feasts of Mary; the fifth is the important Feast of All Saints. Earth festival days honored the Earth as the good mother, the Mother Goddess. The Church established holy days dedicated to Mary on these days in order that the traditional customs would be transferred to Mary, the mother of Jesus, thus drawing to the Church the energy of the people's ancient attachment to their land through local Mother Goddess worship. Lourdes, in France, is an outstanding example. James mentions that there is a Paleolithic cave drawing at Lourdes of men wearing animal heads "engaged apparently in a mimetic dance." [134, 19] The grotto at Lourdes was a holy place long before the name of Mary became attached to it.

Frank Waters gives an excellent example of this attempted transfer of the power of a *place* to the Christian church. He tells of a remote church in the mountains of Michoacán in Mexico, which was a great center of devotion. The Indians would walk for miles over rugged mountain trails to come there. The church authorities were impressed with this devotion until, one day, an earthquake tremor overturned the altar and beneath it was found a stone Aztec idol. The natives had been giving reverence to the power of the *place*, not to the Christian externals. [255]

I began to get a few glimpses into this matter of how the Church supplanted the old local gods while I was still a Catholic. In those days I would often climb down our steep snowy hill in Utah to a tiny Catholic chapel at dawn in order to read Lauds from the Church's Divine Office. The book I used was a shortened breviary of the Hours of the Church, titled *The Church's Year of Grace*. Reading daily Lauds in the early dawn light of the mountains was where I first read Pius Parsch, who wrote such fascinating background on the Church's feast days as, "the Church . . . keeps a genuine 'light feast' on Candlemas. It was instituted to supplant the pagan Lupercalia, a licentious frolic featuring nocturnal torchlight parades." [246, 372] Soon, I discovered the pagan background behind most of the major feasts; furthermore, I noticed that Mary holy days were clustered near solstices and equinoxes throughout the year, but at that time I did not have any background on Mother Goddess rituals.

Understanding the pre-Christian festivals which were held about the time of the earth "balance days" shows how they developed from early people's relationship to the earth of their own *place*. (For more detailed information on how ancient tribal and pagan festivals became Christian feast days, see the appendix.)

To begin your own rituals on the "balance-days" and "quarterdays" you need not follow any system merely because you are of Irish or German descent. You are no longer in the bright green fields of Ireland or the mountains of Southern Germany. It's far better to pay attention to the land of your *place* where you are *now*. Watch where the sun rises and sets through the year and what vegetation manifests during each season.

American Indian tribes, the Japanese *way of the gods*, and many European cultures have a "first foods rite" in the spring. At the time when a wild edible plant becomes ready to eat in the spring, the people gather together in the place where it grows, ritually pick it, cook it if necessary, and ritually consume it together as a sign of returning life. In Japan, to this day, the Emperor and Empress go out to gather "wild vegetables" in the spring.

Henry Bailey Stevens, in his book *The Recovery of Culture*, traces the tributes of flowers and fruit, present at festivals, to the ritual offering of materials for the mulch and compost of trees in the Neolithic tree culture. [309, 61] This ancient practice has continued down to our day in the giving of flowers for weddings and funerals. Instead of throwing such floral arrangements away, use them as compost by burying them under trees accompanied by dancing or chanting.

In mountainous country, spring moves rapidly up the hill, climbing about a hundred feet a day. Spring also moves north approximately fifteen miles a day and in fall warm weather retreats southward at about the same rate. [127] Variations occur due to slope exposure, moisture, and soil conditions.

China has the longest continuous record of seasonal rituals. The Book of Records tells of instructions which "the Perfect Emperor Yao (2254 B.C.) [gave] to his astronomers to ascertain the solstices and equinoxes . . . and fix the four seasons . . ." [38] According to the Chinese, the proper time to worship "goddess Earth" is from early in the morning at the summer solstice because "at this time the *yin* (female) principle is born and begins to wax strong. The *yang* principle begins to wane in power." Likewise at sunrise on winter solstice, the yang principle begins to grow. [125] The equinoxes are the proper times to balance the energies of light and dark, male and female, cold and hot.

Moon festivals are held at either full moon or new moon during any season of the year. In China, the most important moon festival is in the fall. The female principle, which has been growing since summer solstice, is about to give way to the male and the weather is no longer hot. "At no other time is she [the moon] so bright or brilliant . . . Then, and then only, the Chinese say 'she is perfectly round.'" [38, 398] The feast is held at midnight, which is when the moon gives the most illumination. The Full Moon Festival lasts three days. Each evening is devoted to moon viewing, poetry writing, and feasting. (For help in beginning to celebrate solstices and equinoxes, see our first book, *Earth Festivals*.) Here I will give three ceremonies in detail which can be easily adapted to any season.

Specific Seasonal Festivals

Cherry blossom viewing in Japan is one of the most important seasonal festivals. The *Japan Times* prints the expected blossoming dates throughout Japan. People from all levels of society take part in this festival by emulating the old poets who drank sake while sitting under the blossoming trees writing poetry. Okakura in his classic, *The Book of Tea*, refers to the fact that the cherry blossoms "glory in death . . . as they freely surrender themselves to the winds. Anyone who has stood before the fragrant avalanche at Yoshino or Arashiyama must have realized this. For a moment they hover like bejewelled clouds and dance above the crystal streams; then, as they sail away on the laughing waters, they seem to say, 'Farewell, O Spring! We are on to Eternity.'" [237, 60] As well they might, because, until the flower petals fall, the seed cannot develop and thus the new life depends on the death of the flower.

Housman, the English poet, wrote of the importance of viewing cherry blossoms. He wrote that of his alloted span of life of seventy years, twenty had already gone by, leaving him only fifty more springs.

> And since to look at things in bloom
> Fifty springs are little room,
> About the woodlands I will go
> To see the cherry hung with snow.

This is putting things in their proper perspective. In any particular *place* when the most beautiful nature event of the year occurs, all activities should be dropped and everyone should adjourn to view this particular manifestation of Being, as the Japanese go to view their cherry blossoms.

In my own *place*, the Rocky Mountains, the most beautiful manifestation is the aspen turning golden yellow and flickering in the sun under the incredibly brilliant blue of the high-altitude sky. A sacred Tibetan scripture describes "ultimate Reality" (Europeans would say "God") as "absolute identity, similar to *pure crystal*, as the *clear autumnal sky at midday*." [330, 32] Tibet is the same latitude as Silverton, Colorado. From my knowledge of the clear autumnal sky in our mountains, it is easy to see where the Tibetans adopted it as the symbol for "ultimate Reality." That anyone should be required to think of anything else than the aspen when they are at their peak is virtually a crime against nature! The heart of every person feels this, but we have no ritual way for viewing aspen; so it often degenerates into an aimless drive along the highway with stops to take photos. It is not possible to be *present* and await the coming of Being this way. Better that we should copy the Japanese, get out and sit under the trees and write poetry, or at least drink sake or tea. But *be* there—wholly present and aware. The most striking seasonal event in the Eastern United States is the turning of the hardwood trees to brilliant red; in the desert it's the blooming of the cactus. Every *place* has such events. These are the epiphanies we await, and we are never disappointed. All we need do is ritualize them so that the energy generated by this mirroring interaction of earth, sky, god, and human being is fed through the community as a whole and thus benefits all beings of the *place*. This is what Confucius meant when he said that a good

government devotes its efforts only to setting the time for rituals and deciding the music.

In ancient China, government officials performed ritual sacrifices to August Heaven and Sovereign Earth on the sacred mountians of the four directions. [38, 146] This important ritual could be done today in every place where people are beginning to reinhabit the earth. Define the cardinal points by mountains in your vicinity just as the Tewa and Navajo still do. If you have no mountains, designate certain rocks as boundaries or move rocks into such positions. Eliade has written of the importance of boundary stones. They penetrate the earth and thus draw up the energy of the earth mother and reach into the sky and draw down the energy of the sky and focalize this energy within the four quarters of your *place*. [76] This is the real meaning behind Stonehenge and such megalithic centers—not occult metaphysics, but the generating and focusing of energy for the *place*. The Pawnee had such a ceremony to further this relationship of energy between place and human beings.

Pawnee Hako Ceremony

Variations of this ceremony occurred throughout the Caddoan and Sioux tribes and, as was noted in the section on Eleusis in Part I of this book, the ceremony had certain things in common with the rites of the Eleusinian Mysteries, which have inspired humanity from Classical times on. For our purposes here, I will mention only the beginning of the Mysteries, the day-long walk from Athens to Eleusis during which the people passed numerous manifestations of the Mother Goddess, as shown in the horned mountains, and ritually bathed in the sea before arriving at dark amid the forest of pillars which enclosed the central sacred area. Adapting parts of the Hako ceremony to your own place will provide a basis for festivals any time of the year or for reconciling ill feelings between different groups.

Briefly, the ceremony involves ritual adoption between two groups, termed Fathers and Children, who wished to begin friendly relations or to repair such relations. The ceremony consisted of three parts: the Preparation, the Public Ceremony, and the Secret Ceremony. The central part consisted of a journey for the group labelled "The Fathers" to the home of "The Children." When they arrived, there was the Public Ceremony, a sacramental feast, invocations of the power of nature, and other rites. [89] The part which most concerns us here is The Journey. Mother Corn, in the shape of a decorated ear, led the way. The people sang:

Mother Corn, who led our spirits over the path we are now to travel, lead us again as we walk, in our bodies, over the land . . . She led our fathers and she leads us now, because she was born of Mother Earth and knows all places and all people . . .   [89]

141

Underhill tells of the Chaui sub-tribe of the Pawnee:

The party was an impressive one as it set off on foot across the prairie. At the head walked the chief, carrying Mother Corn wrapped in a wildcat skin. [333]

The Hako priest carried two peace pipes in the case of some tribes, or two hako in the Pawnee tribe. The hako were two wands—one symbolized the sky and one symbolized the earth. They were decorated with feathers. Behind them came singers, dancers and all the people. [333, 195–196]

The procession moved over the prairie for days, stopping to contemplate every feature of the landscape and singing songs. There were such songs as: "Song to the Trees and Streams," "Song When Crossing the Streams," "Song to the Wind," and "Song When Ascending Mountains." [89] These songs consisted of a few main phrases describing the natural being, followed by chanting. Underhill gives part of the tree song:

> Dark Against the sky yonder distant line
> Lies before us. Trees, we see, long line of trees,
> Bending, swaying in the breeze. [333, 196]

Remember on Mount Omei, the pilgrims gave picturesque names to all the natural features: "Bridge of Murmuring Waters," "Sombre Dragon Abyss," "Pool of the Gleaming Moon," and "Thundering Cavern."

In a modern-day ritual the group might walk through their place stopping at each noteworthy natural feature, praising it and telling what it does for them, in poetry and chanting. The underlying, deep meaning of this ritual can be explained by referring back to the meaning of the Greek word zoë, as it was explained in the section on Eleusis. It means "not only the life of men and of all living creatures, but also what is eaten . . . Where men draw their nourishment chiefly from plants, the nutritive plants . . . are individually perishable, destructible, edible, but taken together, they are the eternal guarantee of human life." [151, xxv] The Greek word bios means "life, course, or way of living." What this really means is that the life of man is inextricably bound up with the life of place. If the soil is not healthy, the plants are not healthy nor is the human being. The community is, as Aldo Leopold says, the soils, the waters, the plants, and animals, as well as man. The southwest Indians say man was created from corn. Such a journey through your place can become a ritual acknowledgment of the interdependence of human being and place.

Mountains which have a Mother-Goddess shape can be pointed out and openly thanked for their gift of soil. Some goddess-shaped mountains have been created by glaciers. Carl Sauer says that the rock flour produced by long ago glaciers has taken about 25,000 years to become fertile soil [282]; yet, here in the United States, we have lost half of this productive topsoil of our country in about 150 years. [11, 162] Merely throwing these statistics out to be absorbed by the rational brain does little good; but, a ritual setting with chanting and dancing can bring understanding to the older levels of our brain and empathy with the soil itself, as was done in past ages by ritual celebrations. Each living being in the place can be recognized and related to in this fashion. And we, too, can begin to have poetic names for our mountains and streams; because as Gary Snyder says, "Such poetries will be created by us as we reinhabit this land with people who know they belong to it . . ." [300, 42]

Tea Ceremony

Generally, in this country, the tea ceremony is thought of as a social grace which young women acquire in Japan; furthermore, most books written for western readers stress the aesthetic and social aspects of it. Actually, the tea ceremony as it is rooted in Japan's way of the gods, Shinto, is a microcosm wherein the human beings commune with the other beings of their world in a state of total awareness. As such it is an unparalleled setting for beginning to learn total awareness; thus, it is well worth adapting for use as a ritual for a sacred ecology.

Some knowledge of its origins will help in understanding its further possibilities. From the beginning, tea has been associated with the "sacred." The legendary beginnings of tea are connected with Bodhidharma, the Indian patriarch who brought Buddhism to China in the sixth century. It is said that when he found he was becoming sleepy and his eyelids were drooping while meditating, he cut off his eyelids. They dropped to the ground and tea plants sprang up from them. [237, 72] In the year 760, a Buddhist priest wrote the first book on tea, titled Cha Ching. [237, 23]

The tea ceremony is connected with most of the arts of China and Japan, including calligraphy, painting, and pottery. Sung and Yuan priests of China created the first scrolls to hang in tea rooms. It was thought that the serenity and harmony of mind which could be achieved through Zen could also be acquired by the discipline of performing the tea ceremony with total awareness.

Much later, when the Samurai era began after the fall of the Kamakura shogunate in 1333, tea drinking became an important part of the local culture. Each place developed its particular style of ceremony; but most often the tea was served in one large bowl and passed along to each person. Ceremonial incense-smelling came to be associated with it. The participants passed the incense burner among them. Similarly, in Amerindian rites, burning sage, cedar, or sweet grass is passed among the participants.

The tea ceremony became a set of ritualized movements to free the mind from its everyday concerns and "establish a state of tranquil, alert receptivity . . . a state of mind closely akin to that aimed at by monastic discipline . . ." [199, 310] In Japan it is sometimes called *cha-do*, "the way of tea" (*do* indicates a path of discipline). In his book, *The Tea Ceremony*, Tanaka states: "Harmony with nature forms the essential basis of *cha-no-yu* (the tea ceremony)." [315, 80] Serenity and purity are central to the tea ceremony. Serenity means "engaging in life, not withdrawing from it," but knowing that "nothing is permanent except change, that only death is life." Maraini continues, "Purity implies insistence on essentials, aesthetic cleanliness, intolerance of ornamentation and display." [199, 316] The term *fuga* describes this way of life which, according to Suzuki, implies "identification of the self with the creative spirit, the spirit of the beauty of nature. A man of *fuga* finds his friends among flowers and animals, in rocks and water, in showers and the moon." [199, 317]

Because of the serenity and purity necessary for the tea ceremony, everything connected with it must have these qualities. The rooms are of unpainted smooth wood; sometimes the pillars are of wood from trees bent by the wind. The walls are sometimes of natural-colored clays. These special rooms were called *sukiya* and were approached by carefully designed paths which wound past impressive rocks specially placed for their shape or their unique lichens, or were laid out to frame a particular view—such as Mount Fuji. This is reminiscent of the Greek temples, with their stone columns so placed to frame a view of a Mother Goddess mountain.

The word *sukiya* has many meanings, depending on the Japanese character which is used. According to Okakura, the original ideograms meant "the Abode of Fantasy," which the editor explains as being much like the English term, "pleasure house." But, more in keeping with the other meanings of the word and the spirit of the tea ceremony itself, we can see here the influence of the *way of the gods*, in that this is a place where the earthly creative divine spirit and heavenly divine spirit can interact to create the "reality" of this particular experience. Another set of ideograms for the word *sukiya* translate as "Abode of the Void," which shows a Buddhist influence. [199, 313] The "clear light of the void" is a term for "ultimate reality" or Being itself.

In the tea house the human form is not represented in any scrolls or paintings. The human being is already there as the host or guest, while the flower or the bonsai represents the earth. The art of flower arranging grew out of the tea ceremony.

As in any true ritual, nature poetry is of the utmost importance. In fact, the oldest anthology of poems in Japan, compiled at the end of the Nara period, is the *Manyōshū*, which is based on the changing seasons. [315, 80] Poetry in Japan is a totally creative relationship between the writer and the one who listens. This is the essence of *Haiku*. The listener must fill in the details with his own experience.

Directions for the Tea Ceremony

The following are simplified directions which I learned from a friend in Japan. In Japan the real tea masters are almost always men—fiercely dedicated, yet tranquil, ascetics. First of all, the essence of the tea ceremony is simplicity—but simplicity carried out with ritual completeness. There must not be any extraneous sounds or gestures to mar the tranquility. Silence is necessary to increase awareness and so that the sounds of the tea ceremony, such as the gush of poured water, stand out with clarity. (In a Japanese tea ceremony, there are also ritual exchanges between the host and the guests. These I have omitted for simplicity's sake.)

Everything in the tea room must fit the season or particular occasion of the ceremony (such as a moon viewing). Tanaka mentions that it is almost as though the tea ceremony had been created "specially to sing the praises of the passing seasons." [315, 14] The flowers must fit the season, as must also the drawing or painting or scroll. These do not have to be Oriental, but must show reverence for nature. Each tea ceremony should be a unique experience with its own particular mood which cannot be duplicated. The gestures are the same each time (remember the Hopi emphasis on repetition); but the flowers or tree branches used in the room are different, and the artwork is different as well as the season.

The guests are few—ideally five—but from four to six is also good. A single bowl is used, as it is a communion. The guest sips the "froth of the liquid jade," as Okakura calls it. And it is true, that after one has drained the last sip, the remnants of the green foam are curiously like jade carvings. The cleaning of the spoon used to measure out the tea and the wiping of the bowl after each guest uses it are very important. This is done with a small folded silk cloth and signifies a "spiritual cleansing of the mind and heart"; in other words, a ridding of all extraneous thought from the mind and a total awareness of the moment.

Cakes are usually served before the ceremony begins. Eating these begins the preparation for the ceremony. The guest watches the flowers, listens to the fire crackle, and gets into the mood of the room. Incense is always burning for the ceremony.

Utensils Used

All ingredients are laid out ahead of time in order of use:

1. The tea whisk is the only thing you really need to buy. It is of curved bamboo. If you cannot buy one, then make a whisk of some natural plant material from your locality. Tie together short, strong, thin twigs into a whisk. The actual whisk part should be about 3 inches long.
2. The tea bowl is usually about 4-1/2 inches in diameter and 3-1/2 inches deep. It is straight-sided

and flat-bottomed. There should be a design on the front side to facilitate turning the bowl. See below.

3. The tea scoop holds about a rounded half-teaspoon of tea. In Japan it is made of bamboo. It is shaped just about like a ski, with an exaggerated upward curve at the tip. The curved tip of the spoon is not bowl-shaped, as are our spoons, but flat because the powdered tea clings to it. You could use any wooden spoon holding about 3/4 teaspoon.

4. Hot water in an open pan. This could be put in a fondue pan over the fondue burner or over a hot plate.

5. The ladle is made of bamboo in Japan. It holds about 1/4 cup. Any long-handled ladle is good.

6. The tea is put into a decorated tea caddy.
(Where to buy powdered ceremonial tea, see appendix)

Method

When the guests are all seated on the floor you begin.

1. Rinse the bowl with hot water by pouring one ladle of hot water into it.

2. Immerse the whisk into the bowl to warm it, too.

3. Pour off the warm water and wipe the bowl with the cloth.

4. Put 1–1/2 spoons of the powdered tea (from the tea caddy) into the bowl.

5. Add two ladles of hot water.

6. Make a ritual scraping of the bowl with the whisk to be sure all the powdered tea is gathered up. This is done by completely circling the bowl with the whisk and then making two passes through the center of the bowl in a V-shape. Then, lifting the whisk slightly off the bottom of the bowl, whisk it back and forth rapidly for about 15 or 20 strokes, until the tea is frothy. Then make a final slow circle around the bowl with the whisk touching the bottom of the bowl. Turn the whisk upside-down and set it near you.

Serving

1. Turn the bowl three times around toward yourself. The right hand is on the rim of the bowl; the left hand is holding the bowl with the bottom of the bowl resting on the upturned palm of the hand. Then hand the bowl to the first guest with the design in the front of the bowl facing the guest.

2. The guest turns the bowl three times toward himself or herself and then drinks the tea in three swallows. Before the final swallow, take a deep breath and slurp it all down. This is to get all the foam. It should be a real slurp, as this is part of the sounds of the tea ceremony.

3. The guest wipes the edge of the bowl, turns the bowl three times away from himself or herself, and hands it back to the host.

4. The host repeats the making of the tea as outlined above, for each guest.

5. The ceremony is over when the host replaces the lid of the tea caddy. The entire ceremony takes from 12 to 15 minutes.

The pouring of the water from the ladle must be done in a particular fashion. It must pour in one continuous stream, as in a gush. It should look like a waterfall, but should not splash out of the bowl. In the earlier part of this book, in the section on Eleusis, it was mentioned that in the cave stood unstable, tipping vessels. These were tipped over so that the liquid within gushed out onto the ground. Recall also Heidegger's emphasis of the jug on festival days. This sudden flow of abundance, symbolized by the gush of the liquid, is important for festivals because it is a sign of faith in the all-providing goodness of the earth.

During the ceremony, all present maintain absolute silence while observing the host making the tea, watching the light on the flower or as it glints off the implements, and listening to the sound of water and the sip of the tea-drinking. The famous *haiku* describes this aware stillness:

> They spoke no word—the host, the guest and the white chrysanthemum.

When you have practiced sufficiently with indoor tea ceremonies, you can move outside and include a natural being as a guest of honor—a fine old tree or a rock or even a waterfall, as in Hokusai's print of a tea ceremony by the Amida waterfall.

The tea ceremony is the quintessential ritual for the "letting-be-of Being," as Heidegger puts it. It also makes possible Gary Snyder's hope when he said, "What we must find a way to do, then, is incorporate the other people—what the Sioux Indian called the creeping people, and the standing people, and the flying people, and swimming people—into the councils of government . . . If we don't do it, they will revolt against us. They will submit non-negotiable demands about our stay on the earth." [302, 108]

Sweat Lodge Rite of Purification

According to Black Elk, all the "Powers of the universe come together" in the sacred sweat lodge rite. Earth is present in the sacred rocks, the sky is present in the water thrown on the rocks, the bones of the earth, and in the steam created by the relationship of hot rocks and water. The fire outside the lodge, which heats the rocks, represents the sun's energy because it burns the sunlight stored in the wood with the help of the oxygen drawn from the atmosphere. The sweat-lodge ceremony is a continual give-away of all these elements one to the other. The human being is intimately involved in this give-away, and from this total relationship may come the glimpse of the god's message.

"AMIDA WATERFALL": Woodblock by Hokusai (1790–1849).
(Courtesy of The Museum of Fine Arts, Boston. William S. and John T. Spaulding Collection.)

The first four willow poles of the sweat lodge are set up with one pole in each direction. The door is always to the east because that is where the sun comes up, over the "rim of the world."

The wood of the fire is also lined up with the directions. The first four sticks are laid out in the east-west direction; four are laid out on top of them in the north-south line. The remainder of the wood is piled on like a teepee. The east side of the fire is always lighted first.

Inside the tepee, a stick is pushed into the ground in the center of the tepee and a piece of rawhide tied to it in order to make the perfect circle for the sacred center. A round hole is made in the center of this; and using the dirt from the hole, a sacred path is made out to the east through the door to the fire. Black Elk gives the prayer here: "With the help of all things and all beings we are about to send our voice to You . . . I place myself upon this sacred path, and send my voice to You through the four Powers, which we know are but one Power." [41, 34]

The leader of the rite puts a glowing coal into this hole and sweet grass (or sage) is burned over the coal. The smoke is passed over all the body by the hands. The leader lights the sacred pipe and blows the smoke to the four sacred directions, above and below, and then the people all come in, passing around the lodge sunwise to sit on the sacred sage. The hot rocks are passed in along the sacred path. The door is closed, and it is dark.

Four times during the ceremony the door is opened and four times the sacred pipe is smoked. Those who do not wish to use the pipe may hold a stick of natural incense in their hand. Nakatcit, a Delaware Indian, once explained how a period of silence and smoking together was essential: "See, our smoke has now filled the room; first it was in streaks and your smoke and my smoke moved about that way, but now it is all mixed up into one. That is like our minds and spirit too, when we must talk. We are now ready, for we will understand one another better." [23] The mingling of the smoke from each person with the steam rising from the relationship of rock (earth) and water, bring together all the powers of the earth and provide a tangible symbol of the relationships expressed in Black Elk's prayer: "Grandmother Earth, hear me! . . . The two leggeds, the four leggeds, the wingeds, and all that move upon You are Your children. With all beings and all things we shall be as relatives; just as we are related to you, O Mother." [41, 105] The sweat-lodge ceremony is particularly effective for such times as the morning of summer solstice or when the Morning Star is in the sky. At such special times, just before the door is opened for the first time, the leader reads the ritual words of Tahirussawichi, the Pawnee priest:

We call to Mother Earth, who is represented by the ear of corn. [In your sweat lodge you can use the rocks as her symbol, or any plant or tree branch.] She has been asleep and resting during the night. We ask her to awake, to move, to arise, for the signs of the dawn are seen in the east and the breath of the new life is here . . . Mother Earth is the first to be called to awake, that she may receive the breath of the new day.

Mother Earth hears the call; she moves, she awakes, she rises, she feels the breath of the newborn Dawn. The leaves and the grass stir; all things move with the breath of the new day; everywhere life is renewed.

This is very mysterious; we are speaking of something very sacred, although it happens every day . . . Night is the mother of Day . . . The Dawn is the child . . . It gives the blessing of life; it comes to awaken man, to awake Mother Earth and all living things that may receive the life, the breath of the Dawn which is born of the Night by the power of Tirawa [Pawnee name for Great Spirit].

Then the door is closed again and all is darkness for the next pouring of water on the hot rocks. If the Morning Star is expected, just before the opening of the door the second time, these words of the Pawnee priest are said:

The Morning Star . . . comes from a great distance, too far away for us to see the place where it starts. At first we can hardly see it; we lose sight of it, it is so far off; then we see it again, for it is coming steadily toward us all the time. We watch it approach; it comes nearer and nearer; its light grows brighter and brighter . . .

The Morning Star comes still nearer and now we see him standing there in the heavens, a strong man shining brighter and brighter. The soft eagle plume in his hair moves with the breath of the new day, and the ray of the sun touches it with color. As he stands there so bright, he is bringing us strength and new life.

As we look upon him he grows less bright; he is receding, going back to his dwelling place whence he came. We watch him vanishing, passing out of our sight. He has left with us the gift of life which Tirawa sent him to bestow . . .

The day is close behind, advancing along the path of the Morning Star and the Dawn.

The door is closed the second time. When next the door is opened, these are the words: "We sing this song with loud voices; we are glad. We shout, 'Daylight has come!' 'Day is here!' The light is over the earth . . . We call to the Children; we bid them awake . . . We tell the Children that all the animals are awake. They come forth from their places where they have been sleeping . . . Our hearts are glad as we sing—'Daylight has come! The light of day is here!'" The door is closed for the third time.

Before it is opened for the fourth and last time, the Pawnee priest's words are read again: "Whoever is touched by the first rays of the sun in the morning receives new life and strength which have been brought from the power above." Then just as the sun rises, the entire side of the sweat lodge is thrown open. All stand in silence as the sun rises and floods the sweat lodge with light. And those present will truly feel "blessed" as were the initiates in the ancient Mysteries. After the sun has risen, the leader says Tahirussawichi's final words: "While we sing, this ray enters the door of the lodge to bring strength and power to all within . . . Now the ray is walking here and there within the lodge, touching different places. We know that the ray will bring strength and power from our father the Sun as it walks within the lodge. Our hearts are glad and thankful as we sing." The Beatles' song, "Here Comes the Sun," is perfectly appropriate here.

For a sunset ceremony, the order is reversed. The door is opened the first time when the sun has left the lodge itself; the second time, when it has left the tops of nearby trees and these words are said: ". . . Our song can accompany the ray as it leaves the lodge, touches the hills, and finally returns to the sun." The door is shut again. The third time, it is opened, ". . . The sun is sinking in the west, the land is in shadow, only on the top of the hills toward the east can the spot, the sign of the ray's touch, be seen . . . The ray of Father Sun, who breathes forth life is standing on the edge of the hills that like the walls of a lodge, enclose the land where the people dwell." The fourth time, the west wall of the lodge is thrown open and the Pawnee priest's words are said: "When the spot, the sign of the ray, the messenger of our Father the Sun, has left the tops of the hills and passed from our sight . . . we know that the ray which was sent to bring us strength has now gone back to the place whence it came. We are thankful to our Father the Sun for that which he has sent us by his ray." If the Evening Star is expected, all can silently await its coming; otherwise the ceremony ends with the sunset. [All quotations from Tahirussawichi are from reference 89.]

Silence

Ritual silence is a part of all these ceremonies. Silence is very difficult to achieve in our world today. People surround themselves with continuous noise. If no other noise is available, they turn on a radio. Silence terrifies them, as well it might, given the basis of our culture. Wendell Berry says that it raises "all the old answerless questions of origins and ends. It asks a man . . . who he thinks he is, and what he thinks he's doing, and where he thinks he's going. In it the world and its places and aspects are apt to become present to him, the lives of water and trees and stars surround his life and press their obscure demands. The experience of that silence must be basic to any religious feeling. Once it is attended to, admitted into the head, one must bear a greater burden of consciousness, and knowledge—one must change one's life . . ." [27, 41]

I have been luckier than most in experiencing silence in nature, but then an experience showed me that what I thought was silence was not real silence. I had become accustomed to having a sudden drone of a plane's engine interrupting the silence of nature, even in the southwest desert. I thought it didn't matter. But then,

in the northernmost part of Japan's northern island, Hokkaido, I experienced the full glory of silence. With a Japanese professor and some students, we drove for hours in a jeep miles from any habitation. We were north of the paths of all airplanes because there is nothing that far north to draw an airline. The men were all working on the other slope of the mountain doing snow creep tests. I was sitting alone on top of the little mountain, looking out over the ocean toward a small, volcanic island, a castle-like cluster of vertical rock. And I sat and looked out over this startling landscape and was grateful for the total silence. It went on and on, and I sank deeper and deeper into it. Still, nothing broke it: there were no dogs in these far north mountains, no water was running as it was winter, and no airplanes flew over. It was total silence. I discovered that total silence is total awareness and total life. There is no way to explain it, except that I felt I needed nothing but to go on being in that silence. It lasted for hours— until the men returned. But now I know the power of silence. Something of this power can be felt in Peter Matthiessen's description of a young Indian in modern times on a vision quest. He had been told to "face east on the first day, south on the second, west on the third, north on the fourth, until you are at the center of the circle, and then you will know the power of the world." He didn't really believe in it, but his father did. His stomach hurt and he shivered but he remained on the rock a second day and a second night.

. . . and on the third morning he did not feel hungry any more and sat there motionless, letting the sun and wind blow through him. He was as firmly rooted in the ground as the young pine. By afternoon he was growing weak and became filled with apprehension: something was happening. The jays and squirrels had lost all fear of him, flicking over and about him as if he had turned to stone, and the shrill of insects crystallized in a huge ringing silence. The sky was ringing, and the pine trees on the rocks turned a bright rigid green, each needle shimmering; and the pine trees were ringing and beside him a blue lupine opened, breathing. Then the river turned to silver and stopped flowing. The jays trembled on the rock, their eyes too bright, and the squirrel was still, the gold hairs flowing on its tail. He stared at the enormous sky, and the sky descended and the earth was rising from below, and he was soaring toward the center—

Then, in the ringing, far away, rose a flat droning. The airplane unraveled the high silence as it crossed the sky; it disappeared without ever appearing, and when it had gone, the sky no longer rang. He sat a long time on his rock, but the sky had risen, leaving him desolate . . .

And later, he laughed at his vision quest, trying to believe he did not "feel a dreadful sorrow." [209, 89-90]

Personal Rituals

Ritual celebrations involve the community; but, perhaps you have no friends who are interested in rituals, so you think there is no way for you to begin. You are not alone when you celebrate a nature ritual because, as Aldo Leopold pointed out, we belong to the land. It *is* our community. All we need do is get to know it. Edward Abbey says,

The only way to get to know this country (any country), the only way is with your body. On foot. Best of all—after scrambling to a high place—on your rump. Pick out a good spot and sit there, not moving, for a year. Keep your eyeballs peeled and just sit there, through the hours, through the days, through the nights, through the seasons—the freeze of winter, the stunning glare and heat of summer, the grace and glory of the spring and fall—and watch what happens. Pick your place and stay there. You will become a god. [2, 36–37]

Begin your day by greeting that great being, the Sun. Frank Waters tells of John Lansa, a 70-year-old Hopi whose psychic energy

. . . was constantly replenished by long reflective periods alone under sun and stars . . . He would stand in the open doorway facing east, barefooted and stripped to the waist. The first deep yellow to appear in the sky was sun pollen. Four times he would scrape it off the horizon with his cupped hand and put it in his mouth. This fed his body. As the sun began to rise, he breathed deeply four times to cleanse his heart and his insides. Then four times he spread the first rays of the sun over himself from head to feet, clothing himself in its power. Finally, as he faced the sun, now fully risen, he reminded himself to keep his countenance full, benign, and as cheerful as the face of the sun. [351, 76]

In the film, *Black Orpheus*, the hero, with his guitar, played the sun up for his neighbors. He died at the end of the film. A small boy picked up the dead man's guitar and, walking through the dirt, strummed the sun up. A record of Indian flute music from South America has a song, "Pescadores," which provides the perfect music for bringing the sun up over the "rim of the world."

If you cannot see the sun rising from your windows, bore a hole through the wall. This is done both in primitive American Indian shelters and in courtyard walls of modern Japan. In Japan, the rising sun is so important that at a famous Shinto shrine on the coast of Ise a *tori* marks the precise spot at which to stand to view the sunrise over Fujiyama.

As recently as the beginning of this century, in certain Russian villages, it was the task of one man to observe each day's sunset and mark the point where it set as it moved through the year. "The village elders would gather nightly beside the local church to discuss the affairs of the community, and there was always a bench which faced the mountains. The mountain peaks on the horizon formed a profile that was easy for the observer, seated on the bench, to memorize, and thus he identified the turning points of the year." [124, 124] Thus the village affairs were linked with the journey of the sun. The difference between this enlarged viewpoint, the sun as part of the community, and the usual modern viewpoint is shown by Henry Beston when he states, "A year indoors is a journey along a paper calendar; a year in outer nature is the accomplishment of a tremendous ritual. To share in it one must have a knowledge

of the pilgrimage of the sun and something of [a] natural sense of him and feeling for him . . ." [363, 59]

One of the first things one must do to learn to live in true community, by including the other beings of the *place*, is to stop being a "tragic hero." Both our Greek heritage and our Christian heritage have inflicted this viewpoint on us, that man is not part of nature but has higher ideals he must live up to. But as Joseph Meeker says in his book, *The Comedy of Survival*, "The tragic view of man, for all its flattering optimism, has led to cultural and biological disasters, and it is time to look for alternatives which might encourage better the survival of our own and other species." [214, 24] Many human cultures have never produced the philosophical idea of tragedy, while comedy is very nearly universal. The coyote is the Amerindian comic or picaresque hero, while the Chinese Taoist literature is full of wise, comic hermits who retire to nature. Joseph Meeker gives Felix Krull, a character created by Thomas Mann, as an example of a picaresque hero. Felix Krull says, "He who truly loves the world must shape himself to please it." The advantage of the viewpoint drawn from comedy is clear. "Tragedy demands that choices be made among alternatives; comedy assures that all choice is likely to be in error and that survival depends upon finding accommodations that will permit all parties to endure." [214, 33]

In our personal lives, we can quit being "willing to die" for our ideals and instead begin living so that all beings in our community flourish. This is Don Juan's "path with heart." He says, "A man of knowledge chooses a path with heart and follows it; and then he looks and rejoices and laughs; and then he *sees* and knows. He knows that his life will be over altogether too soon; he knows that he, as well as everybody else, is not going anywhere; he knows, because he *sees*, that nothing is more important than anything else. In other words, a man of knowledge has no honor, no dignity, no family, no name, no country, but only life to be lived . . ." [51, 106]

In the cities, it is sometimes difficult to retain contact with the earth. David Leveson, a geologist, says, "But actually the earth is everywhere, and from it, if only we can sense it, there emanates constantly the wherewithal for man to know what he is and where he belongs . . . Even in the heart of cities, brick is from clay, cement derived from the limy excess of antediluvian seas. In moments of hesitation or despair, such knowledge can be a measure of sanity, a route to reality. The 'natural' world is the world, and the products of man extensions of it—always. It helps to remember." [179, 18, 26] He goes on to say that, "We must each develop our own dream of the earth and find a way to it—mystically, empirically, through revelation or evolution—and share our findings with each other. If we don't, then it may be that neither we nor the earth will speak anymore." [179, 146]

Not only the earth is related to us, but as Kablaya, the mythical originator of the Sun Dance, said, "The four paths of the four Powers are your close relatives. The dawn and the sun of the day are your relatives. The Morning Star and all the stars of the sacred heavens are your relatives; always remember this." [41, 100]

Religion

A vast, old religion which once swayed the earth lingers in unbroken practice there in New Mexico . . . For the whole life-effort of man was to get his life into direct contact with the elemental life of the cosmos, mountain-life, cloud-life, thunder-life, air-life, earth-life, sun-life. To come into immediate felt contact, and so derive energy, power and a dark sort of joy. This effort into sheer naked contact, without an intermediary or mediator is the real meaning of religion . . .
[170, 9 and 11–12]

Earlier in this book, I quoted Gertrude Levy: "Religion is the maintenance of abiding relationship." [180, 35] Even as late as Roman classical times, there was no real need to define such a thing as religion because it was so closely bound up with life. The word *religio* existed, derived from the word *religere*, which meant to bind back or bind again, referring to certain religious practices to insure safety in certain places or at certain seasons of the year. In later Roman times, Cicero wrote, "All those things pertaining to the worship of the gods are called religious." [297, 17] By his time culture had become centralized in the city of Rome, loosening the ties of the people to their local place. With this development, the broader meanings of religion—involving the total relationship of people, place, gods and ritual— were already narrowed down to a worship of specific gods, as religion was cut off from its source, the living earth.

Chapter 2 showed that all the major prophetic religions began with one man's relationship to a particular place on earth. Now we are beginning to see that the relationship of *each* of us to our *place* is not only our life but our religion too. There is no other for humanity. Krishnamurti explains that "Religion is a way of life in which there is inward harmony, a feeling of complete unity. As we said, when you walk in the woods, silently, with the light of the setting sun on top of the mountains or on a leaf, there is complete union between you and that. There is no 'you' at all . . . there is no 'observer' . . . So, a religious way of life is the total action in which there is no fragmentation at all." [164, 103] Krishnamurti defines the religious mind as "that state of silence . . . which is not produced by thought but is the outcome of awareness." [162, 119]

Gods are not something to believe in: Gods are "Nature's transcendental powers" coming into contact with man's responsive openness and thus becoming disclosed in man's world. [343, 36] Gods are not just the earth or the sky or the wind or the rain. The energy of the relationship between all these things in a particular *place* names the god. Perhaps an analogy will help here.

You and I are a collection of many different parts (cells at one level of operation, and arms and legs at another level) and many different processes (blood system, breathing system, etc.). The human being *is* the hierarchical organism in this case. Each of the parts cannot be expected to totally understand the whole organism, which is the human being; still the individual parts operate as part of a total relationship which goes to make up the human. So, also, we human beings are parts of the whole system which comprises the earth or the universe. We cannot know the whole, but we can begin to recognize our relationship to the other parts of this whole by naming these relationships. This is what primitives did and still do in such cultures as that of the Pueblo Indians. If we do not name something, it is not communicable among us. Complex relationships between human beings and these other beings are not named in our culture. But once a god is named, meanings can cluster around this god. Lack of understanding here is the reason people find the gods of the ancient Greeks and the Pueblo gods so difficult to comprehend. How can Masau'u, skeleton man of the Hopis, be the god of death and of fire and also of fertility and of boundaries? We demand a cause-effect situation, where there is in fact a complex relationship. [332, 3, 4 and 25–27] In the case of the Greek god, Hermes, there was such a cluster of meanings. He was the god of stones along the road, of merchants, thieves, herdsmen, and a guide for souls. "He is the power which holds everything which partakes in his world in unity . . . All things belong to it [Hermes' world]; however, they appear in a different light than in the realm of the other gods." [242] Frank Waters quotes the Navajo explanation, "When you put a thing in order, give it a name, and you are all in accord: it becomes." [350, 164]

Our culture thinks of Nature as a complex of senseless, spiritless, blind powers, but in a true culture these powers of Nature take their place on festival days. In certain Indian tribes the shaman with his pelt and antlers "speaks for wild animals, the spirits of plants, the spirits of mountains, of watersheds. He or she sings for them. They sing through him." In Pueblo Indian ritual dances "the whole society consults the non-human (in-human, inner-human?) powers and allows some individuals to step totally out of their human roles to put on the mask, costume and *mind* of Bison, Bear, Squash, Corn, or Pleiades; to re-enter the human circle in that form and by song, mime, and dance, convey a greeting from the other realm." [300, 13]

We, too, can have rituals which balance our whole community—not just the human part. Through ritual we can admit these other people:

you people who are always standing, who pierce up through the earth, and who reach even into the heavens, you tree-people!

those-who-walk-upon-the-light, the birds

the "four-leggeds" and the "two-leggeds"

[41, 37; 366, 83; 234]

Ultimately it is the earth itself which teaches us this balance.

As I walk over the hill I'm paying attention to the trees and the ground. The river comes into view and suddenly I'm stunned by the realization that I am not the same person who started the walk! I am transformed by a ceremony residing in the land itself. The place dictates the mandate for human activities there and that mandate can be perceived directly through a ceremony that lives in the woods like an almost tangible creature. I am transformed, transfixed . . . + We have been awakened to the richness and complexity of the primitive mind which merges sanctity, food, life and death—where culture is integrated with nature at the level of the *particular ecosystem* and employs for its cognition a body of metaphor drawn from and structured in relation to that ecosystem. + We have found therein a mode of thinking parallel to modern science but operating at the entirely different level of sensible intuition; a tradition that prepared the ground for the neolithic revolution; a science of the *concrete*, where nature is the model for culture because the mind has been nourished and weaned on nature; a *logic* that recognizes soil fertility, the magic of animals, the continuum of mind between species. + Successful culture is a semi-permeable membrane between man and nature. + We are witnessing North America's post-industrial phase right now, during which human society strives to remain predominant over nature. + No mere extrapolation from present to future seems possible. + We are in transition from one condition of symbiotic balance—the primitive—to another which we will call the *future primitive* . . . a condition having the attributes of a mature ecosystem: stable, diverse, in symbiotic balance again. + + . . . It's very early spring. + + Rain forest. + Hemlock-wapiti-deer-red cedar-sitka spruce biome. + Duff and organic soil is deep. + Wapiti browse, deer browse. Trails through the forest. Beds where they sleep. + The challenge is to fit ourselves to this range in a way appropriate to the strategy and particulars of its regional succession, so that our cultures are once again a ceremony of interaction between species and ecosystem, matching the regional diversity . . . A community of beings joined by rim and basin, air and watershed, food chains—ceremonies. + . . . We will be informed by earthworms and plankton. + We will study that authority which resides in place and act out our lives accordingly. + There is no separate existence.

From Jerry Gorsline and Linn House's
"Future Primitive" in *Planet Drum*   [102]

18. Synergistic Living and Learning

Perhaps, when the new Bible of Science is written, one may read of man as the prodigal son of Mother Nature, flouting for a time her admonition and her wisdom, spending his heritage in riotous living; but at last reduced to the husks upon a barren waste of his own making, he crawls back to his Old Mother's fire-side and listens obediently to the story of a certain wise man whose name was Ecology.

Clark Wissler, Speech to the
Ecological Society, December, 1923   [359]

In Nature a stable ecosystem has two aspects: great diversity but also a symbiotic relationship between all the organisms concerned. The overall effect is synergistic. If human beings wish to fit themselves into this natural community, they must begin to develop similar structures. Such structures should emphasize diversity of approach and at the same time fit Ruth Benedict's definition of synergy as "social-institutional conditions which fuse selfishness and unselfishness, by arranging it so that when I pursue 'selfish' gratifications, I automatically help others, and when I try to be altruistic, I automatically reward and gratify myself." [204, 140]

Cultures such as that of the Pueblo Indians, which have survived for thousands of years, have this synergistic approach. The Taoist strand of Chinese culture is another example. Needham quotes an ancient Taoist text which illustrates this concept:

River Spirit said, "When we are considering either the externals of things, or that which is internal to them, how do we come to make distinctions between them as to noble and mean or as to great and small?" The God of the Northern Sea answered, "When we look at them in (the light of) the Tao, they are all neither noble nor mean . . . To know that heaven and earth are no bigger than a grain of the smallest rice, and that the tip of a hair is as big as a mountain mass— that is to understand the relativity of standards . . . So also we know that East and West are opposed to each other, and yet the (idea of) one cannot exist without the (idea of) the other—thus is their *mutual service* determined . . .

Needham goes on to say, "The Taoists were against the concepts of noble and mean as applied to Nature, but they were also against them as applied to Man . . . Just as there was no real greatness and smallness in Nature, so there should be none in human society. The accent should be on mutual service." [229, 105] Referring to a study by Granet, Needham believes that the custom of "potlatch" was of great importance in ancient Chinese society. Potlatch was also important in our Northwest Coast culture; the prestige of the top man depended on the food, blankets, and ceremonial objects he gave to the community at seasonal festivals. Variations of this culture extended through many Plains Indians tribes—hence Hyemeyohsts Storm's concept of the "give-away." In China the basic trait involved in the "potlatch," that of ceding and yielding, has become a dominant element in the culture. This idea of yieldingness, of giving up in order to get, which is a profound non-possessiveness, is expressed by Lao Tzu when he asks concerning the sage:

Is it not just because he does not strive for any personal end
That all his personal ends are fulfilled.   [229, 61-62]

But as Dr. Schumacher, author of *Small is Beautiful*, said, "Ideas can change the world only by some process of incarnation." [368, 108] This chapter gives some specific examples of structures for living and learning which bring together diverse elements in a synergistic relationship within a particular locality. [Addresses for all organizations may be found in the appendix.]

The Briarpatch Network

The Briarpatch Network is made up of hundreds of people involved in small businesses in the San Francisco Bay area ". . . learning to live in the cracks of society with a joyful consciousness of abundance." [112] Its beginnings date back to when Michael Phillips was still director of Marketing and Planning at the Bank of California. He met Dick Raymond, one of the bank's clients, when Dick was trying to get the bank to provide a space for its customers to get to know one another. Michael and Dick began these meetings. But to get the Briarpatch going, Michael quit his banking job. Dick Raymond's background included managing several businesses connected with the construction tool industry.

The third founder, Andy Alpine (now Bahaudin), has a B.A. in Economics, an M.A. in International Affairs and Chinese Politics, and a doctorate in Law; he served with the United Nations Secretariat researching riparian laws and economics. [112] When I met him I learned that he does Tai Chi and Sufi dancing. Altogether he is a uniquely balanced human being.

Each of these men would be making more money if he were still part of the American competitive scene, but they have a wholistic approach to Right Livelihood. Briars "want to integrate their lives so that all the necessary elements of living are part of their business as well as non-business activities. Naturally, one of those necessary elements is fun, so fun is integrated into business." [7] When they need input from the network as a whole, "a random sample is run on Mike's trusty calculator and fifteen or so Briars are invited to convene and consider a topic . . . with hot tub, a handsome fire, and apple pie with honey ice cream . . ." [372] Special parties are held on Briar holidays such as Groundhog Day, Father's Day, Brazilian Carnival, and Leap Day.

The individual businesses which are members of the network support one another with skills and even interest-free loans when needed. The members of the network feel that living is learning. If a business fails but the people involved have learned a lot, the whole endeavor is considered a success. Michael Phillips and Bahaudin visit individual businesses one day a week to give financial consultation on their problems.

Dick Raymond was the head of Point Foundation, which Stewart Brand and he established to give away the money gained from the *Last Whole Earth Catalog*. They supported many ventures, which mostly failed, and Portola Institute went into a decline. In July, 1974, when he had thought of Briarpatch, Dick Raymond called a meeting with twenty-five others. As Paul Hawken summarizes it: "The camp-meeting was, for Raymond, the beginning of redefining Portola Institute from its whole earth approach, which didn't seem to work any longer, to the more practical and localized concerns of Briardom." [112] This, of course, was Raymond's growing awareness that *place* is what matters. You can only learn to relate to the earth through your local *place*.

The basic principle underlying Briarpatch is "that there should be an alternative to greed, and the best substitute they've found so far is summed up in the word *sharing*." The Briarpatch network is an acknowledgment of the interconnectedness of society and a "willingness of each member to be an open and dynamic interflow of ideas, services, and experience." [112]

Bahaudin and Sherman Chickering put out an issue of *Common Ground* for each season of the year, which lists all kind of services and centers for wholistic living in the Bay area. Each participating member must also distribute *Common Ground*, which not only cuts down on costs but insures wide distribution. *Common Ground*'s unique feature is its *Subject Index*, which permits any one Center to be listed under each of the different services it offers. *Common Ground* provides an excellent model for other areas. Actually, Briarpatch and *Common Ground* both provide learning experiences for those involved, because they help their members to see that it is mutually advantageous to cooperate. Sharing resources is a necessary first step in stopping the destruction of the environment.

Forest Workers

The Forest Workers movement is more directly concerned with preserving the overall environment. Although I had read an article in *Coevolution Quarterly* about the Hoedad movement in Oregon, I had not realized the scope of this movement until I met Linn House, author of "Future Primitive," on Guemes Island in Washington. In talking about rituals, we both agreed that Gary Snyder's poetry reading in Seattle that May had been one of the most powerful rituals we had ever been involved in. (See end of Chapter 11). I asked Linn about the workers who were there. He told me and later I wrote to his friend and co-author of "Future Primitive," Jerry Gorsline, for more information.

Jerry answered me with a fact-filled two-page letter, giving me much of the background of the movement. He had just returned from the Northwest Forest Workers Association conference in Oregon. The NFW association is a regional organization that links together co-ops involved in forest-related work in the northwest. This includes Oregon, Washington, California, British Columbia, Idaho, and Montana. The workers control the profits in these co-ops, which include women as well as men. They work within their own local community-based areas.

Jerry says that what they are trying to do is "to define a biologically-sensitive forestry: industries adapted to land and resource patterns and economic planning that values the economic stability of rural communities and still responds to regional and national needs." [101] They are not loggers but ultimately will include them. They are involved in the more labor-intensive segments of the industry: reforestation, thinning, trail maintenance, and watershed rehabilitation. The logging industry, on the other hand, is involved in the energy-intensive and heavy-machinery approach, which cuts workers out and leaves a large percentage of local people unemployed. Gerald Myers, of the Redwood Creek Renewal Project in California, estimates that as high as 60% of the workers there are unemployed. [224]

The problems which these forest workers are trying to solve are complex. For instance, although tree planting does protect the soil and establish a new forest, under present corporate control it encourages monoculture forestry with the concomitant loss of diversity in forest species. But, as Linn House pointed out, for the first time the latest research in this field is going directly from the upper level to the worker in the forest because these dedicated forest workers study and work to find the best methods for the forest itself and not for the corporate owners. This cannot help but make big changes in the long run. Some of the methods they are aiming for are substituting labor for chemical herbicides in brush control, rehabilitating watersheds and long term changes in the tax structure to encourage employment, and establishing labor as a social benefit instead of a liability. The present system of counting labor as a liability is called "increasing productivity per worker" but really means "decreasing the number of employees." [224] This deprives people of the chance to work and live in the place of their choice.

When I returned on the ferry after talking with Linn House about the forest workers, there suddenly welled-up in me a tremendous feeling of well-being, and I realized that my basic thinking had somehow changed. It dawned on me that my doubt and pessimism of some years past, that the insane course of exploitation of people and land could ever be changed, had now vanished, with these forest coops scattered through the backwoods. (Linn thought there were 2,000 or 3,000 workers in Washington alone and I already knew of the Hoedads in Oregon and a group in Colorado.) There are pockets of intelligent workers, devoted to the land and relatively self-sufficient, scattered throughout the entire West. There is no way they can all be subverted by the system or destroyed by any centralized effort, for they can't be found—they are hidden away in their *place* on their land, not concentrated in cities. A great many of these workers are college graduates, some with advanced degrees. Gerald Myers of the Redwood Creek Renewal Project has a BS in Business Administration and a MBA in Industrial Relations from the University of California at Berkeley.

The Colorado group provides a variation of the other forestry groups. It is known as the Healing Light Foundation. The Cottage Industries, Forestry Specialists branch, gives free voluntary tithing to support the work of the Healing Foundation. The Cottage Industries is a family-oriented collective now in its fifth season. It is a Forestry Cooperative doing thinning, planting, disease control, and fire-fighting. Members work in Colorado, Wyoming, and New Mexico. The healing branch has people involved in herbology diet, nutrition, yoga, polarity, acupuncture, massage, and mid-wifery. They do accept individuals to work in the forests but at least a one-month commitment is required.

In summing up the exciting possibilities of this sharing concept of person and nature, in which both the human and the earth profit from their relationship, I thought of Erik Erikson's concept that in the period between late adolescence and young adulthood, "The resources of tradition fuse with new inner resources to create something potentially new: a new person; and with this new person a new generation, and with that, a new era." [81, 19]

This new era will come about as people learn they can heal themselves by healing the land in a sharing relationship with the earth. No more useful work can be done than planting trees to help heal the land. In my own town of Silverton, Colorado, the local San Juan Women's Club has coordinated contributions for the San Juan Memorial Forest from the statewide membership of the Colorado Federation of Women's Clubs. In 1977 alone, $4,065 was presented to the U.S. Forest Service. Most of the planting paid for by these funds has been done in "Lime Creek Burn" on Molas Pass, near Silverton. The area was burned in the drought year of 1879, and because it is so near the timberline, natural reseeding rarely occurs. Nearly 1.5 million trees have been planted in the Lime Creek area since the project began in 1937. [326] Some of the trees that have been planted are Bristlecone Pine, which thousands of years from now will be just as beautiful as the much photographed, venerable timberline trees which now grow in a few places in the Colorado mountains and in the Sierras.

Advice on How to Save your *Place*

I recommend two books here, the best I have found for immediate help. The first is for those who live in a small town and want to regain control of their lives there. It is *The Town That Fought to Save Itself* by Orville Schell. It's the true story of a town which the inhabitants prefer to call Briones to save further inundation. This factual, photo-filled book tells of the day-to-day battles which the people there fought to gain control over their lives: battles concerning unrealistic energy-wasting building codes, condominiums and other "improvements" which our culture forces on us but which we now know are invalid because the resources of the earth are limited. The depth of the commitment is shown early on in the book where Schell writes, "We cannot escape what men are doing to each other, because they are doing it to the earth and all its creatures as well. This recognition will someday make revolutionaries and fanatics who will die for the earth, rather than for communism or democracy." [283, 42] Further on Schell writes, "So, maybe what we should start doing is deciding where houses should go, if at all, and then start trying to make it happen whether through slope policy, zoning, bond issues, water projects, sewers, or means not yet invented. Face it! We're outlaws. If we obey all the present rules we'll end up just like Los Angeles. LA was built by following the rules! . . . Water and sewage are still the place to grab the growth dragon by the throat. Judges can't sue an entire voting public if they refuse to pass a bond for utilities expansion." [283, 63 and 153]

For your immediate neighborhood there is *Grass Roots Primer*, published by the Sierra Club with the complete story of how local people fought and won battles to save their street, their neighborhood, their bit of open country—legally. [276] Local people are being forced to learn all sorts of ways to save their *place*. Just this summer in wealthy, conservative Bellevue, Washington, a bedroom town for corporate executives, there was a history-making confrontation between a neighborhood and "the system." The article in the local *Daily Journal American* begins "At 11:30 A.M. Thursday, a man in a white short sleeve shirt and jeans walked out of a Bellevue woodland and stepped up to the bulldozer operator who had just pushed down a tree.

"'A person could get shot if another tree goes over,' he said. He turned and disappeared between the trees."

The article goes on to explain that over a year before, in May of 1976, the Bellevue planning commission told a group of neighbors that they had no power to stop a nine-house subdivision which would destroy the 2.6 acres of woods near them. Six months later, the Bellevue City Council turned down the neighborhood request for $55,000 to buy the woods. So, in February the bulldozer came in and started pushing trees down, but the next morning the bulldozer was found "vandalized, the gauges smashed, the fuel fouled with dirt." For six months nothing more happened until the day's events described at the beginning of the article. The driver of that bulldozer "packed up his stuff and took off." The police called it a "fairly sophisticated threat." The developer, asked if he would proceed, said, "No, we wouldn't be doing any building if we had to face this harassment constantly." [322] Unfortunately, this development ultimately was built, but the effort to stop it *was* made, and the developer didn't make as much money as he had planned.

The events described in the Bellevue newspaper have the general name of *ecotage*, sabotage for the good of the environment, which is a very complex matter. Ralph Borsodi pointed out the beginning of the problem which ecotage tries to fight:

Many of the ills that bedevil mankind and the planet today, you know, stem from a statute passed by the New York State Legislature in 1811. That law, for the first time, authorized the formation of corporations for *private* profit. Up until then you could only organize a corporation for public, or quasi-public, purposes: The construction of a toll road or a bridge or something of that nature.

In 1811, however, the New York statute granted corporation the status of artificial persons . . . with special privileges denied to natural people. And that was the start of the tremendous corporate exploitation from which we now suffer." [264]

Almost since this country began, certain men and corporations have been making themselves rich by exploiting our water, our air, our trees, and our topsoil. We are now at the beginning of a new era where the users will have to pay for these up-to-now free resources, as well as for pollution control and waste disposal. [11, 162] Obviously, they aren't going to do this willingly and legal battles will go on for a long time before this concept is accepted because corporations have lots of money. But meanwhile, your own *place* may be destroyed. So ecotage has been independently developed in individual places all over this earth—from the U.S. to Norway to France to Japan. It is a way of making the corporation pay at least something in time lost and legal fees, etc., for their *use* of the air we breathe and the water we drink. A sort of holding action until the law catches up with the times. It has many aspects: some very violent, such as some of the so-called "liberation" groups who don't care who or what is hurt, some tending to violence, such as Edward Abbey's *Monkey Wrench Gang*, and others entirely non-violent.

Arne Naess is an outstanding proponent of non-violent ecological demonstrations in the spirit of Gandhi, in which the demonstrator may be able to teach the opponent more awareness. Naess, a Norwegian specialist in the philosophy of Spinoza, has done a great deal of work toward defining a new philosophical ecology which he refers to as "ecosophy," a combination of the Greek words, *oikos* and *sophia*, meaning *household* and *wisdom*. Household here has the ultimate meaning of the biosphere. [225, 15]

One of Arne Naess's outstanding non-violent protests, which actually produced results, defeated a project to dam a fjord in Norway. Local people had protested and resisted to no avail. Arne is an excellent mountain climber, having climbed in the Himalayas. So one day he went out quietly and bolted his way up the vertical cliff at the edge of the fiord, then anchored himself to the rock and swung a hammock there. He dropped a note pointing out that he was staying there and if they built the dam they would drown him. Since he was a highly respected philosophy professor—and Norway is a small country where such things count—they called the dam off.

In his book, *Gandhi and Group Conflict*, Arne Naess gives some helpful illumination on non-violence in group actions for ecotage. "The essential and most important point in Gandhi's doctrine, taken as a whole, is not a principle or a commandment, but the working hypothesis that the non-violent resolution of group conflict is a practicable goal—despite our own, and our opponent's imperfections; that non-violent means are in the long run more effective and reliable than violent ones, and that they therefore should be trusted even if they seem for the moment unsatisfactory." [226, 15]

According to Gandhi, the supreme goal of each individual is self-realization. To understand this, it must be realized that Gandhi here is referring to "self" in the large sense (the same "self" as Jung postulates.) This greater "self" should be and "can be realized or cultivated maximally." The smaller self, the ego, "should

be and can be reduced towards zero . . . When the egotism-ego vanishes, something else grows, that ingredient of the person that tends to identify itself with God, with humanity, all that lives." [226, 38] The more one learns to discriminate clearly, the more one sees the "universality of Self"—the essential oneness of all. Naess says, "I believe in the essential unity of man and for that matter of all that lives . . . One's own self-realization must therefore somehow include that of others. The requirement of helping the self-realization of others . . . and hurting nobody, follows without further assumptions." [226, 42] In Gary Snyder's words, "May all beings flourish."

When one is up against corporate greed and sees all the beings of the forest destroyed, Gandhi's thought is difficult to follow. Arne Naess's point, though, is that our total self-realization is not complete without the self-realization of others—including our opponents in ecological crises. His advice for particular situations is: "Choose that action or attitude which most probably reduces the tendency to violence in the participants in the struggle." [226, 59]

This is not a simple matter, because the more one realizes the oneness of all life, the more one suffers when any life is needlessly destroyed—even a flower or an insect—and the more one wishes to stop the destruction. This effort can develop into violence, but by the very nature of your feeling for the unity of all life you cannot, in conscience, do violence to others—even those guilty of the destruction.

Education of a new kind is needed, education which puts things together in wholes, instead of taking them apart to analyze and dissect. If we fully realize that the world of the human being comes about through his interaction with the earth, the sky, and the gods of his own *place*, then education must become concerned with *place* itself, not with abstractions and generalizations. We are about to see revolutionary changes in the field of education.

Education

In Childhood

In education, there's an ever-recurring cry of "Let's get back to the basics." I'm for that—but by basics I mean real basics, not just the limited, *half-brained* learning which concentrates on reading and writing, thus making our children right-hemisphere non-literates, a sign of a far more serious deficiency than that defined by the usual word, *illiterate*, which refers to the left hemisphere. To help prevent this half-brained state, children should not be taught to read before the age of eleven, Joseph Chilton Pearce says in his book, *Magical Child,* thus allowing time for the much more important brain functions to develop fully (see Chapter 8). John Holt goes him one better. After more than a decade of trying to reform schools, Holt has come to the conclusion that *no* school for children is the answer. He has started a newsletter, *Growing Without Schooling*, concerned with "ways in which people, young or old, can learn and do things, acquire skills and find interesting and useful work, without having to go through the process of schooling." In the first issue (August 1977), Holt writes that *GWS* will "be looking for ways in which people who want or need them can get school tickets—credits, certificates, degrees, diplomas, etc., without having to spend time in school. And we will be very interested, as the schools and schools of education do not seem to be, in the act and art of teaching, that is, all the ways in which people, of all ages, in or out of school, can more effectively share information, ideas and skills." [126]

In chapter 12, I went into the importance of nature in educating young children. I don't mean the ordinary types of nature study, which do not involve the whole person. Fortunately, there is one book which provides explicit help, so that anyone can begin real nature education. This is Steve Van Matre's book, *Acclimatization, a Sensory and Conceptual Approach to Ecological Involvement*. In the beginning of the book, he writes, "We learned that a sense of the inter-relatedness of life, a respect for the wholeness of the environment, cannot be conveyed piecemeal by the dissection of its parts." Nor are we helped by prophetic statements of the doom which will follow if we don't respect the environment: "All the pollution statistics ever conjured up will not stir the soul of one energetic lad." [338, 9]

His solution is, "Let's help our campers acclimate themselves to their own environment. To understand it on their own terms, and its own merits . . . Let's subject the camper to the most sensory experience imaginable: mud baths, bog crawls . . . the camper should come to 'feel' his environment. To draw it close to him. To love it. To understand it—not for its labels and fables and fears—but as an intrinsic part of himself . . . The rewards: seeing the science of ecology lifted from the realms of the momentary fad; removed from the world of the textbook; to become a meaningful, natural, commitment in the lives of young people." [338, 10–11] The goal of the acclimatization program is "a breaking down of the barriers to the point where one human being can feel himself not only completely surrounded by the environment, but totally involved with it as well. Once he has felt this unity with Nature, he is more hesitant to destroy her; he realizes that to do so would be to destroy himself." [338, 17] The reason I single this book out for special mention here is that Van Matre has adopted techniques from the human growth movement and encounter groups and has used them not only to facilitate interaction between the people involved, but, even more unusual, to facilitate interaction between the human beings and the non-human beings around them—animals, plants, and the environment itself as a living being.

Essentially, what we are concerned with here is education for total awareness. Such an education encompasses all of life, not just that particular segment of it which is spent in school. Thus parents play a large part in educating their children. The most important advice I can give here is based on John David Garcia's premise in his book, *The Moral Society*: "A decent person is immoral when he is deliberately willing to sacrifice anyone's awareness, including his own for anyone's happiness, including his own." [95, 39] Sacrificing awareness for happiness in the long run insures unhappiness, because such a method interposes a buffer between the individual and the reality of that individual as an organism-in-the-world. The following variation of Garcia's maxim provides a guideline for parents: I will not sacrifice my child's awareness for his or her happiness. Or even more to the point, as far as the parent-child relationship goes: I will not put my happiness above our awareness. This, of course, should hold true in any relationship including that of man and woman.

After Childhood

Understanding the importance of *place* leads to an even more startling reappraisal of the higher level of education than of the early childhood level. John Todd gives some of the reasons when he writes,

I'd been in university since 1957, thirteen or fourteen years in academia—and many of these students had been in almost as long as I had—and we simply weren't trained in sensitive stewardship. We didn't know anything. Science hadn't trained us to be able to answer the most fundamental questions: How do you make that piece of earth sing, and how do you make it support those that live there? Degrees in agriculture, disease ethology, ecology . . . nothing!
So I decided we had to figure a way.

He went on to found the New Alchemy Institute with the motto: "To Restore the Land, Protect the Seas, and Inform the Earth's Stewards." Its members seek a world of "decentralized technology based on ecological principles," and they have developed completely self-sufficient communities using wind power, solar power, and fish farming. Their new book, *The Book of the New Alchemists*, provides sufficient information for others to begin learning and living in a similar fashion in their own *place*.

Another approach is mentioned in an article, "Some Utopian Considerations," in *Manas*, which quotes Vinoba Bhave, the Indian land reformer, on his radical idea for decentralized education:

People now think that every village ought to have a primary school, every big village or town a high school, and a big city a college . . . But when all the business of life from birth to death is transacted in villages, why should not the whole learning of life be available also in villages? . . . I ought to be able to get a complete education in my own village, for my village is not a fragment, it is an integral whole. My plan is for a complete and integrated village community where every aspect of life is complete . . . Our motto must therefore be: "Education for self-sufficiency up to sixteen, education through self-sufficiency after sixteen. Unless we make our educational plans on this basis, the evils of our present system will not be overcome.

. . . .

We must re-establish this institution of the wandering teacher. In this way every village can have its university, and all the knowledge of the world can find its way into the villages. We must also reinvigorate the tradition of the *vanaprasthashram* (a state of freedom from worldly responsibility) so that every village gets a permanent teacher for whom no great expenditure will be incurred . . .   [303]

The most utopian and, theoretically, the least likely aspect of Bhave's ideas, is that of the wandering teacher; yet, in modern America we have just such a man and one who is preeminent in his field. Paul Erdös, one of the great mathematicians, claims that to pursue his "ability to prove and conjecture" is to follow the highest possible calling, and so he lives his unique life-style. He has no property, no fixed address, he neither handles money nor fills out income tax forms. Since he was 21 (he is now 64), Erdös has travelled all over the world, collaborating with other mathematicians and giving lectures at colleges and universities. He stays with mathematicians in their homes. All the money he earns is sent directly to a friend in Bell Laboratories in New Jersey, who deals with all debts, as well as sending his W-2 forms off to another friend at M.I.T. who calculates his income tax. According to Persi Diaconis of Stanford University, who was once Erdös' host, "Erdös also gives you everything. He tells you what is on his mind and helps you with your problems." [157]

In a true culture, every *place* could feed and house such wandering scholars in any number of fields, leaving the scholar absolutely free to devote his life to what he loves best, his own further study and his teaching. Education is synergistic, too; if the teacher is not learning, the students aren't really learning either.

International College has already inaugurated a program which is a first step toward implementing another of Bhave's "utopian" ideals. This program goes back for its mode of education to the beginnings of universities in Europe. For instance, if a student wanted to study with Peter Abelard (1079–1142), the student travelled to Paris, where Abelard lived, and stayed there until he had learned what he wanted. Then he might travel on to another place, if necessary, to live near another master.

International College, founded in 1970, is based on the idea that those who compose the faculty teach at home—wherever home is. The student lives nearby. There are no classrooms and no resident faculty. The faculty is composed of over 150 tutors—many of them internationally known thinkers, writers, or artists, such as Buckminster Fuller and Yehudi Menuhin. The administrative office of the College is in Los Angeles, and the paperwork is handled there; however, the actual

teaching relationship is between the tutor and student in the *place* of the tutor, where both may be nourished by the environment.

A new project sponsored by the College is particularly important for the relationship between the earth and human beings. In April of 1977, three International College tutors: Joseph Meeker of Canada, Paul Shepard of California, and Arne Naess of Norway met with representatives of the College to begin outlining *The New Natural Philosophy*. Natural Philosophy, in its classical form was a semi-religious search for divine order as revealed through natural creation. The New Natural Philosophy is the study of human thought and action in the context of evolutionary history and contemporary ecology. During the past year the plans have firmed up and now International College "has assembled a group of distinguished tutors who are prepared to cooperate in guiding serious graduate students through the study of the New Natural Philosophy towards a holistic understanding of relationships between mankind and nature." [371] Some of the other tutors involved in the planning, in addition to those named and the author of this book, are Sigmund Kvaløy of Norway, Vine Deloria, Peter Marin, Loree Rackstraw, Gary Snyder, and Paolo Soleri. [For further information write International College, whose address is on the title page of this book.]

I have space here for only two other innovative ideas connected with "earth learning." One is a course titled "Mystical Ecology," given at Antioch-New England college by Mitchell Thomashow, on the faculty of Environmental Studies. In the course syllabus he writes that "Mystical Ecology will explore the outdoors as a path of transcendence." I find the first set of questions which the course covers highly relevant to this book: When was the first time that you realized that things weren't the way your parents explained them to be? When were your first inclinations of Infinity or God? What constitutes a mystical experience? How do each of us relate to the natural environment? The course goes into Taoism and modern science, the art of seeing, native American cosmology, hunting as a way of life, and death and dying. [319]

Jose Arguelles, author of *Mandala*, has some interesting things to say about the totally new direction education must go. Arguelles explains that our technological culture has made us "peculiarly susceptible to the belief that transmission of information is synonymous with the transmission of knowledge." He further points out that with the modern information industry and computers, which have taken over the transmission of knowledge (as information), the teacher has a totally new role. The teacher "must assume the role of catalyst of new, or *awakening*, experience," which involves going into inner depths of the self and operating on the various planes of consciousness, instead of dealing only with left-hemisphere consciousness. The teacher becomes more of a guide to help others achieve a balance between the knowledge gained from each side of the brain as well as from the earth itself.

The teacher must help students learn to see multi-dimensionally, because as Fritjof Capra pointed out in *Tao of Physics*, modern physics shows us that the universe is a "dynamic web of interrelated events," not a mass of unrelated facts. One of the ways to deal with this kind of material is through ritual, as tribal man has always done in the past. Through ritual, students not only learn from the teachers but from each other and from all the beings of the locality, including the earth itself. Arguelles points out that "group ritual reveals in a condensed, symbolic form/process the structure of interdependence and change which underlies all phenomena." [8]

Alan Watts devised an educational idea that was based on the idea of the teacher as a catalyst to awaken people to new experiences. For many people, their first introduction to Zen was by reading Alan Watts' book, *The Way of Zen*. During his life, Alan Watts helped many toward a non-dualistic understanding of man and nature; furthermore, he had the idea that through electronics there could be a complete liberation of the educational process. In 1973, he founded the Electronic University with the idea that his son, Mark, and Mark's partner, Sandy, would make video-tapes of Alan Watts giving the core of his philosophy. Then, after a group had used them and discussed them, Alan Watts would be available by long distance phone call to answer specific questions. This never worked out while he was alive, but the Electronic University continues under Mark's auspices, distributing films and audiotapes to schools and libraries on Alan and other, related subjects and conducting workshops on how to make better use of electronic media for self-education.

The effects of the new insights gained from modern physics and the larger ramifications of ecology are leading to a new way of looking at the world. Fred Hapgood, explaining the new kind of science writing, pulls this together when he writes,

The theory that I favor is that we sense that the world has changed enough to make a search for new ways of addressing the realities necessary, and what we are seeing now is both the signs of the search and the emerging answers . . .

Perhaps that was the evolutionary origin of religion. If this is true, then perhaps what we are doing now is listening: pulling away from those sense organs that seem to be likely to block nature off, developing others that are more sensitive and open, trying to learn, as we no doubt have thousands of times before, what it is, this time that the world wants us to become. [285]

So we are back again to Gary Snyder's poetic call on us to "*listen*." This must be the core of the new education. If we are going to take this seriously, we can no longer confine learning to the brain alone; learning must be not only whole-brain learning but whole-body/whole-brain learning. This is the reason for the growing importance of certain sports, which I call balance sports.

19. In Balance with the Earth: Skiing, Surfing, Running, and Tai Chi

In skiing and surfing there is a line called a sacred line—the slalom—a line of moving, dynamic balance with the flows of energy in the place. There, for a few moments, one can get close to the streamings of energy that are our universe.

Tom Bender   [23, 55]

A healthy, diverse ecosystem is in a state of dynamic balance. Each being in the system takes part in the great earth cycles: the energy cycle (sun), water cycle, and soil cycle. Food chains, for example, from plant to animal, conduct the energy upward; death and decay return it to the soil. When a change occurs in one part of this ongoing circuit of energy, other parts adjust themselves to the change so that the overall balance is restored. Too much of any one thing is as bad as too little.

The value scale of mammals is likewise exceedingly complex and non-maximizing. Physiologically, for instance, calcium will not replace vitamins. [13] Human beings are mammals and therefore have a value system which is multidimensional and non-maximizing, but today most human beings insist on striving to maximize one or two variables such as money or power.

In the long run this leads to extinction. Instead of maximizing one variable, such as money, the Balinese culture tries to maintain a dynamic equilibrium between all sorts of values—in other words, a steady state.

The Balinese culture has held out most successfully for a very long time against modern technological culture. The secret of its success is due to the value the Balinese place on definite spatial orientation and balance. Bateson says that they "extend to human relationships attitudes based upon bodily balance and that they generalize the idea that motion is essential to balance."

This makes for a society that functions well, "continually undertaking ceremonial and artistic tasks which are not economically or competitively determined. This steady state is maintained by continual nonprogressive change." [13] Their ritual dancing involves total balance, and their music does not build to a climax as western music does, but moves along in a continuous, nonprogressive change.

The more far-seeing economists say that we must move toward a steady-state economy in order to survive. Generally, people think this means stagnation and boredom. Actually it can mean exactly the opposite. For instance, all we have to do is look at those sports which depend on bodily balance—in other words continuous, nonprogressive change in the relationship between the human body and the earth itself—sports such as skiing, surfing, and running.

Skiing, Surfing, and Gravity

Skiing, especially powder snow skiing, provides the ultimate experience of dynamic, complex interrelationship between the members of a human group, the gravity of the earth, and the snow from the sky. As was mentioned earlier in this book, a group can ski very close together in perfect safety if they are aware of the nonhuman factors of the environment, because for any given position on the hill there is only one fall line.

Skiing in the fall line, by the very nature of the terrain, allows the skiers to have much the same movement as a flight of birds—seemingly random but never colliding. Obeying the earth results in perfect freedom. "Real freedom is no choice at all," as Kramer says.

One can never be bored by powder snow skiing because it is a special gift of the relationship between earth and sky. It only comes in sufficient amounts in particular places, at certain times on this earth; it lasts only a limited amount of time before sun or wind changes it. People devote their lives to it, "for the pleasure of being so purely played" by gravity and snow.

Although I've never surfed, I know enough surfers to understand that it provides much the same sort of relationship with nature. In surfing, one rides a line between the chaos of crashing waves in a balanced relationship with waves and gravity. Each surfer is alone with the waves; surfers cannot move as a group in the same fashion that skiers can.

This play with gravity is fundamental to human beings. As was shown earlier, the embryo in the mother's womb is in continual interplay with gravity. Young children play with gravity by walking tree limbs or fences and jumping off heights. All ages delight in skiing, surfing, running, and climbing mountains, all of which intimately involve play with gravity. In fact, "a body can be supported and its function enlarged and improved by gravity," according to Ida Rolf, the founder of Rolfing (Structural Integration). Some would maintain that gravity breaks a body down, but in a recent interview with *Brain Mind Bulletin* Rolf said, "That's only true of random bodies. If a body conforms to a vertical, it is supported and enhanced by gravity . . . The body is an energy field, and the earth has its own energy field around it. The greater energy field of the earth can enhance, support and enlarge the field of the individual human being, in accordance with the lines of force." [83] In her new book, *Rolfing: The Integration of Human Structure,* Rolf writes, "To the extent that its energy fields remain symmetrical, randomizing deterioration of an organic system . . . is slowed. Biological time in such a system expresses itself more slowly than chronological time." [277] This helps to explain why old mountain climbers, old skiers, dancers, and, especially Tai Chi teachers, even into their nineties, are essentially youthful.

In primitive times and even in ancient Greece, sacred sports and games were a part of the culture. Primitives in the new world had sacred ball games and running; Polynesians had surfing; and as for the Greeks, H.D.F. Kitto writes:

The sharp distinction drawn between the body and the soul, the physical and the spiritual, was foreign to the Greek—at least until the time of Socrates and Plato. To him there was simply the whole man . . . it is the Games, local and international which most clearly illustrate this side of the Greek mind. Among us it is sometimes made a reproach that a man 'makes

a religion of games.' The Greek . . . did something perhaps more surprising: he made games part of his religion . . . the Olympian Games were held in honor of Zeus of Olympia . . . Moreover, they were held in the sacred precinct. The feeling that prompted this was a perfectly natural one. The contest was a means of stimulating and displaying human arête, and this was a worthy offering to the god. [153, 173]

Only in a split culture such as ours is the body ignored. Castaneda explains the attitude taken by Don Juan's concept of the sorcerer:

The problem in sorcery is to tune and trim your body to make it a good receptor. Europeans deal with their bodies as if they were objects. We fill them with alcohol, bad food, and anxiety. When something goes wrong we think germs have invaded the body from outside and so we import some medicine to cure it. The disease is not part of us. Don Juan doesn't believe that. For him disease is a disharmony between a man and his world. *The body is an awareness and it must be treated impeccably.* [150]

Earlier in this book, in Chapter 8, we saw how whole-body/whole-mind thinking leads to seeing things in wholes. Examples given there were Giordano Bruno, who was one of the earliest European non-dualistic thinkers, eventually burned at the stake, and the Taoists. Later we saw how Martin Heidegger was influenced in his thinking by skiing in his mountains and Aldo Leopold by looking into the green eyes of a dying wolf while on a hunting trip. Limited left-brain thinking, which is common in our culture, can only see things broken up for analysis.

Running

While skiing and surfing need specialized conditions of the earth, snow, and water, running plays with gravity and can be done anywhere. Primitive men have always run—in hunting, in sacred rituals, and just for fun. Mexican Indians to this day are phenomenal runners, but when they ran in a recent Olympics they did not do well. This was blamed on wrong diet and other causes but, to me, it seems that away from their beloved land and open blue sky, they could not run freely. Lama Govinda tells of an incredible experience he had in Tibet involving running. He had set out in the morning to explore the far end of a lake and to sketch, lightly clad and wearing only his sandals because it was such a beautiful, sunny day. A great deal of his way was along a boulder-strewn narrow ledge of rock which fell perpendicularly into the lake. He had to "boulder-hop" the entire area, but he was fresh and exhilarated and so he continued. Next, he had to cross a steep talus slope (loose rock) which was sliding under him. He finally reached a good vantage point, a dazzling white beach with the "green-blue opal" water nearby against the snowy mountains in the distance. So engrossed was he in his art that he didn't even notice the gathering thunder clouds over the mountains.

When he finished he noticed it was getting very dark, not only because of the clouds but because the sun was setting. He had lost all track of time. He started to run and reached the moving talus slope, but he was very tired. The last of daylight was fast going. He managed to get across with the last of his strength and sat down for a minute. Realizing that in the growing cold and darkness with no warm clothing he would fall asleep and die, "Up I jumped, conscious that it was now a matter of life and death." He had not eaten since morning nor had any water, as the lake was separated from him by precipitous cliffs. It was completely dark; there was no chance to carefully find his way between the boulders that "covered the ground for uncounted miles ahead of me." He was exhausted and frightened, but he started and to his amazement, "I jumped from boulder to boulder without ever slipping or missing a foothold," in spite of the fact that he was wearing sandals. "And then I realized that a strange force had taken over, a consciousness that was no more guided by my eyes or my brain. My limbs moved as in a trance, with an uncanny knowledge of their own . . . Even my own body had become distant, quasi-detached from my will-power . . . and the only thing I knew was that on no condition must I break the spell that had seized me." [103, 77-78] As in a dream, he traversed the miles and miles of boulders and found himself on the easier slope beyond, just as the first star showed over the mountains; thus he could guide himself by that and safely reached his destination.

Later, he found that "unwittingly and under the stress of . . . acute danger, I had become a *lung-gom-pa*, a trance walker, who, oblivious of all obstacles and fatigue, moves on . . . hardly touching the ground, which might give a distant observer the impression that the *lung-gom-pa* was borne by the air (lung), merely skimming the surface of the earth." [103, 78] Govinda refers to Madame Alexandra David-Neel, who, in her early book on Tibet, first gave the West a description of this phenomenon. With her field glasses she saw a moving object in the far distance coming toward her with incredible speed. When he came nearer, she saw that his face was perfectly calm with wide-open eyes and a fixed gaze. "He seemed to lift himself from the ground, proceeding by leaps . . . His steps had the regularity of a pendulum." [103, 80]

Lung-gom

Lama Govinda says that beginners in the art of *lung-gom* "are often advised to fix their mind not only on a mentally visualized object, namely the aim towards which they want to move, but to keep their eyes fixed on a particular star . . ." [103, 80] Even his feet were not bruised or hurt as they should have been. Govinda says "It is the non-interference of normal consciousness which ensures the immunity of the trance walker and

the instinctive sureness of his movements." Training for this art among Tibetan monks involves strict seclusion and mental concentration on certain mantras and all the aspects of air. *Lung* means air and *gom* means "meditation, contemplation, concentration of mind and soul upon a certain subject, as well as the gradual emptying of the mind of all subject-object relationship, until a complete identification of subject and object has taken place." [103, 81] In other words, by shutting off the conscious, rational, little mind, one establishes contact between the rest of the human mind and mind outside the skull—the body and the environment—thus it all "flows."

Govinda states that, contrary to some accounts, the *lung-gom-pa* does not fly through the air; instead *lung-gom* "reveals the dynamic nature of our physical organism and of all material states of aggregation—not in the sense of a self-sufficient dynamism, but as something that depends on the co-operation and interaction of various forces and ultimately on the fundamental (and universal) faculties of consciousness." He also says it is necessary to have "a rhythm that gathers all available forces into its services." This certainly holds for skiing and surfing. A further similarity between powder snow skiing and *lung-gom* is the fact that some expert skiers, even some racers, can never learn to ski really deep powder. They will try, but their control factor is so strong they will not relinquish control to the snow—to let it do what it wills with them—and end up falling or exerting so much strength they are exhausted.

Monty West, whose account of how the Australian aborigines hunt was mentioned earlier in this book, had a similar experience to that of Govinda which could be classified as *lung-gom*. He had been camping by Glacier Peak in the high Cascades. He suddenly decided, shortly before the sun was to go down, that he wanted to see the sunset from Image Lake, some miles away. He began to run, not with an urgent aim, but the thought that he would really like to see the sun there. He entered into a peculiar state and was suddenly surprised to find himself at Image Lake with the sun setting. He stopped only a moment and realized he was in trouble, with the sun's heat gone, since he was in his usual loin cloth, and barefoot, with darkness coming on. He immediately turned back and began running again. He was able to drop back into the same state and skimmed along the ground. Then he noticed a small creature on the trail, just where his foot would come down next; not wanting to kill it, he broke his rhythm—immediately he came out of the special state of consciousness and found himself cold and tired. Still some distance from his camp, he struggled painfully along the last few hundred yards, although he had just skimmed miles in less time. [355]

Carobeth Laird tells of a similar experience, which happened within her husband's lifetime, among the

Chemehuevi Indians in the desert of California. Carobeth Laird, now 83, was first married to John Peabody Harrington, the famous ethnologist; upon divorcing him, she married a Chemehuevi Indian, George Laird, who was twenty years older than she, and lived with him until he died in 1940. She is a trained ethnologist and linguist, and thus her evidence comes from a deeply personal relationship with the tribe through her husband and a background in research. Her husband, George Laird, told of a special group of young men called "The Runners," the remnants of an ancient guild, who in the last two decades of the 19th century ran in one another's company for the fun of it. Only one, whom I will call K., was a true "Runner" in the old way. When he ran with the others, he ran as they did, but alone he used the "old way." It enabled him to "arrive at his destination with no lapse of time." George Laird insisted it was not done by magic but by "the old way."

One morning, George Laird said, they were all near Cottonwood Island in Nevada. The sun had not yet risen, when K. announced that he was going to Yuma. They watched him start off, running in an easy lope and disappear over a sand dune. Someone suggested they track him.

They followed his tracks up to and over the crest of the dune . . . The tracks continued on, but now they were different. They looked as if he had been 'just staggering along,' taking giant steps, his feet touching the ground at long, irregular intervals, leaving prints that became further and further apart and lighter and lighter on the sand. Silently, by mutual consent, the other Runners continued on down-river. When at length they reached the village at the mouth of the Gila, they inquired, "Did K. come here?' 'Yes,' the people answered, 'he arrived on such and such a day (the day he had left them) just as the sun was rising.' . . . K. died of smallpox while still young, possibly under twenty, never having known woman nor communicated his secret; contaminated at last by the white man's disease but never by his culture.   [166, 47-49]

What seems to be the case in *lung-gom*, and certainly in skiing, is that the earth is to be trusted. This feeling is part of the exhilaration of skiing in blizzards. Of course, there's the advantage that during a blizzard one can ski the same area again and again with fresh unbroken snow each time; but a blizzard is essentially one of the most hostile forces a human being can encounter—screaming winds, blinding, horizontal snow, and cold. While skiing down in the glory of powder, all is total bliss; while riding up the lift, I suffer, but I crouch against the wind and contemplate the incredible paradoxes of life.

Balance

Intuitions into some of the deeper meanings behind physical balance between the earth and the human are given by Barbara Meyerhoff in her study of Mexican shamans. [219] She explains that the shaman lives in paradox. His function "is to be the living circuit connecting opposing forces. His problem and his profession coincide—the maintenance of equilibrium and the achievement of mediation." The shaman is a bridge for his people between this world, the underworld and the above world and also between the tribal world of his *place* and the big city world of modern culture. He travels back and forth between all these worlds "with exquisite balance." He mediates between the conscious and unconscious; and he "accomplishes social equilibrium as well, establishing balance between the individual and the group."

Barbara Meyerhoff worked with a shaman, Ramón Medina Silva of the primitive Huichol Indians in Mexico. One afternoon, quite suddenly, he interrupted their taping session to take some friends to a nearby area, where steep banks had been cut by a rapid waterfall, "cascading perhaps a thousand feet over jagged, slippery rocks." Announcing that this was a special place for shamans, he took off his sandals and leaped across the waterfall, from rock to rock, often standing on one foot on the edge of the precipice. Meyerhoff was frightened, but the Indians were not. The next day she began to understand what he had been doing, when he told her that a shaman "must have superb equilibrium . . . otherwise, he will not reach his destination and will fall this way or that"; as he spoke, he marched his fingers up his violin bow. She also mentions a Luiseno Indian shaman on a Southern California reservation who would often climb to the roof and stand immobile for long periods of time, with one leg pulled up and curled to the crook of the other. He did this on weekends, when many people came to visit him, thus "demonstrating his mediating capacity by showing himself to be a specialist in balance."

A demonstration of balance very similar to that of the Mexican shaman, Ramón, is given by don Genaro in *A Separate Reality*. He leaps from rock to rock across the top of a waterfall, plunging Castaneda into "an extraordinary and mysterious terror." Later, don Juan explains that for those who could see, the human being was composed of something like fibers of light which came out of the area around the navel, and Genaro had used these to cross the water by focusing them onto the rocks. He calls Genaro a "master of balance." [51, 126-130]

The various functions of a shaman are split up among numerous specialists in our culture: priests, poets, artists, therapists, and teachers. The real role of the shaman is lost in this splitting up, as the "shaman's function is precisely that of integration." This integration of the person with the group, mind with body, conscious with unconscious, is the basis of all forms of healing, both mental and physical, because it acknowledges a "common causality for man and nature;" but most important, "The shaman reminds us of an alternate world view, a holistic vision in which it is possible to accept, even embrace, ambiguity and paradox." [219]

In the shaman's emphasis on balance, as well as in the integration he brings about between seemingly disparate entities, we are reminded of the Balinese culture and of a mature ecosystem, such as a forest. Both are a process of "continuous, nonprogressive change" wherein the energies of each circulates through the entire system so that all becomes one vast organism living in symbiosis. As Steven Van Matre writes, "Life is divided into producers, consumers, and decomposers. Everything is becoming something else. Everything has a home. Homes in a defined area form a community . . ." [338, 18] If human beings truly want to become a part of the natural community, each person must learn how to take part with balance in the "dance of life."

Tai Chi

Fortunately, there is a specific discipline for developing balance in the "dance of life." This is the dance-like Tai Chi, whose origins are intimately tied up with Nature and even more specifically with mountains. Possibly, the very beginnings of this discipline date back to those ancient Chinese shamans from which Taoism developed. Needham believes that the word *shaman* is a very ancient Tungusic word, which came to Persia as *saman*. The early transliteration into Chinese was *hsien-mên*, which occurs in written form as early as the Ch'in Dynasty (255–207 B.C.) In an ancient classic, the *Shih Chi*, (215 B.C.) it was written that the emperor Chhin Shih Huang Ti "wandered about on the shore of the eastern sea, and offered sacrifices to the famous mountains and the great rivers and the eight Spirits; and searched for *hsien* and *hsien-mên* and the like." [229, 133] The Chinese had their own word for shaman, the word *wu*. Needham says that "it is interesting that the idea of dancing is what binds all these words together." The character for *wu* means to dance or posture and goes back to the oracle-bone forms, "which all depict a dancing thaumaturgic shaman . . . But the same idea is also present in the character *hsien*, which means to caper or hop about . . ." [229, 134]

Chang San-Feng is the person credited with bringing all the elements together into Tai Chi. Because he was a Taoist-Confucianist, he emphasized the breathing system "which had been practiced in China increasingly since the days of Chuan Tzu (369 to 286 B.C.), the greatest of the early Taoists after Lao-Tzu." [131, 45] He combined this ancient breathing system with the art of Shao-Lin, which was developed at the famous Buddhist monastery of Shao-Lin. The art of Shao-Lin focused on the training of the sinews and bones and was based on three classics written by Bodhidarma, who brought Buddhism from India to China. He was against book-learning for monks as he thought it more important for them to be physically fit, because they spent hours meditating. [131, 43]

Chang San-Feng was a famous scholar who was appointed to be District Magistrate of Chung Shan (remember, *Shan* means mountain). "In his leisure time, he often visited K'o Hung Mountain, the headquarters of the Taoists, and eventually he built a cottage in the mountain of Wu Tang, where he concentrated his mind on the study of Tao and finally attained the supreme achievement of creating the art known as Tai Chi Ch'uan." [131, 43]

According to a legend, Chang San-feng heard a hissing noise while meditating and, looking out his window, saw a snake with raised head, hissing in challenge to a crane in the tree above. The crane flew down and attacked, but the snake turned its head aside and attacked the crane's neck with its tail. The bird stabbed with its beak again and again, but the snake, twisting and bending, was always out of reach. Chang San-Feng "realized the value of yielding in the face of strength." In this battle between the crane and the snake he saw the principle of the *I Ching* in action: the strong changing to the yielding, and the yielding changing to the strong. [188, 4]

"The *I Ching* is one of the first efforts of the human mind to place itself in the universe," according to Da Liu. It has influenced China for 3,000 years. "The individual hexagrams were preserved on wood tablets long before they were recorded by King Wen in 1150 B.C." The *I Ching* is a collection of a series of 64 six-line figures called hexagrams. Each hexagram consists of two three-lined figures called trigrams, made up of broken and unbroken lines. "The creation of the eight trigrams is attributed to Fu Shi, the legendary Chinese sage who reputedly lived during the age of hunting and fishing around 5,000 years ago. By studying and observing heaven, earth, animal tracks, and his own body, he devised the broken and unbroken lines as symbols of the fundamental nature of the universe." Each of the eight trigrams stands for an aspect of nature, society, and the individual. [188, 5–6] Here again we see our debt to the hunting-gathering culture.

Tai Chi combines two systems: the training for the sinews and bones and Taoist breathing, with an emphasis on softness and suppleness. T. T. Liang tells of the famous Master Yang Lu Chan in Peking, who was asked about Tai Chi's "lightness and agility." He was about to answer when a swallow entered through the curtain. He shot out his hand and caught it. Then Liang tells what happened next:

He supported it on his right palm and stroked it with his left hand. Then he withdrew his left hand. The swallow spread its wings, ready to fly. The Master's palm stirred ever so slightly, its energy "suddenly concealed, suddenly manifest." The swallow was unable to fly away after all. For any bird, no matter what its kind, must use the stretching energy of its feet in order to help its body take off. The swallow's feet had no place to exert strength; therefore, even though it had wings, it could not fly away.

The Master laughed and explained, "When one has practiced T'ai Chi for a long time and the entire body has become light and agile, then the weight of a feather cannot be added nor can a fly alight." [182, 55–56]

This combination of movement and breathing, combined with softness and suppleness, "makes it possible for man to be in tune with nature's vibrations while in motion . . . When all the principles, techniques and rules are mastered, the results and effects will revolutionize the spirit and the body, leading one to a new sense of harmony and equilibrium of the Yin and Yang forces in the body." [131, 31–32]

All the movement in Tai Chi originates from the center of the body—just below the abdomen (called the *hara* in Japanese, the *tan tien* in Chinese). Tai Chi literally means "the great ridgepole," in other words, that from which all else hangs or is supported. This pelvic region is where all the major muscles are attached.

I have been studying Tai Chi for eight years and teaching it for four years. I have found that Tai Chi gives me the same type of feeling as powder snow, but with Tai Chi this can be achieved any *place* and not just on a mountain while skiing. Tai Chi automatically turns thought off and permits the entire body, the wind, and gravity to take over, and one is whole. Lieh Tzu, in an ancient classic wrote, "I cannot even make out whether the wind is riding on me or I am riding on the wind."

The word *chi*, used for the energy flow developed in Tai Chi, appears in the earliest Taoist classic. Lao Tzu says, "Ten thousand things carry yin and embrace yang; through unification by chi they achieve harmony." More recently, Don Juan said: "Every man is in touch with everything else through a bunch of long fibers that shoot out from the center of the abdomen. Those fibers join a man to his surroundings; they keep his balance; they give him stability." [51, 33] After a few years of doing Tai Chi, I began to experience the reality of those fibers. There's nothing supernatural about it. It's just a part of the natural relationship of human and earth.

The breathing of Tai Chi circulates the chi energy and seems to give almost everlasting youth. My first teacher, Raymond Chung, was over fifty and looked like a man in his thirties; my second teacher, Tchoung ta Chen, is well over sixty and walks just like a baby, with every joint loose and flopping. Master T. T. Liang, who wrote *Tai Chi for Health and Self-Defense* was seventy-five years old when he wrote it and is still teaching Tai Chi. He says, "As long as one has three square feet of space, one can take a trip to paradise and stay there to enjoy life for thirty minutes without spending a single cent." [182, 7]

The special breathing used in Tai Chi, which involves sending the breath down deep into the abdomen on the outbreath, is called "The Great Heavenly Circulation." Chuang Tzu said that the perfect man breathes "through his heels," he breathes so deeply. Don Juan taught this technique to the frightened Castaneda when he said, "Push your belly down, down."

Tai Chi is a continual discovery of new energies and the transformation of these energies to higher levels. Remember, Ida Rolf said that "the body is in an energy field, and the earth has its own energy field around it. The greater energy field of the gravity can enhance, support and enlarge the field of the individual human being . . ." [85]

So what we are concerned with here, in the circling movements of Tai Chi, is a way of balancing the energy of the body and mind with the energy of the earth itself as it comes to us through gravity—all these energies flowing together in dynamic balance, creating true earth wisdom.

There is a movement in Tai Chi, done at the finish of the 108 steps, which is ordinarily called the Grand Terminus or Conclusion of Tai Chi. Al Huang has more aptly used the name "Embrace Tiger, Return to the Mountain," usually applied to an earlier step in the form, for this all-embracing conclusion. [129] In China, tiger refers to energy. The mountain, referred to here, is the spine. Indian yogis call the spine Mount Meru. In Indian cosmology, the world turns about Mount Meru; we turn about our own Mount Meru, the spine. So at the conclusion of Tai Chi, one opens up the arms as if embracing the whole world around and all its energies.

When I do Tai Chi here in Silverton, I face south—the sacred direction in Tai Chi—toward 13,368-foot Sultan Mountain. During the 108 steps which comprise the form, I have opened up so that all of the energy from nature around me is flowing through me. There seems to be no separation between what is inside my skin and what is outside my skin. I come to the last movement, "Embrace Tiger," and I embrace all the energies from my world. Then my arms curve downward and I scoop up all this energy and lift it as my arms cross and rise to my chest. I turn my hands downward and push all that energy into my center, the *tan tien*. Then, as my teachers told me to bow to anyone present, I bow to each of our mountains: Kendall standing in the east, Anvil Mountain in the west, Boulder Mountain in the north, and Sultan Mountain in the south, as I pay homage to the earth wisdom present here in my *place*. Thus I have come to understand what the Tewa Indians mean when they say: ". . . within and around the mountains, your authority returns to you."

20. Dance of the World

In Western culture, our idea of a Supreme Being who hands down laws to all the world goes clear back to the Babylonians—to the god, Marduk, giving laws for the stars. The Taoists of China thought such an idea much too naive "for the subtlety and complexity of the universe as they intuited it." [229, 581] Laws referring to non-human nature in China were called *lü*. The origin of the word has to do with bamboo pitch pipes, which are used for ritual dancing; thus *lü* has more the connotation of harmonious cooperation of all beings. Needham explains that this harmonious cooperation came from the fact "that they were all parts in a hierarchy of wholes forming a cosmic pattern . . ." [229, 582] We in the West are finally coming to this idea, thanks to the new biology and the new physics.

The idea of dance explaining the relationship among the beings of the earth has been almost universal in the past. For instance, representations of how religion began are found in the paleolithic caves, where we find pictures of dancing and masked medicine men dating from 15,000 years ago. A modern Bushman explained that dances "are to us what prayers are to you," and Lame Deer, the Sioux medicine man said, "All our dances have their beginnings in our religion . . . Dancing and praying—it's the same thing." [180, 42 and 167, 243-244] The southwestern Pueblo Indian dances involve not only all the beings of their present world: corn, squash blossoms, animals, thunder clouds, gods, and human beings, but those of the ancient tribal past as well.

The dance reveals "the union of transcendence in immanence. For the dancer, during the ecstasy of the dance, experiences both complete self-expression and complete self-surrender. [298] Or, as Isadora Duncan said, "If I could tell you what it means, there would be no point in dancing it." [20]

Ritual dancing is a message about the relationships between the conscious and unconscious, the past and future, the human consciousness and the consciousness of animals, of plants and even of the earth itself; as well as the relationships between the earth, the sky, the gods, and the human beings: what Heidegger called the "Round Dance" of the fourfold.

In India, this is called the Dance of Shiva. Gregory Bateson referred to this concept when he said, "The truth which is important is not a truth of preference, it's a truth of complexity . . . of a total eco-interactive on-going web . . . in which we dance, which is the dance of Shiva . . ." [37, 33]

Right here in the United States, in George Sibley's world of Crested Butte, Gal Starika told him that

she was either going to have to teach me how to dance right, or kick me out. That was when I learned that dancing right is doing your own thing with a total awareness of the fact that *everyone else* is doing their own thing. When a roomful of people are really *dancing*, everyone is whirling at top speed, moving all over the flow, careening through the narrowest possible openings, and there is no banging and bumping and crashing . . . There is no formal pattern, yet a kind of dynamic structure emerges that is entirely dependent on everyone's sensitivity to everyone else . . . One set of size twelves powered by one who sees himself as set apart from the world can spoil the dancing . . .

"Part of a Winter"   [294]

And what's the meaning of it all? Alan Watts explains:

There is something in common in poetry and in music. In a certain way that both of them are the language of madness—which is to say that the poet and the musician, together, speak a natural and universal language, which Yuerba Buena referred to as the original language, that all creatures spoke before the fall of man. For in the garden of Eden, before Adam and Eve had eaten of the fruit of the tree of knowledge, they understood the language of all the animals and spoke such a language, which was the divine language from the beginning. This language is, of course, the language of the birds. (whistles like a bird)

And what does it mean? What does the shape of a tree mean? What do clouds mean? What is the meaning of the letters that you could make out in the patterns of foam on breaking waves? What is the meaning of the way the stars are scattered through the sky? Of course, we've tried to make sense of the stars—to project upon the scattering—mythological forms, as we see in the big dipper, a dipper or a plow. But, actually, music might express the arrangement of those stars more correctly. (hums a line or two) And what would that be saying? What is Bach saying? (hums a bit of Bach) What's the meaning of that? And when a tree grows—you know it goes kind of z - z - z - uk - ga, and after that it goes chikety, chikety, chikety. And we say, "Oh, isn't that beautiful?" So much so that an artist can copy it and say, "Why, it's a picture!" And when artists have copied trees and the forms of mountains and clouds long enough; why, in every state park there's a place called Inspiration Point, where all the tourists come and look at the view and they say, "Oh, it's just like a picture'" (chuckles)

Because you see both poetry and music lead us to the understanding of what this world is all about. Which is—that it isn't about anything else. You see, the finest music—in both the Eastern and the Western traditions—is not descriptive music. It is not music which is to be understood in terms of something *other* than music. You are not expected, in Hindu rags, to listen for the sound of the rain on the roof, the sound of the galloping of horses, the sound of the murmuring of the sea. You are listening solely to arabesques of the highest complexity—of rhythm playing with rhythm—and, exactly in the same way in our own great musicians of the West, the same game is being played. And if this has any meaning at all, it's merely to draw our attention to the fact that the entire physical universe is doing just the same thing. We always, of course, like to find an explanation for what's going on. We say that butterflies have great big eyes on their wings to scare off birds so that they'll think something rather dangerous is looking at them. Or that a centipede has a hundred legs so that it can get *along* better than an insect with only six or a humanoid with only two. We always find a way of explaining nature in terms of a kind of—social engineering—that it has a purpose and that purpose is, of course, survival.

There are two schools of thought about this, fundamentally. The school of thought about the meaning of life which is most widely acknowledged in the West, today, is that the ultimate goal of physical effort is to survive. It was held in medieval times that the ultimate goal of life was the vision of God. In the end of Dante's *Paradiso*, we come to the vision of the love that moves the sun and other stars. But when Dante saw this vision he made the comment that the angels that were surrounding the vision and singing songs made a sound which he compared to the laughter of the universe because they were singing the word, Alleluia! Alleluia! Alleluia! Alleluia! And what does *that mean*? Alleluia! It's like Hare Krishna. You know—when you say it enough—what a funny sound. Hare Krishna. It'll go on—Krishna, Krishna, Krishna rum - a - rum - a - rum - a - rum-a - rum - a-rum - a - rum - a - rum. What does that mean? (whistles like a bird) Something like that. Cause you see what we're involved in, fundamentally, in this cosmos, is a dance—a rhythm.

Whether you want to express it through the mode of music or whether you want to express it in a poetic mode, by making words play at being something more than words, more than mere sign indicators; because in poetry, the form of words is itself the thing to hear—not simply what it means—because then you could write prose. So both these arts are awakening us to the fact that our own physical organism, for instance, which we think—what do *I* mean? As if I were just a word. It's your own physical organism—with its marvelous hair—with its two jewels, the deep eyes and it's breathing apparatus, its kissing apparatus, its eating apparatus. All this—is a kind of fundamental jazz—which, just as the tree was going z - z - zonk - oop - ee - oop and chikety, chikety—going - uh - like this you see. Just as the stars are shaped in that way and as the goal of music is not the *end*—the finale but all the going along of it. So in exactly the same way, the goal of existence *isn't sensible;* doesn't *have a point;* isn't *serious.* There's not some REAL REASON why all this had to happen. (chuckles)

Why do the angels play harps? What is the harp of the angels? If you look at a harp you see many, many strings, often differently colored and so, in this universe, there are many, many vibrations possible—as the difference between cosmic rays, x-rays, gamma rays, ultra-violet rays, red rays etc.—all the way along—all the different wave lengths of different radio broadcasts—they all are the strings on the harps of the angels. And the angels say, "Now, which strings shall we pluck today and call into being this kind of universe—boing—this kind of universe—this kind of universe. And let's play with the harp with the strings not only going this way but going *this* way and then we'll slide strings that way through them, and so have many dimensions upon which everything can happen. For why?

If you have to ask why, you're not listening. If you are listening, you dance with it. You don't ask why. Then . . . if . . . well—you say what's the point of telling you all that—that all this that we *are* doing, that we *are*, is just some kind of 'thickety boom'? What's the point of saying that? Why do you have to have a point? If you must, I can say, well, if you get *with* that, you'll keep out of trouble; because all the trouble is made by people trying to arrange the world to make it purposive—to improve it—to make everybody serious—to get with that thing. They're the trouble makers . . ."

From a Big Sur tape, "Divine Madness"
(By permission of the Electronic University)   [353]

But if you are still feeling that there's no hope for you—you can't learn the "dance of the world"—perhaps, you should listen to Alan Furst, when he asks:

Have you ever wanted to keep on walking until something happened?

His paycheck always ended with 71 cents and he deposited it without adding that to his balance, so several years of 71 centses probably added up to a tidy sum but there was nothing he wanted. After the child-support check, the rent, the light bill, and the heat, he bought groceries and that was it. He had what he needed and he didn't need much.

Being that much alone, he felt himself an excellent candidate for suicide. But he feared pain and hated the idea of some medical extravaganza with himself as object. He saw himself floating free between life and death, with little to hope for either way. Though he knew others suffered from this disease, he felt no bond with them.

He drove out into the country one Sunday afternoon, following roads as they provided him easy turnoffs, and worked his way finally onto a winding dirt track that climbed part of the way up a mountainside. The road ended suddenly in a thick wall of evergreens. He turned off the engine, and, leaving the key in the ignition, walked into the woods. In times when sameness especially afflicted him, he'd thought of walking into the sea. He pictured drowning as very violent, however, with choking and vomiting and possible last-minute regrets as the sky disappeared forever. Walking into the woods, on the other hand, was a quiet thing. Maybe he'd just keep walking and see what happened.

Nothing did. He got tired. There was nothing much in the woods, just trees and underbrush. He sat against a tree and fell asleep. He knew about hypothermia, where the body's heat simply floats off into the air, and he considered it as good a result of a night's sleep as any other. He woke at sunrise in a drizzle, took off his tie and threw it into a bush, and kept walking.

Soon he got hungry. He'd never read a wilderness survival manual, but he'd read something in the newspaper about it. He recalled that you just cancelled all feelings of disgust and started to eat whatever you could chew and get down. That morning he ate berries, spitting out the really sour-tasting ones and swallowing those that tasted good. Some plants were poisonous, he knew, and some weren't. He munched lots of leaves and, that afternoon, ate some maggots from under a log. Nothing went wrong. It took him a very long time to get filled up, eating this way, and his jaw muscles ached from endless chewing.

He walked for three days, eating as he went. The second night it rained and drenched him. He thought he wouldn't be able to sleep, but was so tired from walking that he slept anyhow. When he awoke, he noticed that he smelled bad. After squatting by a bush, he'd leaf himself daintily but, without soap and hot water, he was getting very ripe.

After the first week he didn't notice it any more. He thought once or twice about his job, a few acquaintances, but he was busier than he'd ever been. Certain shrubs, certain logs, special configurations of leaves on plants attracted him, called out to him to eat. The food itself kept him moving and when the sun went down he'd curl up under whatever branches were about and sleep with exhaustion. Sometimes, to have water, he'd follow streams. But he never went dry for too long. Something in him found water when he was thirsty.

After the first month, several things changed. His clothing was torn and rotted from him but, instead of making him cold at night, he seemed to do better without it. He came upon a place near the crest of a wooded ridge where he knew he'd been before, and so understood he was moving in wide circles within a large range. And once an airplane flew over and he dove in panic beneath a bush. Of that other world he wanted no part whatsoever.

The pains began as the season started to shift. His shoulders ached, his underarms throbbed, and the backs of his legs tied themselves in knots. This aching was faintly remembered. Finally, he recalled that he'd had similar pains in his early teens. He discovered that yawning and stretching helped, and he slept during the day sometimes, though that penalized him in food. The pain went on for several weeks and he suddenly realized what it was. Growing pains. He was growing.

After a long time, several seasons having passed and come again, the pain stopped. His body was dark brown, the color of a walnut. His body hair had grown thick and matted, covering bunchy muscles. His stride was enormous and without effort he trotted miles every day, eating what he found.

That summer turned dry and he was thirsty. His hot throat drove him loping for miles to find trickles of water in streambeds. He circled first the perimeter of his range, which he knew bush by bush, and then worked outward down a mountainside. He found a broad dry creek and headed up it, thinking water might be found near the source. Suddenly a vile smell stopped him dead. His head swiveled in the direction of the wind. There were two men and two horses by the creek bed. One man saw him, yelled excitedly, and pointed a movie camera at him. He ran a few strides in panic, then, for an instant, looked back and faced the men. He heard the whirr of the camera and turned and ran easily into the woods.   [94]

166

Appendix

Ancient Seasonal Festivals and Modern Christian Feast Days

For millenia human beings have celebrated earth festivals around the time of the solstices and the equinoxes. Earlier tribal festivals were gradually absorbed into the celebrations of the classical civilizations of Greece and Rome. During the first few hundred years of Christianity, these pagan festivals were taken over by the church in order to transfer the customs associated with those festival days to the new Christian Church.

As an aid in recovering the meaning of the original earth symbolism, it is instructive to see how the church's liturgy transfer nature symbolism to Christian Feast Days.

1. *Winter solstice celebrations.* These continued from primitive times into Greek and Roman times. In the latter days of the Roman Empire, December 25 was dedicated to the god Mithras, Bull-slayer, the savior beloved by Roman soldiers. Mithras had been an Indo-Iranian god of light, but with his introduction into the Roman Empire he became a Mystery divinity and an invincible god of light, the *sol invictus*. [134, 195] The Christian celebration of the birth of Jesus was given this date to supplant Mithran worship. The sun gods, Apollo and Dionysus, were said to be born on or near the winter solstice. The Roman festival, Saturnalia, originally held for seven days beginning on December 17, was observed in honour of Saturnus, traditionally regarded as the first king of Latium, who introduced agriculture. [134, 175]

Preceding Christmas was the season of Advent, called that because of the importance of the Mysteries at Eleusis. The word *eleusis* means advent. [187, 159] The worship of the Divine Child dates back at least to Minoan Crete. [104, 347]

2. *Winter quarterday.* Candlemas is not as well known in this country as it is in Europe where this great feast-day of the church brings the Christmas season to an end. Explaining the church's liturgy, Parsch states that throughout the Christmas season there has been "a gradual heightening in the season's 'Light' motif and in man's response . . . On Christmas 'the Light shines in the darkness' and only a few 're-ceived it' . . . on Candlemas Day, the Light is placed in our very hands, to hold during the procession and at Mass." [246, v. 5, 370]

The biblical background of the feast of Candlemas is Mary's bringing the baby Jesus to the Temple for the purification rite (a Jewish ritual for new mothers). Simeon, an old man at the temple, said of Jesus that he was "the Light for the enlightenment of the Gentiles." In the Christian church blessed candles were given on this day to the faithful to be taken home.

The basic sun-symbolism is ever-present behind such words in the church's liturgy as, "Today He comes as 'King of the new Light." [246, v. 5, 375] At the winter solstice, the sun turns back on its course and begins to move toward summer. There is a delay of several weeks before the change in the sun/earth relationship becomes noticeable. By the time of this cross-quarter day in early February, the sun's heat is becoming more powerful and the sun has again assumed its full power, and it can be said that the King of Light is again supreme.

The Roman feast of The Lupercalia, (February 15) marking the end of the old Roman year, went back to very ancient times when the people of the early Roman community on the Palatine Hill were shepherds. The ritual began at the cave of Lupercal on the hill where Romulus and Remus, the legendary founders of the city, were nurtured by the female wolf. A sacrifice of goats was made and an offering of new grain (the returning of the earth's gifts back to the earth). Two young Roman nobles, smeared with the blood of the victims and stripped nearly naked, ran completely around the hill, striking all women they met with the strips of hide of the sacrificed goat. This was to ensure the fertility of the women. The strips of hide were called *februa*, from which February was derived. The magic circle the young men made by encircling the hill was a barrier to all evil influences for the coming year. James says that this feast continued to be held "until, in the Christian era, it was transformed into Candlemas by Pope Gelasius in A.D. 494." [134, 179–180]

Another aspect of Candlemas has to do with St. Brigit, actually a renaming of a manifestation of the Mother Goddess type in Ireland. Robert Graves reports that St. Brigit's perpetual sacred fire was kept alight in a monastery at Kildare until the time of Henry VIII. [104, 144] In Rome, there was a Feast of Lights on February 1st, with a fire ceremonial and torches to celebrate the return of the Goddess from the underworld and the rebirth of nature in the spring. [134, 233]

3. *Spring equinox*. Near the time of the spring equinox, the Feast of the Annunciation occurs on March 25. This feast day has to do with the annunciation by the angel to Mary that she was to be the mother of God. On March 25, ancient Rome celebrated the Carnival of Hilaria in honor of the Great Mother Goddess, Cybele. Again, we see a Mother Goddess festival supplanted by a church feast-day dedicated to Mary.

The Christian Easter comes on the Sunday nearest the full moon after the spring equinox. The full moon nearest the spring equinox was the New Year festival in ancient Mesopotamia. Israel followed this custom as did other places in the near east. Easter is based on the Jewish Passover ritual, so it, too, follows this ancient system. [134, 216]

4. *Spring quarterday*. Mayday festivals and maypoles have their origin in very ancient rituals of the Near East marking the rebirth of nature in the spring. In later Roman times, Cybele, the Great Goddess, and Attis figure in the rites. A pine tree was set up near the temple of the Great Mother on the Palatine Hill for this ritual in Rome. Cybele was responsible for the fertility of the fields and so flower offerings were brought to her. The later May Queens in Europe sat in an arbor wreathed with flowers.

In the British Isles, the Celts lit ritual bonfires at the beginning of May. This practice continued until the Eighteenth Century. These fires were known as Beltane fires, and on Walpurgis Night, the Eve of May Day, there was dancing around the fire. Those who took part leaped as high as they could to make the crops grow higher, and burning brands were carried through the fields in order to make the soil fertile. [134, 312–313] Maypole dancing today, in the British Isles, often involves young people dancing around the pole intertwining flower garlands or ribbons as they do so.

Modern Christian rituals involve the crowning of a statue of Mary with flowers. These statues are usually in a rock grotto outdoors. Again, these grottoes are reminiscent of the many rituals to do with the goddess returning from the underworld by means of the sacred cave (such as the Plutonium cave at Eleusis).

5. *Summer solstice*. This is the Vigil of the Feast of St. John the Baptist, the precursor of Christ. A vigil is kept the night before, and on the day following is the feast of the birth of John the Baptist. Parsch states that this feast is part of the "basic structure of the church year . . . It is a kind of advent . . . a joyous anticipation of approaching salvation." [246, v. 4, 204] Thus, this Christian approach kept intact the basic relationship of summer and winter solstice. The summer solstice was the birth of St. John, who told of the coming of Jesus, the savior; and the winter solstice was the birth of Jesus.

Some years ago, while climbing in Europe, we stayed at a hut in order to climb the Matterhorn. We happened to be there on the summer solstice. All the climbers in the hut went outside just at dusk and waited expectantly in the gathering twilight. Then far on a distant mountain we saw a fire suddenly blaze up. Then our hutmaster lit the fire at our hut and soon, far down the valley, another fire was lit. It was a moving ceremony there in the wilderness of snow and rock. I asked the hutmaster and the Swiss climbers what it meant. They said, "That's what we always do on St. John's Eve." It is, of course, what most humans have done on summer solstice, but none of them knew the connection. Pius Parsch makes the connection in the church's liturgy, however: "The birth of Jesus is observed on December 25 at the time of the winter solstice, while the birth of his forerunner is observed six months earlier at the time of the summer solstice. Christmas is a 'light' feast; the same is true today. The popular custom centering about 'St. John's Fire' stems from soundest Christian dogma . . . St. John's Fire symbolizes Christ the Light; John was a lamp that burned and shone . . ." [246, v. 4, 207]

Fires were lit in primitive cultures on summer solstice because, since it is the turn-around position of the sun, its energy must be renewed. The Sun Dance of the Plains Indians in our country has a somewhat similar purpose—to renew the energy of the sun, the vegetation, and the people. The Sun Dance is a fairly recent rite which probably developed in the late Eighteenth Century. As the tribes saw their culture disintegrating because of white encroachment, they tried to renew their powers by the Sun Dance, which actually combines various older rites.

Despite the church's efforts to abolish the old solstice rites, it has been found that many early church basilicas were oriented by their master mason builders to mark the solstices. One example is the Romanesque style basilica of the Twelfth Century in Vezelay, France. The sunlight at winter solstice comes through the upper windows of the nave and lines up directly on the upper capitals of the column; in the summer solstice, the sun "streams down into the nave and creates footprints of itself precisely down the middle," up to the altar. [201]

6. *Summer quarterday*. August 15 is the feast of the Assumption of the Blessed Virgin Mary. Parsch writes that on this day "the Church celebrates the most glorious 'harvest festival' in the Communion of Saints." [246, v. 4, 327] At Lauds on this day the Divine Office reads: "Who is this that comes forth as the rising dawn, fair as the moon, bright as the sun, awe-inspiring . . ." The Assumption concerns Mary's ascension into heaven, there to reign as the Mother of God. An oft-repeated phrase occurring in today's liturgy is: "How could that one taste death . . . from whom the true Life flowed out to all." This could almost be a description of the Mother Goddess, Nature herself. Parsch admits, "Since ancient times vegetables have been blessed on this day, yet its relation to the feast is not readily evident . . . Most probably some pre-Christian Germanic harvest festival was Christianized and associated with her assumption." At the Introit occurs the phrase from the Apocalypse in the Bible: "The woman, clothed with sun, the moon

at her feet, a crown of twelve stars about her head." Perhaps this remnant refers to the twelve moons of the year of the Mother Goddess.

On August 13 Rome celebrated the festival of Diana, when the trees were full of ripened fruit and the grapes were ripe. She was greeted as Our Lady in Harvest. [134, 238]

In Celtic countries Lammas Day is celebrated on August 2. This has to do with Lugh, the Goidelic Sun-god, whose death was commemorated on the first Sunday of August, called *Lugh Nasadh*, "Commemoration of Lugh," later changed to "Lugh-mass" or "Lammas." Llew Llaw Gyffes, a Dionysian-type god, was also associated with Lugh. There were chariot races in medieval times and the "Teltown" marriages in honor of Lugh. These were trial marriages of "a year and a day," which could be dissolved by a ritual in the same place where they were performed. The man and woman stood back to back and then walked apart, one to the north, the other to the south. Lugh probably dates from the early Bronze Age invaders of Ireland, who brought male gods in to replace the matriarchal goddesses. They also brought the institution of fatherhood, according to the Welsh Mabinogian. [104]

7. *Fall equinox*. Near the fall equinox, the outstanding feast in England is Michaelmas, the harvest festival in honor of St. Michael, the archangel, the dragon-slayer. As noted in Part I of this book, tiny chapels, dedicated to St. Michael, were built in particularly wild or rocky parts of Europe. The same symbolism lies behind this feast: Michael slaying the dragon of paganism. This feast was also associated with the beginning of the season of darkness and the death of vegetation.

In the church, as a whole, there are two feasts near the date of the fall equinox: September 24, Our Lady of Ransom, commemorating the founding of the Order of Our Lady of Ransom, which ransomed captive Christian slaves from the Saracens, and September 25, the feast of Judith of the Old Testament. The Assyrian army was advancing toward the Mediterranean Sea conquering new lands for the King of Nineveh. Judith was an Israelite widow who gained access to the Assyrian camp and cut off the head of Holofernes, the leader. This act made her "The glory of Jerusalem, the joy of Israel." According to Parsch, Judith was a "type" of Mary, "Thus did Judith accomplish the deliverance of her people. And all Israel hailed her blessed." [246, v. 5, 232] Judith's victory over the wicked Assyrians is used as a symbol of Mary's victory over sin or, one could say, paganism.

8. *Fall quarterday*. The Vigil of the Feast of All Saints occurs on October 31. This was the end of the Celtic year. On November 1, cattle were brought back from the pastures to be put in stalls for winter, and their new year began. On Samhain, which means "summer ends," fires were lit to counteract the darkness of winter with its fears and dangers for man and beast. In other parts of Europe, there were rites for the dead about this time of year. Thus, we can see why Halloween has become associated with ghosts and witches. Pagan rites for the dead commemorated both past and future tribal life. Thus, the church's epistle on All Saints day states that heaven opens before us and "we see a great host gathered about the throne of God, singing sacred songs." [246, v. 5, 321]

Information: Organizations and Books

Sense of Place

Planet Drum Foundation, Box 31251, San Francisco, California 94131. Peter Berg founded Planet Drum to promote the concepts of "reinhabitation of place" and "bioregionalism." They now publish the journal "Raise the Stakes" and occasional books. Write for information on how to become a member.

Saving Your Place

How to reclaim your rights and those of your land:

1. *Grass Roots Primer,* edited by James Robertson and John Lewallen. Sierra Club Books, 530 Bush St., San Francisco, Ca. 94108. Case histories of how people saved their own neighborhoods or their own bit of nature from destruction by governments and corporations. Contains specific advice on how to begin legal action.
2. *The Town that Fought to Save Itself,* by Orville Schell. Pantheon Books, 455 Hahn Road, Westminster, Maryland. The day-to-day account of how a town, caught on the urban fringe, fought to retain its rights and identity.

Learning the Needs of the Land and Working with It: Urban and Rural

1. *The Earth Manual,* by Malcolm Margolin. Houghton Mifflin Co. The author quotes Patrick Henry: ". . . he is the greatest patriot who stops the most gullies." Such a person is literally saving his country. Contains specific details, with diagrams, on how to return your own bit of land (even a backyard) to nature, how to stop erosion and encourage wild life.
2. *Working with Nature,* by John W. Brainerd. Oxford University Press. An authoritative work which deals with many more problems than the *Earth Manual.* *The Earth Manual* is better for those just beginning; Brainerd's book provides more comprehensive coverage.
3. *Children of the Green Earth* is a non-profit international organization which was conceived in the redwoods in 1980 and later that year held its funding meeting at the United Nations with Richard St. Barbe Baker, Rene Dubos, Dorothy MacLean and others for the purpose of inspiring people to help children plant trees and care for the earth. Director, Ron Rabin explains: "The focus of our work is twofold: to help children develop a deep personal relationship with the natural world and a reverence for all life; and to help children respect and love their friends in foreign countries who share their care for the earth. Our commitment is to work with and through other organizations, sharing our vision and experience to help them develop meaningful children's tree planting and cultural exchange programs.

    Members of the staff are available for workshops, teacher training, curriculum development, and help in networking. A new book, *Start with One Tree* is out this year. For our quarterly newsletter and membership information write Children of the Green Earth, 7635 Tyee Rd., Umpqua, Oregon 97486."

    > "I have a vision of the Earth made green again through the efforts of children. I can see the children of all nations planting trees and holding hands around the globe in celebration of their earth as their home."
    > St. Barbe Baker

4. *The Farallones Integral Urban House in Berkeley* — For the past ten years, the Urban House has served as a model of self-reliant urban living. Converted by a staff of ecologists and architects, the house has solar space- and water-heating; a composting toilet; greywater irrigation in the intensive organic garden; edible landscaping, and "urban livestock": chickens, bees and fish. Farallones Rural Center — includes seven solar cabins, composting toilets, greywater systems, edible landscapes, orchards, several acres of intensive food gardens, kitchen and dining facilities, library, wood, metal, and ceramic shops. It is an active educational resource center, networking and sharing information both locally and internationally. For information or visiting schedules write: Farallones Institute, 1516 Fifth St., Berkeley, Ca. 94710.
5. *New Alchemy Institute,* 237 Hatchville Rd., East Falmouth, MA 02536 provides information on how to make your own bit of land totally self-sufficient.

Synergistic Learning

1. International College, 1019 Gayley Ave., Los Angeles, California, 90024. "The concept of their tutorial program is to bring mature and able students into close association with gifted and established leaders in various disciplines." The college provides maximum possibilities for learning with minimum structure. At the present time there are over one hundred tutors who live and teach in countries all over the world, thus returning higher education to particular localities. Write for general information or their catalog.
2. Electronic University. Box 361, Mill Valley, California, 94941. Founded by Alan Watts in 1973. Write for brochure and list of tapes and films available.

Alternative Food Production

1. *Aquaculture: The Farming and Husbandry of Freshwater and Marine Organisms*, by J. Bardach, J. Ruther and W. McLarney. J. Wiley and Sons, publisher. 868 pages. This is the definitive work on the subject of providing basic protein for humans. Introductory information for beginners is provided in *The Book of the New Alchemists*.
2. *Forest Farming*, by J. Sholto Douglas and Robert A. de J. Hart. How to grow your food and other necessities from trees. Order from Watkins Publishing, 45 Lower Belgrave St., London SW1W OLT England.

Balance

Tai Chi

1. *Embrace Tiger, Return to Mountain*, by Al Chung-liang Huang. Real People Press, Box F, Moab, Utah 84532. Best introduction to the feeling of Tai Chi.
2. *Tai Chi Handbook, Exercise, Meditation and Self-defense*, by Herman Kauz. Doubleday and Co. It's not possible to learn Tai Chi from a book, but if that's the only way you have to learn and you want to try it, get this book. Out of the dozens of books written for the purpose, this is the only one that will help you. Not only does it have clear pictures, it has specific directions for moving from one position to the other, which no other book has.
3. *The Centered Skier*, by Denise McCluggage. Vermont Crossroads Press, Box 30, Waitsfield, Vermont 05673. Denise has taught Tai Chi and was instrumental in starting the Sugarbush Workshops in Centered Skiing, which combines Tai Chi and skiing.

Ritual

1. *Earth Festivals, Seasonal Celebrations for Everyone: Young and Old*, by Dolores LaChapelle and Janet Bourque. Write to Way of the Mountain Center, Box 542, Silverton, Colorado 81433. All you need in order to begin celebrating and learning from your environment.
2. Powdered Ceremonial Tea or *macha* can be bought in any Japanese food store. If there are none near you, order by mail from Uwajimaya, 519 6th Ave. So., Seattle, Washington 98104. Write for cost.

For Children and Adults Together

Tsuga's Children, by Thomas Williams. Random House. Written for children, but equally engrossing for adults. A fantasy story about a hunting-gathering culture, which shows what humanity lost when it moved away from this concept. Two children enter through a waterfall into a secret valley in search of their cow. The children get involved in helping save "the people" from the *Chigai*, who are out to destroy them. The *Chigai* left "the people," became pastoralists and keep animals as slaves, which has led to child sacrifice to appease the spirits of the animals and to other degradations. The *Chigai* leader, Morl, promises the people, "no more hunger," but they find they must turn their lives over to him and live in fear. A microcosm of the whole of humanity's alienation from nature. Just as good as the best of C.S. Lewis.

References/Bibliography

1. Abbey, Edward. *Monkey Wrench Gang.* Philadelphia: J. B. Lippincott Co., 1975.

2. _____. *Slickrock.* San Francisco: Sierra Club, 1971.

3. Aiken, Conrad. *A Letter from Li Po and Other Poems.* New York: Oxford University Press, 1955.

4. Alexander, Hartley Burr. *The World's Rim, Great Mysteries of the North American Indians.* Lincoln: University of Nebraska Press, Bison Book edition, 1967.

5. Anderson, Edgar. "Man as a Maker of New Plants and New Plant Communities." In *Man's Role in Changing the Face of the Earth,* edited by William L. Thomas Jr. Chicago: University of Chicago Press, 1956, pp. 763-777.

6. Anonymous letter. *Seattle Flag,* June 7, 1972.

7. Anundsen, Kristen, and Michael Phillips. "Fun in Business." *Briarpatch Review* (Spring, 1977).

8. Argüelles, José A. "The Believe In—An Aquarian Age Ritual." *Main Currents in Modern Thought,* vol. 26 (June, 1970), pp. 140-145.

9. Aston, W. G. *Shinto, the Way of the Gods.* London: Longmans, Green and Co., 1905.

10. Ballard, Edward G. and Charles E. Scott, editors. *Martin Heidegger: in Europe and America.* The Hague: Martinus Nijhoff, 1973.

11. Barbour, Ian G., editor. *Earth Might Be Fair.* Englewood Cliffs: Prentice Hall, 1972.

12. Bateson, Gregory. "Alfred Korzybski Memorial Lecture 1970." *General Semantics Bulletin,* vol. 37 (1970), pp. 5-13.

13. _____. "Bali: The Value System of a Steady State." In *Social Structure: Studies Presented to A. R. Radcliffe-Brown,* edited by Meyer Fortes, New York: Russell & Russell, Inc., 1963.

14. _____. "Cybernetic Explanation." *American Behavioral Scientist,* vol. 10, no. 8 (April, 1967), pp. 29-32.

15. _____. "The Cybernetics of 'Self': A Theory of Alcoholism." *Psychiatry,* vol. 34, no. 1 (1971), pp. 1-18.

16. _____. "The Logical Categories of Learning and Communication." In *Steps to An Ecology of Mind,* Gregory Bateson. New York: Ballantine Books (1972), pp 279-308.

17. _____. "Pathologies of Epistemology." *Second Conference on Mental Health in Asia and the Pacific,* 1969. Hawaii: East-West Center Press, 1972.

18. _____. "Problems in Cetacean and Other Mammalian Communication." In *Whales, Dolphins and Porpoises,* edited by Kenneth S. Norris. Berkeley: University of California Press, 1966.

19. _____. *Steps to an Ecology of Mind.* New York: Ballantine Books, 1972.

20. _____. "Style, Grace, and Information in Primitive Art." In *Primitive Art and Society,* edited by Anthony Forge. Oxford: Oxford University Press, 1974.

21. _____, and Jurgen Ruesch. *Communication: The Social Matrix of Psychiatry.* New York: W.W. Norton & Co., 1951 (reprint 1968).

22. Beal, James B. *Electrostatic Fields and Brain/Body/Environment Interrelationships.* Lecture delivered at The Rhine-Swanton Interdisciplinary Symposium, "Parapsychology and Anthropology." American Anthropological Association 73rd Annual Meeting, Mexico City, November, 1974.

23. Bender, Tom. *Environmental Design Primer.* Privately published by Tom Bender, 2270 N.W. Irving, Portland, Oregon, 97210.

24. Benedict, Ruth. "Patterns of the Good Culture." *American Anthropologist,* vol. 72 (1970).

25. Benet, William Rose, editor. *The Readers's Encyclopedia.* New York: Thomas Y. Crowell Co., 1948.

26. Berenson, Bernard. *Sketch for a Self-portrait.* New York: Pantheon Books, 1949.

27. Berry, Wendell. *The Long-legged House.* New York: Harcourt Brace & World, 1969.

28. Bettelheim, Bruno. *The Children of the Dream.* Toronto: The Macmillan Co., 1969.

29. Biemel, Walter. *Martin Heidegger, An Illustrated Study,* translated by J. L. Mehta. New York: Harcourt Brace Jovanovich, 1976.

30. Black, Donald M. "The Brocken Spectre of the Desert View Watch Tower, Grand Canyon, Arizona." *Science,* January 29, 1954.

31. Bogen, Joseph E. *"Educating Both Halves of the Brain."* Symposium, May 1, 1977, School of Education and College of Continuing Education, The University of Southern California, in cooperation with The Institute for the Study of Human Knowledge, Los Angeles, Unpublished.

32. _____. "Hemispheric specificity, complementarity, and self-referential mappings." *Proceedings of the Society of Neuroscience,* vol. 3, no. 413 (1973).

33. _____. "The Other Side of the Brain: An Appositional Mind." *Bulletin of the Los Angeles Neurological Societies,* vol. 34, no. 3 (July 1969), pp. 135-162.

34. _____. "The Other Side of the Brain IV. The A/P Ratio." With Dezure, Tenhouten, and Marsh. *Bulletin of the Los Angeles Neurological Societies,* vol. 37, April 1972.

35. _____. "Some Educational Aspects of Hemispheric Specialization." *UCLA Educator*, vol. 17 (Spring, 1975), pp. 24–32.

36. Brand, Stewart. "'For God's Sake, Margaret,' Conversation with Gregory Bateson and Margaret Mead." *Coevolution Quarterly* (Summer, 1976) pp. 32–44.

37. _____. *II Cybernetic Frontiers*. New York: Randam House, 1974.

38. Bredon, Juliet, and Igor Mitrophanow. *The Moon Year*. Shanghai: Kelly & Walsh, Ltd., 1927.

39. Briffault, Robert. *The Mothers*. New York: The Universal Library, Grosset & Dunlap, 1963. (First published in 1927.)

40. Brodsky, Greg. "Workshop on Neural-linguistic Programming." Lecture delivered at Boulder, Colorado, December, 1977.

41. Brown, Joseph Epes, editor. *The Sacred Pipe: Black Elk's Account of the Seven Rites of the Oglala Sioux*. Norman: University of Oklahoma Press, 1953.

42. Bruin, Paul, and Phillip Giegel. *Jesus Lived Here*. New York: William Morrow & Co., 1957.

43. Bryant, Howard C., and Nelson Jarmie. "The Glory." *Scientific American* (July 1974), pp. 60–71.

44. Buonaiuti, Ernesto, "Ecclesia Spiritualis." In *Spirit and Nature, Papers from the Eranos Yearbooks*, vol. 1, Joseph Campbell, editor. Princeton: Princeton University Press, 1954.

45. Burckhardt, Jakob. *The Civilization of the Renaissance in Italy*. London: Harrap, 1929.

46. "The Burdens of the Utopians." *Manas*, vol 30 (February, 1977).

47. Campbell, Joseph. "Bios and Mythos, Prolegomena to a Science of Mythology." *Psychoanalysis and Culture*, edited by G. Wilbur and Warner Muensterberger. New York: International Universities Press, Inc., 1951.

48. Capra, Fritjof. *The Tao of Physics*. Berkeley: Shambhala, 1975.

49. Cardenal, Ernesto. *Homage to the American Indians*. Baltimore: The John Hopkins University Press, 1973.

50. Castaneda, Carlos. *Journey to Ixtlan*. New York: Simon and Schuster, 1972.

51. _____. *A Separate Reality*. New York: Simon and Schuster, 1971.

52. _____. *Tales of Power*. New York: Simon and Schuster, 1974.

53. _____. *The Teachings of Don Juan*. New York: Ballantine Books, 1968.

54. *China, Land of Splendor*. Taipei, Republic of China: Globe International Corp., 1975.

55. Chizhevskii, A.L. "Atmospheric Electricity and Life." In *The Earth in the Universe*, edited by V.V. Fedynskii, translated from the Russian. Jerusalem: Israel Program for Scientific Translations, 1968. (Available from the U.S. Dept. of Commerce, Clearinghouse for Federal Scientific and Technical Information, Springfield, Va. 22151).

56. Chowka, Peter Barry. "The Original Mind of Gary Snyder, Part I." *Eastwest*, vol. 7, no. 6 (1977), pp. 24–38.

57. _____. The Original Mind of Gary Snyder, Part III." *Eastwest*, vol. 7, no. 8 (1977), pp. 18–30.

58. Cobb, Edith. *The Ecology of Imagination in Childhood*. New York: Columbia University Press, 1977.

59. _____. "The Ecology of Imagination in Childhood." *Daedalus*, vol. 88 (Summer, 1959), pp. 537–548.

60. Coleridge, Ernest Hartley, editor. *The Complete Poetical Works of Samuel Taylor Coleridge*. Oxford: Clarendon Press, 1912.

61. Collier, John. *American Indian Ceremonial Dances*. New York: Crown Publishers, Inc. (A revised edition of *Patterns and Ceremonials of the Indians of the Southwest*), no date.

62. Commager, Steele, editor. *Vergil: A Collection of Critical Essays*. Engelwood Cliffs: Prentice Hall Inc., 1966.

63. Coon, Carleton S. *The Hunting Peoples*. Boston: Little Brown & Co., 1971.

64. Couling, Samuel, editor. *Encyclopedia Sinica*. London: Oxford University Press, 1917.

65. Cozza, L., and R. A. Staccioli. *Rome Past and Present*. Rome: Vision Publications, (no date).

66. Csikszentmihalyi, Mihaly. "Play and Intrinsic Rewards." *Journal of Humanistic Psychology*. (Summer, 1975), pp. 44–63.

67. Cushing, Frank Hamilton. "Zuni Breadstuff." In *Indian Notes and Monographs, Vol. VIII*. New York: Museum of the American Indian, 1920.

68. de Angulo, Jaime. *Indian Tales*. New York: Hill and Wang, 1953.

69. Deevey, Edward. "The Human Population." *Scientific American*, vol. 203 (September, 1960), pp. 195–204.

70. de Givry, Grillot. *Witchcraft, Magic and Alchemy*, translated by Locke. London, 1931.

71. Di Cesare, Mario. *The Altar and the City, a Reading of Vergil's Aeneid*. New York: Columbia University Press, 1974.

72. Dickson, Lovat. *Wilderness Man, the Strange Story of Grey Owl*. Scarborough, Ontario: New American Library of Canada Ltd., 1975.

73. Dillard, Annie. *Pilgrim at Tinker Creek*. New York: Harper & Row, 1974.

74. Douglas, William O. *Of Men and Mountains*. New York: Harper & Row, 1950.

75. Dyson, Verne. *Forgotten Tales of China*. Shanghai: The Commercial Press Ltd. (undated)

76. Eliade, Mircea. *Images and Symbols*. New York: Sheed and Ward, 1969.

77. _____. "Mystery and Spiritual Regeneration in Extra-European Religions." In *Man and Transformation, Papers from the Eranos Yearbooks*, vol. 5, edited by Joseph Campbell. Princeton: Princeton University Press, 1964.

78. Emmitt, Robert. *The Last War Trail*. Norman: University of Oklahoma Press, 1954.

79. Erdoes, Richard. *The Sun Dance People*. New York: Alfred A. Knopf, Inc., 1972.

80. Erikson, Erik. *Childhood and Society*. New York: W. W. Norton, 1950.

81. _____. *Young Man Luther*. New York: W.W. Norton Inc., 1962.

82. _____. "Youth: Fidelity and Diversity." *Daedalus*, vol. 91 (Winter, 1962), pp. 5–27.

83. Farnell, L. R. *Cults of the Greek States*, vol. 3. Oxford: Oxford University Press, 1907.

84. Ferguson, Marilyn. "An Editorial." *Brain Mind Bulletin*, vol. 2, no. 16.

85. _____. "Ida Rolf at 81: Still building on the earth." *Brain Mind Bulletin*, vol. 3, no. 2.

86. _____. "Physicists invade psychology, look at mind-brain relationship." Brain Mind Bulletin, vol. 2, no. 6.

87. _____. "Theoretical physics must deal with thought—Bohm." *Brain Mind Bulletin*, vol. 2, no. 21.

88. Flader, Susan, L. *Thinking Like a Mountain: Aldo Leopold and the Evolution of an Ecological Attitude Toward Deer, Wolves, and Forests*. Columbia: University of Missouri Press, 1974.

89. Fletcher, Alice C. "The Hako: A Pawnee Ceremony." Bureau of American Ethnology, *Twenty-second Annual Report*, Part 2 (1904).

90. _____, and Francis La Flesche. "The Omaha Tribe." Bureau of American Ethnology, *Twenty-seventh Annual Report*, (1911).

91. Fiske, Edward B. "Martin Heidegger, A Philosopher Who Affected Many Fields, Dies." *The New York Times,* May 27, 1976.

92. Fraser, Alistair B. "Theological Optics." *Applied Optics,* vol. 14 (April 1975), pp. 92–93.

93. Freeman, Kathleen. *Ancilla to the Pre-Socratic Philosophers.* Cambridge: Harvard University Press, 1966.

94. Furst, Alan. "Have you ever wanted to keep on walking until something happened?" *The Weekly* (Seattle), vol. 2, no. 11 (1977).

95. Garcia, John David. *The Moral Society, A Rational Alternative to Death.* New Nork: The Julian Press Inc., 1971.

96. Gazzaniga, Michael S. "The Split Brain in Man." *Scientific American,* vol. 217, no. 2 (August, 1967), pp. 24–29.

97. Geil, William Edgar. *The Sacred Five of China.* London: John Murray, 1926.

98. Gesell, Arnold L. *The Embryology of Behavior: The Beginnings of the Human Mind.* New York: Harper & Row, 1945.

99. Gesner, Conrad. *On the Admiration of Mountains,* translated by H. B. D. Soulé, edited by W. Dock. San Francisco: Grabhorn Press, 1937.

100. Giles, Herbert A. *A Chinese-English Dictionary.* London, 1912.

101. Gorsline, Jerry. Personal communication, 1977.

102. _____, and Linn House. "Future Primitive." In *North Pacific Rim Alive.* Planet Drum, Box 31251, San Francisco, California.

103. Govinda, Lama A. *The Way of the White Clouds.* Berkeley: Shambhala, 1971.

104. Graves, Robert. *The White Goddess.* New York: Vintage Books, 1948.

105. Grene, Marjorie. *Martin Heidegger.* London: Bowed & Bowed, 1957.

106. Haga, Hideo. *Japanese Folk Festivals, Illustrated,* translated by F. H. Mayer. Tokyo: Miura, 1970.

107. Hapgood, Fred. "The New Reformation in Science." *Atlantic* (March, 1977).

108. Hardin, Garrett. "Nobody Ever Dies of Overpopulation." *Science,* February 12, 1971.

109. _____. *Exploring New Ethics for Survival, the Voyage of the Spaceship Beagle.* New York: The Viking Press, 1972.

110. Harris, T. George. "About Ruth Benedict and Her Lost Manuscript." *Psychology Today* (June, 1970), pp. 51–52.

111. Haug, Martin. *Essays on the Sacred Language, Writings, and Religion of the Parsis.* London: Kegan Paul, Trench, Trubner and Co., Ltd., 1878.

112. Hawken, Paul, Kay Rawlings and Brer Rabbit. "Briarpatch." *New Age* (July/August, 1976), pp. 34–40.

113. Hawkes, Jacquetta. "Paleolithic Art." *History Today,* vol. 8 (1958).

114. _____. *A Land.* New York: Random House, 1951.

115. "Heidegger, Martin." *Current Biography, 1972.* Chicago: Wilson Publication, 1972.

116. Heidegger, Martin. *Early Greek Thinking,* translated by David F. Krell and Frank A. Capuzzi. New York: Harper & Row, 1975.

117. _____. *Poetry, Language, Thought,* translated by Albert Hofstadter. New York: Harper & Row, 1971.

118. _____. *The Piety of Thinking,* translated by James G. Hart and John C. Maraldo. Bloomington: Indiana University Press, 1976.

119. _____. "Preface." In *Heidegger, Through Phenomenology to Thought,* William J. Richardson, S.J. The Hague: Martinus Nijhoff, 1963.

120. _____. *Über den Humanismus.* Frankfurt a.M.: Vittorio Klostermann, 1949.

121. _____. *Unterwegs zur Sprache.* Translated in *Search for Gods,* by Vincent Vycinas. The Hague: Martinus Nijhoff, 1972.

122. Heisenberg, W. *Physics and Philosophy: the Revolution in Modern Science.* New York: Harper & Row, 1958.

123. Heyerdahl, Thor. "How Vulnerable Is the Ocean?" In *Who Speaks for Earth?* edited by Maurice F. Strong. New York: W. W. Norton & Co. Inc., 1973.

124. Hitching, Francis. *Earth Magic.* New York: William Morrow & Co., 1977.

125. Hodous, Lewis. *Folkways in China.* London: Arthur Probsthain, 1929.

126. John Holt, editor. *Growing Without Schooling,* vol. 1, no. 1 (1977).

127. Hopkin, J. "Periodicity and Natural Law as a Basis for Agriculture." *Missouri Weather Review* (July, 1918).

128. House, Linn. "Totem Salmon." In *North Pacific Rim Alive.* Planet Drum, San Francisco, California.

129. Huang, Al Chung-liang, *Embrace Tiger, Return to Mountain, the Essence of Tai Chi.* Moab, Utah: Real People Press, 1973.

130. Huang, Shou-fu and T'n Chung-yo. *A New Edition of the Omei Illustrated Guide Book.* With an English introduction and translation by Dryden Linsley Phelps. Chengtu, Szechuan, 1936.

131. Huang, Wan-Shan. *Fundamentals of Tai Chi Chuan.* Hong Kong: South Sky Book Co., 1973. (Available from U.S. Branch, 5501–5503 University Way N.E., Seattle, Washington 98105).

132. *International Journal of Biometeorology,* vol. 18, pp. 313–318.

133. Jackson, A. V. Williams. *Zoroaster, the Prophet of Ancient Iran.* New York: Macmillan Co., 1901.

134. James, E. O. *Seasonal Feasts and Festivals.* London: Barnes & Noble, Inc. 1961.

135. Johnstone, R. F. *From Peking to Mandalay.* London: John Murray, 1908.

136. "Joseph W. T. Mason, Columnist on War." *The New York Times,* May 14, 1941, p. 21.

137. Jung, C. G. *Analytical Psychology, its Theory and Practice, The Tavistock Lectures.* New York: Random House, 1968.

138. _____. "The Commentary." In *The Secret of the Golden Flower,* by Richard Wilhelm, translated by Cary F. Baynes. New York: Harcourt Brace Jovanovich, Inc., 1970.

139. _____. *Contributions to Analytical Psychology,* translated by H. G. and Cary F. Baynes. London: Routledge & Kegan Paul Ltd., 1928.

140. _____. *Memories, Dreams, Relfections,* edited by Aniela Jaffé. New York: Pantheon Books, 1961. (Paging from the Vintage Books edition, 1963.)

141. _____. "Mind and the Earth." In *Contributions to Analytical Psychology,* translated by H.G. and Cary F. Baynes. London: Routledge & Kegan Paul Ltd., 1928.

142. _____. "On Psychical Energy." In *Contributions to Analytical Psychology,* translated by H. G. and Cary F. Baynes. London: Routledge & Kegan Paul Ltd., 1928.

143. _____. "On Psychic Energy," In *On the Nature of the Psyche.* Princeton: Princeton University Press, 1969.

144. _____. "The Phenomenology of the Spirit in Fairy Tales." In *Spirit and Nature, Papers from the Eranos Yearbooks,* vol. 1, edited by Joseph Campbell. Princeton: Princeton University Press, 1954.

145. _____. "The Spirit of Psychology." In *Spirit and Nature, Papers from the Eranos Yearbooks,* vol. 1, edited by Joseph Campbell, Princeton: Princeton University Press, 1954.

146. _____. "Woman in Europe." In *Contributions to Analytical Psychology,* translated by H. G. and Cary F. Baynes. London: Routledge & Kegan Paul Ltd., 1928.

147. Kahn, Herman. *The Emerging Japanese Superstate.* Englewood Cliffs: Prentice Hall Inc., 1970.

148. Karlgren, B. "Grammata Serica: Script and Phonetics in Chinese and Sino-Japanese." *Bulletin of the Museum of Far Eastern Antiquities* (Stockholm), vol. 12, no. 1 (1940).

149. Kazantzakis, Nikos. *Report to Greco.* New York: Simon and Schuster, 1965.

150. Keen, Sam. "Sorcerer's Apprentice, A Conversation with Carlos Castaneda." *Psychology Today* (December, 1972), pp. 90-102.

151. Kerényi, C. *Eleusis,* translated by Ralph Manheim. New York: Pantheon Books, 1967.

152. Kern, Otto. *Die griechischen Mysterien der klassischen Zeit.* Berlin, 1927. Quoted in Paul Schmitt, "The Ancient Mysteries in the Society of Their Time, Their Transformation and Most Recent Echoes." In *The Mysteries, Papers from the Eranos Yearbooks,* vol. 2, edited by Joseph Campbell. Princeton: Princeton University Press, 1955.

153. Kitto, H.D.F. *The Greeks.* Chicago: Aldine Publishing Co., 1964.

154. Klausner, S., editor. *Why Men Take Chances: Studies in Stress Seeking.* Garden City: Doubleday, 1968.

155. Knight, W. F. Jackson. *Vergil: Epic and Anthropology, Comprising Vergil's Troy, Cumaean Gates and The Holy City of the East,* edited by John D. Christie. London: George Allen & Unwin Ltd., 1967.

156. Kolata, Gina Bari. "!Kung Hunter-Gatherers: Feminism, Diet, and Birth Control." *Science,* September 13, 1974, pp. 932-934.

157. _____. "Mathematician Paul Erdos: Total Devotion to the Subject." *Science,* vol. 196, 1977.

158. Kopp, Sheldon. *The Hanged Man, Psychotherapy and the Forces of Darkness.* Palo Alto: Science and Behavior Books, 1974.

159. Kramer, Joel. *Passionate Mind.* Millbrae, California: Celestial Arts, 1974.

160. _____. *Yoga Workshop.* Vancouver: Cold Mountain Center, August, 1971.

161. Krishnamurti, J. *Commentaries on Living, 1st Series.* Wheaton: Theosophical Publishing House, 1967.

162. _____. *Freedom from the Known.* New York: Harper and Row, 1975.

163. _____. *Talks and Dialogues.* New York: Avon Books, 1970.

164. _____. *Talks and Dialogues, Saanen, 1968.* Berkeley: Shambhala, 1970.

165. LaChapelle, Dolores, and Janet Bourque. *Earth Festivals.* Silverton: Finn Hill Arts, 1977.

166. Laird, Carobeth. *The Chemehuevis.* Banning, California: Malki Museum Press, 1976.

167. Lame Deer, John, and Richard Erdoes. *Lame Deer, Seeker of Visions.* New York: Simon and Schuster, 1972.

168. Lane, Ferdinand C. *The Story of Mountains.* Garden City: Doubleday and Co. Inc., 1951.

169. Laski, M. *Ecstasy, A Study of Some Secular and Religious Experiences.* London: Cresset Press, 1961.

170. Lawrence, D. H. "New Mexico." In *Phoenix I: The Posthumous Paper of D. H. Lawrence,* edited by Edward McDonald. New York: The Viking Press, 1936.

171. Lee R. B. "What Hunters Do for a Living, or How to Make Out on Scarce Resources." In *Man the Hunter,* edited by R. B. Lee and I. Devore. Chicago: Aldine Press, 1968.

172. _____, and I. Devore. *Man the Hunter.* Chicago: Aldine Press, 1968.

173. Legge, James, translator. *The Texts of Confucianism: Part 3. The 'Li Chi'.* In the Sacred Books of the East Series, vol. 27. Oxford: Oxford University Press, 1885.

174. Le Guin, Ursula K. *The Dispossessed.* New York: Harper and Row, 1974.

175. Leonard, J. N. *Early Japan.* New York: Time-Life Books, 1968.

176. Leopold, Aldo. "A Biotic View of Land." *Journal of Forestry,* vol. 37 (September 1939), pp. 727-730.

177. _____. "A book review." *Journal of Forestry,* vol. 32 (October 1934), p. 775.

178. _____. *A Sand County Almanac.* London: Oxford University Press, 1966.

179. Leveson, David. *A Sense of the Earth.* New York: Natural History Press (Division of Doubleday and Co.), 1971.

180. Levy, Gertrude R. *The Gate of Horn, A Study of the Religious Conceptions of the Stone Age and their Influence upon European Thought.* London: Faber & Faber (no date).

181. Lewis, C. S. *Surprised by Joy: The Shape of My Early Life.* London: Collins, 1965.

182. Liang, T. T. *T'ai Chi Chu'an for Health and Self Defense: Philosophy and Practice.* New York: Random House, 1977.

183. *The Life of Muhammad, a Translation of Ishaq's Sirat Rasul Allah.* Karachi: Oxford University Press, 1955.

184. Lilly, John. New Dimensions Tapes, 267 States St., San Francisco.

185. Lindsay, Ron. Personal communication, 1977.

186. Link, Paul. "A book review of *Hamada-Potter,* by Bernard Leach," published by Tokyo Kodansha International, 1975. *Eastwest* (August, 1976).

187. Linton, Ralph. "Marquesan Culture." In *The Individual and His Society,* edited by A. Kardiner. New York, 1949.

188. Liu, Da. *Tai Chi Ch'uan and I Ching.* New York: Harper & Row, 1972.

189. *Living Here.* Frisco Bay Mussel Group, Planet Drum, Box 31251, San Francisco, California.

190. Lorenz, Konrad. "The Role of Gestalt Perception in Animal and Human Behavior." In *Aspects of Form,* edited by L. L. Whyte. London: Lund Humphries, 1951.

191. Lunn, Arnold. *A Century of Mountaineering, 1857-1957.* London: George Allen and Unwin Ltd., 1957.

192. Lutyens, Mary. *Krishnamurti, Years of Awakening.* New York: Farrar, Straus & Giroux, 1975.

193. MacLean, Paul D. *A Triune Concept of the Brain and Behaviour.* Toronto: University of Toronto Press, 1973.

194. Magid, J. "Child Abuse May be Sorriest Problem of All." *Salt Lake Tribune,* February 13, 1977.

195. Mandelbaum, Allen. *The Aeneid of Vergil, a Verse Translation.* Berkeley: University of California Press, 1971.

196. Mann, Thomas. *The Magic Mountain.* New York: Vintage Books, 1969.

197. Maraini, Fosco. "Introduction." In *On Top of the World,* by Showell Styles. New York: Macmillan Co., 1967.

198. _____. *Japan, Patterns of Continuity.* Tokyo: Kodansha International Ltd., 1971.

199 _____. *Meeting with Japan.* New York: Viking Press, 1959.

200. Marianoff, Dmitri. *Einstein—An Intimate Study of a Great Man.* New York: Doubleday, 1944.

201. Marlin, William. "When Ancient Basilica Becomes a Sundial." *Christian Science Monitor,* January 21, 1977.

202. Marsh, George. *Man and Nature.* Cambridge: Harvard University Press, 1977.

203. Marx, Werner. *Heidegger and the Tradition,* translated by Theodore Kisiel and Murray Greene. Evanston: Northwestern University Press, 1971.

204. Maslow, Abraham H. *The Farther Reaches of Human Nature.* New York: Viking Press, 1971.

205. _____. "Metamotivation: The Biological Rooting of the Value-Life." *Journal of Humanistic Psychology,* vol. 7, no. 2, pp. 93-127.

206. _____. *New Knowledge in Human Values.* New York: Harper & Row, 1959.

207. _____. *Toward a Psychology of Being,* 2nd edition. New York: D. Van Nostrand Co. Inc., 1968.

208. Mason, J.W.T. *The Meaning of Shinto.* New York: E. P. Dutton & Co., 1935.

209. Matthiessen, Peter. *At Play in the Fields of the Lord.* New York: Random House, 1965.

210. McCluggage, Denise. *The Centered Skier.* Waitsfield, Vermont: Vermont Crossroads Press, 1977.

211. McHarg, Ian. *Design with Nature.* New York: Natural History Press, 1971.

212. McKenzie, John L. *Dictionary of the Bible.* Milwaukee: Bruce Publishing Co., 1965.

213. Mead, Margaret. *Coming of Age in Samoa.* New York: William Morrow, 1971.

214. Meeker, Joseph W. *The Comedy of Survival: Studies in Literary Ecology.* New York: Scribner, 1974.

215. Menninger, Karl A. "Totemic Aspects of Contemporary Attitudes Toward Animals." In *Psychoanalysis and Culture, Essays in Honor of Géza Róheim,* edited by G. Wilbur and W. Muensterberger. New York: International Universities Press Inc., 1951.

216. Merrell-Wolff, Franklin. *Pathways through to Space.* New York: Julian Press, 1973.

217. _____. *The Philosophy of Consciousness without an Object.* New York: Julian Press, 1973.

218. Merton, Thomas. "The Wild Places." *The Center Magazine* (July, 1968).

219. Meyerhoff, Barbara G. "Balancing Between Worlds: The Shaman's Calling." *Parabola,* vol. 1, no. 2 (Spring, 1976), pp. 6-13.

220. Miller, Henry. *Big Sur and the Oranges of Hieronymus Bosch.* New York: New Directions, 1957.

221. Minnaert, M., *The Nature of Light and Colour in the Open Air.* New York: Dover, 1954.

222. Miura, Yuichiro. "The Great Ski Caper" (as told to Darrell Houston). *Seattle Times,* June 18, 1972.

223. Morgan, Arthur. *Nowhere was Somewhere.* Chapel Hill: University of North Carolina Press, 1946.

224. Myers, Geral. "Healing the Land." *CoEvolution Quarterly* (Winter, 1976/77), pp. 74-77.

225. Naess, Arne. *Ecology, Community and Lifestyle: A Philosophical Approach.* Manuscript, Oslo, 1977.

226. _____. *Gandhi and Group Conflict.* Oslo: Universitetsforlaget, 1974.

227. Nasr, Seyyed Hossein. *The Encounter of Man and Nature.* London: George Allen and Unwin Ltd., 1968.

228. Needham, Joseph. *Science and Civilization in China,* vol. 1. Cambridge: Cambridge University Press, 1954.

229. _____. *Science and Civilization in China,* vol. 2. Cambridge: Cambridge University Press, 1956.

230. _____. *Science and Civilization in China,* vol. 3. Cambridge: Cambridge University Press, 1959.

231. _____. *Science and Civilization in China,* vol. 4, pt. 1. Cambridge: Cambridge University Press, 1962.

232. _____. "Laws of Nature in China and the West." University of Washington, John Danz Lecture, June 28, 1977.

233. Neel, James V. "Lessons from a 'Primitive' People." *Science,* November 20, 1970.

234. Neihardt, John G. *Black Elk Speaks.* Lincoln: University of Nebraska Press, 1961.

235. Nussenzveig, H. Moysés. "The Theory of the Rainbow." *Scientific American* (April 1977), pp. 116-127.

236. Odum, Eugene P. "The Strategy of Ecosystem Development." *Science,* vol. 164 (1969), pp. 262-270.

237. Okakura, Kakuzo. *The Book of Tea.* New York: Dover, 1964.

238. Ornstein, Robert E. *Educating Both Halves of the Brain.* Symposium sponsored by the School of Education and College of Continuing Education, University of California, in cooperation with the Institute for the Study of Human Knowledge. Los Angeles, May 1, 1977.

239. _____. *The Psychology of Consciousness.* San Francisco: W. H. Freeman & Co., 1972.

240. Ortega y Gasset, José. *Meditations on Hunting,* translated by Howard B. Wescott. New York: Charles Scribner's Sons, 1972.

241. Ortiz, Alfonso. *The Tewa World.* Chicago: University of Chicago Press, 1969.

242. Otto, Walter. *Die Götter Griechenlands.* Frankfurt a.M.: Verlag G. Schulte-Bumke, 1947. Quoted in *Earth and Gods,* by Vincent Vycinas. The Hague: Martinus Nijhoff, 1961.

243. _____. "The Meaning of the Eleusinian Mysteries." In *The Mysteries, Papers from the Eranos Yearbooks,* vol. 2, edited by Joseph Campbell. Princeton: Princeton University Press, 1955.

244. Pallis, Marco. *The Way and the Mountain.* London: Peter Owen Ltd., 1961.

245. Parry, Adam. "The Two Voices of Vergil's *Aeneid.*" In *Arion,* vol. 2, no. 4 (Winter, 1963), pp. 66-80.

246. Parsch, Pius. *The Church's Year of Grace,* translated by William G. Heidt, O.S.B. Collegeville, Minnesota: The Liturgical Press, 1954.

247. "A Pattern Laid Up in Heaven." *Manas,* vol. 30, no. 2 (January 12, 1977).

248. Pearce, Joseph Chilton. *The Crack in the Cosmic Egg.* New York: Julian Press, 1971.

249. _____. *Exploring the Crack in the Cosmic Egg.* New York: Julian Press Inc., 1974.

250. _____. *Magical Child.* New York: E. P. Dutton, 1977.

251. Pelletier, Wilfred, and Ted Poole. *No Foreign Land.* New York: Pantheon Books, 1973.

252. Penfield, Wilder. *The Mystery of the Mind.* Princeton: Princeton University Press, 1975.

253. "People and Places." *Rocky Mountain News,* February 26, 1977, p. 34.

254. Perlman, Eric. "I Rescued from Great Danger the Man Who Skied Everest." Ski Magazine (October, 1977).

255. Petersen, James. "Lessons from the Indian Soul, A Conversation with Frank Waters." *Psychology Today* (May, 1973).

256. Phillips, Michael. "The American Anti-Whaling Movement is Racist." *CoEvolution Quarterly* (Fall, 1976), pp. 120-123.

257. Piaget, Jean. Quoted in *Thinking without Language,* by Hans G. Furth. New York: Free Press, 1966.

258. Pieper, Josef. *In Tune with the World, a Theory of Festivity.* New York: Harcourt, Brace & World, Inc., 1965.

259. Pietsch, Paul. "Hologramic Mind." *Quest* (November-December 1977), pp. 124-125.

260. Pinkson, Tom. *A Quest for Vision.* Forest Knolls, California: Freeperson Press, 1976.

261. Pirsig, Robert. "Cruising Blues and Their Cure." *Esquire* (May, 1967).

262. _____. *Zen and the Art of Motorcycle Maintenance.* New York: William Morrow & Co., Inc., 1974.

263. Platt, John R., *Perception and Change.* Ann Arbor: University of Michigan Press, 1970.

264. "Plowboy Interview with Dr. Ralph Borsodi." *Mother Earth News,* no. 26, pp. 6-13.

265. Post, Austin, Personal communication, 1977.

266. Pribram, Karl H. "Holonomy and Structure in the Organization of Perception." In *Images, Perception and*

Knowledge, edited by John M. Nicholas. Dordrecht, Holland: D. Reidel Publishing Company (1977), pp. 155–186.

267. _____. *Languages of the Brain.* Englewood Cliffs, N.J.: Prentice-Hall, Inc., 1971.

268. _____. "Proposal for a Structural Pragmatism: Some Neuropsychological Considerations of Problems in Philosophy." In *Scientific Psychology,* edited by B. Wolman. New York: Basic Books (1965), pp. 426–459.

269. Pritchard, James B., editor. *Ancient Near Eastern Texts Relating to the Old Testament.* Princeton: Princeton University Press, 1955.

270. Rahner, Hugo. *Man At Play.* New York: Herder and Herder, 1967.

271. Rappaport, Roy A. "Energy and the Structure of Adaptation." *CoEvolution Quarterly* (Spring, 1974), pp. 20–28.

272. Rébuffat, Gaston and Pierre Tairraz. *Between Heaven and Earth.* London: Kaye and Ward, (no date).

273. Rexroth, Kenneth. *An Autobiographical Novel.* New York: New Directions, 1969.

274. Richards, M.C., *Crossing Point.* Middletown: Wesleyan University Press, 1973.

275. Richardson, William J. *Heidegger, Through Phenomenology to Thought.* The Hague: Martinus Nijhoff, 1963.

276. Robertson, James, and John Lewallen, editors. *Grass Roots Primer.* San Francisco: Sierra Club, 1975.

277. Rolf, Ida. *Rolfing: the Integration of Human Structures.* Santa Monica, California: Dennis-Landman, 1977.

278. Rolston, Holmes. "Hewn and Cleft from this Rock." *Main Currents in Modern Thought,* vol. 27, no. 3 (1971), pp. 79–83.

279. Sahlins, Marshall. *Stone Age Economics.* Chicago: Aldine-Atherton Inc., 1972.

280. Sallis, John, editor. *Heidegger and the Path of Thinking.* Pittsburgh: Duquesne University Press, 1970.

281. Sanchez, Thomas. *Rabbit Boss.* New York: Alfred A. Knopf Inc., 1973. (Page references to Ballantine Books edition, 1974.)

282. Sauer, Carl O. "Theme of Plant and Animal Destruction in Economic History." *Journal of Farm Economics,* vol. 20 (1938), pp. 765–775.

283. Schell, Orville. *The Town that Fought to Save Itself.* New York: Pantheon Books, 1976.

284. Schmitt, Paul. "The Ancient Mysteries in the Society of their Time, their Transformation and Most Recent Echoes." In *The Mysteries, Papers from the Eranos Yearbooks,* vol. 2, edited by Joseph Campbell. Princeton: Princeton University Press, 1955.

285. "Science for Tomorrow." *Manas,* vol. 30, no. 21 (1977).

286. Scully, Vincent. *The Earth, the Temple, and the Gods; Greek Sacred Architecture.* New Haven: Yale University Press, 1962.

287. Searles, Harold F. *The Nonhuman Environment in Normal Development and in Schizophrenia.* New York: International Universities Press Inc., 1960.

288. Seidel, George J. *Martin Heidegger and the Pre-Socratics.* Lincoln: University of Nebraska Press, 1964.

289. Sharp, Cecil J., and A. P. Oppe. *The Dance, an Historical Survey of Dancing in Europe.* Totowa, N.J.: Rowman and Littlefield, 1972. (Reprint of the book published in 1924 by Halton & Truscott Smith Ltd., London.)

290. Shepard, Paul. "The Cross Valley Syndrome." *Landscape,* vol. 10, no. 3 (Spring, 1961), pp 4–8.

291. _____. *Man in the Landscape, A Historic View of the Esthetics of Nature.* New York: Alfred A. Knopf, 1967.

292. _____. *The Tender Carnivore and the Sacred Game.* New York: Charles Scribner's Sons, 1973.

293. _____, and Daniel McKinley, editors. *The Sub - versive Science, Essays Toward an Ecology of Man.* Boston: Houghton Mifflin Co., 1969.

294. Sibley, George. "Part of a Winter." *Mountain Gazette,* no. 40.

295. Singer, Dorothea W. *Giordano Bruno, His Life and Thought.* New York: Henry Schuman, 1950.

296. Singer, June. *Boundaries of the Soul, The Practice of Jung's Psychology.* Garden City: Doubleday and Co., 1972.

297. Smith, John Holland. *The Death of Classical Paganism.* New York: Charles Scribner's Sons, 1976.

298. Smith, Robert A. "Synchronicity and Syntropy: the Cosmic Psychodrama." In *Fields within Fields—within Fields: the Methodology of Pattern.* vol. 5, no. 1, from The World Institute Council, Julius Stulman, Publisher, 1972.

299. Smith, W. Robertson. *Lectures on the Religion of the Semites,* 1927.

300. Snyder, Gary. *The Old Ways.* San Franciso: City Lights Books, 1977.

301. _____. *Riprap and Cold Mountain: Poems.* Berkeley: Four Seasons Foundation, 1965.

302. _____. *Turtle Island.* New York: New Directions, 1974.

303. "Some Utopian Considerations." *Manas,* vol. 30 (1977), pp. 1–2.

304. Spengler, Oswald. *The Decline of the West.* London: Allen and Unwin, 1918.

305. Spiegelberg, Frederic. *Spiritual Practices of India.* Secaucus, N.J.: The Citadel Press, 1962.

306. Stanner, W. E. H. "Religion, Totemism, and Symbolism." In *Aboriginal Man in Australis,* edited by R. M. and C. H. Berndt. Sydney: Angus and Robertson, 1965.

307. Steiger, Brad. *Medicine Talk.* Garden City: Doubleday & Co., 1976.

308. Steiner, Stan. "The Sun Is Becoming Darker, the Ultimate Energy Crisis." *Akwesasne Notes,* (Autumn, 1974).

309. Stevens, Henry Bailey. *The Recovery of Culture.* New York: Harper & Row, 1949.

310. Stiskin, Nahum. *The Looking-Glass God.* New York: Weatherhill, 1972.

311. Storm, Hyemeyohsts. *Seven Arrows.* New York: Harper & Row, 1972.

312. Styles, Showell. *On Top of the World.* New York: Macmillan Co., 1967.

313. Sze, Mai-Mai. *The Tao of Painting: A Study of the Ritual Disposition of Chinese Painting.* New York: Pantheon Books, 1956.

314. Taimni, I. K. *The Science of Yoga, A Commentary on the Yoga-Sutras of Patanjali in the Light of Modern Thought.* Wheaton: The Theosophical Publishing House, 1967.

315. Tanaka, Sen'ō. *The Tea Ceremony.* Tokyo: Kodansha International, 1977.

316. Taylor, Peggy, and Rick Ingrasci. "'Out of the Body,' A New Age Interview with Elisabeth Kubler-Ross." *New Age* (November, 1977), pp. 39–43.

317. Tennet, Sir James Emerson. *Ceylon.* London: Longmans, 1859. (Quoted in *From Peking to Mandalay,* R. F. Johnstone. London: John Murray, 1908.)

318. Thomas, Edward J. *The Life of Buddha as Legend and History.* London: Kegan Paul, 1960.

319. Thomashow, Mitchell. "Mystical Ecology." Environmental Studies, Antioch/New England, One Elm St., Keene, New Hampshire 03431.

320. Thompson, Ian. Letter in the Telluride, Colorado, *Deep Creek Review,* (Summer, 1975).

321. Thorpe, W. H. *Learning and Instinct in Animals.* New York: Methuen Inc., 1963.

322. "Threat stops bulldozer, another chapter in neighbors vs developed saga." *The Daily Journal American,* Bellevue, Washington, July 2, 1977.

323. Tietjens, Eunice. "The Most Sacred Mountain." In *New Voices,* edited by Marguerite Wilkinson. New York: Macmillan Co., 1929.

324. Tillich, Paul. "The Importance of New Being for Christian Theology." In *Man and Transformation, Papers from the Eranos Yearbooks,* vol. 5, edited by Joseph Campbell. Princeton: Princeton University Press, 1964.

325. Todd, Michael. "Sacred Ecology." In *Earth's Answer,* edited by M. Katz, W. P. Marsh, and G. G. Thompson. New York: Lindisfarne Books/Harper and Row, 1977.

326. "Tree Gifts Hit New High Level." *Silverton Standard,* July, 1977.

327. Tricker, R. A. R. *Introduction to Meteorological Optics.* Quoted in H. Bryant and N. Jarmie, "The Glory." *Scientific American* (July, 1974).

328. Tsunada, R., W. de Bary, and D. Keene. *Sources of Japanese Tradition.* New York: Columbia University Press, 1958.

329. Tsunetsugu, Muraoka. *Studies in Shinto Thought,* translated by Delmer M. Brown and James T. Araki. Berkeley: University of California Press, 1964.

330. Tucci, Giuseppi. *The Theory and Practice of the Mandala.* New York: Samuel Weiser, 1973.

331. Turnbull, Colin M. *The Forest People.* New York: Simon and Schuster, 1961.

332. Tyler, Hamilton A. *Pueblo Gods and Myths.* Norman: University of Oklahoma Press, 1964.

333. Underhill, Ruth M. *Redman's Religion.* Chicago: University of Chicago Press, 1965.

334. Unsoeld family. *Memorial.* Olympia, Washington, 1975. (All quotations from Devi Unsoeld are from the *Memorial.* It is not kown whether she was the author of the poem found in her journal.)

335. Unsoeld, Willi. Personal communication, 1978.

336. Utne, Eric. "Coming of Age on Earth, A New Age Interview with Margaret Mead." *New Age* (May, 1977), pp. 22-29.

337. Van Gennup, Arnold. *Rites of Passage.* Chicago: University of Chicago Press, 1960.

338. Van Matre, Steve. *Acclimatization: A Sensory and Conceptual Approach to Ecological Involvement.* Martinsville, Indiana: American Camping Association, 1974.

339. Vasil'ev, B.D. "Atmospheric Air, Life, and the Blood." In *The Earth in the Universe,* edited by V. V. Fedynskii. Jerusalem: Israel Program for Scientific Translations, 1968. (Available from the U.S. Dept. of Commerce, Clearinghouse for Federal Scientific and Technical Information, Springfield, Virginia 22151.)

340. Vincent, John H., J. Lee, and R. Bain. *Earthly Footsteps of the Man of Galilee.* New York: N. D. Thompson Publishing Company, 1894.

341. Vycinas, Vincent. *Earth and Gods, an Introduction to the Philosophy of Martin Heidegger.* The Hague: Martinus Nijhoff, 1961.

342. _____. *Our Cultural Agony.* The Hague: Martinus Nijhoff, 1973.

343. _____. *Search for Gods.* The Hague: Martinus Nijhoff, 1972.

344. Wahl, Jean. *La Pensée de Heidegger et la Poésie de Hölderlin.* Sorbonne: Tournier & Constans, 1952. Quoted in *Earth and Gods,* by Vincent Vycinas. The Hague: Martinus Nijhoff, 1961.

345. Waley, Arthur, translator. *The Analects of Confucius.* London, 1939.

346. Waller, Robert, "Out of the Garden of Eden." *New Scientist and Science Journal* (September 2, 1971), pp. 528-530.

347. Walton, Evangeline. *Island of the Mighty.* New York: Random House, 1970.

348. Ward, Bernie. "The Scandal of America's Drunken Schoolchildren." *National Enquirer,* 1975.

349. Warshall, Peter. "Turtle Island—1976." *CoEvolution Quarterly* (Winter, 1976/77), 63.

350. Waters, Frank. *Masked Gods.* New York: Random House, 1975. (Page references are to the Ballantine edition.)

351. _____. *Pumpkin Seed Point.* Chicago: Sage Books, 1969.

352. Watkins, T. H. *John Muir's America.* New York: Crown Publishing Company, 1976.

353. Watts, Alan. "Divine Madness." Tape from Big Sur Recordings.

354. _____. "The Individual as Man/World." *The Psychedelic Review,* vol. 1, no. 1 (June 1963), pp. 55-65.

355. West, Monty. *Eyesight Clinic.* Workshop, Experimental College, University of Washington, July 9, 1976.

356. Whorf, Benjamin L. *Language, Thought, and Reality.* Cambridge: The M.I.T. Press, 1964.

357. Whymper, Edward. *Scrambles Amongst the Alps in the Years 1860-1869.* London: John Murray, 1871.

358. Wieger, Leon. *Chinese Characters, their Origin, Etymology, History, Classification and Signification,* translated by L. Davrout. Peking, 1940. (Lithographic reissue of the second edition, 1927.)

359. Wissler, Clark. "The Relation of Man to Nature as Illustrated by the North American Indian." *Ecology,* vol. 5, no. 4 (1924), pp. 311-318.

360. Wittfogel, Karl A. "The Hydraulic Civilizations." In *Man's Role in Changing the Face of the Earth,* edited by William L. Thomas Jr. Chicago: University of Chicago Press, 1956.

361. Zaehner, R. C. *The Dawn and Twilight of Zoroastrianism.* New York: G. P. Putnam's Sons, 1961.

362. Zeckel, Adolf. "The Totemistic Significance of the Unicorn." In *Psychoanalysis and Culture, Essays in Honor of Géza Róheim,* edited by G. Wilbur and W. Muensterberger. New York: International Universities Press Inc., 1951.

363. Beston, Henry. *The Outermost House.* New York: Holt, Rinehart and Winston, Inc. (Paging from the Viking Explorer edition, 1961.)

364. Borland, Hal. *When the Legends Die.* Philadelphia: Lippincott, 1963.

365. Deloria Jr., Vine. *God Is Red.* New York: Grosset and Dunlap, 1973.

366. Douglas, J. Sholto, and Robert A. de J. Hart. *Forest Farming.* London: Watkins Publishing, 1976.

367. Giono, Jean. "Trees." *CoEvolution Quarterly.* (Summer, 1976), pp. 54-59.

368. Katz, Michael, W. P. Marsh and G. G. Thompson, editors. *Earth's Answer.* New York: Lindisfarne Books/Harper and Row, 1977.

369. Lord, Russell. *The Care of the Earth.* New York: Thomas Nelson & Sons, 1962.

370. Margulis, Lynn, and J. E. Lovelock. "Biological Modulations of the Earth's Atmosphere." *Icarus,* vol. 21 (1974), pp. 471-489.

371. Meeker, Joseph, editor. "The New Natural Philosophy." Interim paper, Claremont, California, April, 1977.

372. Parsons, C. "Brer Rabbit Speaks." *Briarpatch Review* (Spring, 1977).

373. Petersen, James. "The Beholder, A Sketch of Rudolf Arnheim." *Psychology Today* (June, 1972), p. 59.

374. Radin, Paul. *The Road of Life and Death, A Ritual Drama of the American Indians.* New York: Pantheon Books, 1945.

375. Sears, Paul B. "Utopia and the Living Landscape." *Daedalus,* vol. 94, no. 2 (Spring, 1965), p. 485.

376. Thompson, Laura. *Culture in Crisis.* New York: Harper and Row, 1950.

377. Warshall, Peter, editor. "The Voices of Black Lake." *CoEvolution Quarterly.* (Winter, 1976/77), pp. 64-69.

Index